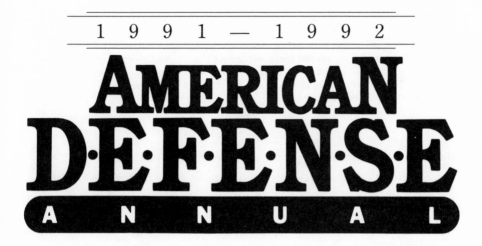

1 9 9 1 — 1 9 9 2

AMERICAN DEFENSE ANNUAL

Edited by
Joseph Kruzel

Mershon Center

The Ohio State University

LEXINGTON BOOKS
An Imprint of Macmillan, Inc.
NEW YORK
Maxwell Macmillan Canada
TORONTO
Maxwell Macmillan International
NEW YORK/OXFORD/SINGAPORE/SYDNEY

1991–92 *AMERICAN DEFENSE ANNUAL*
Photo Credits

The Air Force provided the internal photos in chapters 1 and 4. Northrop provided the internal photo in chapter 10. McDonnell Douglas provided the C-17 photo used in the chapter 3 opener. Wide World Photos provided the photos used in the chapter 2 opener, and the Department of Defense provided all other photos.

The Library of Congress has cataloged this serial publication as follows:

American defense annual. — 1991–1992–   — Lexington, Mass.: Lexington Books, c1992–
    v.;28 cm.
    Annual.
    Sponsored by the Mershon Center at The Ohio State University.
    ISSN 0882-1038 = American defense annual.
    Includes index.
    ISBN 0-669-27282-5. — ISBN 0-669-27281-7 (pbk.)

    1. United States—Defenses—Yearbooks.   I. Mershon Center for Education in National Security.   II. Title: American defense.
UA23.A1A47   355'.033073—dc19   85-646241   AACR 2   MARC-S

Library of Congress [8511]

Lexington Books
An Imprint of Macmillan, Inc.
866 Third Avenue, New York, N.Y. 10022

Maxwell Macmillan Canada, Inc.
1200 Eglinton Avenue East
Suite 200
Don Mills, Ontario M3C 3N1

Macmillan, Inc. is part of the Maxwell Communication Group of Companies.

Printed in the United States of America

printing number
1 2 3 4 5 6 7 8 9 10

Contents

Illustrations

Figures

Photographs

Tables

Preface and Acknowledgments

I n 1990 and 1991 U.S. security policy was buffeted by a variety of contending pressures. Pride in the military's performance in Desert Storm was tempered by the plight of the Kurds and the haunting thought that the Middle East could become as much of a quagmire as Vietnam. Relief at the declining Soviet threat was replaced by concern about the disintegration of the Soviet Union and resurgence of ethnic rivalries long held in check by authoritarian rule. The threats posed by the post–cold war world had not yet been fully assessed, but the United States continued to shrink its military forces and reduce its defense budget.

The decisions made in those early years of the 1990s could very well shape the international order for decades to come. Informed, intelligent debate by military and civilian policymakers, as well as by the public, becomes especially vital in such a critical period to help ensure that those decisions are of high quality. The *American Defense Annual* is uniquely positioned to contribute to that most important debate.

This is the seventh edition of the *American Defense Annual*. Each volume in the series has offered a critical examination of administration thinking about U.S. defense needs, and in doing so has served a useful role. But the great uncertainty of the early 1990s—about the security environment, the force structure appropriate for the new threats, and our collective ability to pay for U.S. defense— makes this edition a most important voice in the debate over U.S. security policy.

Our authors represent a broad spectrum of political views, and address security issues from a variety of perspectives. They disagree with each other, and no reader could possibly agree with all that is contained within these pages. Our purpose is not to provide a comprehensive alternative defense policy, but rather to offer a variety of views that will provoke thought and debate within the defense policy community and the concerned public. This edition of the *Annual* offers a broad coverage of topics at the forefront of the defense debate, and it does so in a timely fashion, with contributors assessing issues such as the performance of reserve forces in Desert Storm and the status of U.S.-Soviet conventional arms negotiations.

Every year the production of a volume such as the *Annual* provides a unique set of challenges, and this year was more difficult than earlier efforts. The buildup of Desert Shield became the conflict of Desert Storm just as we were going to press, and through much of early 1991 conflict in the gulf threatened to rewrite U.S. military strategy. The contributors to this volume performed double duty, rewriting their drafts to include an assessment of the Gulf War and reevaluating if not changing their analyses to make them complete and up to date.

The *American Defense Annual* depends on key staff people to manage the flow of drafts, corrections, page proofs, and other information among contributors, editor, and publisher. We have been fortunate to have the assistance of two extraordinary people to perform these tasks. Mark Wayda, now having assisted with three editions, has taken on ever greater responsibility for editing and overall coordination; he performs these tasks with great skill and dedication. Josephine Cohagen has been a superb administrative assistant, handling all the revisions, corrections, and other paperwork that attends an enterprise such as this.

Once again Terry Ellifritz and his associates at Telcomp Graphic Designs provided much of the aesthetics in the *Annual*. They are responsible for the overall layout, artwork, and design of the book.

Lexington Books has been our publisher through all seven editions of the *Annual*. Our friends and colleagues there—Paul O'Connel, Lyri Merrill, and Richard Tonachel—have always been flexible and helpful in accommodating a much-compressed timetable for production and a manuscript that was in constant flux throughout much of the Gulf War. Their creativity and patience have allowed us to produce the *Annual* in a timely fashion; their understanding and support made it our pleasure to work with them.

Finally, we would like to acknowledge the generous support of the John D. and Catherine T. MacArthur Foundation, which has made it possible for us to produce this volume of the *American Defense Annual*.

Glossary and Abbreviations

AAW Antiair warfare.

ABM Antiballistic missile.

ABM Treaty This 1972 treaty between the United States and the Soviet Union culminated SALT I. Amended by a 1974 protocol, the treaty limits ballistic missile defense systems in each country to one site with 100 ABM launchers and missiles, the location and number of phased-array radar systems, and the development of new ABM systems at the flight testing stage and beyond.

ACM Advanced cruise missile.

AFAP Atomic field artillery projectile.

AIFV Armored infantry fighting vehicle.

ALCM Air-launched cruise missile.

ALPS (accidental launch protection system) A limited SDI system intended to be able to destroy a small number of missiles or warheads as might be associated with an accidental missile launch.

AMRAAM Advanced medium-range air-to-air missile.

APC Armored personnel carrier.

ARG Amphibious ready group.

ASAT (antisatellite) Any system that attempts to render enemy satellites inoperable.

ASPJ (airborne self-protection jammer) A sophisticated on-board electronics suite that jams targeting radars and projects a false target to draw enemy fire away from the aircraft.

ASW (antisubmarine warfare) Any operations conducted with the intent of destroying or denying the adversary effective use of its submarines.

ATA (advanced tactical aircraft) Also known as the A-12. The Navy's proposed replacement for the A-6 was cancelled by Secretary of Defense Richard Cheney in January 1991.

ATF (advanced tactical fighter)   Air Force air superiority fighter under development. The Lockheed/General Dynamics/Boeing YF-22 was selected for production.

ATBM   Antitactical ballistic missile.

ATTU   Atlantic-to-the-Urals.

AVF   All-volunteer force.

B-2 Bomber   The stealth bomber being produced by Northrop. Original plans called for a buy of 132 aircraft. As the cost per unit has escalated to nearly $750 million, the B-2 program is being stretched out, and the total number purchased will not exceed seventy-five.

BBBG   Battleship battle group.

Brilliant Pebbles   An SDI scheme consisting of thousands of orbiting mini-missiles which destroy warheads with kinetic energy.

Budget authority   The amount Congress authorizes the Pentagon to spend, or become contractually obligated to spend, each fiscal year.

Budget outlays   DOD expenditures made in any fiscal year.

C^3I (command, control, communications, and intelligence)   The coordinating functions of a military headquarters, from the battlefield to the national strategic level.

Carter Doctrine   President Carter's declaration that the protection of Southwest Asia and the Persian Gulf was in the vital interest of the United States, resulting in the creation of the Rapid Deployment Force (now CENTCOM).

CAS   Close air support.

CBO   Congressional Budget Office.

CENTAG   Central Army Group.

CENTCOM   Central Command.

CFE (Conventional Armed Forces in Europe talks)   Previously known as the Conventional Stability Talks (CST). Bloc-to-bloc negotiations on various categories of conventional weapons in the ATTU region. Agreement was reached and a CFE Treaty signed in November 1990.

CIC (combat information center)   The area of a warship dedicated to the collection and coordination of information vital to the performance of the ship in battle.

CINCs (Commanders-in-Chief)   Unified and specified commanders.

Conventional weapons   All instruments of war except nuclear weapons, biological weapons, and most chemical weapons. Incendiary and riot-control chemical weapons are considered conventional weapons.

Counterforce   The targeting of enemy military forces, both nuclear and conventional, rather than industrial and population centers. Counterforce targets include strategic C^3I systems. Counterforce targeting is the centerpiece of nuclear warfighting strategies.

Countervalue   The targeting of civilian population and industrial centers, with the goal of disrupting or destroying the social structure of the enemy state. Countervalue strategy is the foundation of mutually assured destruction.

CRAF (civil reserve air fleet)   Civilian passenger and cargo aircraft that can be used to augment military airlift command in times of national crisis. The fleet was called up for the first time during the buildup of Operation Desert Shield.

Crisis stability   A condition in which even during the most intense political confrontation there is no incentive for a state to launch an attack because its opponent's military will survive in sufficient force to inflict unacceptable damage in retaliation.

Cruise missile   A guided missile that maintains a constant velocity once launched and does not leave the atmosphere. A cruise missile is capable of delivering either conventional or nuclear warheads.

CSCE   Conference on Security and Cooperation in Europe.

CTB   Comprehensive Test Ban.

CVBG   Carrier battle group.

D-5   See Trident II.

DACOWITS   Department of Defense Advisory Committee on Women in the Services.

DCA (dual-capable aircraft)   Aircraft that are designed to carry both conventional and nuclear payloads.

DD   Destroyer.

DDG   Guided-missile destroyer.

DOD   Department of Defense.

Dual Track Decision   The decision made at a meeting of NATO foreign and defense ministers on December 12, 1979, approving the deployment of 108 Pershing II and 464 ground-launched cruise missiles in Europe under U.S. control while pursuing arms control negotiations between the United States and the Soviet Union that could limit or even prevent this deployment.

EUCOM   European Command.

EMP (electromagnetic pulse)   A pulse of radio frequency energy resulting from asymmetric ionization of the atmosphere after a nuclear explosion. A high-altitude nuclear blast can blanket a large area of the earth's surface, severely damaging unprotected electrical equipment.

ERIS   Exoatmospheric reentry vehicle interception system.

Flexible response   A strategic concept that gained prominence during the Kennedy administration. The strategy entails developing a military force structure capable of responding to varying degrees of conflict with equally differentiated increments of force. It was originally a response to the Eisenhower administration's apparent reliance on massive retaliation.

FOFA (follow-on forces attack)   A NATO doctrine developed for Central Europe under the supervision of General Bernard Rogers. FOFA emphasizes deep air strikes against enemy second-echelon forces.

FOTL (Follow-On-to-Lance)   Proposed replacement for the Lance missile in Europe, it would have extended the range of the Lance from eighty miles to nearly 250 miles, just under the limit imposed by the INF Treaty. Procurement plans were canceled by President Bush in 1990.

FYDP (Future-Years Defense Plan)   The budget requirements projection established yearly by the Defense Department. The FYDP is a planning document, not binding on either the Defense Department or Congress.

GAO (General Accounting Office)   An independent nonpolitical agency in the legislative branch of the U.S. government. Its responsibilities include legal, accounting, auditing, and claims settlement functions within the federal government and functions as assigned by Congress. It also recommends ways to make government operations more effective and efficient.

GLCM (ground-launched cruise missile)   See cruise missile.

GWEN   Ground wave emergency network.

HACV   Heavy armament combat vehicle.

Hard target   A site constructed to withstand the blast and associated effects of a nuclear attack and likely to be protected against a chemical, biological, or radiological attack.

HASC   House Armed Services Committee.

ICBM (intercontinental ballistic missile)   A land-based ballistic missile with a range capability from about 3,000 to 8,000 nautical miles.

IFF   Identification friend or foe.

INF (intermediate-range nuclear forces)   Nuclear delivery systems with a range between 500 and 5,500 kilometers. INF include intermediate-range ballistic missiles, medium-range ballistic missiles, ground-launched cruise missiles, and medium-range bombers.

INF Treaty   A U.S.-Soviet agreement that entered into force in June 1988 calling for the elimination of U.S. Pershing II missiles, ground-launched cruise missiles, and Soviet INF missiles from all theaters. It was the first agreement to eliminate an entire class of nuclear weapons.

IRBM   Intermediate-range ballistic missiles.

JCS   Joint Chiefs of Staff.

JSTARS   Joint Surveillance Target Attack Radar System.

JTFME   Joint Task Force Middle East.

LCAC   Landing craft air cushioned.

LIC   Low intensity conflict.

LID   Light infantry division.

Long-range bomber aircraft   A bomber designed for a tactical operating radius over 2,500 nautical miles at design gross weight and bomb load.

LRINF   Long-range intermediate-range nuclear forces.

LTBT (Limited Test Ban Treaty)   A 1963 agreement by the United States, Great Britain, and the Soviet Union that prohibits nuclear weapons tests in the atmosphere, in outer space, and under water. The treaty is considered a hallmark event in nuclear arms control.

MAC   Military Airlift Command.

MAD   See mutually assured destruction.

MAG   Marine air group.

MAGTF   Marine air-ground task force.

Maritime strategy The U.S. Navy's strategic policy emphasizing broad-based offensive actions in the event of sustained war against the Soviet Union. There are three prominent themes: aggressive protection of sea-lines of communication, especially the North Atlantic route, which would be used in carrying supplies to NATO forces; a large-scale sea and air campaign in the Pacific to divert Soviet resources and to attack Soviet vital interests; and a great emphasis on the quick and effective nullification of the Soviet submarine threat through an intensive ASW campaign.

MBFR (Mutual and Balanced Force Reductions) Conventional force negotiations that began in 1973 and were supplanted by CFE.

MC 14/2 (Military Committee 14/2) The NATO decision document, approved in 1956, by which the alliance formally adopted the strategy of massive retaliation. This strategy relied heavily on the use of nuclear weapons for the defense of Western Europe.

MC 14/3 (Military Committee 14/3) The NATO decision document, approved in 1967, by which the alliance formally adopted the strategy of flexible response. This strategy called for the NATO nations to confront the Warsaw Pact with a range of capabilities, including stronger conventional forces, tactical nuclear weapons, and American strategic nuclear weapons, thus allowing a variety of responses to Soviet aggression against Western Europe.

MEB Marine expeditionary brigade.

MEF Marine expeditionary force.

Megatonnage The explosive yield of a nuclear weapon in terms of millions of tons of TNT equivalents.

MEU Marine expeditionary unit.

Midgetman (See also SICBM) A mobile, single-warhead missile, weighing approximately 37,000 pounds.

MILSTAR (military strategic and tactical relay system) A network of satellites designed to provide a communications link between the national command authority and the military forces during a nuclear war.

Minuteman A three-stage solid propellant ballistic missile that serves as the foundation of the ICBM portion of the U.S. strategic triad. The Minuteman II is a single-warhead missile; the Minuteman III is armed with three warheads.

MIRV (multiple independently-targetable reentry vehicle) A reentry vehicle carried by a delivery system that can place one or more reentry vehicles over each of several targets.

MLRS (multiple launcher rocket system) Part of the Emerging Technologies Initiative, the MLRS is a self-propelled artillery piece that can ripple-fire twelve rockets in less than a minute at targets up to sixty kilometers away.

MSC Military Sealift Command.

Mutually assured destruction (MAD) A declaratory U.S. nuclear strategic doctrine initiated during the tenure of Defense Secretary Robert S. McNamara. The fundamental premise is that each side in a bilateral nuclear relationship retain a second-strike capability that could devastate the industrial and population centers of the enemy should that enemy initiate a nuclear first strike. The prelaunch nuclear standoff would then create a situation of mutual deterrence.

MX (also known as the Peacekeeper missile) Most recent addition to the ICBM portion of the U.S. strategic triad. The MX weighs 190,000 pounds, carries ten warheads plus decoys, and has a range of over 8,100 miles. The MX is highly accurate, with a circular error probable (CEP) of approximately 165 yards.

NASA National Aeronautics and Space Administration.

NATO North Atlantic Treaty Organization.

NCA National Command Authority.

NDU National Defense University.

NORTHAG Northern Army Group.

NPT Nuclear Nonproliferation Treaty.

NSC National Security Council.

NSWP Non-Soviet Warsaw Pact.

Nuclear Risk Reduction Centers (NRCC) On September 15, 1987, U.S. Secretary of State George Schultz and Soviet Foreign Minister Eduard Shevardnadze signed an agreement establishing these facilities in Moscow and Washington. The centers are staffed by personnel from the host country and serve as transmission and receiving points for notifications and exchanges of information to prevent nuclear war by miscalculation, accident, or misunderstanding. The Soviet NRCC is also the counterpart to the U.S. On-Site Inspection Agency.

O&M Operations and maintenance.

O&S Operations and support.

OMB Office of Management and Budget.

OMG (Operational Maneuver Group) Highly mobile, offensive Soviet armored divisions equipped with state-of-the-art tanks.

OSD Office of the Secretary of Defense.

OTH-B (over the horizon-backscatter) Radar systems that operate by bouncing beams off the ionosphere, eliminating the line-of-sight limitations of conventional radars.

Packard Commission (President's Blue Ribbon Commission on Defense Management) A bipartisan commission established by President Reagan on June 17, 1985, to review Pentagon procurement practices. David Packard, an industrialist and former deputy secretary of defense, headed the commission. The major proposal was the centralization of all DOD procurement responsibilities under the authority of a new under secretary of defense for acquisition, a step the president ordered the Defense Department to implement on April 2, 1986.

PACOM Pacific Command.

PAL (permissive action link) The lock placed on American nuclear weapons to prevent their unauthorized use. Early generation PALs consisted of simple physical impediments to access specifically designed for short-range systems in the European theater. Later-generation PALs are electronic locks requiring special numerical codes and featuring limited-try options. All U.S. nuclear weapons, except those controlled by the Navy, are equipped with PALs.

Patriot Originally designed as an antiaircraft air defense system, it earned a reputation as an effective antitactical ballistic missile system during the Persian Gulf War of 1991. The Patriot is a terminal defense system, operating on nearly one million lines of computer code. Changes to the code, begun in 1984 in response to a perceived increasing threat from Soviet tactical missiles in Europe, allowed the system to respond to the Iraqi Scud threat during the Gulf War.

PGM (precision-guided munition) Popularly known as "smart weapons." Electronically programmed and controlled weapons that can accurately hit a moving or stationary target.

PNET (Peaceful Nuclear Explosions Treaty) 1976 agreement between the United States and the Soviet Union limiting nuclear test explosions for peaceful purposes to a maximum yield of 150 kilotons. PNET was ratified on September 25, 1990, and entered into force on December 11, 1990.

POMCUS Prepositioned overseas material configured in unit sets.

PPBS Planning, programming, and budgeting system.

Presidential Directive 59 (PD-59) The National Security Council decision document that modified official U.S. nuclear strategy. It was signed by President Carter in July 1980 and called for a countervailing strategy that would allow limited nuclear options in case of a limited Soviet attack.

Projection forces Military units capable of rapid and sustained deployment, with the ability to wage low intensity conflict. The Marines, forces of the Central Command, special operations forces in any of the services, airlift and sealift forces, or any combination of these constitute U.S. projection forces.

Rail garrison A mobile basing mode for MX missiles. Fifty MX missiles are to be removed from their silos at F. E. Warren AFB and placed on twenty-five trains deployed at six Air Force bases. In a crisis these trains are to be flushed onto the civilian railways, enhancing the survivability of the missiles and, thereby, preventing preemption.

ROTC Reserve Officers Training Corps.

RV Reentry vehicle.

SAC Strategic Air Command.

SACEUR Supreme Allied Commander Europe.

SADARM (search and destroy armor) A submunition equipped with millimeter-wave radar enabling it to distinguish armored from nonarmored vehicles.

SAG Surface Action Group.

SALT I (Strategic Arms Limitations Talks I) The SALT I agreements, signed by President Richard Nixon and Soviet leader Leonid Brezhnev in 1972, include the ABM Treaty (see ABM Treaty) and an Interim Agreement limiting offensive nuclear forces up to 1977. The 1977 deadline was extended while the follow-on SALT II negotiations continued.

SALT II Continuation of strategic arms negotiations resulting in a 1979 accord never ratified by the U.S. Senate. The United States and the Soviet Union continued formal compliance until 1986. In an effort to meet the challenge of

MIRVing that SALT I did not address, SALT II constraints included a limit of 2,400 strategic nuclear delivery vehicles (to be reduced to 2,250 after ratification), 1,320 of which could be MIRVed. Other constraints effectively limited the number of warheads on each missile to the greatest number tested, with any new ICBM limited to a maximum of ten. Additionally, only one new ICBM model could be introduced to each side's arsenal. To enhance verification procedures, telemetry encryption was to be limited during missile tests.

SASC   Senate Armed Services Committee.

SDI   Strategic Defense Initiative.

SDIO   Strategic Defense Initiative Organization.

SEAL   Navy sea-air-land special forces teams.

SICBM (small intercontinental ballistic missile)   See Midgetman.

SIOP (single integrated operational plan)   The U.S. contingency plan for strategic retaliatory strikes in the event of a nuclear war. Targets, timing, tactics, and force requirements are considered for a variety of responses. The SIOP is prepared by the Joint Strategic Target Planning Staff located at SAC headquarters.

SLAM (standoff land attack missile)   A derivative of the Harpoon antiship missile, the SLAM can be launched by aircraft or from ships. It has a range of sixty nautical miles and carries a 500 pound high-explosive warhead. In the final minute of flight a video link activates, allowing an operator to control the missile with a joystick, seeing through a camera mounted in the nose of the SLAM. It also uses inertial guidance and an imaging infared seeker to acquire its targets.

SLBM   Submarine-launched ballistic missile.

SLCM (sea-launched cruise missile)   See cruise missile.

SLOC(s)   Sea-line(s) of communication.

SNF   Short-range nuclear forces, defined as weapons with a range of less than 500 kilometers.

SOC   Special operations contingency.

SOF   Special operations forces.

SOLIC   Special operations and low intensity conflict.

SOPAG   Special Operations Policy Advisory Group.

SOSUS   Sound surveillance system.

Specified Command   A command that is normally composed of forces from a single service. The Strategic Air Command is an example.

SRAM (short-range attack missile)   Nuclear air-to-surface missile. The Air Force is developing a follow-on known as the SRAM II.

SSBN   A nuclear-powered ballistic missile-carrying submarine.

SSN   An attack submarine.

START (Strategic Arms Reductions Talks)   Negotiations begun in June 1982 with the nominal goal of 50 percent reductions in the strategic nuclear arsenals of the United States and the Soviet Union.

Theater   The geographical area outside the continental United States for which a commander of a unified or specified command has been assigned military responsibilities.

TLAM (Tomahawk land attack missile)   See SLCM. Alternate designation for the conventionally-armed version of the Tomahawk SLCM.

TLAM/N   Designation for nuclear-armed Tomahawk SLCM.

Triad   The foundation of U.S. nuclear deterrence policy, the triad consists of the U.S. Navy's ballistic missile submarine force and the U.S. Air Force's ICBM and strategic bomber forces. The underlying principle of the triad remains the assured second-strike capability of at least one of the three strategic forces following an enemy nuclear attack.

Trident II   Latest U.S. SLBM, also called the D-5, it combines the survivability of the submarine basing mode with the accuracy and throw-weight of ICBMs, making it the first hard-target capable SLBM.

Triple Zero   Refers to the elimination of all SNF from NATO and Warsaw Pact theater forces. The INF Treaty is often credited with having created a "double zero" situation in which the intermediate-range missile forces of both sides were eliminated.

TTBT (Threshold Test Ban Treaty)   A 1974 agreement between the United States and the Soviet Union that prohibits underground nuclear tests with yields greater than 150 kilotons. The treaty was ratified by the U.S. Senate on September 25, 1990, and entered into force on December 11, 1990.

UAV   Unmanned aerial vehicle.

UMT   Universal military training.

Unified command   A command in which the commander has at his disposal the forces of two or more services, usually within a geographic area. The Pacific Command is an example.

USD/A   Undersecretary of defense for acquisition.

USSOCOM   U.S. Special Operations Command.

USTRANSCOM   U.S. Transportation Command.

VLS   Vertical launch system.

V/STOL   Vertical and/or short take-off and landing.

War Powers Act   Passed in 1973, this act requires that the president consult with Congress before committing military forces to actual or imminent hostilities and that he formally inform Congress within forty-eight hours of their introduction. Congress must then approve or disapprove of the deployment within sixty days, although this period can be stretched to ninety days if the president certifies that the safety of the troops requires it.

WTO (Warsaw Treaty Organization)   Official designation of the Warsaw Pact. The military wing of the Warsaw Pact disbanded in 1991.

Wing   An Air Force unit composed of one primary mission group and the necessary supporting organizations.

Zero Option   The Reagan administration's original negotiating position in the INF talks. It called for the elimination of all intermediate-range nuclear missiles from the Soviet and American arsenals and formed the basis for the INF Treaty.

Chapter 1

After the Storm: Perspectives on the Gulf War

Joseph Kruzel

T he 1991 Gulf War raised many questions about American defense policy, and the putative lessons of that conflict will be debated for many years to come. While it will be some time before the combat debriefings, after-action reports, and official histories are compiled and made available to the public, the lessons of Desert Storm are already being invoked and acted upon. Thus it is important to begin sketching out what may have been learned, and what was left unproven, by that brief war and astonishingly low-cost victory by the United States and its coalition partners.

Anyone interested in defense policy should bring a healthy skepticism to lessons so quickly drawn, particularly from a conflict that is unlikely to provide the model for future challenges to the new world order. Iraq is, after all, a country with a population less than that of New York state and an economic output, even before the devastation of the war, less than that of Kentucky. What had been described as the world's fourth largest military establishment revealed itself in battle to be a hollow and ineffective army. Few lessons about combat effectiveness can be learned from engaging with an adversary that declines to fight.

Saddam Hussein also proved to be a near-perfect villain, and the coalition aligned against him had a compelling *casus belli*. There was no Kuwaiti insurgency calling for aid from the Iraqis; Saddam Hussein's invasion was an act of clear military aggression. The Iraqis turned out to be a poorly trained and motivated army using Soviet tactics and equipment with which the United States was familiar. The coalition had unimpeded access to a secure logistics base, and six months to prepare and to lift the needed equipment to a country in the combat theater with good ports and well-developed air bases. One act of great good fortune was Saddam Hussein's decision to release his hostages, those human shields whose continued presence in Iraq would have vastly complicated the air war.

The old saw that generals prepare to fight the last war was dramatically dis-
proved in the gulf. Military leaders and politicians were united in their determination *not* to fight another Vietnam. Defeat in Vietnam taught many powerful
lessons, and military success in the gulf was a direct consequence of failure two
decades earlier. The broad latitude given General Schwarzkopf by his commander-in-chief was a complete reversal of Lyndon Johnson's micromanagement
of operational detail in Vietnam.[1] The steadfast resistance of Central Command
(CENTCOM) briefers to providing "body counts" was a deliberate effort to avoid
a repetition of the grim and ultimately irrelevant fixation on casualty statistics in
Southeast Asia. One lesson of Vietnam taken to heart by President Bush and
senior military officers, and vividly displayed in the Gulf War, was the decision to
commit overwhelming military force, and to use it quickly and decisively once it
was prepared for battle. This stood in stark contrast to the gradual escalation of
Vietnam.

Coalition Diplomacy and Coalition Warfare

One tentative lesson of the war was that American unilateralism would never have
worked. There was considerable grumbling about the conspicuous absence of
some key allies, but the gulf crisis ultimately produced an impressive array of
countries, as seen in table 1–1, that contributed combat troops, support units, or
funding to the collective effort. General Schwarzkopf was not simply making a
political gesture when he thanked by name every nation that contributed military
forces to the coalition.

Another lesson was that the United Nations can play a crucial role. The war
was authorized by United Nations mandate, and Security Council resolutions provided the organizing basis for the allied coalition and the conditions for war termination. Still, Desert Shield did not begin as a U.N. action. It was a unilateral
U.S. deployment undertaken with extraordinary speed that was ultimately ratified
and joined by other states. In effect, the United Nations ratified a U.S. *fait accom-
pli*, and it is doubtful that the United Nations would have authorized the same sort
of military force and delivered the same sort of ultimatum to Saddam Hussein in
advance.

AirLand Battle and the Air War

AirLand Battle, the bible for ground combat developed by the Army and Marine
Corps in the 1970s and 1980s, proved a valuable conceptual guide for the Gulf
War. Anyone who had read Army field manual 100–5 would have had a fairly clear
idea of the ground strategy that allowed allied forces to encircle a demoralized
army in 100 hours.

AirLand Battle combines classical principles of war such as maneuver, surprise, and deception with modern developments in firepower, mobility, and communications. It emphasizes operational art, synchronization, and a focus on centers of gravity.

Operational art matches means to ends. It directs commanders to consider
first the desired end point—what constitutes military victory—and then to begin
fleshing out an operational plan of action. It is not enough to plan individual sorties

Table 1–1. Coalition Equipment and Personnel Contributions,
Operation Desert Storm

	Personnel				
Country	Ground Troops	Navy/Air Personnel	Tanks	Ships	Aircraft
GCC	135,000[1]	50,000	900	36	410
US	370,000[2]	130,000	2,100	72	1,300
UK	35,000	7,000	210	16	96
France	13,000	4,000	40	14	42
Egypt	23,000	—	450	—	—
Syria	19,000	—	300	—	—
Pakistan	7,000	—	—	—	—
Bangladesh	2,000	—	—	—	—
Morocco	1,700	—	—	—	—
Senegal	500	—	—	—	—
Somalia	500	—	—	—	—
Niger	500	—	—	—	—
Czech.	200	—	—	—	—
Honduras	150	—	—	—	—
Argentina	—	300	—	2	—
Netherlands	81	620	—	3	—
Canada	—	2,400	—	3	18
Italy	—	1,600	—	3	16
Belgium	—	400	—	3	—
Spain	—	500	—	3	—
Denmark, Greece, Norway, Portugal	—	—	—	1@	—

Source: Data from *Armed Forces Journal International*, March 1991, p. 25.

[1]Gulf Cooperation Council: Saudi Arabia, 90,000; UAE, 15,000; Kuwait, 10,000; Oman, 10,000; Bahrain, 5,000; Qatar, 5,000.

[2]Includes reserves.

or separate battles in isolation from an overarching conception of how those actions will ultimately contribute to victory. Synchronization refers to the reinforcing
effects of combined arms. AirLand Battle emphasizes attacks on centers of gravity, those elements that keep a military force able and willing to fight. Destroy or
incapacitate those key nodes, and the battle is over. Allied military commanders
identified two centers of gravity for the Iraqi military. One was command and
control, upon which the highly centralized Iraqi military command structure was
critically dependent; the other was the Republican Guard, thought to be the lynch-
pin of Iraqi military strength.

In the Gulf War, the air attacks on command and control centers in the first few hours of the war isolated Iraqi units in the field, and acted as a force multiplier for allied forces in the ground battle that followed. By weakening the overall capacity of the Iraqi armed forces to sustain combat, the various phases of the six-week Gulf War, carried out jointly by the various services, were a true demonstration of the power of AirLand Battle doctrine.

Service coordination and cooperation in Desert Storm was a marked contrast to Vietnam. As a young lieutenant working at Seventh Air Force headquarters during the Vietnam war, this author recalls being told by a general officer that the real war in Vietnam was about "roles and missions"—seizing the high ground for the post-Vietnam bureaucratic battle over which services would be allocated which particular tasks. In contrast to Vietnam, where the Army, Navy, and Air Force waged three separate air wars and the Army and Marines each fought its own war on the ground, Desert Storm saw all U.S. services fighting the same war at the same time. The Goldwater-Nichols Act, the main subject of the "Organization and Management" chapter of previous *American Defense Annuals,* also helped to provide the administrative capacity for the services to work together in a new spirit of harmony and cooperation.

The Air War

Airpower advocates from Guilio Douhet to the present have claimed that massive bombing can subdue an enemy without the need to resort to a ground war. In the gulf, the combination of coalition strength and Iraqi vulnerability made the conflict

a near-perfect test of the efficacy of airpower, and the Gulf War produced the victory that Douhet could only imagine.

The sequential allied air campaign had two parts. The strategic campaign destroyed command and control facilities, as well as Iraq's ability to produce nuclear, chemical, and biological weapons. Coalition forces attacked Iraqi air assets, gaining air superiority in the opening moments of the campaign, and severed supply routes and lines of communication between Baghdad and Kuwait, isolating troops in Kuwait and beginning the efforts to destroy their will to resist.

The architects of the air campaign were determined to inflict as much psychological as material damage. Their around-the-clock sorties—more sorties per average day than the Iraqis experienced during their entire eight years of war with Iran—degraded the fighting capacity of Iraqi divisions by as much as 50 percent, and destroyed the Iraqi capacity to reconstitute the remnants into a viable fighting machine. In addition, industrial targets of military and economic value to the Iraqi leadership were devastated by the air campaign, demonstrating the almost limitless capacity of the coalition air forces to wreak destruction. The air war demonstrated that strategic bombing, while not capable of achieving pinpoint precision, is not quite the blunt instrument that many people believed. Many of the air targets were individual buildings surrounded by apartments and other residences.

The tactical air campaign against the Kuwaiti Theater of Operations (KTO) devastated dug-in troops. The bombing campaign destroyed much of Iraq's artillery and tank force, rendered its air force ineffective, and shattered the morale of Iraqi soldiers. No army had ever before been subjected to such intensive and sustained air bombardment. When the ground war began, coalition air assets flew in support of the ground forces, helping to complete the rout of the Iraqi army with miraculously low allied casualties.

In the six weeks of war, coalition forces flew over 100,000 sorties, dropping an impressive amount of ordnance on Iraqi targets. To perform this task, the U.S. Air Force deployed over 650 aircraft to the region. The Navy's contribution to the air campaign was more modest. Only four of the six aircraft carriers on station in the gulf were available for combat missions (two were being replenished), and more than half of the carriers' fighters were assigned to defending the battle groups from a possible Iraqi air attack. Nonetheless, the U.S. air contingent was formidable, and not alone. In all, eleven countries provided air assets to the war against Saddam Hussein.

The air war was carefully scripted; the daily air tasking order was over 600 pages long. While the air war was meticulously planned, it was also subject to improvisation as strategists attempted to overcome problems encountered. When mobile Scud launchers became a political problem, more than a hundred sorties a day were reassigned to search out and destroy the launchers. The A-10, ordinarily a low-flying tank killer, was pressed into service as a medium-altitude tank finder, a role which it performed quite well. When air planners were dismayed at the slow pace at which Iraqi tanks were being destroyed, they devised new tactics in which "Killer Scout" F-16s visually identified dug-in targets for other aircraft to attack. All of these missions obviously depended on air supremacy.

One surprise in the air war was the difficulty in finding Scud launchers. Skeptics suggested that if allied air forces could not find such sites in a relatively small area with complete air superiority, there was little chance that B-2 bombers would be able to perform their intended mission of finding and destroying mobile missiles in the Soviet Union. That was a lesson of Desert Storm the Air Force had obviously hoped to avoid.

Still, for all the remarkable success of the air war, it cannot be said that airpower won the war, or if it did, which aspect of airpower was responsible for success. Did airpower destroy the Iraqis' ability to fight or shatter their morale? Many Iraqi soldiers disliked Saddam Hussein, were weary after eight years of fighting with Iran, and did not accept the argument that Kuwait was the "lost province" of their homeland. If the psychological toll of incessant bombing forced the rout of the Iraqi army, then the precision-guided munitions (PGMs) and other high-tech weaponry performed brilliantly in a role that was peripheral to the defeat.

Friendly Fire

Coordinating the waves of allied aircraft from eleven countries was impressively executed. One measure of success is that the 100,000 combat sorties did not produce a single plane brought down by "friendly" fire. By way of comparison, some analysts expected that in a North Atlantic Treaty Organization (NATO)–Warsaw Pact air war, up to 40 percent of NATO losses in the first week would be to friendly fire.[2]

Two factors contributed to the astonishing outcome. First, careful tracking of coalition air assets isolated threat aircraft and reduced the risk of misidentification. Second, the Iraqi air force, reckoned in prewar planning to be a significant threat, never seriously challenged the coalition air forces. The near-total absence of a real air-to-air threat reduced the chance that a friendly aircraft would be misidentified and targeted.

CENTCOM also gave high priority to minimizing friendly fire casualties on the ground. Helicopters were trained with gun-camera footage to distinguish allied vehicles from Iraqi forces. Front-line U.S. tanks and armored vehicles were conspicuously marked with a "V," making them more easily identifiable. The close coordination of ground and air forces, as well as the multinational nature of the Gulf War, made inevitable some number of casualties by friendly fire; in one incident, an AH-64 Apache helicopter mistakenly launched a Hellfire missile at a Bradley Fighting Vehicle, killing two and wounding six infantrymen. At the conclusion of Desert Storm, however, the leading cause of death was neither friendly fire nor combat with the enemy, but traffic accidents, which killed well over 100 soldiers.

Intelligence and Warning

The inability of U.S. intelligence agencies to predict Saddam Hussein's invasion of Kuwait, or even to alert senior policymakers to the possible consequences of the Iraqi leader's posturing and threats over the summer of 1990, raised questions about the nation's ability to collect and evaluate intelligence in the post–cold war world. It also supports the growing pressure in Congress to overhaul the intelligence system with an eye toward improving efficiency, eliminating duplication, and improving accountability.

One suggestion would revise the current structure in which the director of the Central Intelligence Agency (CIA) also serves simultaneously as director of central intelligence (DCI). The DCI has nominal responsibility for all intelligence, but most of the $30 billion-a-year intelligence budget is allocated to agencies over which the DCI has no real control. A new position of national intelligence director would have authority over the CIA and all other intelligence agencies including the Defense Intelligence Agency, the National Security Agency, and the National Reconnaissance Office.

Beyond organizational change the U.S. intelligence community needs to refocus its strategic priorities, as well as its sources and methods, in the post–cold war era. When the Soviet military threat was the primary target, U.S. intelligence could rely on sophisticated technology for intelligence: satellites and communications eavesdropping devices. Now that problems of Third World instability are becoming increasingly important, the U.S. intelligence effort must reevaluate its sources and methods to determine those most appropriate for the new requirements. Satellites and other high-tech collection methods may not provide the intelligence needed for new, post–cold war threats.

Intelligence assessments of Iraq's military capability, at least those that became public, also appeared wide of the mark. The soldiers of the vaunted Republican Guard fought no more effectively than their less elite comrades. The number of Scud missiles in the Iraqi arsenal was apparently vastly underestimated. The lethal "Saddam Line" along the southern and western borders of Kuwait turned out to be militarily insignificant: minefields alleged to be a mile deep turned out to be only 400 feet deep; the impenetrable sand berms were so eroded by desert winds that they could easily be traversed by jeeps.

Figure 1-1. World Conflicts, 1990

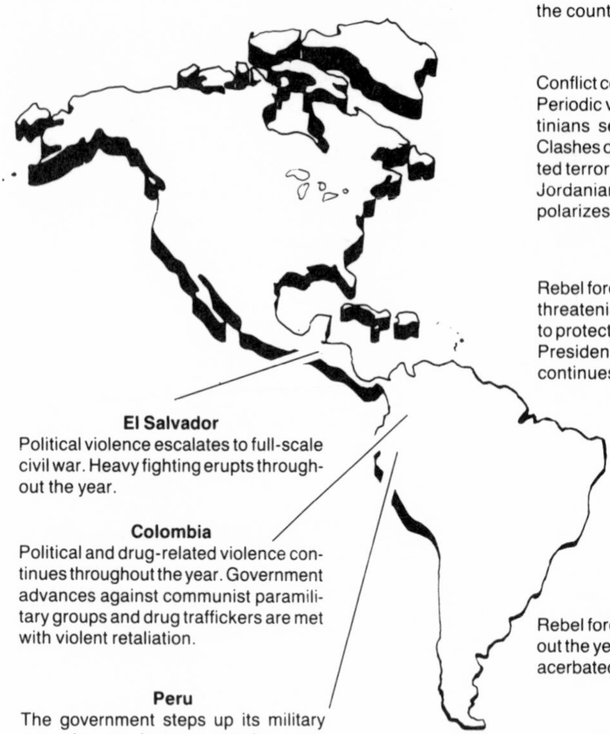

Lebanon
Christian and Muslim forces continue to clash for control of the country. Political resolution appears unlikely.

Israel
Conflict continues on a number of fronts throughout the year. Periodic violence erupts in the occupied territories as Palestinians seek to prevent Israeli settlement of the region. Clashes on the border with Lebanon and air strikes at suspected terrorist camps in Lebanon continue. Clashes along the Jordanian border intensify as the Iraqi occupation of Kuwait polarizes the Middle East.

Liberia
Rebel forces pursue military advantage throughout the year, threatening the capital in early May. U.S. Marines are sent to protect and evacuate U.S. nationals. The capital falls and President Samuel Doe is captured and killed. Unrest continues.

El Salvador
Political violence escalates to full-scale civil war. Heavy fighting erupts throughout the year.

Colombia
Political and drug-related violence continues throughout the year. Government advances against communist paramilitary groups and drug traffickers are met with violent retaliation.

Peru
The government steps up its military operations against suspected communist groups and drug traffickers.

Sudan
The civil war continues with conflict spilling over the border, intensifying the Ethiopian conflict with Eritrean rebels.

Ethiopia
Rebel forces continue to battle government troops throughout the year. Thousands die in the fighting and in famines exacerbated by the war and its disruptive effect on relief efforts.

Angola
U.S. support to UNITA accelerates. Political violence continues as a number of major offensives are launched throughout the year.

Soviet Union

The shaky foundation of *perestroika* continues to take a pounding as the Baltic states and the Central Asian Republics push for independence from Moscow. Soviet troops are given the option to use deadly force and numerous clashes between Soviet troops and pro-independence demonstrators leave many casualties. Resurgent ethnic tensions result in violent clashes in several republics.

Kuwait

Longstanding political conflict explodes when Iraqi troops and tanks occupy Kuwait. 500,000 U.S.-led forces take up positions in Saudi Arabia to blunt further Iraqi advances and provide the capacity to liberate Kuwait. The United Nations sets a January 15 deadline for Iraq to withdraw and authorizes the use of force. By year's end, hope for a political settlement all but disappears.

India/Pakistan

Political agitation continues over the control of the Kashmir region. Tensions and military alerts at mid-year threaten all out war. Artillery battles and skirmishes between troops occur throughout the year.

Cambodia

Negotiations prove ineffectual. Khmer Rouge forces make important military gains throughout the year. The intensity of the conflict declines but solutions remain difficult to achieve and escalation remains a possibility.

Somalia

Civil war continues to rip the country with battles intensifying late in the year. End-of-the-year fighting in Mogadishu, the capital, leaves countless dead.

South Africa

The complexities of South African tribal politics become apparent as conflict between blacks and whites is joined by black-on-black violence. Nelson Mandela is released from prison, and tribal conflict escalates throughout the year.

Sri Lanka

Tamil separatists continue to battle government forces throughout the year. Charges of chemical weapons use surface in late summer.

If long-term strategic information about Iraq's capabilities and intentions was less than desired, tactical intelligence on the battlefield was of a far higher quality. PGMs and other modern munitions require real-time precision intelligence, and one legacy of the Gulf War will almost certainly be a greater emphasis on the dissemination of surveillance information, especially those satellite links that can pass information directly to users in the field.[3]

One clear winner was the Army-Air Force joint surveillance target attack radar system (JSTARS). Originally conceived as the primary deep sensor for NATO's follow-on forces attack strategy, and still in the development and testing phase, the two JSTARS E-8 aircraft were ordered to the gulf in December 1990. The results, according to the services, were spectacular.[4] By providing high-quality images of the battlefield in real time, JSTARS enable ground commanders to select targets and intercept Iraqi military vehicles on the move. Fitted with a new communications system, the JSTARS aircraft were able to pass data directly to various command units, enhancing the real-time provision of intelligence. The political battle over the need for a multibillion dollar system like JSTARS will continue, but the system's performance in the gulf certainly shifted momentum in its favor. The Air Force will continue development and testing, looking eventually to field up to twenty JSTARS aircraft, with production beginning in 1993 and initial operational capability to be achieved in 1997.[5]

Space systems also performed well in Desert Storm. Every military satellite program was involved in some manner with U.S. and coalition military activities in the war.[6] U.S. imaging and signals intelligence satellites gave real-time information to commanders and troops regarding Iraqi positions and movement. A critical factor in the success of space operations was the use of mobile down-link stations, permitting data to be processed by analysts in the field. Some information, including targeting information generated by the Global Positioning System (GPS) could be downloaded directly to the troops via miniaturized personal GPS receivers.[7] Space-based assets also provided critical weather information and battle damage assessment in addition to routine command, control, and intelligence.

There were, however, potentially critical shortcomings in tactical intelligence that came to light in the months after the war. Interoperability, the capacity to connect to other services and systems, was limited. Some nine different intelligence gathering and analysis systems were fielded in Desert Storm. In many cases these systems could not communicate with each other, thus repeating one of the most glaring errors of the Grenada invasion of 1983.

Military Quality and Quantity: Better versus More

One perennial dispute in the defense community has been over quality versus quantity of military equipment. The United States has traditionally favored technology over numbers, arguing that U.S. scientific superiority holds the key against adversaries that may well be numerically superior. Military reformers have contended that U.S. security interests would be better served by greater numbers of weapons of less sophisticated design, along with more innovation in tactics. They have argued that high-tech weapons, in addition to their high cost, are too complex to operate on the battlefield and too prone to break down under combat conditions.

The reformers will have a difficult case to make in the post–Gulf War era, for one clear lesson of the war was that high-tech weapons worked. And while it is true that many of the decisive weapons were not that sophisticated—the Air Force and Navy aircraft, the Abrams main battle tank, and the Patriot and Tomahawk missiles were developed decades before and employed technology that would hardly be considered "high tech" by scientists in the 1990s—other weapons, especially stealth fighters and PGMs—justified the U.S. investment in sophisticated high unit-cost systems. In fact, inexpensive "dumb bombs" may have been one of the great losers in the Gulf War. Pilots found it very difficult, even with air superiority, to destroy targets with unguided munitions.[8] In terms of cost-effectiveness, gravity bombs that miss the target more often than not and expose pilots to repeated air defense and antiaircraft fire may be far more expensive than PGMs.

According to Lt. General Charles Horner, the coalition air commander, the performance of the stealthy F-117 fighter not only vindicated the aircraft's high cost but also fundamentally changed the nature of air warfare. The F-117 accounted for only 3 percent of allied aircraft but struck 43 percent of the Iraqi targets that were hit. Air Force officials claimed that the F-117 hit about 95 percent of its targets. And none of the stealth fighters was hit by Iraqi surface-to-air missiles or antiaircraft fire. Clearly, stealth technology was one of the big winners in the desert.

The next-generation Air Force tactical fighter, heavily dependent on the stealth advances pioneered by the F-117, is certain to receive greater attention in the wake of the Gulf War. Also in line for increased attention is the Navy's plan for a fighter to replace the aging A-6. In January 1991 Secretary Cheney canceled the A-12 Avenger, the McDonnell Douglas-General Dynamics design for this role. The A-12 was to use the same stealth technology as the F-117. It was not the high-tech character of the aircraft that forced its cancellation, but its skyrocketing cost (more than $90 million per plane) and delays in production (about eighteen months behind schedule). There were allegations of fraud and deception in the management of the program, and several Navy officers were fired. Secretary Cheney's decision was a surprising one for a secretary so congenially supportive of the military, but it did not signal a turn away from high technology—only that incompetence and excessive cost overruns will not be tolerated in any program. In fact, in light of the success of stealth technology in the gulf, Cheney revived the search for an A-6 replacement, renamed the AX (at roughly the same cost and probably with the same contractors).[9]

The Gulf War brought praise for the Reagan buildup of the 1980s, without which, it was implied, the U.S. military could not have mounted Desert Storm. But, as Secretary Cheney noted, much of the technology so successfully employed in the gulf was the product of efforts by the Carter administration and especially Harold Brown, Carter's secretary of defense.[10]

The Gulf War also underscored a new range of security threats for the 1990s. As many as forty nations are reportedly seeking radar-evading stealth technology, and many already have the capability of building a "poor man's cruise missile."[11] The proliferation of these dangerous technologies—nuclear, chemical, and biological, as well as missile—will increase the destructiveness of regional conflicts and, by increasing the advantage of preemption, decrease crisis stability.

One generally overlooked first in Operation Desert Storm was the first firing of a U.S. cruise missile in combat. The dazzling success of the Tomahawk cruise missile had some military analysts wondering why $100 million airframes like the F-117 were necessary. Cruise missiles are, in some ways, superior to manned aircraft, and leave behind no downed pilots to become prisoners of war.[12] Cruise missiles have limitations—small warhead, no search-and-destroy capability—but Desert Storm should give cruise missile research and development a great boost.

Finally, there have long been concerns that advanced U.S. equipment were laboratory successes, but that the strains of war and the harsh conditions of the desert would render them impotent. Those concerns proved unfounded in the Gulf War. Many systems performed at or above specifications. Fighters, for example, averaged three sorties per day, and the Air Force maintained over 90 percent of its aircraft in commission in the war zone during Desert Storm.[13] In the end, Desert Storm proved that with necessary maintenance high-tech systems can perform well even under harsh battlefield conditions.

The Total Force Concept

One clear lesson of the Gulf War was the fundamental value of well-trained and highly capable personnel. Generals Colin Powell and Norman Schwarzkopf were officers of great skill and uncommon intellect. Lt. General Sir Peter de la Billière, the British commander in the gulf, called General Schwarzkopf the "man of the match" for his "brilliance, leadership, drive, determination and occasional rudeness."[14] All of the forces, from the senior military leadership down to troops on the front line, performed with diligence and distinction.

The skill and professionalism of U.S. forces in the Gulf War seem vindications of the all-volunteer force. One of the lessons of Vietnam was to abolish the draft and field a force of willing soldiers. Senior military officers said repeatedly through the 1980s that the all-volunteer force produced the best quality troops in memory, and Desert Storm proved them right. It was, however, a less successful first combat test of the Total Force concept.

Secretary Cheney claimed that the Gulf War was a vindication of the total force concept, but most of the guardsmen and reservists called to active service in the gulf were in support positions. The reserve forces performed with distinction. Air Force reservists provided much of the airlift and refueling capability, and flew a significant number of combat missions. Army reservists provided a number of support functions: military police, civil-military affairs, and medical support. But in real combat roles the reserve forces performed less effectively. The 48th Infantry Brigade of the Georgia National Guard spent the entire war at the National Training Center trying to become certified as combat-ready and join the 24th Mechanized Infantry Division as its "roundout" brigade. The "round-out" concept that Lewis Sorley discusses in Chapter 11 needs to be reassessed. The experience of Desert Storm suggests that two days a month and two weeks a year are not enough time to keep trained and qualified soldiers at an acceptable level of readiness, and the antipathy of regular Army troops toward "weekend warriors" creates a cultural divide that makes smooth and rapid integration very difficult.[15]

America's Role in the New World Order

The most important lesson of the Gulf War was not to be found in the study of military tactics or weapons technology, but in the broader question of what the war suggested about America's role in the new world order. The collapse of communism and victory in Desert Storm combined to focus attention once again on a question that in one way or another has been vigorously debated throughout most of U.S. history, but was muted during the cold war: the debate between internationalism and isolationism.

There is a lively dialogue in the scholarly community between these two groups, but as Stephen Van Evera notes in Chapter 7, almost no such discussion within the Bush administration. Even before the success of Desert Storm, President Bush and his closest advisors were committed to continuing America's past internationalist policies.

The internationalists believe that the United States has no choice but to play an active role in world affairs. There is no going back to a political and military detachment from world problems and other centers of power. America's own security requires an activist role, and so do the interests of the rest of the world. The United States is increasingly dependent on international trade and unfettered access to raw materials, not the least of which is oil. Without oil available at reasonable prices, the entire industrialized world would quickly collapse. The United States also has a moral and a political obligation to promote democratic values and to support democratic regimes. Simply put, the world needs a dominant power. An international system without a hegemonial power is doomed to anarchy and instability. It is America's responsibility, as well as its good fortune, to provide hegemonic stability to the post–cold war world.

Modern-day isolationists do not argue for an American withdrawal from world politics, but rather for a less expansive conception of vital American interests and a greater appreciation of the growing disutility of military force in securing and protecting those interests. What the United States really needs from the rest of the world is free trade with Western Europe and the countries of the Asian rim. Military power is irrelevant to achieving that objective, and may indeed erode U.S. economic competitiveness. The United States and the rest of the industrialized world need oil, but the declining price of oil during the Gulf War—with no oil coming from Iraq and Kuwait—demonstrated how well the market can correct itself. In economic terms, the rest of the world simply does not matter. The promotion of democratic values through national example and rhetorical support abroad is commendable, but military intervention to support democracy is both morally suspect and practically counterproductive. Democracy requires social and economic preconditions which are generally lacking in the Third World. There are problems enough to occupy Americans at home—drugs, a crumbling infrastructure, a crisis in education—without taking on intractable problems overseas. With the collapse of the Soviet military threat, the United States can return to the security position it enjoyed in the 1920s, when President Calvin Coolidge took note of the country's favored geopolitical position. "We have no traditional enemies," Coolidge observed. "We have no possessions that are coveted by others; they have none that are coveted by us. Our borders are unfortified. We fear no one; no one fears us."[16]

Paradoxically, while internationalists and isolationists begin from opposite positions, many from the two camps reach a common ground in assessing the likelihood of conflict in the post–cold war environment. Both agree that the world is likely to be a more dangerous place. As noted earlier, as many as forty countries are striving to acquire sophisticated high-technology arms—chemical, nuclear, and biological—as well as ballistic and cruise missiles with which to deliver these weapons of mass destruction. Conventional munitions that only a few years ago were exclusively in the hands of major powers are becoming increasingly easy to purchase on the international market. Internationalists see this less stable and more dangerous world as a threat to vital U.S. interests, underscoring the importance of vigorous American efforts to impose order and tranquility. For the isolationists this vision of global chaos is all the more reason for the United States to stand apart from conflicts that threaten no tangible U.S. interest.

For forty years internationalism prevailed in the United States because its proponents held the trump card of anticommunism, which proved to be an unassailable rationale for activism and military intervention. With the collapse of communism, internationalism has lost its trump card, and American foreign policy has

By permission of Don Wright, *The Palm Beach Post*

no comparable organizing concept. In the early 1900s a British diplomat asked von Bülow, Germany's foreign minister, why the Germans, traditionally a continental power, were building such a large navy. "We are building it," von Bülow replied, "for general purposes of greatness." But greatness in world politics is measured not only by raw military power but also by ideas and principles. Greatness derives not so much by what is opposed as by what is championed.

In his postwar address to Congress, President Bush cautioned that the war against Iraq "was not waged as a 'war to end all wars,'" thus distancing himself from any Wilsonian notion of solving the problem of world politics once and for all. But the president also said that "enduring peace must be our mission." The war was waged for some moral purpose, and that purpose should be the cornerstone of the new world order. The United States stood squarely against Saddam Hussein's specific act of aggression against Kuwait, but what it stood for is less clear. What might be the new lodestar of American foreign policy in the post–cold war era? Three principles suggest themselves as candidates: (1) the promotion of democracy and democratic values; (2) securing the right of nations to self-determination; and (3) maintaining the inviolability of existing international borders.

While the United States has long championed human rights and democratic values, Desert Storm was not waged to make the Middle East safe for democracy. The Arab world boasts few democracies, and Kuwait is not among them. Many Arab states persecute minorities and women, and deride the personal, political, and intellectual freedom that is the essence of Western democracy. The end of the war brought the emir back to Kuwait (once his palace was repaired) and permitted Saddam Hussein to continue his butchery inside Iraq's borders. The treatment of minorities and progress toward representative democracy were internal matters, the Bush administration suggested, not issues for international action. The new world order may not have been intended to preserve governments that deny political and economic freedom, but that was its immediate consequence post–Desert Storm.

It is also clear that the Gulf War was not fought to secure the right of ethnic self-determination. President Bush repeatedly made clear that he opposed the political disintegration of Iraq, but the "Lebanonization" of Iraq, so greatly feared before the fighting began as a likely consequence of war, had been a geopolitical fact long before Saddam Hussein came to power. The country has always been a hodgepodge of ethnic and religious communities: Shiites, Sunnis, Kurds, Christians, and secular Iraqis joined together in a state with no overarching sense of national identity. President Bush's unwillingness to help the Kurds reflected his determination not to open the Pandora's box of Middle Eastern ethnic rivalry. Emboldened Kurds in Iraq would cause trouble for Turkey and Iran with their own Kurdish populations. A Shiite revolt would extend Iranian influence, hardly a comforting prospect to Saudi Arabia and the emirates.

Desert Storm was waged in defense of existing territorial boundaries and the right of small states not to be gobbled up by larger neighbors. But American policy, so explicit on this right with respect to Kuwait, has been ambiguous about the right of small captive nations to secede from multinational empires. The powerful force of nationalism, far from disappearing in contemporary international relations, threatens to tear apart states in many regions of the world. Until Iraq's invasion of Kuwait, Arab countries accepted each other's territorial boundaries, however artificially drawn. (This same accord has kept African states from disintegrating along tribal lines.) If this pragmatic rule of contemporary international relations were to be abandoned, the collection of states put together in the drawing rooms of European capitals in earlier times would begin to collapse. If the new world order is simply a defense of the political status quo, then the United States should have as little sympathy for Lithuanian independence as it did for Iraq's annexation of its would-be nineteenth province.

The fundamental lesson of Vietnam was that the United States could not be the world's policeman—there are limits to American power. The "specter of Vietnam" kept the United States out of Angola, Somalia, and a substantial ground war in Central America, but it did not long deter America from playing the role of global hegemon. U.S. military involvements in the 1980s were quick in-and-out affairs: Grenada, Libya, and Panama. The Gulf War can now be added to this list, and the tentative lesson of these post-Vietnam conflicts points too enthusiastically in the opposite direction: that military power is a generally quick and inexpensive way of achieving political objectives. It would be ironic and dangerous if the Vietnam syndrome were replaced with an Iraq syndrome—the notion that military power can be used easily, effectively, and with low cost to U.S. forces.

Saddam Hussein will be remembered as one of the most incompetent military commanders of all time: leaving his troops in dug-in positions in a desert over which his enemy had absolute air superiority and a tremendous advantage in ground maneuverability. Rarely before in history has a military commander played so diligently to his enemy's strength. The next test of the new world order will not likely involve so inept an adversary. The military strategy that worked so well in the deserts of the gulf will not work so effectively in the mountains of Peru or the rice paddies of Cambodia, and the price in U.S. lives may be far higher.

Fighting the Gulf War was the easy part; fashioning a durable peace proved far more difficult. When a nation chooses to go to war in defense of collective values it must have, in addition to a reasonable prospect of winning, some plausible vision of how to secure a durable postwar peace. The Bush administration hoped that humiliation on the battlefield would incite the Iraqis to depose Saddam Hussein and bring to power a less brutal leader. But that gamble did not pay off, and the decisive military victory compounded rather than reduced political chaos in the region.

The United States cannot lay down rules for world order and take unilateral responsibility for enforcing them. There may be no competitor to the United States for the position of world hegemon, but there are serious challenges to the U.S. ability to exert power. Other nations will not accept coercive American leadership, but they will respond to consensus building. In the new world order the United States will have to do what Harry Truman said he did as president: "I sit here all day trying to persuade people to do the things they ought to have enough sense to do without my persuading them."

The military lesson of Vietnam was not to tie the military's hands. If committed to war, don't subject military decisions to political second-guessing; allow the military to use military means to achieve a decisive victory. These lessons were

learned well and applied with great success in the Gulf War. But there is another lesson of Vietnam, a political lesson that should not be forgotten in the euphoria of Desert Storm, and that is to take a cautious skepticism to the use of American military power. The next war to preserve the new world order may well be more like Vietnam than the gulf. Guerrilla insurgencies in Cambodia, the Philippines, or Peru and ethnic conflicts in Eastern Europe will be less amenable to American military force. Americans can be proud of the professionalism, courage, and prowess displayed by their military forces in Desert Storm, yet should bear in mind that long-term peace and stability rarely grow out of the barrel of a gun.

Chapter 2

Toward the Post–Cold War World: Structure, Strategy, and Security

John Lewis Gaddis

F or the first time in over half a century, there is no single great power, or coalition of powers, capable of posing a "clear and present danger" to the national security of the United States. The end of the cold war has left Americans in the fortunate position of being without an obvious major adversary, and that—given the costs of confronting adversaries who have been all too obvious since the beginning of World War II—is a condition worthy of greater appreciation than it has so far received.

It would be foolish to claim, though, that the United States after 1991 can return to the role it played in world affairs before 1941. For as the history of the 1930s suggests, the absence of imminent threat is no guarantee that threats do not exist. Nor is the isolationism of that era possible in the 1990s: advances in military technology and the progress of economic integration have long since removed the insulation from the rest of the world that geographical distance used to provide. The passing of the cold war world by no means implies an end to American involvement in whatever world is to follow; it only means that the nature and the extent of that involvement are not yet clear.

Whatever else one might say about them, wars—hot or cold—do have the advantage of concentrating the mind. The existence of an adversary forces one to think about strategy in the way it should be thought about: as the calculated adaptation of desired ends to available means. We can now see that containment, the strategy the United States and its allies followed throughout most of the cold war, met that standard: it proved remarkably successful in maintaining the post–World War II balance of power without war and without appeasement until the Soviet Union, confronting the illogic of its own system and its own position in the world, simply gave up.

But victories in wars—hot or cold—tend to unfocus the mind. They encourage pride, complacency, and the abandonment of calculation; the result is likely to be disproportion in the balance that always has to exist, in strategy, between what one sets out to do, and what one can feasibly expect to accomplish. It is sometimes a dangerous thing to have achieved one's objectives, because one then has to decide what to do next. Past successes provide no guarantee against future failures.

Interests

"We have no eternal allies, and we have no perpetual enemies," Lord Palmerston once memorably proclaimed. "Our interests are eternal, and those interests it is our duty to follow."[1] After a year in which old adversaries have become allies and old allies have become adversaries—for that is what the end of the cold war and the crisis in the Persian Gulf brought about—we would do well to keep Palmerston's familiar maxim in mind. Conceptions of interest, if they are to be of any value, ought at least to be durable: the national interest is not something that shifts back and forth from crisis to crisis, or from adversary to adversary, or from administration to administration.

Definitions of interest, however, tend toward the bland, the abstract, and often the perfectly obvious. It is easy to assert, for example, that all nations have an interest in survival, security, and the maintenance of a congenial international environment. The proposition is universally valid, but it is also so skeletal as to be analytically useless; these bones require meat if we are to make anything of them. One way to provide it is to specify the conditions nations have historically found to be necessary in order to safeguard such fundamental interests.[2]

For the United States, these have largely boiled down to the balancing of power. One need not look far to find the roots of this tradition: they are evident in the practice of eighteenth-century British politics and diplomacy from which the American system of government emerged,[3] and they are firmly enshrined in the Federal constitution of 1787, based as it is on the premise that individual liberty survives only when the powers of the state are separated, and hence held in careful equilibrium.[4]

The Founding Fathers were themselves adept balancers of power: witness the relative ease with which they shifted from allegiance to Britain before 1776 to alliance with France after 1778, then back to alignment with Britain in the wake of the French Revolution. Nor did Americans abandon their concern with the balance of power during the "long peace" that followed the Congress of Vienna after 1815;[5] isolationism existed, but only because the European balance maintained itself for the next century. When challenges to that balance did materialize, in 1917, in 1940–1941, and again in 1945–1947, the United States took decisive action to restore it, twice by military intervention and the third time through economic and military assistance in support of containment.

Other fundamental American interests follow from this concern with international equilibrium. This country's sympathy—and sometimes support—for democratic forms of government abroad traces back, at least in part, to the conviction that such governments are less likely than their authoritarian counterparts to upset balances of power.[6] American efforts to open the world to trade and investment derive not just from the search for profits, but also from the conviction that the prosperity capitalism generates prevents war and revolution.[7] Even the Wilsonian principle of collective security reduces, in the end, to the task of balancing the power of the rest of the world against those few who would commit aggression.

The American commitment to democracy, capitalism, and collective security has never been absolute: the nation has, at one time or another, compromised all of these principles. But these compromises, too, relate to maintaining a balance: an absolutist crusade to make the world democratic, or to make market economies universal, or to impose a collective security system everywhere, would bring about another form of imbalance, which is the one between ends and means. Interests are—potentially at least—infinitely expandable; means never are. It can serve the interests of no state to allow ends to outstrip means.

The traditional American conception of a national interest rooted in the balancing of power—whatever form that "power" takes—is likely to persist into the post–cold war world.

Palmerston's dictum about eternal interests ought not to be read as precluding the emergence of new ones. Advancing technology—as well as advancing morality—can change the nature of power over time, and these shifts can affect interests in significant ways. It would not have occurred to Palmerston to make the abolition of great-power war itself a national objective; but to anyone living in a nuclear age, such an interest has become, tacitly at least, widely shared.[8] Nor would that statesman have foreseen the need to end racial and sexual discrimination, or to defend the biosphere against greenhouse warming, ozone depletion, and diminishing biodiversity. Progress, if we can call it that, does occur, and the interests of states do enlarge to accommodate it.

Even so, the traditional American conception of a national interest rooted in the balancing of power—whatever form that "power" takes—is likely to persist into the post–cold war world, it having served the United States well in the world in which it has functioned as an independent state for more than two centuries. Just what the post–cold war world will look like, however, is not yet clear.

Cartography

Finding one's way through an unfamiliar environment generally requires a map of some sort. But that is only to point out that we need to simplify complexity, for what is a map if not a vast simplification of the environment in which we find ourselves? Nobody would claim that a map replicates reality: if one were to have a map that accurately represented, say, the Persian Gulf, it would have to be the same size and have all of the same characteristics as the Persian Gulf, which would defeat the purpose of having the map in the first place.[9] Cartography, like cognition itself, is a necessary simplification that allows us to see where we are, and where we may be going.

If we are to devise a strategy for safeguarding American interests in a post–cold war world, the first thing we will need is a geopolitical map. We have had such maps in the past. The assertion that the world was divided between the forces of democracy and those of totalitarianism—to use the precise distinction made in President Harry S. Truman's announcement of the Truman Doctrine—was, of course, a vast simplification of what was actually happening in 1947.[10] But it was probably a necessary one: it was a starting point, an exercise in geopolitical cartography, if you will, that depicted the international landscape in terms everyone could understand, and that by so doing prepared the way for the more sophisticated strategy of containment that was soon to follow.

The end of the cold war was too sweeping a defeat for totalitarianism—and too sweeping a victory for democracy—for this old geopolitical map to be usable any longer. But another form of competition has been emerging that could be just as stark, and just as pervasive, as the rivalry between democracy and totalitarianism was at the height of the cold war: it is the contest between forces of integration and fragmentation in the contemporary international environment.[11] The search for a new geopolitical cartography might well begin here.

Integration

I use the term *integration* in its most general sense, which is the act of bringing things together to constitute something that is whole. It involves breaking down barriers that have historically separated nations and peoples in such diverse areas as politics, economics, religion, technology, and culture. It means, quite literally, the approach to what we might call—echoing some of the most visionary language of World War II—one world.[12]

Integration is happening in a variety of ways. Consider, first, the communications revolution, which began over a hundred years ago when it first became possible to transmit information instantly from one part of the globe to the other, but which has taken on a vastly greater impetus from the more recent development of such things as Xerox copiers, television satellites, fax machines, and computer linkages, along with the tendency of this technology, once developed, to come down dramatically in price.

We have in fact become one world as far as communications are concerned: it is no longer possible for any nation to deny its citizens access to what is going on elsewhere, and that is a new condition in international politics, the importance of which became clear as revolution swept rapidly through Eastern Europe in the fall of 1989. A new kind of domino theory has emerged, in which the achievement of liberty in one country causes repressive regimes to topple, or at least to wobble, in others. Integration through communications has largely brought that about.[13]

Consider, next, economics. There have, of course, been international commercial and financial contacts for centuries, but it was not until after World War II that a true global market began to develop. Americans bear a good deal of the responsibility for this: convinced that the war had come because of the breakdown in the international economy in the 1930s and the social and political fragmentation that grew out of it, the United States used its postwar hegemony to create the basis for a worldwide integrated trade and financial network whose importance has continued to grow since that time. The incorporation of two former adversaries—Germany and Japan—into that network was, in particular, an American decision; whatever we think of it today, the current prominence of those nations in the global economy comes close to what the strategists of containment after World War II hoped would happen. [14]

The result of this movement toward economic integration is that no nation—not even the Soviet Union, or China, or South Africa, or Iraq—can for very long maintain itself apart from the rest of the world: that is because individual nations depend, for their own prosperity, upon the prosperity of others to a far greater extent than in the past. Integration also means that transnational actors like multinational corporations or cartels like OPEC or even humanitarian organizations like Amnesty International—through the economic (and in the case of the latter, also moral) pressures they bring to bear—can have a powerful effect on what happens to national states. And in Europe at least, integration has led to the creation of a potential new superpower in the form of the European Community: Europe as a whole, not just Britain, or France, or Germany, is already a major player in the world economy, and there are those who believe that, after the final removal of trade barriers in 1992, it could become one in world politics as well.

Consider, as a third manifestation of integration, security. It used to be the case that nations relied on their own strength or on that of allies to provide for their security, and that is still primarily the case. But Woodrow Wilson began the movement toward collective security on a global scale with his proposal for a League of Nations after World War I, and although that organization proved inef-

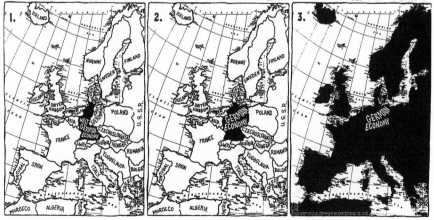

UNIFICATION

By permission of Ranan R. Lurie, 1991 International
Copyright by Cartoonews, Inc., NYC, USA.

fective—in part because of the Americans' refusal to join it—the League did give rise to the United Nations, which in recent years has become a major force in world politics. The U.N. has helped in rapid succession to resolve a series of longstanding conflicts in southern Africa, Central America, the Middle East, and South and Southeast Asia. It is highly significant that the United States waited to gain U.N. approval for the use of force in the Persian Gulf; Washington has not always been so solicitous of the world organization in the past, and the fact that it proceeded in this way suggests that the Bush administration has come to see important advantages in collective as opposed to unilateral action in such matters.

Another form of cooperative action to achieve security has existed for years alongside the U.N.: it is the North Atlantic Treaty Organization (NATO), itself an example of seeking security through integration that has managed to keep the peace in Europe for over four decades. Many people forget that it was NATO— together with the movement toward economic integration mentioned earlier— that ended the protracted and deeply rooted rivalry between France and Germany.[15] On those grounds alone NATO would have to be considered a success for integration, quite apart from whatever it has or has not achieved in deterring the Soviet Union.

Then consider the integration of ideas. The combination of easy communications, unprecedented prosperity, and freedom from war—which is, after all, the combination the cold war gave us—made possible yet another integrationist phenomenon, which is that ideas now flow more freely throughout the world than at any other time in the past. The United States has particularly benefited from this process, for even as its military and economic power has gone into relative decline, its influence as a source of ideas and as a shaper of culture is as great, if not greater, than it has ever been. This "soft" form of power ought not to be ignored.[16] We may deplore the fact that much of the rest of the world gets its image of this country from watching reruns of *Dallas* or from listening to rock music, but that does not prevent much of the rest of the world from aspiring to emulate—or even to emigrate to—this country. That simple fact continues to be a major element in the international power balance.

One particular aspect of the integration of ideas is the fact that people are better educated than at any time in the past. This trend has had a revolutionary effect in certain authoritarian countries, where governments found that they had to educate their populations in order to continue to compete in a global economy, only to find that the act of educating them opened their minds to new ideas and ultimately worked to undermine the legitimacy of authoritarianism itself.[17] The consequences can be seen in Chinese students who prefer statues of liberty to statues of Mao, in Soviet citizens who taunt their own leaders in front of Lenin's tomb, and in the truly remarkable sight of a president of Czechoslovakia—himself a living symbol of the power of ideas—lecturing the Congress of the United States on the virtues of Jeffersonian democracy.[18]

Finally, consider peace. It has long been a central assumption of liberal political philosophers that if only one could maximize the flow of ideas, commodities, capital, and people themselves across international boundaries, then the causes of war would drop away. It was an idea based more on faith than on reality: the outbreaks of both World War I and II severely called it into question, since those wars arose among precisely the nations that had had just those kinds of extensive contacts with one another.

But there is some reason to think that a by-product of integration since 1945 has indeed been peace, at least among the great powers. The prosperity that is associated with market economies tends to encourage the growth of liberal democracies; and one of the few patterns that holds up throughout modern history is that liberal democracies do not go to war with one another.[19] From this perspective, then, the old nineteenth-century liberal vision of a peaceful, integrated, interdependent, and capitalist world may, at last, be coming true.

Fragmentation

Would that it were so. Unfortunately, however, the forces of integration are not the only ones active in the world: there are also forces of fragmentation at work that are resurrecting old barriers between nations and peoples—and creating new ones—even as others are tumbling. Some of these forces have begun to show unexpected strength, just when it looked as though integration was about to prevail. The most important of these is nationalism.

There is, to be sure, nothing new about nationalism: given the fact that the past half-century has seen the number of sovereign states expand from something like fifty to over 170, it can hardly be said that nationalism was in a state of suspended animation during the cold war. Still, many of us did have the sense that, among the great powers at least, nationalism after World War II had been on the wane.

The very existence of two rival superpowers—which is really to say, two *supranational* powers—created this impression. We rarely thought of the cold war as a conflict between competing Soviet and American nationalisms: we saw it, rather, as a contest between two great international ideologies, capitalism and communism; or between two antagonistic military blocs, NATO and the Warsaw Pact; or between two geographical regions we imprecisely labeled "East" and "West." One could even argue that the cold war discouraged nationalism, particularly in Western Europe and the Mediterranean, where the mutual need to contain the Soviet Union moderated old animosities like those between the French and the Germans, or the Greeks and the Turks, or the British and everybody else. Much the same thing happened, although by different and more brutal means, in Eastern Europe, where the Soviet Union used the Warsaw Pact to suppress longstanding feuds between Hungarians and Romanians, Czechs and Poles, and the (East) Germans and everybody else. Nationalism might still exist in other parts of the world, we used to tell each other, but it had become a historical curiosity in Europe; there were even those who argued, until recently, that the Germans had become such good Europeans that they were now virtually immune to nationalist appeals and so had lost whatever interest they might once have had in reunification.[20]

Today, in the absence of the cold war, the situation looks very different. Germany has reunified, and no one—particularly no one living alongside that new state—is quite sure what the consequences are going to be. Romanians and Hungarians threaten each other regularly now that the Warsaw Pact is defunct, and nationalist sentiments are manifesting themselves elsewhere in Eastern and Southeastern Europe, particularly Yugoslavia, which appears on the verge of breaking up.[21] The same thing could even happen to the Soviet Union itself: nationalist pressures the regime thought it had smothered as far back as seven decades ago are coming to the forefront once again, to such an extent that we can literally no longer take for granted the continued existence of that country in the form that we have known it.

Nor should we assume that the "West" is immune from the fragmenting effects of nationalism. The Irish question ought to be a perpetual reminder of their durability; there is also the Basque problem in Spain, and the rivalry between the Flemings and the Walloons in Belgium. Growing nationalism is undermining the American position in the Philippines, and similar pressures are building in South Korea. Nationalism is even becoming an issue in Japan, what with recent controversies over the treatment of World War II in Japanese history textbooks and the Shinto ceremonies that officially began the reign of the Emperor Akihito. And consider, most astonishingly of all, how close the Canadian confederation came during the summer of 1990 to breaking up—as it may yet do—over the separatist aspirations of Quebec. We are even at the point now where the Mohawk Indians have been demanding—from Quebec, no less—recognition of their own rights as a sovereign state.[22]

But the forces of fragmentation do not just take the form of pressures for self-determination, formidable though those may be. They also show up in the field of economics, where they manifest themselves as protectionism: the effort, by various means, to insulate one's economy from the workings of world market forces. They show up in the racial tension that can develop, both among states and within them: the killing of blacks by blacks in South Africa, *after* the release of Nelson Mandela, illustrates the problem all too clearly. They certainly show up in the area of religion: the resurgence of Islam might be seen by some as an integrationist force in the Middle East, but it is surely disintegrationist to the extent that it seeks to set that particular region off from the world in general by reviving ancient and not-so-ancient grievances against the West, both real and imagined.[23] They can show up with respect to language: speakers of French, both in France and in Quebec, have become increasingly determined to maintain the purity of that tongue against alien Anglo-Saxon intrusions. They can even show up as a simple drive for power, which is the only way I can make sense out of the fiendishly complex series of events that has torn Lebanon apart since the civil war began there in 1975.[24] Indeed, one can look at Beirut as it has been for the past decade and a half and get a good sense of what the world would look like if the forces of fragmentation should ultimately have their way.

Fragmenting tendencies are also on the rise—they have never been wholly absent—within American society itself. Expressions of alarm about the self-centering seductiveness of popular culture are probably exaggerated.[25] But it would be difficult to overestimate the disintegrationist effects of a worsening drug crisis in this country, or of the breakdown of our system for elementary and secondary education, or of the emergence of what appears to be a permanent social and economic "underclass."[26] Well-intentioned efforts to decrease racial and sexual discrimination have increased racial and sexual—as well as constitutional—tensions.[27] Linguistic anxieties lurk just beneath the surface, as the movement to make English the official language of the United States suggests. Immigration may well be increasing at a faster rate than cultural assimilation which has itself been a less than perfect process. Regional economic rivalries are developing over such issues as energy costs and the bailout of the savings and loan industry. And the rise of special interest groups, together with their ability to apply instant pressure through instant communications, has so fragmented the American political process that elections are reduced to the unleashing of attack videos and the preparation of the budget has come to resemble the endless haggling of rug merchants in some Oriental bazaar. When the leading light of American conservatism has to call for a return to a sense of *collective* interest,[28] then disintegrationist forces have proceeded very far indeed.

What all of this suggests, then, is that the problems we will confront in the post-cold war world will more likely arise from competing processes—integration versus fragmentation—than from the kinds of competing ideological visions that dominated the cold war. Unlike the old rivalry between democracy and totalitarianism, though, the new geopolitical cartography provides no immediately obvious answer to the question of which of these processes might threaten the future security interests of the United States.

Threats

It would appear, at first glance, that the forces of integration should be the more benign. Those forces brought the cold war to an end. They provided the basis for the relative prosperity we and most of the rest of the developed world enjoyed during that conflict, and they offer the most plausible method of extending that prosperity into the post–cold war world. They combine materialism and idealism in a way that seems natural to Americans, who tend to combine these traits in their own national character. And they hold out the promise of an international order in which collective, not unilateral, security becomes the norm. But is the trend toward integration consistent with the old American interest in *balancing* power? Has that interest itself become obsolete in the new world that we now confront?

The longstanding American commitment to the balance of power was based on the assumption that the United States would survive most comfortably in a world of diversity, not uniformity: in a homogeneous world, presumably, one would not need to balance power at all. No one would claim that the progress of integration has brought us anywhere close to such a world; still the contradiction that exists between the acts of balancing and integrating power ought to make us look carefully at the post-cold war geopolitical map. Jumping to conclusions—in favor of either integrationist or fragmentationist alternatives—could be a mistake.

The United States is not likely, for the foreseeable future, to see threats to the balance of power arising from the actions of a single hostile state, as it did from the Soviet Union during the cold war or from Germany during World Wars I and II. But balances of power could still be imperiled by three more general kinds of threat that are sure to exist in the post–cold war world: ecological, regional, and internal. All of them, in one way or another, reflect the tension between integrative and fragmentative processes that characterizes the new geopolitical cartography.

Ecological Threats

Ecological threats are those that could imperil the international system as a whole, but that do not arise from the actions of any single state. An asteroid or comet hitting the earth and wiping out whole species—as some scientists think actually happened some 65 million years ago—would be an extreme example of an ecological threat. So too would be the "Martian" scenario that Ronald Reagan is said to have described to Mikhail Gorbachev at their first summit conference in Geneva in 1985: if the Martians—or some other all-powerful extraterrestrial force—should land, Soviet-American differences would evaporate overnight.[29]

The possibility of all-out nuclear war, of course, served as the equivalent of a "Martian" threat during much of the cold war, causing the United States and the Soviet Union to find common cause in a surprising number of areas. The development of permissive action links on nuclear weapons, of secure second-strike capabilities, of tacitly tolerated satellite reconnaissance, of intrusive verification, and ultimately the mutually agreed-upon destruction of nuclear-armed missiles themselves all grew out of a concern that an uncontrollable nuclear war might someday take place, thereby threatening the continued existence of both cold war competitors as well as everyone else. Weapons developed for, quite literally, disintegrative purposes came to have strongly integrative effects.[30]

The twin ecological threats of global war and global depression will not disappear with the end of the cold war.

Similarly, it was the specter of global depression—and the conviction that war might erupt from it—that led the United States and its allies after World War II to construct an integrative system of economic structures, including the World Bank, the International Monetary Fund, and the General Agreement on Tariffs and Trade, all of which were designed to preserve the international economic system against the forces that led to its collapse, with such devastating results, in the 1930s.[31] Within that framework—whether because of it is a more controversial matter[32]—much, though by no means all, of the postwar world has enjoyed unprecedented levels of prosperity and productivity for an unprecedented length of time.

The twin ecological threats of global war and global depression will not disappear with the end of the cold war. The first danger now appears considerably diminished, to be sure, but as long as nuclear weapons exist—and there is no reason to think they will not continue to exist for some time—the possibility of their use in some form will remain.[33] The second danger, a worldwide economic collapse, is more difficult to make judgments about. On the one hand, our understanding of how modern economies work is better than it was at the time of the last great depression. But, on the other hand, integration has linked the world economy together more closely than it was in the 1930s, so that even small disintegrative perturbations—the Iraqi seizure of Kuwait, for example—can produce widescale ripple effects. The need for a collective consciousness of these dangers, and for collective safeguards against them, has, therefore, by no means disappeared.

Nor is it difficult to conceive of other ecological threats that might require collective action. The possibility of global warming looms as a long-term constraint upon future economic development conducted in traditional—which is to say, polluting—ways: integration here, in the form of expanding industrialization and increasing agricultural productivity, may have created a new kind of danger. The worldwide AIDS epidemic illustrates how one integrative force—the increasing flow of people across international boundaries—can undermine the effects of another, which is the progress that has been made toward the conquest of disease. Population pressure, the product itself of progress in agricultural productivity and in conquering disease, is in turn exacerbating differences in standards of living that already exist in certain parts of the world, with potentially disintegrative results.[34]

The forces of integration, therefore, provide no automatic protection against ecological threats: indeed, they are a large part of the problem. Despite classical liberal assumptions, we would be unwise in assuming that an ever-increasing flow of people, commodities, and technology across international borders will necessarily—at least from the ecological standpoint—make the world a safer place.

Regional Threats

The sources of regional violence in the world remain as various as they have always been: they include the divisive forces of nationalism, ethnicity, religion, as well as economic and social inequality, together with the always-present possibility of incompetent leadership. But superpower crisis management provided an integrative framework within which to contain these forces during the cold war: it is striking how many regional crises there were after 1945, and yet not one of them escalated into a direct military conflict between the United States and the Soviet Union.[35]

This system of accommodating regional crises within a structure of global stability—which is one of the things the "long peace" was all about[36]—depended, however, upon the existence of two functioning superpowers. Now that the Soviet Union no longer qualifies in this regard—and now that some are questioning the continued capacity of the United States to play this role as well[37]—regional conflicts could become more difficult to contain than they were during the cold war. The failure to contain them, in turn, could produce dangerous consequences for the international balance of power in the post–cold war era.

One such consequence could be a return to violence in a part of the world that has, for years, been remarkably free of it: Europe from the Atlantic to the Urals.[38] The reunification of Germany, together with the impending breakup of the Soviet Union, is one of the most abrupt realignments of political, military, and economic power in modern history. It has come about as a result of those integrative forces that ended the cold war: the much-celebrated triumph of democratic politics and market economics.[39] And yet, this victory for liberalism in Europe is producing both integrative and disintegrative consequences.

In Germany, demands for self-determination have led to reunification, to be sure, but the economic effects could be disintegrative: there are concerns, now, over whether the progress the European Community has made toward removing trade and immigration barriers by 1992 is going to be sufficient to tie the newly unified Germany firmly to the West; or whether the new Germany will build its own center of power further to the East, with the risk that this might undo the benefits of 1992. What happens, for example, if Germany invests heavily in Eastern Europe—as seems likely—and then some of the economies of that part of the world collapse as a result of their exposure to market forces—as also seems likely: will the new Germany be prepared to tolerate disorder and financial losses in the countries that border it to the east, or will it attempt to reimpose order and profitability there? If it does the latter, what will the Soviet Union—and indeed the rest of the world—think of that? The future of Europe, in short, is not at all clear, and it is the increasing tension between the forces of integration and fragmentation that has suddenly made the picture there such a cloudy one.

In the Soviet Union, the "triumph of liberalism" has had profoundly disintegrative consequences: we are witnessing nothing less than the dismantling of that once-mighty superpower. Here we face a painful dilemma, for while our hearts tell us that we ought to be supporting the aspirations for self-determination of groups like the Georgians, or the Moldavians, or even the Russians themselves, our heads should be asking how far are we prepared to see this process go. The Abkazians and the South Ossetians, after all, seek their independence from Georgia, as do the Gagauz from Moldavia. The Bashkirs and the Yakuts have proclaimed their independence—as could dozens of other nationality groups—from the Russian Republic, just as it in turn has been moving toward independence from the Soviet Union. The central Soviet government is sinking into irrelevance as power diffuses down to the level of the republics, and even below.[40] No one knows what the future political configuration—to say nothing of ideological orientation—of the various successor states is going to be. Civil war, and even international war growing out of civil war, are by no means unrealistic prospects; and these possibilities will be all the more dangerous because the Soviet Union's massive arsenal of nuclear and conventional weapons will not disappear even as the Soviet Union itself does.[41] The wholly admirable principle of self-determination, which has drawn strength from the commendably integrative forces of education and communication, is having disturbingly disintegrative practical results.

There is yet another danger to be kept in mind in connection with these European developments. The combination of German reunification with Soviet collapse, if it occurs, will involve the most dramatic changes in international boundaries since the end of World War II. It is not at all clear what precedents this may set for other parts of the world, notably the Middle East and Africa, where boundaries inherited from the colonial era do not come close to coinciding with the patterns of ethnicity, nationality, or religion that exist there. If the Lithuanians are going to get their own state, it will not be easy to explain why the Palestinians or the Kurds or the Eritreans should not have theirs also. If the boundaries of the dying Soviet empire are to be revised, then why should boundaries established by empires long since dead be preserved?

This brings up the problem of conflict in the Third World. When regional violence has arisen there in the past—whether in the long and bitter Arab-Israeli dispute over Palestine, or clashes between India and Pakistan over Kashmir and what is now Bangladesh, or the protracted and costly Iran-Iraq war of 1980–

1988—the superpowers used their influence to prevent it from spreading more widely, with the result that these conflicts remained limited in their scope, and also (with the exception of the 1971 war that produced the independence of Bangladesh) in their consequences.

The Iraqi invasion of Kuwait, however, has produced a different pattern of regional violence with disturbing implications for the post–cold war era. (First,) Saddam Hussein did not wait to exhaust diplomatic alternatives before attacking: in what seemed a throwback to pre–cold war behavior, he simply seized a small, rich, and defenseless neighboring country without bothering to conceal the fact that an old-fashioned act of aggression had taken place. (Second,) it was Iraq's integration into the international market in sophisticated military technology that made it possible for him to do this. Saddam's arsenal of chemical and biological weapons, to say nothing of his SAMs, Scuds, Mirages, the nuclear weapons he probably would have had if the Israelis had not bombed his reactor in 1981, and the long-range artillery he certainly would have had if the British had not become suspicious of his orders for very thick "oil pipes" early in 1990—all of this hardware was not forged by ingenious and self-reliant Iraqi craftsmen working tirelessly along the banks of the Euphrates. He obtained it, rather, by exploiting an important consequence of integration, which is the inability or unwillingness of states to control what their own entrepreneurs—even those involved in the sale of lethal commodities—do to turn a profit. (Third,) the global energy market—another integrationist phenomenon—created the riches that made Kuwait such a tempting target in the first place; it also brought about the dependency on Middle Eastern oil that caused so rapid a military response on the part of the United States, its allies, and even some of their former adversaries. The eagerness of this improbable coalition to defend the principle of collective security would hardly have been as great if Benin had attacked Burkina Faso, or vice versa.

There is, of course, no assurance that Saddam Hussein would have refrained from invading Kuwait if the cold war had been at its height, but there is a good chance that under these circumstances either the United States or the Soviet Union—depending upon which superpower Iraq was aligned with at the time—would have sought to exert a restraining influence, if only to keep its principal rival from exploiting the situation to its own advantage.[42] Certainly it is sobering to consider that 1990—the first post–cold war year—saw, in addition to the occupation of Kuwait, the near outbreak of war between India and Pakistan, an intensification of tension between Israel and its Arab neighbors, a renewed Syrian drive to impose its control on Lebanon, and a violent civil war in Liberia. Conflict in the Third World, it appears, is not going to go away just because the cold war is over; it may well intensify.[43]

There is yet another form of regional conflict that is likely to affect the post–cold war era: it is what we might call the "post-Marxist revolution" crisis. A central assumption of American foreign policy during much of the cold war was that the processes of decolonization and modernization made Third World countries vulnerable to Marxist upheavals; communism, Walt Rostow used to argue, was "a kind of disease which can befall a transitional society if it fails to organize effectively those elements within it which are prepared to get on with the job of modernization."[44] Few people worry about that prospect today, because there are so few parts of the world left in which revolutionaries would voluntarily align themselves with a Marxist movement to overthrow an old order. Revolution itself, in the collectivist form in which we have most often witnessed it in the twentieth century, appears to be passing from the scene.[45]

The new "revolutionary" force in the Third World may well be democracy: certainly the trend in Latin America is noticeably in that direction, and one can even make the argument that there is a long-term historical tendency for the number of democratic governments worldwide roughly to double with each half century.[46] But it is no clearer in the Third World than it is in Europe that the emergence of democracy—the supposedly integrative "triumph of liberalism"—will necessarily promote peace. For just as the United States used to justify its intervention in "less developed" countries as a means of "inoculating" them against the "bacillus" of communism, so the post–cold war era could see military interventions by democracies for the purpose of confirming in power—or restoring to power—other democracies.

It is no clearer in the Third World than it is in Europe that the emergence of democracy—the supposedly integrative "triumph of liberalism"—will necessarily promote peace.

As democracy spreads more widely in the Third World, observers from the old "first" and "second" worlds as well as from the United Nations will be invited to monitor elections and thereby legitimize the governments that emerge victorious from them: the pattern has already manifested itself in Namibia, Nicaragua, Panama, Pakistan, and most recently Haiti. But as the outcome of the 1989 Panamanian election shows, undemocratic elements may still succeed in subverting democratic processes. In such situations, the pressures for international condemnation, for the application of sanctions, and even for the use of military force in support of democracy, may become irresistible. The violent—but overwhelmingly popular—American military operation to apprehend General Manuel Noriega in December 1989 could well be a portent of things to come.

Internal Threats

Threats can arise, though, not only from external sources, for the way in which a nation chooses to respond to threats—whether real or imagined—can, under certain circumstances, pose as much of a danger to its long-term interests as does what is happening beyond its borders. The United States did not *have* to involve itself, to the extent that it did, in the Vietnam War. It did not *have* to become as dependent as it has on foreign oil. It did not *have* to accumulate such massive budget deficits that the government will have no choice but to allocate a large percentage of its revenues, well into the twenty-first century, to paying off the accumulated debt. All of these were decisions we ourselves made, not our adversaries; and yet their consequences have constrained, and in the case of energy dependency and the national debt, will continue to constrain, American freedom of action in the world for years to come.

The difficulty here arises from a curious unevenness that exists, within the United States these days, in the willingness to bear pain. Americans have readily accepted pain in connection with this country's integrative role as a global peacekeeper. Washington has repeatedly sent troops and resources overseas for the purpose of resisting aggression, even in situations where the probability of an attack was remote and where the states it was defending did not always see fit to contribute proportionately to their own defense. To the extent that such interventions have been necessary to redress imperiled balances of power, they can be justified in terms of the national interest. But American interventionism has too often become an instinctive, not a considered, response: the United States has tended to jump into situations where the balance of power was not really threatened, and it has tended to do this unilaterally. We have found it difficult, in short, to distinguish between being a global policeman and a global nanny.

Americans have been unwilling to accept even moderate pain, though, when it comes either to raising the taxes necessary to support the government expenditures we demand, or to cutting back on those expenditures to bring them into line with the taxes we are willing to pay. The United States is generous, even profligate, with its military manpower and hardware, but it is selfish to the point of irresponsibility when it comes to issues of life-style and pocketbook.[47] As a result, a kind of division of labor has developed within the international community, in which Americans contribute the troops and the weaponry needed to sustain the balance of power, while American allies finance the budgetary, energy, and trade deficits we incur through our unwillingness to make even minimal sacrifices in living standards.[48]

Whatever the causes of this situation—certainly they include the disintegration of our domestic political process into special interest constituencies that lack any sense of the collective interest—the long-term effects cannot be healthy ones. Americans will not indefinitely serve as "mercenaries" overseas, especially when the troops recruited in that capacity come, as they disproportionately do, from the less fortunate social, economic, and educational classes.[49] Resentment over this pattern—when it develops—is certain to fragment whatever foreign policy "consensus" may remain; pressures will eventually build for *all* Americans to bear their fair share of *all* the burdens that are involved in being a world power, and that may considerably diminish the attractions of continuing to be one.

The end of the cold war, therefore, brings not an end to threats, but rather a diffusion of them: one can no longer plausibly point to a single source of danger, as one could throughout most of that conflict, but dangers there still will be. The architects of containment, when they confronted the struggle between democracy and totalitarianism in 1947, knew which side they were on; the post–cold war geopolitical cartography, however, provides no comparable clarity. In one sense, this represents progress: the very absence of clear and present danger testifies to our success in so balancing power during the past four and a half decades that totalitarianism—at least in the forms we have considered threatening throughout most of this century—is now defunct. But, in another sense, the new competition between the forces of integration and disintegration presents us with difficult choices, precisely because it is by no means as clear as it was during the cold war which tendency we should want to see prevail.

Choices

Consider, for a moment, the most extreme alternatives. A fully integrated world would be one in which the United States—and other countries as well—would lose control of their borders and would be dependent on others for critical resources, capital, and markets. It would mean, therefore, a progressive loss of national sovereignty, and ultimately the loss of whatever remained of national identity. A fully disintegrated world would closely approximate the Hobbesian state of anarchy that theorists of international relations assume exists but that, in practice, never has: the world would be reduced to a gaggle of quarreling principalities, with war or the threat of war as the only means of settling disputes among them. Both of these extremes—for these are obviously caricatures—would undermine the international state system as we now know it: the first by submerging the autonomy of states within a supranational economic order; the second by so fragmenting state authority as to render it impotent.

No one seriously claims that, with the end of the cold war, we can abandon the international state system or relinquish national sovereignty: not even our most visionary visionaries are prepared to go that far. This suggests, therefore, that the United States retains the interest it has always had in the balancing of power, but that this time the power to be balanced is less that of states or ideologies than of the processes—transcending states and ideologies—that are tending toward integrationist and fragmentationist extremes. Instead of balancing the forces of democracy against those of totalitarianism, the new task may well be to balance the forces of integration and disintegration against each other.

What would this mean in practical terms? How can one translate this abstraction into policy recommendations? In the best of all possible worlds, one would need to take no action at all, because integrationist and disintegrationist forces would balance themselves. Unfortunately, though, in the imperfect world in which we live things rarely work out this neatly. Gaps generally exist between what one wants to have happen and what seems likely to happen; and it is here that the choices of states—and of the leaders who govern them—make a difference.

These choices, in the post–cold war world, are likely to center on those areas where integrationist and disintegrationist forces are not now balancing themselves; where the triumph of one over the other could imperil the conditions of international stability upon which rest the security interests of the United States, its allies, and other like-minded states, and where action is therefore needed to restore equilibrium. They include the following:

Reconstructing the Soviet Union and Eastern Europe

Over the next decade, the most serious source of instability in world politics is likely to be the political, economic, and social disintegration that is already developing where communism has collapsed. It is true that integrationist forces—the idea of self-determination, the appeal of market economies, the rise of mass education—helped bring about that collapse; but as we have seen integrative causes can produce disintegrative consequences, and that is what is happening in this case.

Marxism-Leninism could hardly have suffered a more resounding defeat if World War III had been fought to the point of total victory for the West;[50] fortunately victory, this time, did not require a war. The trouble with victory, though, is that it tends to produce power imbalances: it was precisely to avoid this danger that the peacemakers of 1815 and 1945—who designed the two most durable peace settlements of modern times—moved quickly after their respective triumphs to rehabilitate defeated adversaries and to invite them back into the international state system. Perhaps because the communist regimes of the Soviet Union and Eastern Europe have not actually suffered a military defeat, we in the West are not focusing as carefully as we should on the problems of reconstruction and reintegration in that part of the world.[51] But if the forces of fragmentation should prevail there, the resulting anarchy—and mass emigration away from anarchy[52]—could destabilize any number of power balances: the situation then would certainly have our attention, even if it does not now.

The peoples of the Soviet Union and Eastern Europe will of course have to bear the principal burdens of reconstruction; but they will not be able to accomplish this task alone, and already discouragement and demoralization have set in among them. It is in dealing with this kind of despair that aid from the "West"—including Japan—can have its greatest impact. A multinational Marshall Plan for former communist states sounds impractical given the extent of the problem and the existence of competing priorities at home, but the "highly leveraged" character of that earlier and highly successful enterprise ought not to be forgotten. The Marshall Plan worked by employing small amounts of economic assistance to produce large psychological effects: it restored self-confidence in Europe just at the point—some two to three years after the end of the war—at which it was sagging. What was critical was not so much the extent of the aid provided as its timing, its targeting, and its publicity: it shifted the expectations of its recipients from the belief that things could only get worse to the conviction that they would eventually get better.[53]

It will serve no one's interests in the West now, anymore than it would have served the interests of the victorious allies after World War II, to allow despair, demoralization, and disintegration to prevail in the territories of our defeated cold war adversaries: what happened in Germany after World War I ought to provide a sufficiently clear example of the consequences that can follow when victors neglect the interests of those they have vanquished, and thereby, in the long run, neglect their own.

Creating New Security and Economic Structures for Europe

Glaciers, when they invade a continent, not only obscure its topography but, through the weight of the accumulated ice, literally press its surface down into the earth's mantle. Retreats of glaciers, when they occur, cause old features of the landscape slowly to rise up again, sometimes altered, sometimes not. The expansion of Soviet and American influence over Europe at the end of World War II had something of the effect of such a glacier: it froze things into place, thereby obscuring old rivalries and bringing peace—even if a "cold" peace—to a continent that had known little of it throughout its history.

But now that the cold war is over, geopolitical glaciers are retreating, the situation is becoming fluid once again, and certain familiar features of the European landscape—a single strong German state, together with ethnic and religious rivalries among Germany's neighbors to the east—are once more coming into view. The critical question for the future stability of Europe is the extent to which the cold war glacier permanently altered the terrain it covered for so long. Integrationist structures like the European Community and NATO suggest permanent alteration; but these could also have been artifacts of the glaciation itself. If so, these organizations are likely to become increasingly vulnerable as the forces of fragmentation revive.

No economic or security structure for Europe can hope to be viable over the long term unless it incorporates—and provides benefits to—all of the major states on that continent: the classic lesson is the Versailles Treaty of 1919, which sought to build a peace that treated Germany as a pariah and excluded Soviet Russia altogether. But neither the European Community nor NATO has given sufficient attention to how each might restructure itself to accommodate the interests of the former Warsaw Pact states, including whatever is left of the Soviet Union itself; few efforts have been made to think through how these integrative organizations might expand the scope of their activities to counter the disintegrationist challenges—coming from the reunification of Germany, the liberation of Eastern Europe, and the collapse of the Soviet Union—that are already evident.[54]

The United States has used its influence, over the years, to favor integrative over fragmentative processes in Europe; indeed without that influence, it is difficult to see how integration could have proceeded as far as it has. But Americans cannot expect to maintain the authority the cold war gave them on the continent for very much longer, especially now that the Soviet "glacier" is so obviously retreating. We would do well, then, to consider what new or modified integrative structures might replace the role that we—and, by very different means, our former adversaries—played in "freezing" disintegrative forces in Europe during the cold war. Otherwise, serious imbalances could develop in that part of the world, as well.

Deterring Aggression

One thing the "long peace" did was to make the use of force by the great powers against one another virtually unthinkable. It created inducements that caused states to seek to resolve peacefully—or even to learn to live with—accumulated grievances that could easily, prior to 1945, have provoked major wars.[55] It did this by appealing more to fear than to logic, but patterns of behavior that arise out of fear can, in time, come to seem quite logical. Few today would question the desirability of perpetuating, and if necessary reinforcing, the inhibitions that arose, during the cold war, against once violent patterns of great-power behavior.

The unprecedented multinational response to Saddam Hussein's aggression in Kuwait suggests that an opportunity now exists to extend disincentives to war beyond the realm of the great powers. The need to do this is urgent, not just because of the crisis in the Persian Gulf but also because the end of the cold war is likely to end the informal crisis-management regime the United States and the Soviet Union have relied on in the past to keep such regional conflicts limited.

Woodrow Wilson's vision of collective international action to resist aggression failed to materialize in 1919–1920 because of European appeasement and American isolationism, and again after 1945 because the United Nations fell victim to the great-power rivalries that produced the cold war. Neither of these difficulties exist today: the world has a third chance to give Wilson's plan the fair test it has never received, and one could hardly have found a more appropriate occasion than by acting through a reinvigorated United Nations—not through the unilateral action of the United States—to restore the independence of Kuwait and to call to account the aggressor who extinguished it. The example that has now been set could even advance us some distance toward placing the conduct of international relations within the framework of international law that has long existed alongside it, but too often apart from it.[56]

The unprecedented multinational response to Saddam Hussein's aggression in Kuwait suggests that an opportunity now exists to extend disincentives to war beyond the realm of the great powers.

Can such a legalistic vision sustain the realistic security interests of the United States? Whether rightly or wrongly, the answer was negative after World Wars I and II; but we may have reasons, this time, for giving a more positive reply. The "long peace," after all, has already created in the *practice* of the great powers mechanisms for deterring aggression that have worked remarkably well: these did not exist prior to the cold war. There could be real advantages now— before the foundations of the "long peace" erode completely—in codifying and extending these practices as widely as possible: the evolution of a new world order designed to deter aggression could ensure that the most important benefits of the "long peace" survive the demise of the cold war. It could also counteract the dangerous conviction—which American leaders still at times appear to feel— that only the United States has the will and the capacity to take the lead in policing (or nannying) the world.

Finding the Appropriate Limits of Interdependence

The Iraqi invasion of Kuwait raises another issue, though, that will involve more difficult choices: it has to do with just how far we want economic integration to proceed. The purpose of having global markets is to ensure prosperity, not to compromise national sovereignty. And yet, it was the international market in oil and armaments that made it possible for Saddam Hussein to violate Kuwaiti sovereignty: economic integration, in this instance, produced literal political fragmentation. This unexpected and dangerous juxtaposition suggests strongly the need to think, more seriously than we have to this point, about how the economic and political forces that are shaping our world intersect with one another, and about where our own security interests with respect to these lie.

Certainly there is much to be said, from a strictly economic perspective, in favor of reducing barriers to trade, investment, and even labor flows across international boundaries if the result is to maximize production, minimize prices, and ensure that consumer needs are satisfied. But what if the result is also to allow despots easy access to sophisticated military technology, or to increase the West's reliance on energy resources it does not control? If integration is really a good thing, then should we not applaud Iraq's enterprise in exploiting the international arms trade as well as our own craftiness in relying on cheap foreign oil? Such behavior is consistent, after all, with the principles of free markets and comparative advantage, the benefits of which Adam Smith and David Ricardo illustrated so graphically as the Industrial Revolution was getting underway. But do market principles also require that we welcome, on a continuing basis, the dispatch of American troops to safeguard critical supplies halfway around the world? There are political costs to be paid for economic integration, and we are only now beginning to realize what they are.

These issues are, in turn, only part of the much larger problem of how one balances the advantages of economic integration against its political and social disadvantages. Are we really sure, for example, that we want to integrate our own economy into the world market if the result of doing that is to shut down industries we have historically relied upon for both jobs and national defense? When the most viable effects of integration are to transform once-diversified industrial complexes into strings of fast-food outlets and shopping malls, with the reduction in wages that kind of employment normally brings, one can hardly expect people to be out in the streets cheering for these developments, however ingeniously professional economists may rationalize them. What about the foreign ownership of American facilities? Japanese manufacturers have made valiant efforts to integrate themselves discreetly into the national economy, but when their presence becomes critical to the survival of local economies, as is the case with Japanese automobile plants throughout much of the midwest, or when Japanese companies begin raiding universities to hire scarce computer designers, as is happening on the east and west coasts,[57] it is not at all difficult to see how a backlash against this kind of integration could arise.

Increasing labor mobility, together with the liberalized immigration policies that facilitate it, provides yet another example of how economic integration could produce political fragmentation. There are undeniable advantages to allowing immigration, not just because it provides cheap labor, but also because in some instances the host nation can gain a diverse array of sophisticated skills as a result. But immigration also risks altering national identity, and the forces of integration have by no means advanced to the point at which one can dismiss concerns over that issue as anachronistic.[58] Certainly the Japanese have not done so: they long ago devised ways to be integrationist in international trade and investment, but rigidly protectionist (which is to say, fragmentationist) when it comes to matters of national culture. The difficulties confronting Turks in Germany, Arabs in France, and Pakistanis and West Indians in Britain suggest that the problem has by no means been solved in Europe; indeed, it could get much worse as the final removal of restrictions on the movement of labor within the European Community coincides with the mass emigration from the Soviet Union and Eastern Europe that the collapse of communism may bring.[59] As a nation of immigrants, the United States can probably handle such problems of cultural assimilation more easily than most nations.[60] Still, they are real problems, and attempts to write them off as reflections of an antiquated "nationalism," or even "racism," are not likely to make them go away.

What all of this suggests, therefore, is that we need better mechanisms for balancing integrative and disintegrative processes at those points where economic forces intersect those of politics and culture. The increasing permeability of boundaries is going to be an important characteristic of the post–cold war world,[61] and it would be a great mistake to assume—as market principles encourage us to assume—that in such an environment an "invisible hand" will always produce the greatest benefits for the greatest number. As in most other areas, an equilibrium will be necessary: if imbalances of power are not to develop, then a certain amount of protectionism, within prudent limits, may be required.

Regaining Solvency

The principle of balancing power also requires that ends be balanced against means. National security, even in the most auspicious of circumstances, rarely comes cheap. This country's reluctance to bring the costs of providing for its security into line with what it is willing to pay—that is, its unwillingness to regain solvency[62]—suggests that integrative and disintegrative mechanisms are imperfectly balanced within the United States as well as beyond its borders.

The last American president to preoccupy himself with solvency, Dwight D. Eisenhower, regularly insisted that the National Security Council specify, as "the basic objective of our national security policies: maintaining the security of the United States *and* the vitality of its fundamental values and institutions." To achieve the former without securing the latter, he warned, would be to "destroy what we are attempting to defend."[63]

Too often during the years that have followed Eisenhower's presidency, the quest for security has overwhelmed concern for the vitality of fundamental values and institutions. The military-industrial complex has, as he warned it that it might,[64] taken on a life of its own, producing weapons systems in search of purposes, bases in search of missions, strategies in search of objectives, and organizations—both military and civilian—in search of their own perpetuation. We fought the Vietnam War, which came close to tearing this country apart, for geopolitical reasons that remain obscure to this day. The Watergate and Iran-contra scandals revealed how excesses committed in the name of national security can subvert constitutional processes. And no one would be more appalled than Eisenhower himself to see the extent to which we now finance the costs of defense—as well as everything else—on credit extended by the unborn (who cannot object to the process) and by foreigners (who someday may).

Again, integrationist phenomena—in this case, the attempt to hold on to our cold war role as global policeman while relying on our ability to borrow to stabilize the economy at home—have produced fragmentationist effects; only what appears to be fragmentating now is nothing short of the national consensus that used to exist on what role the United States should play in the world that surrounds it.[65]

A return to solvency in its broadest sense—by which I mean not just balanced budgets but bearing the full pain of what one is doing at the time one is doing it—might discipline our thinking about national security in the way that it should be disciplined: through the constantly annoying—but also intellectually bracing—demands of stringency. For the concept of security is, as interests are, infinitely expandable: the more widely one projects one's interests in the world, the more threats there will sooner or later be to them. One winds up, figuratively at least, chasing one's own tail. But the pursuit of security along with solvency is a much more manageable enterprise. By requiring specifications of interests in terms of available (and not future, or even imaginary) means, it guards against the principal occupational hazard of being a great power, which is paranoia and the exhaustion it ultimately produces. The result might well be less grandiose visions, but more sustainable policies.

Strategy

Which is going to win—integration or fragmentation? At first glance, it would seem that the forces of integration will almost certainly prevail: one cannot run a modern post-industrial economy without such forces, and that, many people would say, is the most important thing in the world. But that is also a parochial view: running a post-industrial economy may not be the most important thing to the peasant in the Sudan, or to the young urban black in the United States, or to the Palestinian who has spent his entire life in a refugee camp. For those people, forces that might well appear to us to be disintegrationist can be profoundly integrationist, in that they can give meaning to otherwise meaningless lives. One person's fragmentation may be another's integration, and we need to be keenly aware of that fact.

We should also recognize that the forces of integration may not be as deeply rooted as we like to think. It comes as something of a shock when one realizes that the most important of them—the global market, collective security, the "long peace" itself—were products of the cold war. Their survival is by no means guaranteed into the post-cold war era. Disintegrationist forces have been around much longer than integrationist forces have been, and now that the cold war is over, they may grow stronger than they have been at any point in the last half century.

We should not necessarily conclude from this, though, that it will always be in our interest to try to ensure that the forces of integration come out on top. Surely, in the light of the Persian Gulf war, we will want to restrict future sales of arms across international boundaries, and it would not be a bad idea to develop alternatives to the worldwide marketing of oil as well. The increasing permeability of borders—the very thing we welcome when it comes to the free flow of ideas—will by no means be as welcome when commodities, capital, and labor begin flowing with equal freedom. And we are already, in this country, beginning to move away from the view that we can leave everything—international trade, energy resources, and especially the regulation of the savings and loan industry—to the "invisible hand" of market forces that the integrationist model in principle recommends.

But swinging to the other extreme—toward autarchy, nationalism, or isolationism—will not do either. The forces of fragmentation are always lurking beneath the surface, and it would take little encouragement for them to reassert themselves, with all the dangers historical experience shows would accompany such a development. We need to maintain a healthy skepticism about integration: there is no reason to turn it into some kind of sacred cow. But we also need to balance that skepticism with a keen sense of how unhealthy fragmentationist forces can be if allowed free rein.

So we are left, as usual, groping for the middle ground, for that rejection of extremes, that judicious balancing of pluses and minuses on both sides that is typical of how essays like this are supposed to end. This one will be no exception to that rule. I would point out, though, that practical statecraft boils down, most of the time, to just this task of attempting to navigate the middle course, while avoiding the rocks and shoals that lie on either side. Certainly we Americans, of all peoples, should find this a familiar procedure. For what is our own constitution, if not the most elegant political text ever composed on how to balance the forces of integration against those of fragmentation? It had been necessary, Madison wrote in *The Federalist* number 51, so to contrive "the interior structure of the government as that its several constituent parts may, by their mutual relations, be the means of keeping each other in their proper places."[66] That would not be a bad strategy to follow with regard to the external world as we think about how we might come to grips—as the Founding Fathers had to do—with the combination of centripetal and centrifugal forces that are already shaping our lives.

How Many? How Much?

Chapter 3

The Economics
of Defense
in the 1990s

Murray Weidenbaum

T he pattern of U.S. defense spending over the past half century has followed a frantic stop-and-go (or rather go-and-stop) cycle, oscillating between accelerated spending and periods of declining military budgets. In 1991 the United States experienced an unusual variation of that cycle: generosity for Operation Desert Storm simultaneous with cutbacks in the rest of the military budget. The post–Gulf War outlook is that the downward phase of the military budget cycle will continue.

Historical Perspective

Since the beginning of World War II, the military budget has never experienced an extended period of stability. Eras of rapid growth have alternated with times of austerity. The military buildup associated with the Korean War came while memories of World War II were still fresh. In turn, the end of that war was followed by a much slower pace of defense spending in the 1960s.

It is easy to forget the uncertainty that exists during each phase of the stop-and-go cycle. For example, in 1969, John Kenneth Galbraith tried to explain to a congressional committee that large-scale military spending was a thing of the past: "Finally, it must be recognized that the big defense budgets of the 1950s were a unique response to the conditions of that time."[1]

Often the change in the size and direction of military spending has mirrored the shift in the national security environment facing the United States. This was the case after the Vietnam War when the end of hostilities permitted a substantial

This chapter draws on his forthcoming book, *Small Wars, Big Defense,* to be published by the Oxford University Press in the fall of 1991.

reduction in military spending. At other times, the shifting internal response to a relatively constant set of external factors has been more subjective. Witness the rapid buildup in the early 1980s and the abrupt decline starting in the middle of the decade, all of which occurred during a period when the threat to U.S. national security remained relatively constant.

That start-and-stop cycle began in early 1981, when Congress approved almost all of the Reagan administration's proposed five-year defense program calling for spending $1.5 trillion in fiscal years (FY) 1982–1986. Between FY 1980 and FY 1985 the size of the defense budget doubled, rising more than 50 percent in real terms. By the middle of the decade, U.S. military procurement expenditures exceeded those of the Soviet Union for the first time since the late 1960s. That rapid buildup of weapon systems in the first half of the 1980s was greater than the peak pace of military production at the height of the Vietnam War.

Congress reversed direction on the military budget for FY 1986, cutting the funds requested by 10 percent. Appropriations for defense have continued on that downward path since then.

The Reagan administration tried to ignore the intent of the congressional reductions in the Department of Defense (DOD) budget. The basic reaction was to leave the long-term plans of the Pentagon unchanged and merely add the shortfall in a given year's funding to the amount requested in future years. Planned expenditures for hundreds of programs were each reduced slightly with the expectation that large increases would resume in the following year. The administration repeated this procedure each time Congress reduced the military budget request, which served both to widen the gap between military planning and fiscal reality and to aggravate the relationship between the legislative and the executive branches.

When Frank Carlucci became secretary of defense late in the Reagan Administration, he was faced with the challenge of reconciling the extremely expensive force structure embedded in the Pentagon plans that he had inherited with the lower, but still substantial, sums being appropriated by Congress. His main response was to "stretch out" the procurement of major weapon systems—an approach whose costs and benefits will be discussed later.

On taking over the Pentagon leadership in the incoming Bush administration, Secretary of Defense Richard Cheney made a series of budget changes, responding to the lower levels of congressional funding. This meant eliminating construction of one new aircraft carrier and canceling or cutting back several major aircraft procurement programs. Nevertheless, the gap between plans and funding remained. The General Accounting Office reported that President Bush's five year defense plan for fiscal years 1990–1994 exceeded available or allocated funds by almost $114 billion.[2] Simultaneously, the relative "famine" in the basic military budget was accompanied by generous outlays for the U.S. effort to contain Iraqi aggression in the Persian Gulf.

Current Military Budget Developments

In February 1991, Secretary Cheney submitted to the Congress the military budget for FY 1992, together with preliminary estimates for FY 1993–1995. In current-year dollars, the DOD request totaled $278 billion in new budget authority or $5 billion above the FY 1991 amount. The 1 percent annual decline in real terms is the smallest drop in seven years (the real declines in budget authority averaged a bit over 4 percent during the period 1986–1991). The reduction in military funding over the next four years (FY 1993–1996) is estimated to average in excess of three percent.[3] All of these figures exclude the costs assigned to Operation Desert Storm.

The costs of the U.S. participation in the Persian Gulf conflict are hard to estimate with any degree of precision. First of all, most of the weapons and equipment used came out of preexisting inventories and most of the troops were already serving in the armed forces. It is fair and proper for America's Gulf War allies to share the costs incurred in producing these arms and in training the military personnel who participated in the conflict. Thus, the United States did not make a profit from the war. In any event, the incremental costs including the costs of transportation from peacetime stations to the gulf, combat pay, calling up reserve units, and procuring special equipment to enable U.S. personnel to operate in a desert environment, were substantial. Estimates of the gross cost of Desert Storm range up to $60 billion. The Congressional Budget Office (CBO), using DOD data, estimated that, as of February 27, 1991, the added costs of U.S. military activities in the Persian Gulf came to roughly $45 billion. That estimate included $7 billion for a phase-down period after the war and $5 billion for transporting all U.S. troops and equipment back to their home stations. The $45 billion figure also assumed that all of the equipment and munitions lost in the war would be replaced.[4]

To a very large extent, these immediate costs are being covered by U.S. allies in the gulf conflict. More than $50 billion has been pledged, although far lesser amounts were received by the end of the first quarter of 1991 (see table

3–1). Not all of the pledges may be fully redeemed, but the reimbursements clearly are substantial. In the case of the material taken from the North Atlantic Treaty Organization (NATO) stockpile, the Congress and the administration will have to decide the extent to which the items used in the gulf conflict need to be replaced.

Because outlays for Operation Desert Storm are excluded from the congressionally-mandated limits on the military budget, there is a natural tendency for the Department of Defense to be generous in allocating its costs to the Persian Gulf conflict. For example, some question has been raised as to whether all of the higher price of fuel since August 1, 1990, has been assigned to Operation Desert Storm, including the petroleum used by troops in the continental United States and elsewhere.

By way of comparison, the Vietnam War, in the peak year of 1969, cost the equivalent of $85 billion in 1991 dollars, according to Gordon Adams, director of the Defense Budget Project. That came to about $233 million each day, measured in 1991 dollars. In comparison, the Yom Kippur War cost Israel about $750 million a day (in 1991 dollars) over three weeks.[5]

In any event, the post–Gulf War trend of U.S. military spending is most likely to continue downward. Table 3–2 shows the dramatic reductions from President Reagan's last five-year military budget plan (submitted in January 1989) that have been made by the Bush administration. If carried through, the contemplated cutback is larger than it appears, because the numbers are in current dollars, which

Table 3–1. Contributions to the U.S. Effort in the Persian Gulf
(in millions of dollars)

Country	Cash paid to U.S.	Materials delivered to U.S.	Pledges to U.S. 1990	Pledges to U.S. 1991	Aid to other nations[a]
European community					
Germany	272	66	1,072	5,500	2,300
Japan	870	206	1,740	9,000	2,100
Korea	50	11	95	280	125
Kuwait	2,500	6	2,500	13,500	2,500
Saudi Arabia	760	854[b]	3,300	13,500	3,000
United Arab emirates	870	111	1,000		
Gulf nations					4,000
Totals	5,322	1,254	9,707	41,780	14,025

Source: Department of Defense, Congressional Budget Office, Defense Budget Project.

[a]Mainly aid to Egypt, Jordan, and Turkey.

[b]Saudi Arabia also supplied American troops with food, water and oil at a cost estimated by the Saudis at $1.2 billion a month.

Table 3–2. The Downward Trend in the U.S. Military Budget
(budget authority by fiscal year, in billions of nominal dollars)

Date Budget Submitted	1990	1991	1992	1993	1994	1995	1996	Total
January 1989	306	321	336	351	366			1680
April 1989	296	311	322	336	350			1615
January 1990		295	300	304	308	312		1519
February 1991			278	278	278	281	283	1398

Source: U.S. Department of Defense

include an allowance for future inflation. In terms of constant purchasing power, the current military budget represents a substantial reduction from the plans made two years earlier.

The Unfortunate Side Effects

Over the years, the stop-and-go approach to military budgeting has generated serious repercussions. During the "go" times, defense planners assume that rapid increases in military funding will continue indefinitely and plan accordingly. Then along come the austere years when substantial cuts are made. There is natural reluctance, of course, to cancel new weapon systems that only recently had been approved. Hoping that the time of budgetary austerity will soon pass, military decision makers respond by slowing down and stretching out the production plans for all the systems underway, even though such a response raises unit costs and makes the full completion of all the production plans infeasible.

As a result of the inefficiencies resulting from the start and stop cycles since the end of World War II, the United States has enhanced its national security far less than might have been expected from the vast resources devoted to defense programs.

In the 1980s, Congress and the Pentagon also attempted to adjust to lower military budgets by squeezing government contractors. In the mid-1980s, a host of outrageous examples of waste and inefficiency (not all of them accurate) created an atmosphere conducive to imposing more stringent requirements on the companies providing materials for defense.

As is inevitable when hundreds of billions of dollars are being spent in a limited period of time, many shortcomings in military procurement, ranging from outright dishonesty to unintentional inefficiency, emerged in the 1980s. Prosecution of the lawbreakers was clearly appropriate, but imposing more detailed and burdensome regulation did little to reduce the overall cost of weapons acquisition. The immediate impact was what experienced observers of the Washington scene would expect: an increase in the expense of producing the goods and services ordered by the military establishment. A more basic—and unexpected—response to the increasingly onerous regulation was an exodus of defense contractors and sub-contractors from the military market.

Given the continuing fiscal mismatch in the Pentagon, key decision makers on national defense have only a few effective choices (none of them pleasant) to maintain a sustainable defense production effort: (1) reduce the number of air-craft, missiles, ships, etc., being bought, (2) reduce the operational readiness of the military force in being, (3) increase military budgets, or (4) some combination of the three.

The sensible approach is to tailor the military's demand to match the limited supply of fiscal cloth. Surely, the quaint notion of producing more weapon systems by paying defense contractors less is a futile exercise in wishful thinking. Mean-while, the continued erosion of the U.S. defense industrial base is one of those quietly undramatic events that deserves more attention than it has been receiving.

Stretching out production programs over longer periods of time sounds harm-less. Producing, say, 500 fighter aircraft over a five-year period does cost less in each year than producing the same number in four years. This sounds like an easy way to curtail defense spending. But quick fixes in federal budgeting are rarely satisfying. The economic effect of stretch-outs is adverse: the total cost of pro-ducing those 500 aircraft will rise—and by far more than the rate of inflation. That is so because the aerospace industry is characterized by a "learning" or "improve-ment" curve in its production cycle. Companies and their employees learn how to improve the work they do as they do more of it.[6] Relatively fixed overhead costs are spread over more units of production.

Much of this benefit of mass production is lost when fewer units are produced in any given time period.[7] The Department of Defense estimates that reducing the annual numbers of Black Hawk helicopters produced from eighty-two to sixty-one (a 26 percent reduction) increases the cost of each helicopter by 25 percent. Similarly, cutting back production of the M-1 tank by 25 percent raises the unit cost by 13 percent (see table 3–3 for detail).

Table 3–3. Changes in Unit Cost of Weapon Systems, 1987–1988

Weapon System	Percent Change in Annual Quantity Produced	Percent Change in Unit Cost
M1 Tank	− 25%	+ 13%
Blackhawk Helicopter	− 26	+ 25
Harrier Jet Airplane	− 24	+ 25
EA-6B Electronic Warfare Plane	− 50	+ 61
E-2C Warning Plane	− 40	+ 45
Sidewinder Missile	− 54	+163

Source: Derived from data contained in Congressional Budget Office, *Effects of Weapons Procurement Stretch-Outs on Costs and Schedules* (Washington, D.C.: U.S. Government Printing Office, 1987).

The Need for New Policy Approaches

Clearly, the cycles of feast and famine in military budgeting force executives within the Department of Defense to make unsound management decisions. The unpredictability and instability discourage Pentagon managers from developing stable and realistic procurement plans.

The attitude of decision makers toward defense spending needs to be redefined. The nature and intensity of the threats to national security do change substantially over time and so, reasonably, should the American response. But the pattern of those changes should be made with the knowledge that the underlying threats to U.S. national security are likely to continue beyond the immediate period for which specific plans are being made.

International Considerations

Surely the cyclical nature of international relations over the years provides little justification for basing our defense plans either on the assumption of an uninterrupted downward spiral in the arms race, or the reverse—that the United States will invariably be engaged in active hostilities. The possibility of reversals in the state of international tensions surely remain, as does the need to be able to alter our response to the changed external environment.

The harsh crackdown by Soviet troops in Lithuania and Latvia in early 1991 is very disturbing, especially as it may indicate a shift in power relationships within the Soviet Union to a harder line. Moreover, even with the victory of U.S. and allied forces over Iraq, the most casual examination of the strategic and political situation in the Middle East confirms that it remains an extremely dangerous area.

There is an especially perilous twist to recent developments (in a sense, good news is also bad news) with the slowing of weapon system production by the two superpowers. The substantial pool of Western and Western-trained scientists, engineers, and technicians may be tapped on a larger scale than ever by Third World nations eager to acquire their expertise for missile, nuclear, chemical, and other weapon projects. With the Soviet military threat receding, the spread of advanced weaponry to the developing countries has become the greatest danger to stability in the world. It is sad to learn that, no sooner had the American-led coalition begun to destroy Iraq's equipment (some of which had been purchased earlier from members of the coalition), than Iran announced the signing of new contracts for the procurement of long-range missiles.[8]

Domestic Considerations

If substantial albeit fluctuating or declining levels of U.S. military outlays are here to stay, defense spending should neither be viewed as something to be abhorred vehemently nor embraced enthusiastically. Rather, the military budget is an important factor in the nation's economic development, whether or not it is a particularly efficient one. Military procurement shifts resources from consumption to research and development and high-tech production. Whether we agree with them or not, decisions on the size and composition of defense spending have important impacts on the overall pace of innovation and, hence, on national productivity and international competitiveness.

Important policy conclusions flow from this line of reasoning. The investment process is a long-term affair and military budgeting is an important case in point. Hence, both the military and civilian sectors would benefit by replacing the practice of quick fixes in defense policy with fundamental, slower-acting reforms.

As a general proposition, the long-run effectiveness of the resources that are devoted to military purposes will be increased by lowering the peaks of military funding and raising the valleys. Wild fluctuations in the levels of defense budgets make it extremely difficult to carry out such desirable reforms as multiyear production contracting. In turn, the present state of affairs discourages private contractors from making the long-term investments in new factories and production equipment necessary to increase the efficiency and reduce the costs of procuring the weapon systems that are needed.

Much of the present array of regulation of military contractors results from attempting to alleviate short-term pressures on the military budget. Efforts to reduce the cost of defense purchasing should focus instead on an overhaul of the basic procurement system.

True multiyear budgeting—not limited to twenty-four months—is only the most obvious example of the efforts needed. Compared to the continuous modernization of private industry, investments in new military production facilities have been neglected. This deficiency leads to the high levels of costs and numerous quality shortcomings, which, in turn, erode public support for the military effort. The experiences, both positive and negative, with deregulation and privatization in the civilian sectors of the economy should be drawn upon.

It has become fashionable in recent years to lament the trend of increased congressional "micromanagement" of the military establishment, especially given the excessively detailed nature of the restrictions imposed. Yet we must understand the basic reason for the increasing degree of legislative involvement in what historically has been executive branch decision making. Both the pressure and the opportunity for congressional micromanagement have arisen from the virtual abdication by the Office of the Secretary of Defense (OSD) of its earlier role in reviewing and questioning the proposals initiated by the individual military services. Surely, the buildup of OSD under Secretary Robert McNamara may have been excessive and a greater role for the services desirable, but the shift to the opposite extreme under Secretary Caspar Weinberger is hard to defend.

Nevertheless, it is fundamentally wrong to view the task of OSD as merely packaging and selling (both to the White House and the Congress) the wish lists developed by the services. Without that tough-minded Pentagon review of individual system proposals that characterized earlier periods, it is hardly surprising that Congress stepped in to try to fill the analysis gap.

But congressional committees and their staffs are the wrong place to exercise that analytical function. We have a vivid current example of the shortcoming that result from OSD's abdication of its analytical responsibilities: despite the multitude of congressional hearings, committee reports, and statutory provisions, the recent buildup of U.S. forces in the Persian Gulf was delayed because key units of the Army's motorized equipment did not fit into the Air Force's transport aircraft which were intended to move the material to trouble spots. The Army had to wait for slower ships to do the task. It is the Office of the Secretary of Defense that should review the proposals of the Army, Navy, and Air Force to assure consistency and thus avoid duplication and waste. Secretary Cheney has begun to reassert the earlier role and power of OSD. He has done that in a series of tough-minded decisions—ranging from firing the chief of staff of the Air Force to canceling high priority service weapons (such as the F-14 modernization and the A-12 development and production). Yet, the purpose of strengthening OSD is not merely to express personal pique at poor performance—no matter how well or ill justified—but to conduct and act on serious analysis. Moreover, the concern over cost overruns that has motivated recent cuts in defense seems to have dissipated with the reports from the Persian Gulf of the outstanding performance of some of our high-tech weapon systems such as the Patriot and Tomahawk missiles.

Real stability in military expenditure levels is not always going to be the most likely outcome, therefore, the military establishment needs to learn how to accommodate its long-term plans to short-term funding fluctuations. It could do so by capitalizing on the "up" periods to build stocks of the high-priority weapons most likely to be needed during the coming "down" period. This approach would avoid the Department of Defense becoming committed to so many different weapon systems when money is very generous that chaos ensues during the inevitable downturns in funding availability. The continuing efforts of members of Congress to saddle the military budget with costs of unrelated civilian objectives cannot be ignored, either. The attitude that the Department of Defense should fund social objectives (ranging from promoting small business to favoring domestic producers) because it supposedly has the money is no substitute for sensible budgeting of civilian activities. There is a close connection between ever-expanding regulation and the rising dropout of defense contractors and subcontractors. The trivia of such military requirements as the fourteen-page specification for buying a fruitcake lends itself to ridicule. But, far more important, in the aggregate this overregulated, bureaucratized procurement process politicizes the behavior of the contracting firms that have adapted to that unique set of ground rules.

More fundamentally, old-fashioned political pressures too often override the choice of weapon systems and selection of contractors to produce them. Members of Congress too often become uncritical cheerleaders for the weapon being produced in their districts. Use of the military budget as the premiere political gravy train is a luxury that this nation should abandon.

Cutting Back the Defense Sector

Decisions on the military budget—especially its overall size—need to be related to the national economy. Although the military budget has continued to grow in nominal terms, making an allowance for inflation shows that the level of "real" military appropriations declined at about two percent a year from fiscal 1986 through fiscal 1990. Ignoring the special costs of Desert Storm, that decline continued in the early 1990s. The steady shrinkage in new funding has been both quiet and real. The drop in actual military spending has been slower, because in part the Defense Department could live off its substantial backlog of unspent appropriations. A scenario of minimum change is to assume that, following the Persian Gulf conflict, the downtrend in the military budget will resume the pace of the late 1980s. That is, we can forecast that, over the five-year period from 1991 to 1995, the military budget will rise in nominal terms, but not rapidly enough to offset the full effects of inflation. Thus, no substantial change would be made in the basic trend of funding for the military establishment. In real terms, defense spending would follow the trend of appropriations and decline at the rate of 2 percent a year. Over the coming five-year period, CBO estimates that this policy would generate a nominal dollar saving of approximately $80 billion compared to a stable level of defense outlays. An additional saving of $11 billion would arise from lower interest costs because of the reduced budget deficit.[9]

A second possible scenario is to assume that a lower overall level of military tension is achieved with the end of the war against Iraq. As a consequence, Congress will refrain from voting any increase in the military budget at all, even in nominal terms. If the United States continues to experience an average inflation rate of approximately 4 percent a year, this would mean an annual decline at the same 4 percent rate when the outlays are measured in real terms, or double the scenario of minimum change. Over the 1991–1995 time period, this approach would generate a nominal dollar savings of $158 billion plus an additional reduction of $20 billion in interest on the public debt (see table 3–4). Prior to the invasion of Kuwait, some military experts recommended larger cuts in the defense budget. General (ret.) Andrew Goodpaster, former supreme allied commander in Europe, proposed a 50 percent reduction in NATO forces by 1995. Senator Sam Nunn (D-Georgia) and former Secretary of Defense James Schlesinger urged planning on a residual U.S. military force in Western Europe on the order of 75,000 to 100,000 troops within five years.[10] Former Assistant Secretary of Defense Lawrence Korb called for reducing the Navy's fourteen carrier battle groups to the more traditional force of twelve.[11] In light of more recent developments, however,

Table 3–4. Savings from Alternative Defense Paths Compared with the CBO Baseline
(fiscal years, in billions)

Category of Spending	1991	1992	1993	1994	1995	Total 1991–95
2 Percent Annual Real Decline in Budget Authority						
Change in defense spending	$ − 4	$ − 9	$ − 15	$ − 22	$ − 30	$ − 80
Change in interest spending	a	− 1	− 2	− 3	− 5	− 11
Total change in deficit	$ − 4	$ − 10	$ − 17	$ − 25	$ − 35	$ − 91
4 Percent Annual Real Decline in Budget Authority						
Change in defense spending	$ − 8	$ − 18	$ − 30	$ − 44	$ − 58	$ − 158
Change in interest spending	a	− 1	− 3	− 6	− 10	− 20
Total change in deficit	$ − 8	$ − 19	$ − 33	$ − 50	$ − 68	$ − 178

Source: Compiled from Congressional Budget Office data.

a = Less than $500 million.

reductions of these magnitudes would likely be accompanied by some offsetting increases in weapon systems geared to an Iraq type of confrontation.

CBO has identified sixteen areas of the military budget that could be reduced substantially. Table 3–5 contains CBO's estimates of potential dollar savings in military personnel and procurement for the years 1991–1995. A fundamental rationale for massive cuts in the procurement of new weapon systems is the assurance that for some time the United States can rely on the powerful arsenal of modern aircraft, missiles, tanks, and ships acquired in the 1980s.

Table 3–5. Potential Defense Savings
(outlays in billions of dollars)

Item	1991	1992	1993	1994	1995	5-Year Savings
Cancel B-2 bomber	1.1	2.6	3.8	4.4	4.8	16.7
Cancel C-17 transport	.6	1.4	2.1	2.4	2.6	9.0
Cut Trident sub production 50%	.1	.2	.4	.4	.6	1.7
Limit SDI to research	.5	.7	.7	.5	.2	2.6
Cancel national aerospace plane	.1	.2	.3	.3	.3	1.2
Reduce procurement staff 10%	.1	.5	.9	1.3	1.8	4.7
Retire 4 battleships	.2	.3	.4	.4	.4	1.6
Reduce military personnel by 250,000	1.1	3.6	6.7	11.0	15.9	38.4
Reduce drills for noncombat reserves	.2	.3	.3	.3	.3	1.3
Reduce procurement of F-16 aircraft to 72 yearly	.1	.2	.5	.7	.7	2.2
Reduce procurement of DDG-51 destroyers to 3 a year	—	.2	.5	.8	.8	2.3
Cancel amphibious lift vehicles	.1	.2	.4	.5	.7	1.8
Eliminate increase for supporting procurement	.7	1.6	3.3	4.6	5.7	15.9
Eliminate dual compensation for selected reservists	.1	.1	.1	.1	.1	.5
Eliminate BAQ payments to reservists	.1	.1	.1	.1	.1	.5
Redefine reservists pay for drills	.6	.6	.6	.6	.6	3.0
Total	5.7	12.8	21.1	28.4	35.6	103.4

Source: Estimated from budget baseline computed by Congressional Budget Office.

An important limitation on the size and speed of reductions in the U.S. military budget is political—most dovish members of the Congress quickly become hawks when the bases or defense plants in their districts are threatened by budget cuts. An article in *The New York Times* on the congressional response to the fiscal year 1991 military budget is very revealing. Under the headline, "Plan for Closing Military Bases Alarms Capitol," the front page article sounds like a wartime communique: "D-day in the battle of the military budget came to Congress three days early as lawmakers mobilized today to protect bases in their districts."[12]

Adjusting to Defense Cutbacks

Reductions in defense spending during the next several years are likely to be substantially less—in terms of economic importance—than the cuts made after either the Korean or Vietnam Wars. After both of those wars, defense spending as a percent of GNP fell approximately 4 percentage points, bringing that ratio to about ten percent of GNP after the Korean War and approximately 6 percent after the Vietnam War. A swing of 4 percent in today's massive $6 trillion GNP would be awesome. But such a reduction in defense outlays from the FY 1991 projected level of 5.5 percent of GNP is unrealistic. To reduce U.S. defense spending to 1.5 percent of the GNP would require dismantling virtually the entire military establishment.

A more reasonable expectation is that the annual "peace dividend" in the 1990s will be in the neighborhood of one-quarter to one-half of one percent of GNP—accomplished by annual budget cuts in the neighborhood of 4 percent. A cumulative savings of 1.25 to 2.5 percent of the GNP over a five-year time period would be substantial—$75 to $150 billion. Yet it would neither constitute a great bonanza for the advocates of civilian spending increases nor the overwhelming problem of "conversion" to a peacetime economy feared by others. As Charles Schultze of the Brookings Institution put the matter, "We can clearly shift this modest amount of resources between military and civilian pursuits without any significant macro-economic problems."[13]

There are important lessons to be learned from the experiences of the "peace dividends" generated by ending the Korean and Vietnam Wars. The fundamental point is that nobody remembers any special use of those "dividends," and for good reason. By and large, the funds were absorbed by expansions of ongoing federal civilian programs, such as social security and Medicare. The fiscal problem that emerged resulted from the fact that a one-shot savings in defense was used to justify a relatively permanent commitment to a higher level of civilian spending.

Devoting any peace dividend to bringing the budget deficit down has the added benefit of not tying the hands of the next generation if it chooses to shift to a different set of priorities.

Contingency Planning

Given the vagaries of human experience, a modest amount of contingency planning is wise. Indeed, the highly cyclical pattern of this nation's past defense spending reflects the sharp and abrupt changes that can occur both in the international environment facing the United States and in our reaction to it.

A skeptical attitude underscores the need for maintaining the capability of reversing fairly quickly the direction of military policy. As we have seen since August 1990, effective reversibility requires a basic military force in being, which can be augmented fairly quickly by calling up the reserves and national guard units.

A period of sustained reductions in the level of defense spending would underscore two key aspects of reversibility: a healthy defense manufacturing base and an ongoing research and development effort focusing on the design of new and improved weapon systems. That does not require continuing every weapon system or military supplier. The military budget for 1992 does request a $5 billion increase in research and development, a 15 percent rise from 1991.

The proposed level of funding would provide significant support for a new generation of weapon systems such as the B-2 bomber, the advanced cruise missile, the advanced tactical fighter, the SSN-21 attack submarine, and advanced armored vehicles. In addition, substantial funds are allocated to such varied projects as the Strategic Defense Initiative and SEMATECH, the semiconductor industry consortium.[14] Reversibility does point up the need to maintain an adequate industrial base containing an array of strong prime contractors and subcontractors that can compete effectively for the design and production of the equipment needed by the substantial military force that will be required for the indefinite future. Despite the well-publicized cases of cost overruns and production delays, the U.S. defense industry continues to contain the nation's largest concentration of scientific and technological talent. The outstanding performance of the high-tech weapons our armed forces used against Iraq underscores that point.

The notion of reversibility, nonetheless, is consistent with closing down or converting defense plants that are no longer needed. The defense industry is coming off an all-time peak; thus, a substantial reduction in its volume of activity is to be expected. In view of the sad history of most of their previous diversification efforts, the large specialized military contractors will do better in reacting to defense cuts by slimming down to more sustainable size. Conversion is worse than mere empty talk. It is a costly snare and delusion.

Since many of the industry's production facilities are ancient by the current standards of the commercial economy, the opportunity to phase them out should be welcomed. Some defense plants may be useful in civilian endeavors, while a select few may have to be mothballed for contingency planning purposes. It is vital that the remaining defense suppliers in the aggregate be financially viable and that they possess the ability to meet the likely design and production needs of the military establishment in the years ahead. That can be done without subsidizing them. Congress must reduce the many costly burdens that it unnecessarily imposes on the defense procurement process generally and on defense contractors specifically. The defense dollar can go much further if military budgeting is no longer viewed as an extension of governmental service to constituents.[15]

There is a far more basic reason to improve the economic efficiency of the military establishment: to secure the continuing public support needed to maintain a high level of defense spending for the foreseeable future.

MX Missile
Test Launch

Chapter 4

Strategic Forces

Michael E. Brown

Although East-West relations were transformed by the events of 1989 and 1990, American strategic nuclear policy exhibited more continuity than change as the last decade of the millennium got under way. Modernization efforts proceeded, albeit in the face of stringent and frequently arbitrary fiscal constraints, and operational doctrine continued to be based on the political assumptions and targeting requirements of previous years.

There were four main reasons why American strategic policy followed a familiar trajectory in 1990. First, although Soviet leaders agreed to radical changes in the conventional balance of power in Europe, they made comparatively few changes in their strategic force posture. American policymakers were consequently reluctant to make major changes in their own forces and plans. Second, although the Strategic Arms Reductions Talks (START) made significant progress in 1990, the cuts built into the START framework will not have to be fully implemented until long after the treaty goes into effect. Overhauling the force structure in order to bring it in line with START limitations was therefore not an immediate concern in 1990. Third, the U.S. Air Force and Navy aggressively resisted attempts to scale back cherished procurement programs, such as the B-2 bomber, Trident ballistic missile submarine (SSBN), and sea-launched cruise missile (SLCM). This contributed to the considerable momentum these endeavors already enjoyed. Fourth and last, civilian policymakers in Washington, not unnaturally, were preoccupied with events in the Soviet Union, Eastern Europe, Germany, and the Persian Gulf. Rethinking the strategic equation was not at the top, or even close to the top, of the policy agenda.

Important decisions loom on the horizon, however. Policymakers in the administration and Congress have yet to resolve their differences over the fate of the B-2 bomber, the MX intercontinental ballistic missile (ICBM), and the small intercontinental ballistic missile (SICBM). This deadlock is driving up the price of each program at a time when excessive costs are increasingly difficult to sustain.

In addition, decisions have to be made about restructuring U.S. strategic forces in light of impending START limitations. In all probability, the number of strategic nuclear weapons deployed in the U.S. arsenal will decline from over 12,000, the level in 1990, to around 9,000 (if seventy-five B-2s are built) or 8,000 (if only fifteen or twenty B-2s are built). These arms control cuts, while less grandiose than many had originally anticipated, will nonetheless obligate policy-makers to overhaul the U.S. force posture. Many older systems will have to be retired, and modernization decisions will have to be made with care. In particular, policymakers will have to decide if the 1,000 additional warheads provided by a large force of B-2 bombers is worth the tens of billions of dollars it would cost to build and operate such a fleet.

Finally, a comprehensive review of U.S. nuclear war plans and targeting policies must be undertaken in light of the fact that the deterrence problem the United States faces is easing in fundamental ways. The Warsaw Pact has ceased to exist, the Soviet Union's ability to launch a surprise attack on Western Europe is rapidly eroding, and the Soviet political system itself is changing. American strategic thinking should reflect these developments. It no longer makes sense, for example, for the United States to target military facilities in Eastern Europe, or to plan to use American nuclear weapons in a way that would undermine the Communist party's ability to control events in the Soviet Union. Many believe that Washington no longer needs 9,000 or even 8,000 strategic weapons to deter Moscow from attacking vital American interests. If events in Eastern Europe and the Soviet Union continue on course and if strategic arms control negotiations between the superpowers reconvene after the signing of the START Treaty, as they are expected to do, it might be possible to reduce weapon levels to between 2,000 and 4,000 per side by the end of the 1990s.

In short, American strategic nuclear policy in 1990, in the grips of entrenched dogma and established plans and programs, is on the verge of major, perhaps radical, change.

Programmatic Developments

Strategic modernization efforts begun in the 1970s and 1980s continued to mature in the early 1990s. However, most programs were affected by budgetary constraints imposed, first, by the Department of Defense (DOD), which anticipated congressional opposition to high spending levels, and then by Congress itself. As a result, modernization plans were determined more by fiscal pressures and political compromise than by an assessment of strategic needs and priorities. One DOD official called the budgeting process "a Brazilian rain forest drill," a slash and burn exercise. According to Congressman Les Aspin (D-Wisconsin), the chairman of the House Armed Services Committee, any resemblance the budgeting and planning process bore to a rational debate on defense priorities was "purely accidental."[1]

ICBMs

As they have done for many years, policymakers in Washington failed in 1990 to make a firm decision about adding a mobile ICBM to the force structure. Two main options for deploying a mobile ICBM remain under consideration. One is to deploy fifty ten-warhead MX missiles on twenty-five trains, which would be flushed from their garrisons in time of crisis. The other option is to develop and deploy 500 single-warhead SICBMs on road-mobile launchers, many of which would be widely dispersed on a regular basis.

The main advantage of the MX rail garrison option is financial. The MX missile itself has already been developed and deployed in silos, and the rail garrison basing system would be relatively inexpensive to build and operate. Rail garrison procurement costs are estimated to be $6.9 billion ($1.7 billion of which has already been spent), and twenty-year operating and support (O&S) costs would be $5 billion. The SICBM, on the other hand, would cost $41.9 billion to develop and deploy ($3.4 billion of which has already been spent), and $11 billion in twenty-year O&S costs.[2]

The main advantage of the SICBM option is strategic. SICBM launchers randomly dispersed over wide areas would probably have high survival rates even if the Soviet Union successfully executed a massive surprise attack. MX trains, on the other hand, would be vulnerable, even more vulnerable than silo-based systems, unless strategic warning of an impending attack provided decision makers with enough time to flush them from their garrisons.[3]

The DOD plan, as of mid-1990, was to deploy fifty MX missiles on rail cars by 1994 (figure 4–1). Concurrently, it would continue to develop the SICBM, which just began flight testing in 1989, and start deploying this more survivable system in 1997. The Pentagon consequently asked for $2.8 billion for the MX in its fiscal year (FY) 1991 budget request. This would enable the Air Force to build twelve more MX missiles, seven trains, several alert shelters, and some rail lines. The Defense Department also asked for $202 million for development of the SICBM.

Congress, which for some time has been highly critical of DOD's attempts to promote MX rail garrison at the expense of the SICBM, slashed and redirected the Pentagon's ICBM modernization budget. It authorized $674 million for procurement of twelve MX missiles, but it provided no money at all for rail garrison procurement; this was one issue on which the Senate and the House of Representatives agreed completely. In addition, Congress provided $687.7 million for continued development of both MX rail garrison and the SICBM.

Although many in Congress hoped that these actions would derail the Pentagon's plans for the MX and give a boost to the SICBM, the Defense Department is unlikely to embrace the SICBM option. It recognizes that building a road-mobile missile would inevitably cut into the amount of money available for other strategic systems, many of which, such as the B-2, have powerful and determined bureaucratic backers. In fact, some congressional leaders are beginning to have second thoughts about the SICBM, given its cost and the prospect of declining defense budgets through the 1990s. But rather than embrace MX rail garrison, they, along with some administration officials, are beginning to explore the idea of deploying large numbers of single-warhead ICBMs in silos. These missiles would be vulnerable to an all-out attack, but once START warhead limits are put into effect,

Soviet war planners would probably be disinclined to dedicate a large portion of a comparatively modest arsenal to an attack that would require two warheads for each single-warhead target. This option, therefore, would enhance stability, in that it would not present an attacker with a small number of highly valuable targets, the main limitation of the MX rail garrison option. At the same time, it would not involve exorbitant procurement or O&S costs, because large numbers of mobile launchers would not have to be built and operated. The idea of deploying single-warhead missiles in silos will probably attract more support as the deadlock over the MX and SICBM drags on, and when the implications of the START framework for the U.S. force structure become better understood.

The Soviet Union, for its part, continued to develop and test a more accurate and more powerful version of its heavy SS-18 ICBM. This modernization effort led conservative American analysts to charge that the Soviet Union will be able to compensate for the fact that it will have to cut its SS-18 force in half under the terms of the START Treaty. The Soviet Union also doubled the number of ten-warhead, rail-capable SS-24 ICBMs in its inventory; sixty SS-24s were operational at the end of 1990, although some of these were based in silos. The Soviet leadership promised to end SS-24 production in early 1991, however. Finally, deployment of the single-warhead, road-mobile SS-25 continued in 1990 as the size of this force grew from 165 to 225 missiles. The Soviet leadership has not indicated that it plans to terminate SS-25 production.[4]

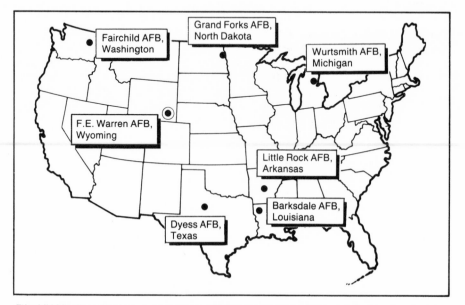

Fifty MX Missiles would be removed from F.E. Warren Air Force Base and deployed on twenty-five trains which would be stationed at the Air Force facilities shown above and flushed onto civilian tracks during crises.

SSBNs and Submarine-Launched
Ballistic Missiles (SLBMs)

The Trident submarine and D-5 SLBM programs continued to be among the least controversial components of the U.S. strategic modernization program. The Trident is needed to replace the aging Poseidon fleet, as most policymakers and analysts recognize, and the D-5 will provide survivable, hard-target kill capabilities that vulnerable silo-based ICBMs can no longer guarantee. Although some contend that the deployment of counterforce systems is destabilizing, the D-5 retains strong backing in DOD and, by and large, in Congress.[5]

The D-5, which had to have its first-stage nozzle redesigned after problems emerged in 1989, completed its submerged firing trials and was accepted into service in 1990. Three Tridents were equipped with D-5s by the end of the year.[6] New Tridents will henceforth be equipped with D-5s, and Tridents equipped with C-4 SLBMs before 1990 will eventually be retrofitted with the more advanced missile. Congress provided $1.34 billion in procurement funds for fifty-two D-5s in the FY 1991 budget, which is what the Defense Department requested, as well as $192 million for procurement of long-lead items for more D-5s. No decision was made on the size of the overall production run.

Congress also authorized $1.15 billion in funds for the eighteenth Trident SSBN, but it did not provide any money for the nineteenth and twentieth as the Pentagon had hoped. Congressional leaders maintained that the United States would throw its strategic force structure out of balance if it deployed more than eighteen Tridents in a START regime. This action does not preclude construction of additional Tridents, but it would slow production should additional submarines be placed on order.

The Soviet Union continued to retire large numbers of old ballistic missile submarines, while adding smaller numbers of modern boats to its fleet. In 1990 it added a sixth Delta IV SSBN (each of which is equipped with sixteen SS-N-23 SLBMs) to its inventory, as well as the sixth and last of the Typhoon series (each of which is equipped with twenty SS-N-20 SLBMs). The decision to terminate Typhoon production was probably influenced by the fact that under the START counting rules each SS-N-23 will be counted as having only four warheads, while each SS-N-20 will be counted as having ten. Each Delta IV, therefore, will be counted as having sixty-four warheads, while each Typhoon will be credited with 200. This means that the Soviet Navy will be able to deploy a larger number of boats, and a more survivable SSBN force, if it emphasizes Delta IVs instead of Typhoons.[7] Delta IV production is therefore expected to continue.

Bombers

Efforts to modernize the bomber leg of the triad continue to be routine in some respects. By late 1990, half of the FB-111 fleet had been transferred from strategic to tactical units. B-52Gs equipped with short-range attack missiles (SRAMs) and air-launched cruise missiles (ALCMs) were being retired outright, a process that will continue in the early 1990s.[8] At the same time, the B-52H fleet was being modified to carry the ALCM's successor, the advanced cruise missile (ACM). This modification program is expected to conclude in April 1992. Interestingly, the Air Force, which has long maintained that structural fatigue will force the B-52 out of the strategic inventory in the mid-to-late 1990s, announced that additional modifications could extend the B-52's operational life to the year 2030.[9]

The B-1B program has resolved virtually all of the offensive avionics problems that plagued it in the late 1980s, but some defensive avionics deficiencies still await corrective action. The bomber's main electronic countermeasures suite is in the process of being modified, but flight testing of the modified system has been delayed. In addition, the B-1B's tail warning radar has not performed as expected.[10] Even so, the Air Force, which originally claimed that the B-1B's effectiveness as a penetrator would be suspect after the mid-to-late 1990s, new plans to use the B-1B in a penetrating role well past the year 2000. The failure of Soviet air defenses to improve as rapidly as expected more than compensates for the B-1B's lingering technical limitations.

The B-2 was far and away the most controversial element of the DOD strategic modernization program, and the debate over the B-2 reached a fever pitch in 1990. This debate focused on two main issues: the strategic rationale for the new bomber, and its stupendous cost.

Supporters of the stealth bomber claim that there are ten strategic rationales for fielding it.[11] First, they argue that, if the United States fails to build the B-2, the bomber leg of the triad will atrophy and the triad itself will eventually disintegrate. Opponents of the B-2 point out that the B-1B has just been added to the force structure, and that the Air Force itself claims that the B-1B will be an ef-

fective penetrator for years to come. In addition, B-52s and B-1Bs will be able to serve as cruise missile carriers for decades.

Second, supporters of the B-2 maintain that it is important to have bombers in the force structure because this complicates the Soviet attack problem. Opponents maintain that even if this is true it does not translate into a case for the B-2 because existing bombers, including cruise missile carriers, already fill this role.

Third, B-2 enthusiasts argue that bombers enhance strategic stability for a number of reasons. They are not first-strike systems; they can be generated quickly in crises; they are recallable; and they give national leaders options for signalling adversaries. Critics of the program note that these are not compelling reasons for deploying the B-2 because existing systems, including cruise missile carriers, also have these attributes.

Fourth, supporters of the B-2 contend that it would be risky for the air-breathing leg of the triad to rely exclusively on cruise missiles because this would allow the Soviet Union to concentrate its air defense efforts on a single threat. B-2 opponents argue that, since the Soviet Union has been unable to develop effective defenses against the ALCM, there are good reasons for being confident about the effectiveness of the ACM. The ACM takes full advantage of stealth designs and materials that will make it much harder to detect than the ALCM or, for that matter, the B-2. In addition, the ACM will have better range than its predecessor, which will enable ACM carriers to stay even farther away from the Soviet air defense perimeter and which will allow the missile itself to go around heavy concentrations of air defenses, instead of through them. The ACM, therefore, will be a highly survivable system.

Fifth, B-2 backers hold that penetrating bombers are more flexible than other strategic systems because pilots can determine if silos and bases are occupied before attacking them, and because they can evaluate the amount of damage caused by earlier attacks before executing new attacks. Opponents of the B-2 point out that operations such as these will depend on the development of long-range sensors that can be used without giving away the location of the attacking bomber. Pilots could move in close to their targets and make visual checks during daylight attacks, but doing so would increase the bomber's exposure to terminal air defenses.

Sixth, supporters of the B-2 argue that only penetrating bombers carry the high-yield gravity bombs that are needed to destroy superhard targets. Critics maintain that few targets require high-yield weapons, and that ballistic missiles could be equipped with high-yield warheads or earth-penetrating warheads for those that do. Critics also point out that since targets valuable enough to warrant superhardening are likely to be protected by strong terminal air defenses, the B-2 would attack these targets with SRAMs rather than gravity bombs.

Seventh, B-2 defenders maintain that it has more potential than any other strategic system to hold at risk mobile targets such as Soviet SS-24 and SS-25 ICBMs. Many of the B-2's opponents contend that it is profoundly destabilizing to try to hold the other side's survivable forces at risk, while others argue that the point is moot, given the magnitude of the search problem and the unpromising prospects for sensor technology.

Eighth, B-2 advocates argue that the United States needs to deploy the B-2 in order to take full advantage of the bomber counting rule in the START framework. This treaty provision does not count every gravity bomb and SRAM carried by penetrating bombers against the 6,000-weapon ceiling that the agreement will impose on each side. Instead, it counts each bomber as one weapon against this cap. A bomber-heavy force structure could consequently have 9,000 to 10,000 nuclear weapons at its disposal. The Air Force insists that it needs this many weapons to cover the Soviet target set adequately. Some Air Force leaders have said that, because of these targeting requirements, they would not support a START Treaty without a favorable bomber counting rule and a commitment to build the B-2.[12] Opponents of the B-2 believe that American targeting requirements could be lowered significantly in light of international developments that took place in 1989 and 1990. They further argue that if lower levels of forces are adequate to deter the Soviet Union, then the bomber counting rule in the START framework should be renegotiated. It would be ridiculous, they insist, to build a bomber the country does not need simply to take advantage of a counting rule over which the U.S. government has considerable control.

Ninth, B-2 supporters maintain that the new bomber will be needed for conventional operations in various parts of the world. Critics argue that the B-1B more than fills the bill. The B-1B, like the B-2, would not be dependent on foreign bases, and the Air Force expects the B-1B to be effective against the most sophisticated air defenses in the world for years to come. Interestingly, General John Chain, at the time commander-in-chief of the Strategic Air Command (SAC), disparaged the idea of using the B-2 in conventional operations. According to Chain, "Because of the value of the unit, I can't see putting very many at risk in a conventional conflict."[13]

Tenth and last, supporters of the B-2 argue that it is needed because its "stealthy" capabilities will be needed to penetrate Soviet air defenses in the future. Setting aside the question of whether there is a legitimate military requirement for a penetrator, critics of the program maintain that the B-2's impressive penetration capabilities would not be needed to overcome Soviet air defenses in an all-out nuclear war. Air defenses would be suppressed by ICBM, SLBM, ALCM, and SRAM attacks tailored to clear out penetration corridors for B-1Bs, which could then use SRAMs against targets surrounded by heavy terminal defenses and gravity bombs against lightly defended targets.

As the debate over the FY 1991 budget heated up, many in Congress concluded that the Air Force, which had changed its arguments for building the B-2 many times over the years, failed to present a compelling case for going ahead with the program. The B-2's fate, therefore, hinged to a considerable degree on its cost. By early 1990, the Air Force cost estimate for building 132 B-2s had risen to over $70 billion. Critics of the program pointed out, though, that this estimate assumed that the program's technical problems were behind it, which was not the case, and that Congress would provide $8 billion per year in B-2 procurement funds in the early 1990s, which it was unlikely to do.[14] In addition, the Air Force estimate left out the cost of non-baseline items (military construction, facilities, flight simulators, and other critical equipment) as well as postproduction modification efforts, which equalled 19 percent of the B-1B's baseline costs. Finally, the Air Force's estimate left out O&S costs, which would undoubtedly be very high because manned aircraft are expensive to operate and maintain. Critics contended that the cost of building 132 B-2s and operating them for twenty years would total more than $150 billion.[15]

With the cost problem in mind, Secretary of Defense Richard Cheney decided in April 1990 to build only seventy-five B-2s. This brought the official DOD procurement cost estimate down to $62.8 billion (although critics contended that total procurement and twenty-year O&S costs for seventy-five B-2s would exceed $106 billion).[16] Cheney's decision backfired in two respects, however. First, since research and development costs were the same for 75-aircraft and 132-aircraft programs, reducing the production run drove up the system's unit costs from $530 million to $837 million. Many in Congress found the idea of spending this much money for a single bomber unpalatable. Second, Air Force leaders had already gone on the record saying that they needed 132 B-2s to cover the Soviet target set adequately.[17] Now they were forced to admit that seventy-five B-2s would do the job. The Air Force's credibility consequently suffered, and rightly so.

Cheney, who had scaled back his B-2 budget request when he scaled back the size of the overall program, still hoped to get $4.65 billion and authorization to start work on two new B-2s, the sixteenth and seventeenth in the series, in FY 1991. The Senate went along with Cheney, although a resolution to halt B-2 production was only narrowly defeated. The House of Representatives, however, voted to stop production with the fifteenth aircraft. In the end, Senate and House conferees approved $4.15 billion for development and production, but they disagreed sharply over how B-2 production funds could be spent. The Senate maintained that work could start on two new B-2s, should Cheney so desire. The House insisted that B-2 production funds could only be spent on the fifteen aircraft that Congress had already approved. Some in the House threatened to take the matter to federal court if the Pentagon tried to start work on two new bombers.[18]

Congress will grapple with this issue again in 1991, but there is no guarantee that it will make a final decision on the fate of the B-2. The worst-case scenario, as some in Congress see it, is that the Senate and House will keep coming to an impasse on the B-2, allocating just enough money to build one or two new aircraft every year but not enough to build them at an efficient rate. Should this come to pass, and the events of 1990 suggest that it might, the Air Force will probably end up with a total of twenty to thirty B-2s, each costing in the neighborhood of $2 billion.

Bomber modernization has been somewhat less eventful in the Soviet Union. The Soviet Air Force continues to field a force of around 160 TU-95 Bear bombers, which are roughly comparable in vintage and capability to the U.S. B-52. A significant part of the Soviet Bear force is equipped to carry long-range ALCMs. The Soviet Union also fields a small force of approximately fifteen TU-160 Blackjack bombers, which are roughly comparable to the U.S. B-1B in age and capability. Ironically, the Blackjack, like the B-1B, has experienced development problems, apparently with its avionics. This might explain why Blackjack production has proceeded slowly to date. The Blackjack, which would probably be an effective penetrator, given that the United States deploys thin air defenses, is also capable of carrying ALCMs.

Cruise Missiles and SRAMs

In 1983, the Defense Department decided to terminate ALCM production and begin work on a follow-on system, the ACM. Unfortunately, the ACM development program experienced serious technical difficulties; problems with avionics software and hardware were particularly troublesome and led to a series of crashes in the late 1980s. In 1989 Congress tied the release of production funds to successful flight testing, and threatened to cancel the program outright if its prospects failed to improve.

Since then, the ACM program seems to have turned the corner. Full-scale development has virtually ended, and the first operational ACMs were delivered to SAC in June 1990. Congress subsequently approved DOD's FY 1991 request for $365.8 million in ACM production funds, enough for 100 missiles.[19] Full-rate production (250 missiles per year) is scheduled to begin in FY 1992. The total production run of 1,461 missiles is expected to cost $6.7 billion, which would make the cost of each missile $4.6 million.[20] In short, the ACM's prospects appear to be bright. There is general agreement that a follow-on to the ALCM is needed, and that the ACM program is progressing well. Those in Congress who would like to replace the penetrating bomber force with a cruise missile force are, not surprisingly, strong supporters of the ACM.

The Air Force is also in the process of developing a follow-on to the SRAM. The SRAM II is expected to be stealthier, more accurate, and longer-legged than its predecessor. But the SRAM II development program, which got under way in 1987, has experienced serious problems, most notably with the missile's rocket motor and propellant. The program was two years behind schedule at the end of

1990, and first flight of the SRAM II had been pushed back to April 1991. The new missile is not scheduled to enter the force structure until April 1994. Plans call for the Air Force to buy 1,633 SRAM IIs at an estimated total cost of $2.4 billion. [21]

The SRAM II's prospects are clouded only by its stubborn development problems. It is widely recognized that SRAMs make an important contribution to the effectiveness of the bomber leg of the triad; they can be used to suppress air defenses or attack heavily defended targets. It is also widely recognized that the SRAM I needs to be replaced in short order. Since the START framework gives both sides a powerful incentive to deploy short-range attack missiles, production and deployment of the SRAM II is virtually inevitable once its technical problems are resolved.

The U.S. Navy continues to deploy nuclear-armed, land-attack cruise missiles. Over 350 such SLCMs have already been built, and a production run of 758 is planned. By the end of 1990, fifty-three submarines and thirty-five surface ships were equipped with launchers capable of handling this system. [22] After years of wrangling over the SLCM issue in the START negotiations, the United States and the Soviet Union agreed, in a decision that was formalized at the May–June 1990 summit, that neither side would deploy more than 880 nuclear-armed SLCMs. As things stand, therefore, this agreement will not interfere with Navy plans for SLCM procurement and deployment.

The Soviet Union continues to modernize in this area as well. It deployed a long-range ALCM, the AS-15, in 1984, and it continues to work on a supersonic ALCM, the AS-X-19. Its first long-range SLCM, the SS-N-21, entered service in 1987, and a large, supersonic SLCM, the SS-NX-24, is being developed.

Ballistic Missile Defenses

The Strategic Defense Initiative Organization (SDIO) continued to lobby aggressively in 1990 on behalf of "Brilliant Pebbles," its latest scheme for a ballistic missile defense. According to SDIO, a Brilliant Pebbles system would consist of several thousand space-based interceptors. Each three-foot rocket would be equipped with its own package of sensors that would enable it to spot, home in on, and destroy its target on impact. These interceptors, therefore, would not be dependent on a centralized battle-management system; each would be capable of independent operations. SDIO maintained that the technology to build a Brilliant Pebbles system is "at hand," and that sensor and guidance testing could be moved out of the laboratory. [23]

SDIO argued, moreover, that a Phase I system designed to destroy 15 percent of a massive Soviet attack could be built for $55 billion. This system would include 4,614 Brilliant Pebbles, as well as a ground-based interceptor (which began flight testing in January 1990) and a new early warning satellite system. It would not, however, include any laser or beam weapons. In order to pave the way for a Phase I deployment decision in 1993, with deployment following in the late 1990s, SDIO planned to increase Brilliant Pebbles funding by more than 250 percent and Phase I funding significantly in FY 1991. [24]

Many in Congress complained that although SDIO paid lip service to the problem of protecting the United States against an accidental launch or an attack from the Third World, an issue of growing concern, its not-so-hidden agenda was to deploy a system designed to defend against an all-out attack from the Soviet Union. Congressional leaders felt that these priorities should be reversed, and they opposed the idea of making a deployment decision, especially for a Phase I system, in the near future. The idea of taking steps that would violate the terms of the Anti-Ballistic Missile (ABM) Treaty was, as far as Congress was concerned, even more problematic. Analysts pointed out, moreover, that SDIO's cost estimates for Phase I systems have, in the past, left out inflation, the cost of operating the system while it is being deployed, and the cost of system upgrades. The true cost of a Phase I system, therefore, would undoubtedly be much higher than SDIO's preliminary figures.[25]

It would not be in the Soviet national interest to enter into a defensive arms race with the United States.

SDIO's total budget request for FY 1991 was $4.66 billion, $1 billion more than it had received in FY 1990. The Senate voted to give SDIO $3.7 billion in FY 1991, and the House authorized only $2.3 billion. Senate and House conferees more or less split the difference, and settled on a figure of $2.89 billion for the new budget. In addition, they took steps to discourage SDIO from emphasizing near-term deployment of Phase I at the expense of long-term research and development. In an innovative departure from past practice, Congress broke SDIO's budget down into five mission areas: Phase I systems, including Brilliant Pebbles, that would provide modest capabilities against a large-scale attack ($817.3 million); follow-on systems that might lead to the deployment of highly effective defenses in the next century ($754.3 million); limited protection systems that would be compliant with the narrow interpretation of the ABM Treaty ($389 million); theater defenses and tactical ballistic missile defenses ($180 million); and support activities ($749.4 million). Congress gave SDIO discretionary authority to shift funds between these accounts, as long as no account increased or decreased by more than 10 percent. This gave SDIO some funding flexibility while ensuring that long-term research and limited protection systems would not be neglected in the Pentagon's enthusiasm for Brilliant Pebbles and Phase I development efforts.

The Soviet Union continues to work in this area as well. The Moscow ABM system was recently upgraded and, although some Soviet analysts contend that it contributes little to Soviet security, concerns about ballistic missile attacks from the Middle East and Asia might lead Soviet decision makers to keep it up and running. In addition, the Soviet Union conducts a vigorous program of research on a variety of defensive systems, including exotic technologies with potential defensive applications.

At the same time, the Soviet leadership in 1990 seemed to be deeply committed to preserving ABM Treaty limitations on permissible research and development. It recognized that it would not be in the Soviet national interest to enter into a defensive arms race with the United States. The Soviet Union is ill-equipped technologically and economically to compete in, let alone win, such a race. Moscow's commitment to the ABM Treaty was reflected in its September 1989 decision to dismantle its controversial radar at Krasnoyarsk, which it later acknowledged violated the terms of the agreement.

Although the Soviet Union is unlikely to launch a defensive arms race itself, it will not remain idle if the United States takes steps to deploy space based defensive systems. Moscow has made it clear that if the United States proceeds down this path, it will withdraw from the START Treaty and deploy appropriate offensive and defensive systems of its own. [26]

Air Defenses

In 1990 the United States, unbeknown to many policymakers and analysts, was in the process of modernizing and expanding its air defense system. The Distant Early Warning system in Alaska and northern Canada is being replaced by the North Warning system, a network of advanced radars designed to detect cruise missile carriers and low-altitude bombers. This system has a limited ability to detect cruise missile attacks and is scheduled to be fully operational in 1992.

In addition, the United States made plans to add four over-the-horizon back-scatter (OTH-B) radars to its early warning network. OTH-B radars, unlike conventional radars, are not hampered by line-of-sight limitations because they operate by bouncing beams off the ionosphere. This gives them long-range and wide-area coverage, but their performance can be spotty due to changing atmospheric conditions. The first of these complexes, the eastern system based in Maine, was completed in April 1990. The western system, based in California and Oregon, was nearly finished. The central system, based in North Dakota, was still on the drawing board, as was the Alaskan complex. Budgetary limitations, however, have placed the entire OTH-B program in jeopardy. [27]

The United States is also exploring the possibility, in accordance with its Air Defense Initiative, of deploying a more comprehensive air defense system in the future. Space-based radars are now in development, for example, but it is not yet clear if systems powerful enough to detect stealthy bombers and cruise missiles can be built. Full-scale testing of a space-based radar is still several years away. Systems that could engage attacking bombers, cruise missile carriers, and cruise missiles, such as the advanced tactical fighter and a long-range surface-to-air missile (SAM), are also under development. Cost estimates for a comprehensive air defense system range from $54 to $170 billion, depending on the architecture of the system. Given these technical and fiscal obstacles, deployment of an enduring defense in depth against air-breathing systems is at least ten to twenty years away. [28]

The Soviet Union's air defense system is extensive, and impressive on paper, but largely ineffective against low-altitude and especially low-observable systems. Many Soviet fighters lack true look-down/shoot-down capabilities, and many Soviet SAMs are ineffective against low-altitude threats. Advanced systems, such as MiG-31 and Su-27 fighters and SA-10 SAMs, are being deployed, however, and others, such as the SA-12B SAM, are in development. Still, the Soviet Union is many years away from being able to neutralize stealthy bombers and cruise missiles; a long-term research and development effort will be required to overcome Soviet sensor and data processing limitations.

A growing number of Soviet analysts argue that, since air defenses will contribute little to national security in the foreseeable future, and since they consume 10 to 15 percent of the defense budget, Moscow's commitment to air defense should be reconsidered. The huge Soviet air defense infrastructure would certainly seem to be a prime candidate for military *perestroika*.[29]

Impending Arms Control Constraints

The START Treaty, nine years in neogitation, was signed by presidents Bush and Gorbachev at the Moscow summit in July 1991. The main provisions of the treaty are as follows:[30]

- Each side will be allowed to deploy no more than 1,600 ICBMs, SLBMs, and heavy bombers. Within this total, each side will be allowed to deploy a maximum of 154 heavy ICBMs.[31]

- The total number of nuclear weapons attributed to these launchers cannot exceed 6,000. Of these, no more than 4,900 can be deployed on ICBMs and SLBMs, no more than 1,540 on heavy ICBMs, and no more than 1,100 on mobile ICBMs.[32]

- Heavy bombers that are not equipped to carry nuclear-armed ALCMs will count as one delivery vehicle against the 1,600 limit and one weapon against the 6,000 limit.

- Heavy bombers equipped to carry nuclear-armed ALCMs will be counted as one delivery vehicle against the 1,600 limit. Each of the first 150 American ALCM carriers will be counted as ten weapons against the 6,000 ceiling, and each additional ALCM carrier will be counted as carrying all of the ALCMs it is equipped to carry. Each of the first 180 Soviet ALCM carriers will be counted as eight weapons against the 6,000 ceiling, with each additional Soviet ALCM carrier counted as carrying all of the ALCMs it is equipped to carry. Maximum loading for American ALCM carriers is twenty, and sixteen for the Soviets.[33]

- SLCMs will not be limited by the START Treaty itself. However, each side agrees to make an annual statement about its deployment plans for long-range, nuclear-armed SLCMs, with the understanding that at no point will either side make plans to deploy more than 880 of these missiles.[34]

- The START framework is to be implemented in three phases over a period of seven years.

The current U.S. force structure exceeds START limits in a number of areas, as table 4–1 indicates, but many of these problems can be addressed by retiring old systems. Table 4–2 shows what the U.S. strategic force structure might look like after it is modernized and brought in line with START constraints. Minuteman II and Minuteman III ICBMs would be taken out of the inventory. Large numbers of single-warhead ICBMs would be deployed, and fifty MX ICBMs would stay in

Table 4–1. U.S. Strategic Forces, December 1990

Delivery Vehicle	Deployed Launchers	Attributed Weapons	Likely Loadings
ICBM Minuteman II	450	450	450
Minuteman III	500	1,500	1,500
MX	50	500	500
SLBM Poseidon C-3	176	1,760	1,760
Trident C-4	384	3,072	3,072
Trident D-5	72	576	576
Subtotal	1,632	7,858[a]	7,858[b]
(START limit)		(4,900)	
Bombers (ALCM)			
B-52G	77	814	924
B-52H	95	950	1,520
Bombers (non-ALCM)			
B-52G/H	39	39	546
B-1B	95	95	1,330
Subtotal	306	1,898[c]	4,320[d]
Grand Total	1,938	9,756	12,178
(START limit)	(1,600)	(6,000)	
SLCM	357		
(Agreed limit)	(880)		

Source: IISS, *Military Balance, 1990–1991*, p. 212, updated.

[a]At the December 1987 Washington summit, the United States and the Soviet Union agreed that Minuteman II missiles would be counted as having one warhead; Minuteman IIIs three; MXs ten; C-3s ten; C-4s eight; and D-5s eight.

[b]Actual ICBM and SLBM warhead loadings may not exceed START attribution numbers.

[c]The first 150 U.S. ALCM carriers will be counted as having ten weapons; each additional carrier will be counted as carrying all of the ALCMs which it is equipped to carry. In this case, ninety-five B-52Hs and fifty-five B-52Gs (a total of 150 ALCM carriers) would be counted as having ten weapons each. The remaining twenty-two B-52Gs would be counted as having twelve weapons each, the maximum number of ALCMs for which they are equipped. Non-ALCM bombers are counted as one weapon.

[d]Assumes that B-52Gs will be equipped with twelve ALCMs, and B-52Hs with sixteen. Also assumes that non-ALCM B-52s and B-1Bs will carry fourteen weapons each, which is what the Air Force says the B-1B will carry as a penetrator. See Rice, "Manned Bomber and Strategic Deterrence," pp. 125–26.

the force structure. The number of ICBM warheads deployed on mobile launchers could range from zero to 1,100 and would depend on the extent to which policy-makers were concerned about the Soviet Union's still-formidable hard-target kill capabilities, on the one hand, and fiscal constraints on the other. Poseidon submarines, as well as C-3 and C-4 SLBMs, would be retired. The modernized SSBN and SLBM force would consist of eighteen Trident submarines, each equipped with D-5 missiles. Since American policymakers will probably want to field close

Table 4–2. U.S. Strategic Forces, Modernized, START-Compliant

Delivery Vehicle	Deployed Launchers	Attributed Weapons	Likely Loadings
ICBM Single-Warhead	850	850	850
MX	50	500	500
SLBM Trident D-5	432	3,456	3,456
Subtotal (START limit)	1,332	4,806[a] (4,900)	4,806[b]
Bombers (ALCM) B-52H	95	950	1,520
Bombers (non-ALCM) B-1B	95	95	1,330
B-2	20	20	320
Subtotal	210	1,065[c]	3,170[d]
Grand Total (START limit)	1,542 (1,600)	5,871 (6,000)	7,976
SLCM (Agreed limit)	758 (880)		

[a]At the December 1987 Washington summit, the United States and the Soviet Union agreed that MX missiles would be counted as having ten warheads; D-5s would be counted as having eight.

[b]Actual ICBM and SLBM warhead loadings may not exceed START attribution numbers.

[c]The first 150 American ALCM carriers will be counted as having ten weapons. Non-ALCM bombers are counted as one weapon.

[d]Assumes that B-52Hs will be equipped with sixteen ALCMs. Also assumes that non-ALCM B-1Bs will carry fourteen weapons, and B-2s sixteen. See Rice, "Manned Bomber and Strategic Deterrence," pp. 125–26.

to 4,900 ballistic missile warheads, there will be some pressure to reduce U.S. bomber forces, especially ALCM forces, given START's 6,000 weapon cap on total forces. Retiring the B-52G force and non-ALCM B-52s would address this problem. One should note that, given the treaty's bomber and ALCM counting rules, the United States will have a strong incentive to use the B-1B as a penetrator as long as B-52Hs are used as ALCM carriers. One should also note that there will be room for the B-2 under these ceilings, the assumption being that only twenty B-2s will be built. SLCM limits would have no effect on U.S. forces, given current procurement plans.

Tables 4–1 and 4–2 distinguish between "attributed weapons," which count against START ceilings, and "likely loadings," the number of weapons a delivery vehicle would carry on an actual mission. Because of START's unusual bomber and ALCM counting rules, attributed numbers for bombers and ALCM carriers bear little relation to actual weapon loads. The current force structure would consequently be credited with only 9,756 weapons, according to START counting rules, even though it has the capacity to deliver over 12,000 nuclear weapons.

Similarly, the modernized force structure depicted in table 4–2 would be credited with meeting the START Treaty's 6,000 weapon cap, even though it would have the capacity to deliver almost 8,000 nuclear weapons, plus several hundred SLCMs. It is important to note that this modernized force is formidable—it provides 2,000 weapons above and beyond the formal cap—even though it assumes that only twenty B-2s will be built. A force that included a fleet of seventy-five B-2s would provide war planners with an additional 880 weapons, or a total of almost 9,000 weapons, but it would, of course, be substantially more expensive to build and operate.

Soviet force planners will have a strong incentive to take advantage of START counting rules (and thin American air defenses) and deploy large numbers of Blackjack bombers.

In short, a modernized, START-constrained force structure will be quite different from the one that exists today. Smooth implementation of the START Treaty will therefore depend on timely retirement and modernization decisions. Several questions, in particular, will have to be addressed: Do the risks of fielding a silo-based ICBM force outweigh the costs of building and operating a mobile force? Are eighteen SSBNs enough? Is the B-2 a strategic necessity or an expensive luxury? How should these force structure decisions be influenced by START considerations? Unfortunately, the linkage between retirement and modernization decisions, on the one hand, and implementation of the START agreement, on the other, has received insufficient attention in Washington.

The Soviet Union will have a difficult time bringing its strategic force structure in line with the terms of the START framework because it currently deploys very large ICBM and SLBM forces, as table 4–3 indicates. In order to get launcher and weapon totals down to START levels, Soviet policymakers will have to retire their large stock of old ICBMs and SLBMs, streamlining their force structure considerably. Even so, the Soviet Union will retain impressive hard-target kill capabilities, and it will have room under the START ceilings to build up its bomber and ALCM forces substantially.

Table 4–4 shows what the Soviet force structure might look like after it is modernized and brought into line with the terms of the START agreement. This table assumes that Soviet policymakers will retain the 154 heavy SS-18 ICBMs they will be permitted under the terms of the treaty, and deploy as many weapons on mobile ICBMs as the framework permits. These are reasonable assumptions given Soviet negotiating positions and recent force structure decisions. It is also reasonable to assume that Soviet policymakers will retain essentially the same mix of ICBM and SLBM forces, and that they will want to keep their six Typhoon-class SSBNs in the force structure. Should Soviet decision makers proceed down this path, they will be forced to retire their old SS-11, SS-13, and SS-17 ICBMs,

Table 4–3. Soviet Strategic Forces, December 1990

Delivery Vehicle	Deployed Launchers	Attributed Weapons	Likely Loadings
ICBM SS-11	350	360	360
SS-13	60	60	60
SS-17	75	300	300
SS-18	308	3,080	3,080
SS-19	320	1,920	1,920
SS-24	60	600	600
SS-25	225	225	225
SLBM SS-N-6 (Yankee I SSBN)	192	192	192
SS-N-8 (Delta I, II)	280	280	280
SS-N-17 (Yankee II)	12	12	12
SS-N-18 (Delta III)	224	1,568	1,568
SS-N-20 (Typhoon)	120	1,200	1,200
SS-N-23 (Delta IV)	96	384	384
Subtotal	2,322	10,181[a]	10,181[b]
(START limit)		(4,900)	
Bombers (ALCM)			
Bear	75	600	900
Blackjack	15	120	180
Bombers (non-ALCM)			
Bear	95	95	380
Subtotal	185	815[c]	1,460[d]
Grand Total	2,497	10,996	11,641
(START limit)	(1,600)	(6,000)	
SLCM	150		
(Agreed limit)	(880)		

Source: IISS, *Military Balance, 1990–1991*, p. 213.

[a]At the December 1987 Washington summit, the United States and the Soviet Union agreed that SS-11s would be counted as having one warhead; SS-13s one; SS-17s four; SS-18s ten; SS-19s six; SS-24s ten; SS-25s one, SS-N-6s one; SS-N-8s one; SS-N-17s one; SS-N-18s seven; SS-N-20s ten; and SS-N-23s four.

[b]Actual ICBM and SLBM warhead loadings may not exceed START attribution numbers.

[c]The first 180 Soviet ALCM carriers will be counted as having eight weapons; each additional carrier will be counted as carrying all of the ALCMs which it is equipped to carry. The non-ALCM bombers are counted as one weapon.

[d]Assumes that Bears and Blackjacks will carry twelve ALCMs, and that non-ALCM Bears will carry only four weapons, a standard load for that system.

Table 4–4. Soviet Strategic Forces, Modernized, START-Compliant

Delivery Vehicle	Deployed Launchers	Attributed Weapons	Likely Loadings
ICBM SS-18	154	1,540	1,540
SS-19	40	240	240
SS-24	75	750	750
SS-25	350	350	350
SLBM SS-N-20 (Typhoon)	120	1,200	1,200
SS-N-23 (Delta IV)	192	768	768
Subtotal	931	4,848[a]	4,848[b]
(START limit)		(4,900)	
Bombers (ALCM)			
Bear	75	600	900
Blackjack	40	320	480
Bombers (non-ALCM)			
Bear	95	95	380
Blackjack	60	60	840
Subtotal	270	1,075[c]	2,600[d]
Grand Total	1,201	5,923	7,448
(START limit)	(1,600)	(6,000)	
SLCM	???		
(Agreed limit)	(880)		

[a]At the December 1987 Washington summit, the United States and the Soviet Union agreed that SS-18s would be counted as having ten warheads; SS-19s six; SS-24s ten; SS-25s one; SS-N-20s ten; and SS-N-23s four.

[b]Actual ICBM and SLBM warhead loadings may not exceed START attribution numbers.

[c]The first 180 Soviet ALCM carriers will be counted as having eight weapons; each additional carrier will be counted as carrying all of the ALCMs which it is equipped to carry. Non-ALCM bombers are counted as one weapon.

[d]Assumes that Bears and Blackjacks will carry twelve ALCMs. Also assumes that non-ALCM Bears will carry four weapons, and that non-ALCM Blackjacks will carry fourteen, the same as the B-1B.

as well as their aged SS-N-6, SS-N-8, and SS-N-17 SLBMs. The SS-19 force will have to be cut significantly, and SS-N-18s on Delta III submarines will probably be retired as SS-N-23s and Delta IVs come on line. Because ten-warhead SS-18, SS-24, and SS-N-20 missiles will consume much of the Soviet Union's ballistic missile weapon allotment, Soviet policymakers will be not be able to deploy large numbers of ICBMs, SLBMs, or SSBNs in a START regime. In fact, the number of SSBNs in the Soviet Navy's fleet could shrink from sixty-one, which is what it deployed in 1990, to less than twenty. However, Soviet force planners will have a strong incentive to take advantage of START counting rules (and thin American air defenses) and deploy large numbers of Blackjack bombers as penetrators. They would be able to deploy 100 (or more) Blackjacks without complicating their position with respect to the START framework.[35]

Changing Strategic Circumstances

What deters? What does the United States need to do to deter the Soviet Union from launching a conventional war in Europe or a nuclear attack against the United States itself? Since the late 1970s, American nuclear war planners have maintained that the United States must threaten four main sets of targets in order to deter Soviet aggression: (1) Soviet strategic nuclear forces, (2) conventional and other military forces, (3) Soviet industrial and economic facilities, and (4) the Soviet political leadership.[36] The events of 1989 and 1990 have brought about important changes in most of these areas. A reassessment of American deterrence requirements is therefore in order.

The idea behind leadership targeting, according to President Reagan, was to place "at risk those political entities the Soviet leadership values most: the mechanisms for ensuring the survival of the Communist party and its leadership cadres, and for retention of the party's control over the Soviet and Soviet Bloc peoples."[37] Bunkers built to protect the party's elite were targeted, and attacks were designed to undermine the party's ability to control nationalistic aspirations in the Soviet empire. Now that the Communist party of the Soviet Union has voluntarily relinquished its constitutional monopoly on power, the authority and legitimacy of the party have collapsed, and centrifugal forces in the Soviet federation have reached the breaking point, the idea of using American nuclear weapons to undermine the party's ability to control events in the Soviet Union seems more than a little anachronistic. American targeting requirements, including requirements to drop high-yield gravity bombs on large numbers of superhard bunkers, should consequently ease significantly in the 1990s.

The objective of industrial and economic targeting was not to inflict indiscriminate damage on Soviet urban centers but to destroy the Soviet Union's war-supporting industry and, with it, the Soviet capacity to wage a protracted war in Europe. Again, this idea seems anachronistic in light of the events of 1989 and 1990. The disintegration of the Warsaw Pact, the withdrawal of Soviet military power from Eastern Europe, and the restrictions that the Conventional Forces in Europe (CFE) Treaty places on Soviet forces west of the Urals have undercut the Soviet Union's ability to wage a protracted war in Europe. In addition, the Soviet economy itself has collapsed, which makes the idea of targeting war-supporting industries largely moot. It is worth noting, moreover, that some Soviet defense industries have been converted to civilian use, and more will undoubtedly follow as the leadership in Moscow continues in its efforts to restructure Soviet economic affairs. This, therefore, is another area where American targeting requirements should ease significantly in the 1990s.

Similarly, Soviet and Eastern European conventional forces were targeted so that Warsaw Pact forces would not be able to prevail in a war, short or otherwise, in Europe. Given the political transformation that has taken place in Hungary, Poland, Czechoslovakia, and what used to be known as East Germany, it now makes little sense for the United States to target East European forces and facilities for destruction. In addition, as noted earlier, Soviet conventional (and tactical nuclear) forces are being withdrawn from Eastern Europe, and Soviet forces west of the Urals are being streamlined. Thousands of pieces of conventional hardware will be destroyed under the terms of the CFE Treaty. As a result, the number of conventional targets worthy of attention is dropping rapidly.

The one area where targeting requirements have changed little is the strategic nuclear arena. The Soviet Union has not reduced the size of its strategic force structure, and the START Treaty will not have a dramatic impact on the targeting picture. In implementing the START agreement, Soviet force planners will be forced to retire hundreds of silo-based ICBMs, but they will probably compensate for this by deploying more bombers and mobile ICBMs, as discussed earlier. Submarines bases and facilities will be targeted as before.

That said, one aspect of the strategic equation needs to be reevaluated: the extent to which American war plans will target mobile ICBMs and command facilities. American planners devoted more and more attention to Soviet mobile targets as the 1980s wore on. The ability to hold this target set at risk, it was said, would help deter the Soviet leadership from contemplating aggression in the first place. In addition, according to this school of thought, having the ability to destroy mobile targets would limit damage to the United States in the event of a protracted nuclear war. The logic behind this argument, which was never easy to follow, will be increasingly difficult to sustain when the United States and the Soviet Union begin implementing the START Treaty. In a world where Soviet leaders will rely heavily on mobile ICBMs for secure retaliatory capabilities, any threats, potential threats, or perceived threats to these forces will be highly destabilizing. Giving up the ghost on this war-fighting mission will therefore make sense from a strategic standpoint. It will also pull American targeting requirements away from the artificially high levels of late 1990.

Targeting requirements are not set in concrete. In 1982, the number of potential targets in the American nuclear war plan was 50,000. In 1987, there were 14,000 targets on this list. In 1989, Air Force officials insisted that they had to have 132 B-2s in the force structure and a favorable bomber counting rule in the START framework—which would give American war planners over 10,000 nuclear weapons with which to work—in order to cover the Soviet target set. In 1990, Air Force officials insisted that they had to have seventy-five B-2s in the force structure and a favorable bomber counting rule in the START framework—which would give American war planners around 9,000 weapons with which to work—in order to cover the Soviet target set. Other informed commentators have argued that "even the most demanding conception of deterrence" would not require the United States to be able to destroy more than 1,500 to 2,000 Soviet targets.[38]

If targeting requirements can be reduced significantly in the 1990s—and, it is argued here, there are good reasons for thinking that targeting requirements are easing in several important respects—then force structure requirements can be reduced significantly as well. START weapon levels, which will probably settle at around 8,000 weapons per side, could be reduced in subsequent negotiations to 2,000 to 4,000 weapons per side. In addition to addressing concerns about first-strike incentives, warhead concentrations on ballistic missiles, and system survivability, which it is mandated to do, the START II negotiations could lead to even deeper cuts in strategic forces later in the 1990s.

U.S. Forces
Train in Europe

Chapter 5

Conventional and Theater Nuclear Forces in Europe

Robert D. Blackwill

E vents in Europe in 1990 so fundamentally changed the postwar paradigms regarding European security that traditional modes of military analysis can no longer capture the security situation on the Continent. Recall for a moment the principal elements of the conventional and theater nuclear postures of the two alliances during the years of the cold war:

- Two heavily militarized blocs facing each other across a divided Germany and a divided Europe.

- The massive forward deployment in Eastern Europe of about thirty Soviet armored and motor-rifle divisions representing, along with Soviet reinforcement capabilities, a clear Warsaw Pact conventional and short-warning attack advantage over the North Atlantic Treaty Organization (NATO).

- A NATO defense along the inner German border, which most Western analysts believed would be ground down and pushed back by a Warsaw Pact conventional attack.

- The deployment in Europe, and especially in West Germany, of hundreds of thousands of U.S. Army and Air Force personnel meant to deter a Soviet attack and to ensure if deterrence failed the immediate entry of the United States into the third major European war of the century.

- A North Atlantic Alliance that for nearly twenty-five years had not, for very good reasons, fundamentally reexamined its approach to the East.

- A NATO–Warsaw Pact conventional arms control negotiation that for almost twenty years had delivered no agreement, no reduction in conventional forces, and no alteration of the conventional balance in Europe.

- The positioning on both sides of the dividing line in Europe of thousands of U.S. and Soviet theater nuclear weapons.

So complete has been the transformation of the postwar order on the Continent, so definitive the end of the cold war, that 1990 saw the collapse of every one of these alliance, conventional force, and theater nuclear verities in Europe.

The End of the Warsaw Pact

By the end of 1990 the Warsaw Pact ceased to exist as a functioning military alliance and therefore as an instrument of Soviet national security policy. The decades-long debate in the West over whether Eastern European armies would fight on behalf of the Soviet Union in an attack on Germany was rendered moot by the democratic revolutions in Eastern Europe and their profound impact on Soviet military planning. The immediate security concerns of Czechoslovakia and Hungary in 1990 were centered on their demand for the rapid and total withdrawal of all Soviet forces from their territory, an objective likely to be met by the end of 1991. Fears of a resurgent Germany led Poland to lag somewhat behind its two neighbors in this regard, but Soviet military deployments are also no longer welcome in Poland.

Thus, in 1990 the eleven Soviet divisions with their integrated air force and ground support units in these countries that preoccupied NATO military analysts for more than twenty years were on their way home. Indeed, between 1988 and 1990, the Soviet High Command must have recategorized Polish, Czech, and Hungarian conventional forces from ally, to doubtful ally, and then to likely adversary in the event of a European war. In short, in most contingencies, in the event of conflict with NATO the Soviet military would have to plan to fight its way across Eastern Europe before it reached the forces of the Western Alliance.

Events in Germany had an even greater impact on conventional and theater nuclear forces in Europe and eroded Soviet conventional capabilities vis-à-vis NATO even further. With events in Eastern Europe and the July 1990 agreement between Chancellor Kohl and President Gorbachev that all 380,000 Soviet forces would withdraw from united Germany by 1994, Moscow's short-warning attack threat to NATO in purely military terms became very nearly a thing of the past and by 1995 should disappear altogether. This weakening Soviet military capability in Germany, and thus its diminished threat to the West, is quite apart from the political turmoil across the Soviet Union, which also reduces dramatically the likelihood that Moscow would contemplate any of the conventional attack scenarios westward that have dominated NATO threat assessments since the alliance's inception.

What Is the Threat?

The most pressing challenge for NATO in the 1990s is to define the threats in the new Europe to which alliance forces must be ready to respond. Given the factors mentioned above vis-à-vis Soviet forces in Eastern and Central Europe, and given that the Soviet Union is on the edge of internal political revolution and well into systemic economic and nationalities crises, it is difficult to visualize a plausible scenario in which massive and ready Soviet armored forces slice through Eastern Europe, then Germany, on their way to the English Channel. This is not to dismiss the reality of a large residual Soviet military capability in the 1990s. The Soviet Union will continue to have millions of men, tens of thousands of tanks, artillery pieces, infantry fighting vehicles, and thousands of attack aircraft, and will be easily the strongest military power on the Continent. And events within the Soviet Union could push to the political leadership an individual or group very different from Mr. Gorbachev: xenophobic, hostile to the West, intensely bitter about Soviet strategic losses in Eastern and Central Europe and beyond, and ready to try to pull the country together through external adventure. But it appears that even in such unlikely worst-case projections, warning time in the West of a Soviet attack across the Polish border would be measured not in days or weeks, but rather in many months or, more likely, even years.

That being the case, this is obviously a very different sort of Soviet threat than the one that animated Western publics and parliaments to support NATO's conventional and theater nuclear forces during the cold war. Indeed, a significant portion of European and especially German public opinion is well on the way to dismissing the potency of the Soviet military threat in the 1990s, given the extraordinary Soviet internal difficulties.

Those very internal difficulties have led some to worry, however, about a less traditional Soviet threat to the West. This scenario centers on the political disintegration of the Soviet Union in the 1990s and the danger to Western interests posed by the possibility of civil war in the Soviet Union. Here, major conflict would erupt, perhaps over whether the Ukraine and its forty million Ukrainians would be allowed by the central Soviet government to declare national independence and, if so, how the ten million Russians who live in the Ukraine would be treated. Western governments and publics might well wish to have a viable NATO conventional force in place should Ukrainian-Russian war spill into Eastern Europe. However, one wonders if a contingency so removed from the way the West has thought about the Soviet military threat since the late 1940s can be sufficiently plausible to inject new life into the alliance in the 1990s.

Another array of threats to Western interests in the new Europe could come from the new democracies east and south of the Oder-Neisse and from the Balkans. Repressed for a half-century or more, these countries are finding it difficult and painful to develop democratic institutions and habits and at the same time to confront the immense difficulties they all face: crushing foreign debts by Poland and Hungary; the dead hand of communist bureaucracy everywhere; too little foreign assistance; growing inflation; few patterns of parliamentary compromise on which to develop national consensus; and in Czechoslovakia, two peoples, the Czechs and the Slovaks, struggling to work out a tolerable unitary state.

These daunting trends, along with a rebirth of nationalism and acute ethnic identity, could produce serious internal disruption in Eastern Europe in the 1990s as in Yugoslavia in 1991. In addition, the smoldering dispute between Hungary and Romania over the two million ethnic Hungarians in Transylvania might conceivably erupt into conflict. This would inject further instability into the area between Western Europe and the Soviet Union. Such developments could threaten Western interests: cutting off markets and some raw materials; producing floods of refugees westward; triggering violence that would be quite painful to watch, especially for West Europeans; trampling Western democratic values. But none of these sorrowful contingencies regarding Eastern Europe seem to pose a threat appropriately relevant to NATO's military forces (as opposed to diplomatic efforts). It is difficult to imagine a consensus within the alliance to commit NATO forces to affect the outcome of any of these Eastern European scenarios and equally hard to see how any such events in Eastern Europe would pose a military threat to the West that NATO conventional and nuclear forces would help deter.

The final security threats to which the alliance's military forces might be an answer were frequently articulated by President George Bush during 1990.

Western governments and publics might well wish to have a viable NATO conventional force in place should Ukrainian-Russian war spill into Eastern Europe.

Pressed on why NATO should retain a viable military organization after the cold war, President Bush enumerated his list of threats to Western security: uncertainty, instability, and the unanticipated. Stressing that none had foreseen the transforming events of 1989–1990, he advised caution in such a turbulent period, a caution later born out by the Gulf War and the threat to NATO territory in Turkey by Iraq from outside the treaty area. It was no time, President Bush counselled, to dismantle NATO's conventional and nuclear posture, which had performed as a deterrent so well and for so long, and which had kept the peace in Europe for the most extended period in centuries. While a powerful strategic and historical insight on the president's part, it remains unclear whether such a generalized and indistinct objective will serve to sustain public support, especially in Germany, for the necessary resources and inconveniences inherent in ready NATO army and air forces in Europe.

Challenges to NATO's Military Capability

Thus, 1990 witnessed the end of the classical postwar Soviet military threat to NATO, the functional demise of the Warsaw Pact, and the emergence before the gulf crisis began of a Western debate on the future of the alliance. With the Eastern pillars of the cold war order gone, the principal elements of NATO defense strategy and the U.S. conventional and theater nuclear contribution to European security are under the most exacting questioning in forty years.

NATO's formal defense line has moved from the inner German border to the German-Polish frontier since the whole of united Germany is protected by the alliance collective defense commitment embodied in the North Atlantic Treaty. Concurrently, the July German-Soviet agreement on German unity stipulated that no NATO-committed forces could be stationed within the territory of the former German Democratic Republic. Therefore, NATO conventional forces in Germany, unlike in the past, will be far from the border they would defend in the event of conflict. The traditional advantage for the defender of familiarity of terrain would be significantly reduced for NATO in this situation. But this is only the beginning of the military problems that the alliance faces in redefining its defense mission in the new Europe.

With a united Germany properly reassessing its view of the future of European security, a second military problem concerns the future readiness of NATO forces on German soil. For decades, West German citizens were willing, if increasingly reluctant, to accept the notion that deterring the Soviet threat required disruptions and irritations in their daily lives caused by frequent NATO military exercises. U.S., British, and other Western tanks from time to time clogged and sometimes tore up roads in the Federal Republic. Long convoys of NATO vehicles tied up traffic as Western troops moved from their permanent garrisons to exercise areas. German farmers, though compensated, accepted with no enthusiasm the environmental damage done to their fields by tank treads, heavy artillery pieces, and other armored vehicles. And, most politically problematical of all, the citizens of West Germany suffered the discomforting effects of low-level training flights by NATO aircraft as Western pilots sensibly sought to establish the advantage of terrain familiarity over their potential Soviet adversaries.

German support for these activities was waning rapidly before German unification and the end of the cold war. As West Germans perceived a diminished Soviet danger in the post–1985 era, ordinary Germans in the Federal Republic of Germany (FRG) increasingly asked why they should continue to tolerate the significant interference in their lives that such NATO military activities represented. And, of course, all this occurred in a country without the vast, largely empty spaces found in the American West and Southwest where the United States primarily holds these kinds of exercises. German voters pointed out ever more often and forcefully to the government in Bonn and to their parliamentary representatives that the people of no other industrial democracy anywhere, including the United States, were asked to make such tangible sacrifices affecting negatively the quality of their daily lives in order to deter an increasingly unconvincing Soviet military threat.

With these domestic German factors in mind, NATO military authorities reduced the number and size of Western military activities and reinforcement exercises to Germany from the United States, and sought to rely increasingly on computer simulations to capture the requirements, challenges, and uncertainties of modern warfare. However, contemporary armies cannot adequately maintain their readiness, much less their fighting edge, if they are primarily confined to their garrisons. In such a circumstance in Germany, the professionalism and morale of all forces, foreign and German, would be sure to fall. This could be particularly true of American servicemen and women confined to caserns an ocean away from home. This unhappy situation would certainly not escape the attention of the U.S. Congress. Indeed, the difficulties of retaining a militarily plausible Western force in a united Germany and in Western Europe as a whole in the 1990s without an obvious external threat led some analysts to predict the emergence at best of a hollow NATO army deployed in Germany. This weak alliance force would be meant to rely on long warning time to meet any threat that might emerge in the future, an approach that could fail in an extended crisis.

But the emergence of such potential technical deficiencies of NATO forces, especially in Germany, may not be the most serious military problem the alliance will face in the course of the next decade. As indicated above, all Soviet forces will be withdrawn from the former territory of the German Democratic Republic by 1994. Until that time, it seems likely that the German public will support the continued deployment of Western and particularly American military personnel on German soil. How much longer after the mid-1990s this German willingness to accept foreign forces of any militarily significant size will continue is one of the major imponderables at the end of 1990.

Added to this uncertainty is one generated by decreasing defense budgets in the United States and Britain, the two NATO nations most heavily engaged during the postwar period in the defense of Germany. In the United Kingdom's case, Her Majesty's government announced that the British Army on the Rhine will be significantly cut from its 1990 size of 55,000. Whether the British public will support even in the medium term a force of twenty-odd thousand in a Germany bound to be richer and more prosperous than the United Kingdom is an open question. The same is certainly true for the smaller Belgian, Dutch, and Canadian contingents stationed in Germany. And France has indicated its intention to withdraw most if not all of its three divisions from Germany within several years.

As for the United States, the size, character, and location of future military deployments in Europe were, as 1990 ended, also uncertain. Roughly half of the 300,000 U.S. forces deployed on the Continent went to the Persian Gulf, including two of the four U.S. Army divisions stationed in Germany. Given the reduction in the immediate threat and the American budget and deficit crisis, it seems unlikely all or even most of these forces will return permanently to their European garrisons. According to media accounts, Pentagon planners, even before the gulf crisis, were projecting a U.S. force in Europe in the second half of the 1990s, of about 80,000–100,000, built around a corps concept and two U.S. divisions in Germany for as long as the German and American publics and politicians would agree.

Impact of the Gulf Crisis and War

The successful outcome of the situation in the Persian Gulf will affect this Department of Defense projection. Because the gulf crisis ended positively for the

United States as seen by American and Western public opinion, maintaining a militarily significant U.S. presence in Europe will only, because of the above factors, be a challenge. But if the Bush administration had mismanaged this crisis, if Saddam Hussein had come out on top in the gulf at the expense of the United States, or if the war there had been bloody for the coalition and most of the casualties U.S. and not European, the willingness of the American people to pay for any U.S. troops to defend Western Europe could have eroded quickly. Thus, the stakes in the Persian Gulf confrontation for NATO and its future, and for the American military presence in Europe, were significant. Happily, the Gulf War was a triumph for the United States and its world role.

The London NATO Summit

It was with these many challenges to the alliance in mind that President Bush sought at the July 5–6, 1990, NATO summit in London to alter fundamentally the relationship of NATO to the countries of Eastern Europe and the Soviet Union. In a document filled with initiatives drafted in Washington, changed very little in internal alliance discussions, NATO reached out boldly to its former adversaries by (1) inviting the governments of the Soviet Union, Poland, Hungary, Czechoslovakia, Bulgaria, and Romania to establish regular diplomatic liaison with NATO, thus seeking to create a new and much greater transparency in the alliance's deliberations and decisions vis-à-vis the East; (2) proffering an invitation to President Mikhail Gorbachev to visit Brussels and address the North Atlantic Council; (3) proposing to the member states of the Warsaw Pact a joint declaration in which the signatories would solemnly state that they were no longer adversaries and affirm their commitment to nonaggression, a pledge later formally made at the Conference on Security and Cooperation in Europe (CSCE) summit in Paris in November 1990; and (4) suggesting that the member states of NATO and the Warsaw Pact expand and intensify military-to-military contacts throughout Europe, to include visits by senior NATO military officers to Moscow and Eastern European capitals.

With these diplomatic initiatives as a backdrop, NATO leaders in London also announced important, if generally phrased, decisions concerning changes in the alliance's conventional strategy and force structure in the post–cold war period. These included smaller, restructured active forces with greater mobility and versatility to give allied leaders maximum flexibility in a crisis. NATO would also reduce the readiness of its active forces, lowering training requirements and the number of exercises. Thus, in the 1990s, as warning time significantly increased because of events in Eastern Europe and the Soviet Union, the alliance would rely more heavily on its capacity to generate larger reserve forces.

In addition, Western heads of government in London stated NATO would increasingly depend on multinational corps composed of national units to maintain the common defense. This hesitant step, carefully hedged to emphasize that sovereign control over a country's military operations would remain in national capitals, nevertheless represented two important acknowledgments by the alliance: first, that allied forces stationed in Germany would likely be more acceptable to the German public in the decade ahead if they increasingly had a multinational rather than a national character; and second, that multinational military procurement and organization would be at the core of any serious European defense cooperation that might grow out of the Western European Union and the European Community in the 1990s.

Whether such a multinational corps concept can take root in the alliance, or indeed in European defense cooperation, remains an open issue. The tide of German public opinion could sweep away Western forces stationed in that country whatever their organizational structure. France continues to be highly skeptical of multinational integration under the NATO umbrella, and also apparently is unwilling to cede much French control over its military forces in the intra-European context. The United States, too, may well be reluctant to move toward real integration of its ground forces in Europe in a multinational corps not commanded by an American general officer. The success or failure of this multinational concept is likely to be one of the crucial litmus tests in the 1990s of the capacity of the United States to maintain sizable numbers of troops in Germany; of NATO's ability to continue to deploy a militarily plausible force on the Continent; and of the European Community's attempts to add, in the following ten to twenty years, a defense dimension to its culture, organization, and mission.

The Future of CSCE

In addition to conventional and theater nuclear arms control that will be addressed subsequently in this chapter, the final set of initiatives at the London summit concerned the CSCE. With an eye to striking the correct, if difficult, balance between a vital NATO and expanding CSCE institutions, Western leaders agreed on six steps to strengthen the thirty-four-nation CSCE process:

- Annual meetings of CSCE Heads of Government or Foreign Ministers.
- Full CSCE review conferences every other year.
- A small secretariat.
- A mechanism to monitor free elections.
- A prevention-of-conflict center to exchange military information, discuss worrisome military activities and help resolve disputes among CSCE member states.
- A CSCE parliamentary body, the Assembly of Europe.

Some on the Continent hope that the CSCE rather than NATO could become the new hub of European security. The six London NATO summit initiatives and the CSCE summit in Paris in November may have given a mild boost to these advocates. However, an international organization that has no military forces at its disposal, no previous experience in collective threat assessment or deterrent action, and operates entirely on the basis of unanimous agreement is unlikely to be a reliable foundation for European stability in the 1990s or to provide a solid institutional base for the continued deployment of American forces in Europe.

Thus, a stronger and essentially political CSCE can serve European security, but not at the expense of a weaker North Atlantic Alliance. To put it differently, it is NATO that provides the fundamental strategic stability in which the CSCE can exist. If NATO were to erode seriously in the early 1990s, a period of European uncertainty, the CSCE would likely be not the inheritor of the NATO mantle, but rather a parallel victim of the decline of the alliance.

Conventional Arms Control

At the July London summit, the West indicated its determination to conclude a Conventional Armed Forces in Europe (CFE) Treaty by the November Paris CSCE Heads of Government meeting. Although there were many bumps along the way, the treaty was completed and signed in Paris by the member states of NATO and the Warsaw Pact on November 19. This treaty represents the most militarily significant arms control agreement ever reached and, if entirely implemented, will codify a dramatic alteration in the postwar conventional military balance in Europe.

It is NATO that provides the fundamental strategic stability in which the CSCE can thrive.

The agreement, which covers equipment in the Atlantic-to-the-Urals (ATTU) area, allows NATO and the Warsaw Pact each to hold 20,000 tanks—the primary instrument of modern offensive warfare. According to the Arms Control Association this will mean a reduction in U.S. tanks from 5,100 to 3,840 and in other NATO forces from 17,130 to 16,160. Eastern European tank totals will drop from 11,900 to 6,850 and, as noted earlier in this chapter, should in any case no longer be counted on the Soviet side of the ledger. Most importantly and although all the following numbers on the Soviet side remain to be confirmed, Soviet tank totals in the ATTU area will apparently be reduced from 24,898 to 13,150, and by the mid-1990s all of these tanks will be deployed only on Soviet territory. From a Soviet military planner's standpoint, these CFE totals translate into a Soviet tank total in Europe to the Urals of 13,150 and a potential NATO–Eastern European tank aggregate of 26,850.

Through a series of complicated definitions the artillery ceilings are set at 20,000 per side. This will mean no reduction in NATO's holdings of 18,500 artillery pieces. Eastern European artillery numbers will decline from 13,700 to 6,825. The Soviet Union will reduce its artillery from 18,300 to 13,175, a critical cut in essential firepower for conducting combat operations.

The limits for armored combat vehicles are 30,000 each for NATO and the Warsaw Pact. This category of vehicles, which provide infantry mobility and support during combat, includes armored personnel carriers (APCs), the more capable armored infantry fighting vehicle (AIFVs), and heavy armament combat vehicles (HACVs). Each of these three subcategories has agreed ceilings but the most significant point is that NATO faces no reductions in these systems. Eastern European countries will reduce their armored combat vehicles from 14,900 to 10,000, and the Soviet Union's total will drop from 32,320 to 20,000. Again, if

Figure 5–1. CFE Reductions

Weapons	Alliance/ Country	Pre-CFE Level	Treaty Limit
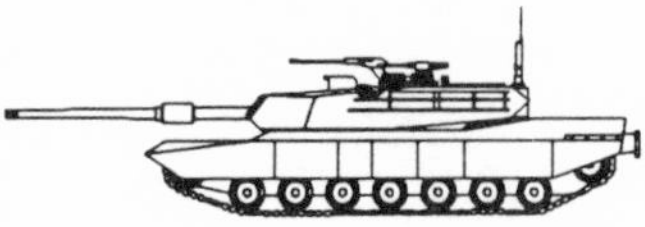	NATO	22,230	20,000
	Eastern Europe	11,900	6,850
	Soviet Union	24,898	13,150
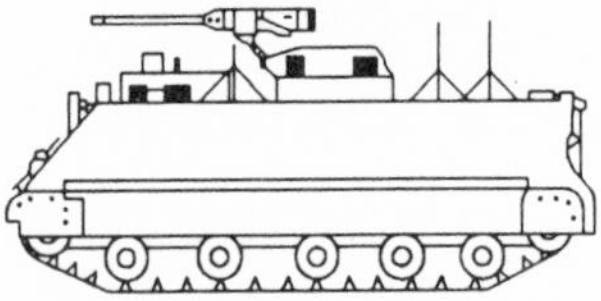	NATO	30,000	30,000
	Eastern Europe	14,900	10,000
	Soviet Union	32,320	20,000
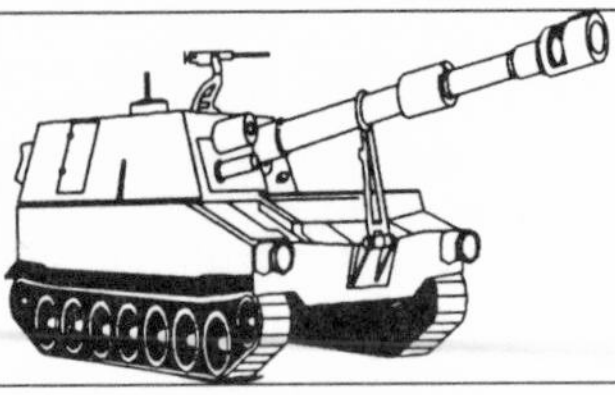	NATO	18,500	20,000
	Eastern Europe	13,700	6,825
	Soviet Union	18,300	13,175
	NATO	5,700	6,800
	Eastern Europe	1,600	1,600
	Soviet Union	8,190	5,150
	NATO	2,235	2,000
	Eastern Europe	700	500
	Soviet Union	2,850	1,500

NATO totals are added to those of Eastern European nations, the holdings of countries west of the Soviet/Polish border will outnumber Soviet armored combat vehicles in Europe by a two-to-one margin.

NATO had 5,700 combat aircraft in 1990, while Eastern Europe had 1,600. The CFE ceilings allow 6,800 such aircraft and an additional 430 land-based naval aircraft, meaning that only the Soviet Union will be required to reduce its combat aircraft inventories. The Soviet total will drop from 8,190 to 5,150. There will be a ceiling on helicopters at 2,000 per side with a reduction of 235 for NATO, 200 for Eastern Europe, and about 1,350 for the Soviet Union.

Although there are no general manpower ceilings in the CFE Treaty, unified Germany has agreed in the context of the treaty to reduce its total armed forces from 560,000 to 370,000. This commitment on Germany's part was an important element in persuading President Gorbachev to accept the end of Four Power Rights in Germany and to acquiesce to a united Germany's full membership in NATO.

An extensive verification regime accompanies the reduction requirements of the CFE Treaty and should promote compliance on the part of all signatories. An added complication, however, is increasing evidence that the Soviet Union moved tens of thousands of pieces of ground equipment out of the area of reduction and east of the Urals before the treaty was signed and went into effect, thus reducing the amount of Soviet equipment to be destroyed. NATO argues correctly that this was a serious violation of the spirit of the agreement. In addition, the data on its forces in the ATTU area that the Soviet Union provided at the time of treaty signature seemed to have under counted Soviet equipment. Most importantly, Moscow had, through early 1991, refused to count roughly 5,000 pieces of treaty-limited equipment held by Soviet naval infantry divisions and strategic rocket forces, an unambiguous violation of Article III of the CFE Treaty. This last issue, resolved in mid-1991, allowed the CFE ratification process to proceed in the United States.

If the CFE reductions are completed, the conventional military map of Europe will be utterly transformed. To sum up, as represented in figure 5–1, in the ATTU area, NATO will take a 13 percent cut in its tanks; Eastern Europe 42 percent; and the Soviet Union 47 percent. NATO will be required to reduce no artillery, while Eastern Europe's holdings will decline by 50 percent and the Soviet Union's by 28 percent. NATO will lose no armored combat vehicles; Eastern Europe will cut 33 percent; and the Soviet Union 38 percent. Neither NATO nor Eastern Europe will take reductions in combat aircraft, while the Soviet Union will reduce these systems in the ATTU area by 37 percent. NATO will reduce its helicopters by 11 percent, Eastern Europe by 29 percent and the Soviet Union by 47 percent. In total weapons in these five major conventional categories, NATO will, in the ATTU area, reduce 4 percent of its current total of 79,335 to 76,162; Eastern Europe 40 percent of 42,800 to 25,680; and the Soviet Union 39 percent of 86,558 to 61,456.

The Future of CFE

At the London NATO summit, Western leaders agreed that once CFE I was completed, new conventional arms control negotiations should aim toward further, far-reaching measures to limit the offensive capabilities of conventional forces in Europe, to prevent any nation from maintaining disproportionate military power on the Continent. This lofty goal of another round of deep negotiated cuts is unlikely to be achieved.

Indeed, there are a number of reasons why most conventional force reductions in Europe beyond CFE I will probably be unilateral in character—a product of the lessened threat and not of formal arms control talks. Most importantly, CFE was barely finished before the end of the cold war swept away its conceptual basis of opposing blocs. A new conceptual framework for reductions is not apparently available. On the Western side, the need to keep NATO forces at a militarily viable level will further complicate negotiated decreases. Greece and Turkey will be especially attentive to how cuts in their forces might alter the conventional balance between them. Eastern European nations will want further reductions in the size of both German and Soviet forces, neither of which could be easily negotiated.

CFE was barely finished before the end of the cold war swept away its conceptual basis of opposing blocs.

Western cuts beyond CFE I would have to take account of Soviet conventional forces and stored equipment east of the Urals, a particularly difficult problem because of Moscow's enduring concern about a possible Chinese threat and because of the equipment transferred out of the ATTU area in 1990. If ground forces and equipment were cut even deeper in CFE II, combat aircraft numbers and capabilities, which were not significantly affected in CFE I, would have to become a central element in the follow-on talks lest airpower begin to weigh disproportionately in the European conventional balance. As numbers of ground-based combat aircraft declined further, the Soviets would surely insist on the inclusion of U.S. carrier-based aircraft, a possibility that the United States has always firmly rejected with good reason. With its postwar conventional advantages in Europe a thing of the past, the Soviet Union will undoubtedly worry about Western technological edges and probably attempt somehow to include that extraordinarily complex subject in the new negotiation. Finally, the influence of the Soviet military will also slow further progress beyond CFE I.

All these factors make likely an exceedingly complicated and lengthy next phase of negotiated conventional arms control. This phase will lag far behind unilateral reductions likely to be made by the nations involved because of budgetary constraints and a dramatically lessened threat perception, assuming that a serious attempt will be made to negotiate subsequent conventional cuts in Europe (which may not turn out to be true). In short, further large conventional force reductions are quite likely in Europe in the 1990s but national offices of management and budget and treasuries rather than foreign ministries will provide the primary impetus.

Theater Nuclear Forces

The final crucial subject treated at the London NATO summit was the future of nuclear weapons in Europe. Western leaders agreed that the alliance would prepare a new allied military strategy that would reduce reliance on nuclear weapons and modify the strategy of flexible response. In the new Europe, NATO announced, the alliance's nuclear forces would truly become weapons of last resort. In addition, the London summit proposed that talks on short range nuclear forces (SNF) in Europe begin shortly after the signing of the CFE Treaty and that an objective of that negotiation should be the elimination of all NATO and Soviet nuclear artillery shells from Europe. With the earlier U.S. decisions not to modernize either the Lance surface-to-surface missile or nuclear artillery shells deployed in Europe, the 1990s are sure to see a sharp drop in the American nuclear presence on the Continent. Most experts believe that by the mid- to late 1990s, U.S. nuclear weapons in Europe will at best be confined to those that can be delivered by aircraft—including perhaps a new theater air-to-surface missile (TASM) to be deployed in about 1995 with a range of somewhat less than five hundred kilometers. As indicated earlier, even this minimal American nuclear presence in Germany and elsewhere in Western Europe, and especially TASM deployment, might prove politically impossible across the Atlantic. Nevertheless, there remain powerful reasons why such a continued and modernized, if greatly reduced, U.S. nuclear presence would promote stability in Europe. Such a minimum American nuclear deployment through the end of the century would:

- Provide a balance for the thousands of nuclear weapons that will be deployed in the European portions of the Soviet Union, including air-delivered weapons.

- Hedge against residual Soviet Russian conventional capabilities, which will remain the most potent in Europe.

- Protect against the possible disintegration of the Soviet Union, the extension of civil war there westward, or some loss of the Soviet central authority's command and control over its nuclear weapons.

- Promote the maintenance in Europe of stabilizing U.S. ground forces.

- Reduce the likelihood that in the 1990s non-nuclear nations in Europe will decide to acquire nuclear weapons.

- Maintain nuclear risk sharing on both sides of the Atlantic, including in Germany.

- Increase the chances that France and Britain will continue to maintain small nuclear arsenals which contribute to stability on the Continent.

- Deter countries on Europe's southern rim that, having developed nuclear weapons and delivery systems, might attempt to coerce Europe or individual nations therein.

The central question that the West should ask about the impending SNF negotiations is whether these talks will perpetuate the presence of U.S. nuclear weapons in Europe or hasten their early departure. Unilateral announcements by the United States and Soviet Union concerning their respective SNF reduction, deployment, and perhaps modernization plans might be preferable to a long, drawn-out negotiation that could have the effect of further eroding Western public support for American nuclear deployments of any kind in Europe. Indeed, an urgent if steeply uphill effort ought to be made by the alliance, and especially by the United States, to persuade the Soviet leadership that minimum nuclear deterrence in Europe and the continued deployment of U.S. nuclear weapons in Germany and elsewhere on the Continent serve Soviet interests by promoting stability in Europe. In any event, the negotiations on SNF, which are to begin in 1991, should be short, uncomplicated, and reflect the fact that it is far too soon for the West to rid itself of nuclear deterrence in Europe which has helped keep the peace for almost forty years.

U.S.-European Security Objectives in the Period Ahead

As this exposition makes clear, uncertainties dominate analysis of Europe's security in the early 1990s as they have at no time since the late 1940s or early 1950s. In such a time, it is important for the United States to set firmly its own security objectives concerning the new Europe in the 1990s. The central tenets Washington should follow include:

- Maintaining an influential U.S. voice on broadly defined issues of European security.

- Sustaining NATO, including its integrated military structure, as an effective instrument of European stability and U.S. national security.

- Continuing the presence of substantial numbers of U.S. Army and Air Force personnel in Germany and elsewhere in Western Europe.

- Maintaining a small number of modernized, air-delivered U.S. nuclear weapons in Europe, including in Germany.

- Reducing further conventional and nuclear weapons in Europe in stabilizing ways.

- Developing the CSCE as a viable transatlantic institution, but not as a replacement for NATO.

- Supporting, with the European Community, in every way possible the growth of democratic institutions in Eastern Europe and the Soviet Union.

- Developing, with the government of united Germany, a joint tactical and strategic agenda regarding the future of European security because Germany has now clearly become, for the long term, America's most important partner in building the new Europe.

USS Wisconsin
Roars to Life
in the Persian Gulf

Chapter 6

Seapower

Norman Friedman

G iven the vast change in circumstances since the U.S. Navy adopted its explicit maritime strategy in the mid-1980s, the great question for the 1990s is the extent to which some new strategy is required. After all, the main enemy of the past, the Soviet Union, seems to be in deep trouble. Although the Soviets continue to build new ships, particularly submarines, it is difficult to imagine a U.S.-Soviet war in the near future. On the other hand, the operations in the Persian Gulf in late 1990 are likely to be the prototype for much of the future. What sort of fleet is needed now?

The Changing Strategic Environment

What sort of world is the United States entering? Until quite recently the United States tended to prepare for war against the Soviet Union on the theory (which seems less and less valid) that forces designed for that purpose would suffice in any lesser scenario. Even if the United States was not to fight the Soviet Union, it often assumed that those it would fight would be Soviet proxies, and the United States would be able to call upon its allies to provide support and bases in such conflicts. Although they often did not like to support the United States (e.g., in the Middle East), U.S. allies generally provided the requested assistance. It would not be too much to assume that they did so on the theory that the United States stood between them and assault by terrifyingly powerful Soviet forces.

Most U.S. allies assume that the Soviet threat is gone. Although that view is probably naïve in the long term, it was certainly well accepted in 1990. To the extent that its allies help the United States specifically to avoid being overrun by the Soviet Union, their reason for cheerful assistance, particularly in the matter of bases, is now gone. There is some expectation that the North Atlantic Treaty Organization (NATO) will turn from concern with the Soviet threat to a more general stance against Third World turbulence, but the historical record is not terribly encouraging. For example, although the Iraq-Kuwait response has been impressive, note that most of the European allies shrink from the military response the United States supports.[1]

The most likely outcome, then, is the loss of virtually all base rights outside the United States or U.S.-controlled territory. That might well include Diego Garcia, a British possession now under long-term lease. Such a development will *not* coincide with the end of problems in the Third World. A student of the interwar period would have to expect that the bases would be lost just about the time the Soviets recovered from their disasters and became a nascent threat.[2]

Such a change would have profound implications for U.S. defense, and particularly for the role of the Navy in that defense. If it is assumed that the United States retains its interests in the Third World (because so much of what the United States uses comes from there, and that so much of U.S. exports go to the Third World), then within a short time literally the only U.S. military forces capable of operating abroad will be naval formations and very long range bombers. To the extent that military presence is more often intended to present a latent threat than actually to kill anyone, the bombers have only a limited capability. Troops and shorter-range aircraft can operate only at the sufferance of countries in the area of interest, and experience shows that such states more often want U.S. pressure than U.S. presence in their own countries. For example, even at a time of greatest threat from Saddam Hussein, the Saudis apparently feared the effect of large foreign contingents in their country almost as much as they feared the Iraqis. This is not a unique reaction.

With restricted access to overseas bases, the Navy must become in fact what it has always been in theory, the primary means by which the United States exerts military influence abroad. The difference in the 1990s and beyond is that this Navy must behave more like the Navy the United States built before World War II (i.e., operating without fixed overseas bases) than like the Navy of the postwar period (which always enjoyed a plenitude of bases worldwide). For example, the United States operates carriers at relatively high intensity, refueling them about every week (the aircraft require fuel even if the carrier itself is nuclear powered). That is possible because resupply ships can shuttle between the carrier battle group and a rear base. The typical future operating pattern may be one of much more intermittent flight operations, the ships exploiting the endurance associated with nuclear power but flying their aircraft only when necessary. That in turn is possible only if the fleet enjoys sufficiently early warning of air attack, and only if its surface-launched weapons are sufficiently effective that it can survive the consequences of insufficient warning. This requirement can be met in the early 1990s, due largely to the emergence of the Aegis missile fire-control system. Any approach to this sort of operating style would entail some alternative to constant air operations in order to keep pilots sharp, and that suggests a much more stringent requirement for flight simulators.

At the same time, the nation requires the sort of Navy that can respond relatively quickly to shifts in alliances which may force it again to confront a major power. It must be able to maintain the security of sea transport for large ground-

based forces and also to exert influence by attacking around an enemy's periph-
ery. In some conceivable cases of alliance shift, it may also have to destroy an
enemy's seaborne trade.

The difference between the two missions is partly geographical. Limited warfare in the Third World is geographically limited. Enemy forces are unlikely to be
found very far from their bases or from other natural points of concentration.
Although it would be foolish to leave sea lanes entirely unprotected in such a
conflict, the consequence of such a lapse is unlikely to be very serious. By way
of contrast, war against a major power is almost inevitably oceanic. The shipping
needed to support forward operations becomes an attractive target.

There is another important difference. Any operation in the Third World is
both a response to an immediate problem and a demonstration of capability intended to dissuade numerous potential troublemakers. If it is conducted smoothly
and at low cost, then many potential problems simply will not arise. If it is costly
(if, for example, U.S. warships are sunk), then the conflict encourages others and
tends to discourage the United States from further intervention.[3] By way of contrast, a major war is conducted on just one level: the United States wins or loses.
If the enemy is powerful, the United States expects to lose ships, aircraft, and
men in some numbers, and such losses are seen as a necessary cost rather than
as an embarrassment.

This consideration has a significant potential consequence. In the past, U.S.
tactics for antisubmarine warfare (ASW) have emphasized the destruction of submarines before they approach close enough to fire their torpedoes. That will
often, but not always, be possible. However, any submarine commander knows
that once he has fired, he will be detected and may well be killed. The combination
of early detection and deterrence should hold down the effect of submarine action,
but it cannot be expected to neutralize all submarines. The combination should
suffice in a major war. However, because the standard of self-protection is actually
higher in a Third World intervention, it would seem that the new strategic circumstances should encourage greater interest in specifically antitorpedo measures.
They impose difficult technical problems (which is why only limited measures of
this type exist in the early 1990s), but they should be more, rather than less,
important in the future.[4]

Similarly, it becomes more important to limit the effects of hits. In the past,
the great-power war was generally conceived as a very short war, terminated by
some sort of mutual nuclear threat. In such combat, even relatively limited damage puts a ship out of action for the duration. Passive protection is not too important. In the Third World, passive protection limits the consequences of a hit.
Some hits are likely because political circumstances may well prevent U.S. naval
forces from firing first, and because purely reactive weapons (such as Phalanx)
cannot be credited with 100 percent performance. Such lapses would hardly be
remarked in a big war, but every lapse counts in the Third World. The United
States is already moving in the right direction with the new Arleigh Burke–class
destroyer, but much more can be done (mainly by enlarging the next generation
of surface combatant to accommodate more passive protection).[5]

Another besetting problem of modern warfare is identification friend or foe
(IFF). As the speed of combat increases and the consequences of not shooting
down an airplane that may be carrying a missile become more serious, IFF errors
are easier to make. In a Third World setting such errors may have disastrous

political consequences, and the political dimension is always extremely important in such limited conflicts. No one reviewing the effects of the 1987 downing of the Iranian Airbus by the USS *Vincennes* should find that surprising. Similarly, shooting down friendly forces by accident, the most common IFF error, becomes much more embarrassing when relatively few friendly forces are lost to enemy fire. By way of contrast, IFF errors in a major war are swamped by the larger issues raised by the war. About a quarter of all U.S. air losses in World War II were to friendly fire, for example, but that was not seen as a crippling problem.[6]

Force Posture

To what may seem a surprising extent, the fleet was not too far in 1990 from what this sort of future requires. Because the United States, far more than most of its NATO allies, has had to project power into the Third World since 1945, it has always maintained the sort of fleet adaptable to that purpose. The question has always been whether that power-projection fleet was also what was needed for central war against the Soviet Union or, for that matter, against some future major power adversary. The maritime strategy answered this question largely in the affirmative, rejecting an alternative view—the sea-control Navy—which had gained credibility through the 1970s and which was espoused by most of the other NATO navies (with the major exception of the French Navy). Possibly more importantly, the maritime strategy was a return to classical seapower concepts.[7]

The central fact of naval warfare has always been that the sea is so large and naval forces so few in number that they are difficult to find and thus to bring to battle. Submarines are the most extreme example of this concept, but the tracklessness of the sea also applies to surface ships. Even in an era of satellites, surveillance is at best discontinuous, and deception is relatively easy. In a major war the great prize for seapower is free use of the sea. Ultimately, that requires that the enemy fleet be neutralized in some way. One way is classic blockade (denying the enemy fleet access to the sea so that it never has the opportunity to vanish). Another is to force the enemy to fight a decisive battle by threatening one or more of its vital interests. A third is to provide continuous close cover for groups of ships at sea (convoy escorts) so that the enemy must fight every time it tries to attack the ships being covered. In a sense, convoy is a continuous series of decisive battles in small scale. The economics of convoy require that the escorts, which must be cheap in order to be numerous, are yet powerful enough to destroy the enemy forces attacking them.

A fleet designed to project power (e.g., into the Third World) is necessarily built around a small number of very powerful warships. In the early 1990s, carriers remained the only way to concentrate firepower deep inshore because their aircraft shuttle bombs back and forth. To deliver an equivalent load of ordnance by missile is very expensive, since unlike an airplane a missile must expend its airframe and guidance with every shot. But such a fleet makes it difficult to carry out the convoy mission. Since naval resources are finite, a fleet built around carriers can provide few surface escorts beyond those required by the carriers themselves. Since modern carriers are expensive, moreover, there can never be enough for them to escort convoys.

The traditional U.S. approach to naval warfare, which was applied in the Pacific during World War II, was to force the enemy fleet into a decisive battle.[8] Once the enemy fleet was gone, the U.S. fleet was free to support operations around the enemy's coastline. In the Pacific war that meant amphibious operations that succeeded partly because the Japanese could not reinforce their scattered garrisons. In the cold war era, the advantage of neutralizing Soviet antiship forces was to free U.S. mobile strike forces, which could tie down and disperse Soviet air and missile defense forces. It could be further argued that in the absence of a decisive engagement even a vastly superior fleet could be tied down to the point of impotence (as in the case of the British Grand Fleet in World War I and, to a lesser extent, the Home Fleet in World War II). In this view, as long as it survived, the weaker enemy fleet could provide cover for antishipping forces (U-boats, in both the cases cited above). In the absence of a surviving enemy fleet, the stronger fleet could have been risked in operations against the bases of the enemy's antishipping forces or, for that matter, in amphibious operations to turn the enemy's land flank and thus end a disastrous stalemate on land.[9]

All of this history was applied after World War II. In the first postwar decade, the U.S. Navy pursued its traditional policy in which sea control and power projection, the threat of which was intended to force a decisive battle, were blended together. Such a policy automatically resulted in a fleet adapted to Third World operations, so little effort was required to adapt the Navy to a combination of central and limited warfare. In the Soviet case, the covering force for the submarine fleet was largely a naval air arm (which, had it assaulted convoy escorts,

would have wiped them out). The U.S. carrier groups could force the Soviet bombers out into the open, and the fighters it carried could destroy them in the air. If the Soviets chose not to fly out, their bases could be bombed from the sea. Destruction in the air was always preferable to the attacking force, since that would kill the pilots, so much more difficult than the airplanes to replace.[10]

As for Soviet submarines, the hope was that U.S. submarines operating in forward areas could wear them down. Carrier aircraft, moreover, could attack their bases and mine the approaches to those bases. By the mid-1950s it seemed that the new long-range ocean-bottom detection systems could help by directing maritime patrol aircraft against whatever submarines survived the forward offensive. Convoy tactics, the mainstay of much of World War II ASW, seemed less than effective in the face of fast modern submarines.

Unfortunately, the synergistic combination of what might be seen as pure projection forces (carriers and their consorts) and pure sea-control forces (maritime patrol aircraft directed by seabed sensors, and some attack submarines) did not fit the sort of analysis that Secretary of Defense Robert S. McNamara introduced into U.S. defense policymaking in the early 1960s.

McNamara had to make major economies because the numerous high-technology projects begun by the three services during the 1950s had proven far more expensive than expected. Cost overruns were tolerable as long as they were development projects, but became impossibly expensive when many programs reached production status more or less simultaneously. McNamara was convinced that the only solution was to reduce or eliminate duplication among the services. His chosen technique was to evaluate the alternative systems or weapons being bought for each particular role, e.g., strategic-strike or general-purpose warfare.[11]

Although this technique was at least rational in its assumptions, it had a peculiarly unfortunate consequence for naval forces. It seemed to force the Navy to relate specific ships or systems to specific missions, sea control *or* power projection. Because the strategy then in force was only rarely stated, this sort of division was not seen at the time as the deadly mistake it turned out to be.

The error became public during Admiral Elmo Zumwalt's tour as chief of naval operations. Between 1970 and 1974, much of the existing fleet became obsolete. It could not be replaced on anything like a one-to-one basis because money was scarce. Funding became even scarcer when the end of the draft drove up the cost of manpower. Such an environment inevitably breeds intense interservice rivalry, and this period was no exception.

Admiral Zumwalt made two related choices. First, he realized that with the withdrawal from Vietnam the U.S. government could not easily support any Third World power projection mission. The only legitimate military mission was defense of NATO, and to most in the government that meant defense of the inner-German border. Second, Admiral Zumwalt seemed to have thought that, of all possible naval missions, sea control was the one most clearly naval and therefore safest from attack by the other services. He was willing to follow the McNamara-era distinction between sea control and power projection. It is not altogether clear how seriously Zumwalt personally took that distinction, but the idea gained momentum and became particularly important under President Carter.[12]

The Carter administration was especially opposed to intervention in the Third World. To the extent that the carriers and their fast escorts conferred a capability to do that and little else, they became objects of suspicion. The administration sought a pure sea-control policy. Its choice resonated with those who wished to emphasize European security at the expense of the Pacific and the Third World, since the carriers also represented the ability to intervene in those more remote areas. This view changed only as the Carter administration discovered a real threat in just such a remote area, Southwest Asia, in 1979.

The emblem of sea control under Carter was the Perry-class frigate, a convoy escort. In theory the frigate was valuable because it could be built in numbers, and numbers were an essential element of convoy-style defensive sea control. The frigate could also serve as a second-rate carrier escort, but it could not really stand up to intense air attack. That required something like an Aegis cruiser, which cost three or four times as much as a frigate. Without high-quality escorts, the carriers could not execute any offensive sea-control/power-projection operation against the Soviets because they could not survive long enough to do so.

The central weakness of Zumwalt's strategy was that the Soviet threat to shipping consisted of naval aircraft (long-range land-based bombers carrying stand-off missiles) as well as submarines—the Soviet surface fleet would have had little effect on shipping. The bombers were, in effect, the main Soviet battle fleet, and they could be defeated only by carrier-based aircraft. Once that was understood, the U.S. Navy had to revert to a classical strategy—to the maritime strategy of the Reagan years. The maritime strategy seemed radical at the time only because the earlier strategy had never really been made explicit, at least not in the terms understood by modern analysts.

Power projection was inseparable from the maritime strategy, because it was both the threat expected to drive the Soviets to a decisive engagement (or series of engagements) and the benefit to be derived from the early destruction of Soviet naval forces. It was also a very natural bridge into Third World operations, which would correspond to the sort planned in central war after the destruction of the enemy's main fleet. The main differences between the maritime strategy fleet and a fleet optimized purely for the Third World are in its nuclear dimension and in its approach to ASW.

The nuclear dimension was mainly for deterrence. The maritime strategy was designed to be part of a U.S. approach to protracted non-nuclear warfare, and that in turn made sense only if the U.S. deterrent against escalation to nuclear war was credible and survivable. That task required the Navy to field Trident submarines in some numbers. The strategic submarines had the additional (unintended) virtue of tying down the best of the Soviet attack submarine fleet, which would inevitably be assigned to sinking them. Deterrence had the important effect of limiting any Soviet interest in the one really devastating anti–surface ship weapon, nuclear attack at sea. There was good reason to believe that the Soviets were not particularly anxious to begin nuclear warfare of any kind, so deterrence was likely to be robust, at least early in a war. Ideally, the Soviet antiship forces would be wiped out early enough that any Soviet decision to initiate a nuclear exchange later in the conflict would not matter.

As noted above, the ASW aspect of the strategy depended on submarines operating in forward areas and on open-ocean patrol planes, both in some numbers. It might also be that submarines would be invaluable in killing Third World submarines before they could approach offshore carriers, so that element of the maritime strategy might be relevant in limited conflict. The patrol planes, even if they could fly out of Third World airfields, would not enjoy the support of fixed seabed sensors. To some extent mobile surveillance ships (SURTASS) could compensate for that deficiency, although ocean conditions in much of the Third World do not really support the sort of long-range operations developed by the U.S. Navy for the North Atlantic and North Pacific.

Overall, adaptation to Third World conflict would involve smaller numbers of specialist ASW units. The great question would be to what extent these units were adaptable to other tasks more in keeping with Third World scenarios. Certainly the submarines will be useful for covert operations; they have been used in that way throughout the cold war. That may even have been their greatest cold war virtue, albeit a publicly unarticulated one. Submarines have another virtue as well: they carry Tomahawk land-attack missiles (TLAM).

Although a single Tomahawk carries only a very small warhead, it may be very usefully employed in destroying a key target ashore, particularly since the submarine may fire from an unexpected direction. For example, carrier strikes are useful only as long as they are very inexpensive. One way to help insure that is to use cruise missiles, which are inherently fairly stealthy, to destroy an enemy's coastal radars and low-level command centers. No submarine will carry very many Tomahawks, but then again few enemies will present very many crucial targets suitable for attack by their small warheads. Tomahawks were particularly useful during the 1991 Gulf War, destroying long-range Iraqi radars as a precursor to manned air strikes.

The ideal fleet of the 1990s, then, is built around carriers and their consorts.

The more Tomahawks (or successor missiles) a submarine carries, the more useful it is in supporting power projection. That fact tends to favor a fleet composed of large submarines as opposed to small ones. It also favors nuclear submarines, which can rapidly transit very large areas to reach unpredictable points of tension in the Third World, over slower diesel submarines with their lesser combat endurance. In particular, these considerations favor the new Seawolf-class submarine, though not in the numbers that might be considered appropriate to a fleet balanced more for conflict with the Soviets.[13]

As for the patrol aircraft, their great virtue in limited conflict is as long-endurance surface surveillance platforms. They quite possibly would not have been bought had the Navy been designed purely with Third World conflict in mind, but they are in the inventory, and they remain valuable. They also probably represent a resource absolutely essential if the international situation shifts back towards the cold war.

The ideal fleet of the 1990s, then, is built around carriers and their consorts. The United States has been operating carriers singly, simply because it has to be in so many places nearly simultaneously. To keep a single carrier forward-deployed in the Mediterranean or in the Western Pacific, the United States must maintain at least three: one is always in overhaul, one is always en route back to the United States, or working up, or en route forward. In a crisis it can forward deploy up to two out of the three, but that cannot be sustained. If the carrier must be farther from home, e.g., in the Persian Gulf, then transit times are so long that permanent deployment requires more than three carriers in all. The classic postwar pattern of two carriers in the Mediterranean and three to cover the greater reach of the Far East equates to a force of at least fifteen in all, and even that force can be stretched (e.g., by the Indian Ocean deployments).

In reality, the carrier shortfall is even worse. Carriers should be operated in pairs or in groups of three, not singly. Concentrated forces allow a sharing of the operational burden. For example, twenty-four-hour operation for air defense is best done in twelve-hour shifts. A carrier flying off fighters for combat air patrol cannot easily concentrate a big strike, so the ideal strike formation consists of three or four carriers operating together. All of this suggests two conclusions. First, the fifteen-carrier figure is not a ceiling but rather a floor. As bases recede, it will take more carriers to maintain forward deployments. If the bases go, the number of carriers should rise rather than fall. They are, after all, cheaper than a network of fixed bases abroad. Second, even if the numbers grow, it will be more and more difficult to maintain permanent forward deployments of carriers. Unfortunately, in the early 1990s carrier deployments are equated with U.S. presence. The withdrawal of a Seventh Fleet (Far East) carrier was equated, in the region, with a withdrawal of U.S. interest. The battleships were recommissioned so that there was some alternative to a carrier in an area. Given that alternative, carriers could be concentrated where they were needed.[14]

The carrier force contributed six ships to the Gulf War; carrier-based aircraft conducted about one third of all strike and other combat sorties. It is tempting to imagine that, as in the gulf, ground-based aircraft can always be employed, and that the carriers, therefore, are a luxury of sorts. That is very far from the case. Until well into the crisis, the carriers were the *only* effective source of tactical airpower in the theater. It was only Saddam Hussein's relative docility (he eschewed the obvious tactic of a spoiling attack) which permitted the ground-based air to be brought into position and then built up.

It takes eighteen carriers to maintain six on station for any extended period. The Defense Department planned in 1990 to scale back to twelve carrier battle groups. Given the instability of the Third World, it seems foolish to imagine that the Gulf War was unique or, indeed, that the experience would not soon be repeated by some enemy substantially more alert than Saddam Hussein.

Funding Options for the Post–Cold War Navy

A big carrier force is inevitably expensive. The ships cost a great deal to build and maintain, and the aircraft cost about as much as a ship. This cost is aggravated by any decision to shift to a new generation of airplanes, such as the now-defunct

A-12.[15] Some of the money can come out of more efficient procurement and maintenance, but much has to come out of some other part of the overall budget.

There are several approaches. One is to cut cold war naval forces drastically, on the theory that they will not be needed for some years. On that basis the pure ASW frigates of the Knox-class could be laid up. The Perry-class could largely be transferred to the reserves. Submarines prior to the Los Angeles–class could be laid up, with emphasis shifting to the more capable, newer units, which are also less expensive to operate.[16] The patrol plane force could be cut. It might even be possible to reduce undersea surveillance expenditures, although since the Soviet submarine force remains quite potent in the 1990s, such cuts may be short sighted. It would be essential, however, to maintain a high investment in ASW research and development against the likely day when a great-power threat will reemerge.

These are all cuts in operating or maintenance costs; they make sense only if some or all of the money saved could be shifted into new construction for new carriers or for carrier refits, or for high-capability carrier escorts like Arleigh Burke–class destroyers.

When a carrier arrives on station, it can fight. When army troops arrive in a country, they are tourists in uniform.

Another possibility is that an enlightened Defense Department or Congress could recognize that times are changing, and that the interservice balance is wrong. The fleet could be enlarged and modernized easily if, say, B-2 funds were transferred to the Navy account. After all, about four B-2s cost the same as a new carrier. This sort of approach seemed likely before the Kuwait crisis. But the transfer of troops and land-based aircraft to Saudi Arabia seems to have proven their value in the Third World. Cuts in those forces could still be justified, however, since whatever the value of those forces in Third World contingencies, the numbers are far less than what was needed for the cold war in Europe.

Independently, no land-based force really reacts quickly to crisis. When a carrier arrives on station, it can fight. When army troops arrive in a country, they are tourists in uniform. They become a fighting force only when enough weapons and munitions and other materiel have been built up. That generally takes some time because most of the Third World is so far from U.S. sources of supply. Western Europe was an exception only because the United States deliberately stockpiled materiel there, to be married up in an emergency with troops airlifted into the area. The lengthy interval between the beginning of the Kuwait crisis and the point at which the United States had anything like a military option is likely to be typical of future situations.

Naval forces, moreover, can appear in areas of interest at the discretion of the U.S. government, with little or no local agreement or consent. Since their role is much more often to exert influence than actually to fight, that ability to appear and to remain in an area is very valuable. It can also be stabilizing. Since the naval forces can remain for a protracted period, there is little or no question of using them before they begin to degrade, unlike the pressures that were beginning to face the U.S. forces on the ground in the Middle East at the end of 1990.

Another approach is to change the relationship between the elements of the naval budget itself. The budget can be broken down into a few large elements: shipbuilding/conversion (SCN), aircraft/weapons procurement (APN), operations/maintenance (OPN), and personnel. It may be possible to cut the OPN cost per ship or airplane, both on a platform (overhaul) basis and on a day-to-day basis. The submarine community claims that it has been able to reduce the ownership cost of the submarine fleet in just this manner, largely by improving reactor cores to the point that they must be replaced only once during the lifetime of a submarine (the core-replacement overhaul accounts for much of the OPN cost of the submarine). Reliable electronics ought to be an important factor here as should the design of new ships specifically for easy overhauls (as is happening, for example in the Seawolf class).

It may be that some new technology can change relationships within elements of the budget. For example, the stealthy new A-12 attack bomber was justified on the grounds that, although it was terribly expensive, it would be dramatically more survivable than its predecessor, and thus that it could reduce the need to buy expensive stand-off weapons and their associated targeting systems. That would allow for more APN at the cost of WPN funding.

The A-12 proved too expensive, and it was canceled. The Navy still needs a new attack bomber, however. Cancellation was no more, in effect, than a delay in procurement. The new bomber will still be stealthy, which means that it will be something like the A-12. Indeed, given the claims of success for the Air Force's stealthy F-117, the A-12 may even be revived. Ironically, one lesson of the war in the gulf may be that stealth is less useful that had been imagined. If, as in Iraq, U.S. forces were able to demolish the Soviet-style national air defense systems of the Third World, then stealth may be almost irrelevant in future conflicts. All aircraft, including stealthy ones, will be at risk when attacking at low altitudes. The key consideration for the future, therefore, may well be to ensure that virtually all missions can be conducted at higher altitudes to avoid small-caliber guns and shoulder-fired missiles—antiaircraft systems that are not tied into a national command, control, and communications (C^3) system.

Quite aside from the political or geopolitical change, the underlying technology of sea power is undergoing major changes. The most important of these changes is that electronics finally work reliably, often with minimal maintenance. Many observers of the military scene will scoff, but reliable electronics is a proven fact for millions of computer users. Many do not even remember a time when much less capable machines required daily or weekly visits from repairmen carrying what amounted to doctors' bags. At sea, such visits translated into limited reliability and also into high costs in spares and in expert maintenance personnel.

The prospect of cheap but reliable electronics has some interesting implications. First, the economics of procurement may be changing. The last such revolution saw combat systems, largely electronic, come to consume the largest single chunk of the cost of the average ship or airplane. At that time hardware accounted for the bulk of system costs, so that there was little hope for economies of scale. By 1991, however, software, which can easily and cheaply be copied, accounted for up to 85 percent of the cost of any given system. The more systems the United States buys, the less the cost of the software per system. This sort of economics occurs on a daily basis: it costs millions to develop standard software packages for micro computers, but so many such packages are sold that the unit cost is comparatively low. As electronics become substantially cheaper, it may even be possible to maintain systems on a throw away basis, drastically reducing the specialized maintenance force.

Computers offer other possibilities. Much of the cost of a shipyard overhaul can be attributed to the time it takes just to plan a specialized job. By the early 1990s the Navy began translating its plans into computer form. Specialized software should be able to assemble work plans automatically, and even to instruct robot production systems to manufacture the required spare parts.

Another possibility is a drastic reduction in the number of specialist technicians through greater reliability and easier maintainability. This is a long-term trend. For example, many systems incorporate built-in test equipment (BITE). Ultimately, it ought to offer economies in personnel. That in turn ought to make it possible to reduce the size of the shore training establishment.

Reliability can have another interesting effect. Those persons serving aboard a ship are rotated through the fleet so that a ship is unable to build up a core of long-term personnel. This practice is often described as an artifact of the Bureau of Naval Personnel, simplifying the task of manning a ship. It can probably be traced to the shortage of qualified technicians in an increasingly complex post–World War II fleet. If the pressure to provide technicians could be relaxed then the Navy would be able to return to the classical pattern in which a ship's crew was extremely stable. That sort of stability ought to make for better crew spirit and therefore for better retention and lower training costs. It also ought to make for greater tactical (i.e., group) expertise. After all, once weapons and sensors are reliable, the Navy can concentrate on tactics rather than on bare operability.

Conclusion

For the near term, then, the United States faces two alternatives. Clearly the overall military budget must be cut. If the cut is spread uniformly among the services, as though each service is a pressure group requiring its share of attention, then the national capability to project power into the Third World will surely suffer. The Navy may make some savings by reorientation, but they will be minor compared to the costs of new construction. New technology presents the possibility that the ownership costs of the new ships and aircraft will be considerably lower than those of the present generation, but those economies will be realized only over the lifetime of a ship, submarine, or airplane.

The alternative is for the Defense Department to make a basic strategic choice, in favor of power projection into the Third World and away from the forces, particularly those based on land, bought primarily to fight the cold war and its hot extension in Europe. This alternative would require the acceptance of a basic but unhappy fact of life: that the network of foreign bases is a fleeting asset.

NATO may well survive, but as a political rather than a military alliance. Its members may even allow us to use facilities in their countries, but only on a very transitory basis, and only for operations consistent with their foreign policy. For true freedom of action in pursuit of its own national security interests, the United States should reconfigure and expand its Naval forces.

Postscript: The Gulf War

The fight against Iraq was dominated, at least publicly, by forces fighting on land and by air forces based largely on land. That was unfortunate because it obscured the reality that the war could not have been fought in the first place had naval forces not arrived in the region almost immediately after Saddam Hussein seized Kuwait. Similarly, the ground-based forces could not have been built up or functioned without guaranteed access to Saudi Arabia *by sea*. In this particular case, such access was not overtly threatened, but it should be remembered that much of what was deployed to the gulf had to pass through the Mediterranean, within reach of Iraq's ally, Libya. Libya did not interfere with the build up of U.S. forces because of its own experience with U.S. seapower several years earlier.

Once the war had begun, the naval forces in the Persian Gulf and the Red Sea struck heavily at Iraqi targets. Its Tomahawks were crucial precursors to the large, manned air strikes, and there are no equivalent land-based systems. The Marine amphibious group in the gulf pinned down several Iraqi divisions and also forced them to concentrate on the gulf itself, so that ultimately the flanking attack, conducted in large part by other Marines, rolled them up into Kuwait City. Without the presence of U.S. naval forces, Iraq would have had the option of striking at the sea flank of the allied forces. It actually tried to do so, albeit ineptly, and its operation, of which the attack on Khafji was a part, was frustrated by British and U.S. naval aircraft.

It is much too easy to imagine that somehow the Gulf War proved that heavy army divisions and a large air force can solve U.S. problems in the Third World. Certainly, the personnel and the airplanes can appear very quickly, and indeed their appearance seems to have impressed a naïve Saddam Hussein. Without seaborne logistics, however, those are empty forces. In contrast, when the carriers and Marines with their prepositioning ships arrived, they were combat ready. It seems unlikely that future enemies will graciously grant U.S. forces five months to prepare for battle.

Troops and Equipment Deploy to the Persian Gulf

Chapter 7

The United States and the Third World: Policies and Force Requirements

Stephen Van Evera

[handwritten annotation: This chapter is full of B.S. (bias, errors, + erroneous assumptions) — it is not worth reading!]

Introduction

What policy should the United States pursue toward the Third World in the post–cold war era? Three harbingers suggest that the Bush administration intends to continue America's past interventionist policies. First, a large chunk of the Bush administration's defense budget for fiscal year (FY) 1991 is allocated to forces optimized for Third World intervention, including fifteen aircraft carriers and eight light Army and Marine divisions and the administration's proposed cuts for the mid-1990s would impose only small cuts on these intervention forces.

Second, the Bush administration has continued four gruesome wars-by-proxy against leftist Third World regimes and movements, long after a cold war rationale for fighting has disappeared. In Cambodia the administration supports a coalition dominated by the Khmer Rouge, which seeks to oust the Vietnam-installed Hun Sen government. In Afghanistan it sustains a rebellion by seven *mujahideen* groups against the Najibullah regime. In El Salvador it supports the right-wing National Republican Alliance (ARENA) government against the Marxist Farabundo Marti Front for National Liberation (FMLN).[1] In Angola it has backed a violent rebellion by the National Union for the Total Independence of Angola (UNITA). (This war was suspended by an uneasy truce in May 1991, but a secure peace has not yet been achieved.)

Third, during the latter half of 1990 the administration deployed a large mili-

---

This chapter is adapted from "Wars of Intervention: Why They Shouldn't Have a Future, Why They Do," *Defense & Disarmament Alternatives* 3, no. 3 (March 1990), pp. 1–4, 8; and from "The Case Against Intervention," *Atlantic Monthly*, July 1990, pp. 72–80.

tary force to the Persian Gulf, and it used this force in early 1991 to rout Iraqi forces from Kuwait, which Iraq had seized on August 2. By January 1991 this American force totaled some 515,000 troops, including some eight Army divisions, one and two-thirds Marine divisions, six aircraft carriers, roughly 2,000 tanks, and 1,500 planes. About one-fourth of all American military personnel, and two-fifths of U.S. ground units, were deployed.

Widespread American intervention in the Third World made little sense even at the height of the cold war, and it makes even less sense with that war's demise. Accordingly, the United States should avoid further interventions except in a narrow range of circumstances. Iraq's invasion of Kuwait presented these circumstances; hence the gulf deployment deserved support, although the Gulf War was perhaps unnecessary, since economic sanctions also might have forced Iraq from Kuwait. The case for the four proxy wars is much weaker, however. These wars should be ended, and intervention forces should be sharply cut. Such cuts would save more than $30 billion per year.

Intervention for National Security?

Throughout the cold war, proponents of U.S. intervention made two principal claims: that Third World interventions protect American security by preserving the global balance of power, and that interventions promote democracy, thereby promoting human rights. Both arguments were false in the past, are false now, and would remain false even if the Soviet Union regained its strength and returned to an aggressive foreign policy.

The national security argument for intervention rests on three main assumptions:

- The Soviet Union seeks an empire in the Third World.

- It could gain such an empire, either by direct intervention or by sponsoring the expansion of proxies, unless the United States intervenes to stop it.

- Such an empire would add significantly to Soviet military strength, ultimately tipping the world power balance in the Soviet Union's favor, thus threatening American national security.

All three assumptions must be valid to uphold the security case for intervention. If any fails the global balance of power is not threatened, leaving no security problem for intervention to solve. In fact, however, all three assumptions are defective. The first assumption crumbled with the waning of Soviet expansionism under Mikhail Gorbachev. Soviet tolerance of the democratic revolutions in Eastern Europe in 1989 signaled the ebbing of Soviet expansionism worldwide, and perhaps its total abandonment. Eastern Europe matters far more to the Soviet Union than any Third World region; Soviet leaders who concede their empire in Eastern Europe cannot be planning to colonize much less valuable Third World areas. Soviet cooperation against Iraq—an erstwhile Soviet ally—during the Persian Gulf crisis also illustrates the change in Soviet policy. In short, there is little Soviet imperial thrust left for American interventions to blunt.

The second assumption fails because the Soviet Union lacks the capacity to colonize the Third World. It can barely control its inner empire as unrest in the Baltic republics, Transcaucasia, and Central Asia reveals. Overseas colonialism is unthinkable.

But even if the Soviets recovered their unity and their appetite for Third World empire, they could not seize it. Soviet military forces are designed primarily for land war in Europe and for intercontinental nuclear war with the United States, not for Third World intervention. This leaves the Soviet Union with scant means to intervene directly.[2] Nor can the Soviet Union gain empire by promoting leftist revolution or expansion by Soviet "proxy" states, because the centrifugal force of nationalism tears the bonds between proxy and master. As a result, Third World leftists tend to be unruly proxies, seldom following Soviet dictates except when pushed into the Kremlin's arms by American bellicosity. This is underlined by the unfraternal relations among communist states, and illustrated by the conflicts that have often flared between the Khmer Rouge and Vietnam, Vietnam and China, China and the Soviet Union, the Soviet Union and Yugoslavia, and the Soviet Union and Albania. In fact, communists have fought each other as much or more than they have fought others, indicating that Third World "Soviet proxies" are largely fictitious. Moreover, the Soviet Union is evolving away from communism. This further discredits fears that the Soviets can organize a transnational communist empire, since the leaders of the empire are themselves discarding the ideology that would allegedly glue it together.

The third assumption fails because the Third World has little strategic importance, hence even large Soviet gains in the Third World would not shake the global balance of power. By the best measure of strategic importance—industrial power—the Third World ranks very low. All of Latin America has an aggregate gross national product (GNP) less than half that of Japan. All of Africa has an aggregate GNP below that of Italy or Britain. The aggregate GNP of the entire Third World is below that of Western Europe.[3] Modern military power is distilled from industrial power. The Third World has little industrial power, hence it has little military potential, and correspondingly little strategic significance. As a result, Third World realignments have little impact on the global power balance.

Moreover, the nuclear revolution has further reduced the Third World's strategic importance to a level far below even what its industrial strength might indicate. Nuclear weapons constitute a defensive revolution in warfare. They make conquest among great powers almost impossible, since a victor now must destroy almost all of an opponent's nuclear arsenal—an enormous task, requiring massive technical and material superiority. As a result, the nuclear revolution has devalued the strategic importance of all conquered territory, including Third World territory, because even huge conquests would not provide the conqueror with enough technical or material assets to confer decisive nuclear superiority over another great power. Hence industrial regions that mattered greatly before the nuclear age now matter little, and Third World regions that formerly mattered little now matter even less.

Some interventionists assert that the Third World has strategic importance despite its lack of industrial power because the West allegedly depends on Third World raw materials, or because military bases in Third World areas allegedly have considerable strategic value. Both claims are much overdrawn. Oil is the only Third World material on which the West depends to any degree. The West imports many other materials from the Third World, but at modest additional cost all could be produced locally in the West, synthesized, replaced by substitutes, conserved and recycled, or acquired from alternative Third World sources if supplies from current producers were interrupted. Bases, too, can be replaced by longer-range forces, or moved to new locations, if a given country denies basing rights to the United States. Soviet bases in the Third World are vulnerable to Western blockade and destruction since the West holds naval superiority. This leaves the Soviet Union unable to defend or resupply forces based overseas, hence Third World bases add little to Soviet military capability.[4] Finally, the nuclear revolution renders such strategic arguments largely obsolete. Even if the United States depended heavily on Third World imports, and even if bases mattered for conventional war, the American nuclear deterrent would still give the United States nearly absolute security from conquest.

The failure of all three assumptions creates a redundant, and therefore a very strong, case against intervention. Moreover, the latter two assumptions were false before the Gorbachev revolution, and would remain false even if that revolution were reversed. Hence the security case for intervention was very weak before Gorbachev appeared, and would remain very weak even if the changes he instituted were swept away.

In short, no national security justification exists for U.S. commitment to Third World intervention.

The security case for intervention was very weak before Gorbachev appeared, and would remain very weak even if the changes he instituted were swept away.

Intervention for Democracy?

During the 1980s proponents of intervention supplemented security arguments with claims that American interventions promote democracy. This argument fails on both logical and historical grounds.

Deductive logic indicates that the United States lacks the means to implant democracy by intervention. Democracy requires suitable social and economic preconditions: a fairly equal distribution of land, wealth, and income; high levels of literacy and economic development; cultural norms conducive to democracy, including traditions of tolerance, free speech, and due process of law; and few deep ethnic divisions. Most of the Third World lacks democracy because these preconditions are missing. Moreover, it would require vast social engineering, involving long and costly post-intervention occupations, to introduce them. American taxpayers clearly would not support extravagant projects of this sort.

The historical record shows that past U.S. interventions have generally failed to bolster democracy. These interventions have more often left dictatorship than democracy in their wake. Moreover, Washington has often subverted elected governments that opposed its policies, and many U.S.-supported "democratic" governments and movements were not at all democratic. Overall, this record suggests that the United States lacks the will and the ability to foster democracy.

The legacy of American interventions and occupations is not wholly undemocratic: Germany, Japan, Italy, Austria, and Grenada are significant exceptions. But these were easy cases, since each country had some previous experience with democracy, and all but Grenada were economically developed. Elsewhere the American record is bleak.

The U.S. governed Cuba, Nicaragua, Haiti, and the Dominican Republic in a generally undemocratic fashion during the intermittent occupations in the period 1898–1934, and then allowed brutal dictators to seize power after it left. South Korea has seen far more dictatorship than democracy since American forces arrived in 1945. Following the era of U.S. colonial rule (1899–1946), the Philippines experienced a corrupt and violent perversion of democracy and a long period of repression under Ferdinand Marcos's U.S.-supported dictatorship.[5] Even in the post–Marcos era, violence has marred Philippine elections, and the threat of a military coup has hung over the elected government. Iran and Guatemala have been ruled by cruel dictatorships since the CIA-sponsored coups of 1953 and 1954. Chile is only now emerging from years of harsh military dictatorship under Augusto Pinochet, who was installed by a U.S.-supported coup in 1973.

Some would argue that the United States brought democracy to Panama in 1989 and Nicaragua in 1990, but the United States deserves less credit than appearance suggests. The legacy of the 1989 U.S. invasion of Panama is still uncertain. The Bush administration's invasion deposed dictator Manuel Noriega and installed an elected government in his place, but the administration also installed a sinister Noriega henchman, Col. Eduardo Herrera Hassan, as the commander of the new Public Force (PF), the successor to Noriega's corrupt Panamanian Defense Forces (PDF).[6] Herrera staffed the PF almost exclusively with former PDF members, raising the risk that corrupt military cliques will continue to dominate the country's politics.[7] Moreover, by invading, the United States merely sought to undo a mess of its own making. The United States created and trained the PDF; then, in 1968, the PDF destroyed Panamanian democracy, installing a junta that later gave rise to the Noriega dictatorship.[8] Overall, U.S. policy toward Panama has not fostered democracy.

The 1990 Nicaraguan elections have apparently put Nicaragua on the road to democracy for the first time in its history. The U.S.-sponsored *contra* war and U.S. economic sanctions contributed by pressuring the Sandinistas to hold earlier and freer elections than they otherwise would have, but the social conditions required for democracy were created by the Sandinista revolution over American opposition. In 1979, when the Sandinistas took power, 50 percent of the adult population of Nicaragua was illiterate; land was very maldistributed (5 percent of the rural population owned 85 percent of the farmland, while 37 percent of the rural population was landless); and the country was terrorized by the Somoza dictatorship's brutal National Guard.[9] The Sandinistas reduced adult illiteracy to 13 percent, redistributed the land, and disbanded the National Guard.[10]

Had the United States gotten its way, these changes never would have happened. As the Somoza regime crumbled in 1979, the Carter administration tried to forestall a Sandinista victory by replacing Somoza while preserving his National Guard in power.[11] A Guard-dominated regime surely would have left intact the old oligarchic social and political order—an order in which widespread coercion, voter ignorance, and vote fraud made elections meaningless.

The United States also gets mixed reviews for its role in arranging the 1990 Nicaraguan elections. The Reagan administration preferred a military victory to any compromise solution, including one providing for elections. It therefore disrupted the 1984 Nicaraguan elections by persuading the opposition not to run.[12] It also resisted the peace plan proposed by Costa Rican president Oscar Arias in 1987, which launched the process that led to the 1990 elections. This resistance ended only when the Bush administration took office.[13] In short, the impetus for the Nicaraguan election process came from Central America against U.S. opposition, while the conditions for democracy were established by a social revolution that the United States sought to prevent. Hence, U.S. claims of authorship for Nicaraguan democracy ring hollow.

The United States lacks the means to institute democracy by intervention, and apparently lacks the will.

The undemocratic effects of American policies result partly from their pronounced bias in favor of elites. The Carter administration's support for the Nicaraguan oligarchy was not unique; in many other Third World countries American policy has bolstered the power of local antidemocratic upper-class elements, who then blocked the social leveling that democratization requires. In South Korea, U.S. policies favored the rightist elite from the early days of the postwar occupation.[14] In the Philippines the United States aligned itself with the upper-class *ilustrado* elite after seizing the islands in 1898–1899, and again when it recovered the Philippines from Japan in 1944–1945.[15] In Guatemala the CIA-sponsored Castillo Armas government (1954–1957) repealed universal suffrage and dispossessed peasant beneficiaries of earlier land reforms, leaving Guatemala among the most stratified societies in the world.[16] Throughout Latin America the Alliance for Progress, founded partly to promote social equality, was coopted by oligarchic governments that ran it for the benefit of wealthy elites. As a result, the Alliance in fact increased social stratification.[17]

America's ambivalence toward Third World democracy is more starkly manifest in its recurrent subversion of elected Third World governments that pursued policies distasteful to the United States. There have been eleven prominent instances since 1945 in which Third World democracies have elected nationalist or leftist regimes whose policies disturbed Washington. In nine of these cases—Iran (1953), Guatemala (1954), British Guiana (1953–1964), Indonesia (1957), Ecuador (1960–1963), Brazil (1964), the Dominican Republic (1965), Costa Rica (in the mid-1950s), and Chile (1970–1973)—the United States attempted to overthrow the elected government (or, in the Dominican case, to prevent its return to power), and in most cases succeeded. In the other two cases—Greece (1967) and Jamaica (1976–1980)—evidence of American subversion is less clear-cut, but is nevertheless substantial.[18]

In short, American leaders have favored democracy only when it produced governments that supported American policies. Otherwise they have sought to subvert democracy.

American ambivalence toward Third World democracy is also revealed by the thuggish character of America's Third World clients. America's client regimes in Central America are illustrative. The U.S.-backed governments of El Salvador, Guatemala, and Honduras hold regular elections, which qualifies them as "small and fragile democracies" in Ronald Reagan's view.[19] But none pass the first test of democracy—that those elected control government policy. Instead, the army and police effectively rule all three countries; the civilian governments are hood ornaments on military vehicles of state. Civilian officials who defied the military would be removed promptly by assassination or coup. Knowing this, they obey the military. Moreover, the preconditions for fair elections—free speech, a free press, and freedom to vote, organize, and run for office—are denied by government death squads that systematically murder critics of the government. The official terror has reached vast proportions in El Salvador, where the government has murdered 40,000 Salvadorans since 1979, and in Guatemala, where the government has murdered 140,000 since 1970.[20] Fair elections are impossible amid such slaughter.

In sum, the United States lacks the means to institute democracy by intervention, and apparently lacks the will. There is little reason to expect more democratic results from future interventions. Accordingly, the advancement of democracy is an unpersuasive reason for intervention.

When Not to Intervene: The Case against Bush's Proxy Wars

These criticisms of the case for intervention apply directly to the Bush administration's proxy wars. The Bush administration did not create these wars; they were inherited from the Carter and Reagan administrations. Nor is the United States solely responsible for past fighting; it became directly involved only after all four wars began. However, U.S. responsibility for past fighting is sizable, and the United States now plays a key role in sustaining the three wars where active fighting continues. These wars have taken a huge human toll: 341,000 killed in Angola since 1975, including 320,000 civilians (thanks to the war, Angola has 50,000 amputees, the most per capita in the world); 65,000 killed in Cambodia since 1978; thousands killed in Afghanistan since the Soviets withdrew in 1989; and 75,000 killed in El Salvador since 1979.[21] Such enormous violence requires a compelling justification, but the cases for these wars are extremely thin.

Their main rationale vanished with the waning of Soviet expansionism. The Reagan administration claimed that these wars were required to blunt the Soviet Union's "imperial thrust" in the Third World, in order to preserve the global balance of power. This rationale—dubious even during the cold war, since there was little power in the Third World to add to either side of the balance, and little Soviet capacity to exert imperial control—wholly dissolved once the abatement of Soviet imperialism became clear, leaving these wars without strategic purpose.

Moreover, the administration's client groups are dominated by brutal elements who will rule by terror if they win on the battlefield. Democracy won't be helped, and human rights will be harmed, if the Bush policy succeeds.

In Cambodia the administration claims to oppose the return of the Khmer Rouge, while working to oust the Hun Sen government. But the Khmer Rouge are Hun Sen's only real competitors for power, and his most likely successors. In effect, then, the administration supports the Khmer Rouge's bid for power. These same Khmer Rouge killed over one million Cambodians when they held power during 1975–1978.[22] In contrast, Hun Sen leads a pluralist, fairly popular regime that is accepted as legitimate in most of Cambodia.[23]

UNITA leader Jonas Savimbi preaches democracy and capitalism to credulous conservative audiences in America, but he runs a brutal, quasi-Stalinist autocracy in the territory he controls in Angola. He has murdered UNITA dissidents, and once burned alive an entire family at a public bonfire as "witches."[24] As a youth, Savimbi was a communist organizer in Portugal, and UNITA defectors warn that he remains an unreformed Maoist. The training manual for UNITA leaders has a communist flavor, defining UNITA domestic policy as "democratic centralism," and UNITA's structure includes a central committee and a politburo.[25] UNITA also favors Savimbi's tribal kinsmen against others, leading one commentator to label his movement "nepo-Leninist."[26] (Americans who mistook Savimbi for a supply-side conservative can probably blame Black, Manafort, Stone, and Kelly, the high-powered public relations firm that Savimbi paid over $2 million to give him a suitably Reaganite American public image.)[27]

The Afghan *mujahideen* are a fractious group dominated by Moslem extremists and drug traffickers. The strongest *mujahideen* group, Hizbe-Islami, is led by Golbuddin Hekmatyar, an extreme fundamentalist described by some Afghan specialists as an "Afghan Khomeini."[28] His fundamentalist cohorts have launched a reign of terror among Afghan exiles in Pakistan, murdering those who criticize their views.[29] Hekmatyar has also scornfully castigated the United States and its "immoral" society, even while the United States lavished him with aid.[30] Another *mujahideen* leader, Nasim Akhunzada, was known as the "heroin king" because he controlled the Afghan heroin routes to Iran.[31] In 1989 rebel-controlled Afghan areas exported 700 tons of opium, the raw material for heroin, making Afghanistan the world's second-largest opium producer, after Burma.[32] These "founding fathers" are not the type to build democracy if they win power.

The Salvadoran government is dominated by ARENA party founder Major Roberto D'Aubuisson and his military colleagues. President Alfredo Cristiani is largely a figurehead who distracts the American Congress with moderate rhetoric while D'Aubuisson and the military run their savage war. D'Aubuisson is widely regarded as the mastermind of El Salvador's official death squads, and was personally implicated in the 1980 murder of Archbishop Oscar Romero and the 1981 murders of two American labor officials.[33] He also authored a plot to assassinate the U.S. Ambassador to El Salvador, Thomas Pickering, in October 1984.[34]

In short, victory by the administration's clients would lead to rule by violent elements who have committed gross human rights abuses and have shown no commitment to democracy.[35]

Why Does War Continue?

One would expect even an interventionist administration to cut off such odious groups once the wars they waged no longer served a strategic purpose. But the Bush administration presses on with its wars. Perhaps most striking, it has pressed on even after winning its main demands.

As the price for a settlement in Cambodia, the United States has long demanded that Vietnam withdraw the occupation forces it left in Cambodia after it overthrew the Khmer Rouge regime in 1978–1979. Vietnam finally agreed and withdrew its forces in September 1989. But the Bush administration upped its demands, first insisting that Hun Sen include the Khmer Rouge in his government as coalition partners, and later demanding that his government step down under a complex and expensive scheme involving an interim United Nations' administration—a solution that would raise the risk of a Khmer Rouge return to power since Hun Sen's regime is the main barrier in their way.[36] Meanwhile, the Hun Sen government has been prepared since late 1989 to accept internationally supervised elections conducted, as they were in Nicaragua, Namibia, and Poland, with the incumbent regime in office.[37] These three cases, and several others, show that fair elections are feasible under such conditions. The administration has nevertheless rejected this solution, insisting instead on Hun Sen's prior departure. It also continued supplying the Khmer Rouge coalition armies, which forced Vietnam to counter by sending forces back to Cambodia in the fall of 1989—thereby defeating America's main declared aim.[38]

As the price for a settlement in Angola, the United States has long demanded that Cuba withdraw the troops it sent there in 1975 to bolster the new Angolan government. In late 1988 the Cubans agreed to withdraw, and all were gone by June 1991.[39] The Angolan government also offered to give amnesty to all UNITA members, and to integrate UNITA personnel into the government.[40] But then, in September 1989, the Bush administration for the first time demanded that the government also hold elections as the price for peace.[41] This is a nice-sounding afterthought, but a pointless complication, since even foreign-sponsored elections will not bring real democracy to Angola. Angola is a very poor country with a largely illiterate and deeply divided population, hence it lacks important preconditions for democracy.[42] In late 1990 the Angolan government accepted multiparty democracy in principle,[43] in early 1991 both sides accepted most elements of a U.S.-Soviet plan that would resolve the war through elections to be held in late 1992,[44] and both sides also agreed to observe a ceasefire in the meantime.[45] Even if this peace process succeeds, however, Angola surely won't become a democracy; thus the Bush administration's late demand for elections merely prolonged a war that could have ended sooner.

In exchange for an Afghan settlement, the United States asked the Soviet Union to withdraw the invasion force it sent to Afghanistan in 1979. The Soviets did so in February 1989, leaving behind an Afghan regime that offered moderate peace terms, including a broad coalition government and U.N.-supervised elections.[46] Elections cannot bring real democracy in Afghanistan, for the same reasons as in Angola—intense poverty, widespread illiteracy, and deep tribal divisions.[47] A peace based on power sharing that reflects the relative military strength of the parties would probably prove more durable. Whatever the shortcomings of an electoral solution, however, the administration has impeded even that road to peace by demanding that the Najibullah regime step down before elections are held—a solution that Najibullah predictably rejects.

The United States said it sought to build a democratic political system in El Salvador. The FMLN has progressively softened its demands, and now agrees in principle with Washington's declared objective, pledging to lay down its arms if conditions for free elections are established. The FMLN's main demand is the dismantling of the government death squads to allow the opposition to organize and campaign without fear.[48] But the Bush administration has not pressed the Cristiani government to accept such a settlement. Until the November 1989 FMLN offensive, the administration opposed any settlement that would give the left a significant share of political power.[49] Later it began to express more support for negotiations, but still failed to apply strong pressure on the government— without which a settlement is unlikely.[50]

Why has the Bush administration waged these wars so stubbornly? One theory holds that the administration has ceded control of Third World policy to the far right in a bid to appease ultraconservatives for their exclusion from arenas of foreign-policy decision making in which the stakes are higher for the United States, such as U.S.-Soviet relations. The far right favors a *jihad* against all Third World leftists, even if this means aiding barbarians or wrecking the targeted societies. To win this *jihad* it will even use Marxist movements to destroy other Marxists if non-Marxist clients are not available—hence its peculiar willingness to back the Marxist Khmer Rouge and UNITA. In contrast, American peace groups have shown little interest in these wars, except for the Salvadoran conflict, allowing the administration to make more friends than enemies by fighting on.

When to Intervene: The Case for the Gulf Deployment

The case for the 1990–1991 Persian Gulf deployment is far stronger than the case for these proxy wars. Like these wars, the gulf deployment did not protect American sovereignty or advance democracy, nor did it protect American prosperity. The gulf deployment did advance secondary American interests, however, and was justified for this reason.

Had Iraq gone unchecked, its seizure of Kuwait might have foreshadowed its seizure of the rest of the Arab Persian Gulf. Iraq could have easily overrun the other Arab gulf states (Saudi Arabia, the United Arab Emirates, Qatar, Bahrain, and Oman), especially if it had retained Kuwait's large resources and converted these resources to military capability.[51] Iraqi expansion would have been eased by the common Arab culture that Iraq shares with the gulf states; this common identity would have dampened popular resistance to Iraqi occupation, allowing Iraq to digest Arab conquests at modest cost, and then move on to take more. Moreover, an Iraqi campaign of this sort was not implausible. Iraq has launched two wars of choice since 1980, and the ideology of the Iraqi Baath party stresses the importance of achieving Arab unity, thus justifying a campaign of expansion against Iraq's Arab neighbors.[52]

Had it seized the other Arab gulf states, Iraq would have gained control of 20 percent of world oil production—a vast increase from the 4.4 percent that Iraq controls alone.[53] Iraq's GNP would have more than quadrupled.[54] In short, by expanding, Iraq would have greatly increased its strength.

This enlarged Iraq would have remained a minor world power, too weak to directly threaten American security. It still would have produced only 1 percent of Gross World Product (GWP), leaving it dwarfed in economic strength by the major industrial states. (In contrast, the United States produces 27 percent of GWP; the North Atlantic Treaty Organization (NATO) states together produce 50 percent of GWP.)[55] With this small economic base, even an enlarged Iraq could not have built a military machine that could match the militaries of the industrial West. Iraq could have developed a modest nuclear deterrent, and could have emanated power in the Mideast region under the umbrella provided by this deterrent, but Iraq would have remained vulnerable to Western military power since even a nuclear-armed state cannot build a robust defense against determined opponents with economies twenty-seven to fifty times larger than its own. As a result, the Western countries could have blocked further Iraqi expansion, or even crushed Iraq if they were willing to pay a steep price and to run some risk of nuclear retaliation.

Nor could an enlarged Iraq have extracted much wealth from the West by forcing a large permanent oil price increase. Such an increase would have triggered new non-OPEC oil production, alternative energy development, and wider energy conservation. These events would have devalued oil held in the ground by current oil producers, including Iraq. Such considerations have led Saudi Arabia to pursue a moderate oil pricing policy; the same considerations would have compelled Iraq to adopt similar policies. Moreover, with just 20 percent of world oil production even an enlarged Iraq would have lacked the market power required to force more than a marginal rise in longterm oil prices. Had it cut its oil production completely it might have caused a large oil price rise, but other producers would have harvested all the profits. Had it pumped enough oil to make money from the price rise, its own pumping would have kept that rise to a minimum. In short, the price of oil was not at stake in the gulf.

Thus, Iraq's seizure of the gulf would have posed little direct threat to American sovereignty or prosperity. Overall, an expanded Iraq would have become a dominant regional power, but would have remained a minor world power, with little influence beyond the Middle East. It could not have jeopardized the security of the United States or its western industrial allies. Nor would it have directly threatened democracy since the gulf states are not democratic.

The United States does have secondary interests that would be jeopardized by unchecked Iraqi expansion, however, which were protected by the gulf deployment. These include the protection of human rights, the preservation of peace among other states, the deterrence of terrorism, the prevention of nuclear proliferation, and the fulfillment of its moral commitment to Israel. If these interests are considered separately, each by itself can seldom justify the use of force, but here their cumulative importance was substantial, and unchecked Iraqi expansion would have threatened them quite directly. Hence the gulf is an instance where the limited use of force was appropriate.

An expanded Iraq would have become a dominant regional power, but would have remained a minor world power.

Iraqi occupation forces cruelly violated the human rights of the residents of Kuwait. The United States has acquiesced to far more serious human rights violations by other governments, and American opposition to Iraq's lesser violations reflects a double standard.[56] Nevertheless, the fact that the gulf deployment ended these violations weighs in its favor. Iraq's aggression against Kuwait was unusually blatant—U.N. members have very rarely tried to conquer and annex one another—and American action to reverse it helps deter similar acts by others in the future; this bolsters peace. Iraq has sponsored international terrorism and has escaped punishment for this sponsorship; the gulf crisis provided an opportunity to correct this oversight. Kuwait's financial resources would have allowed Iraq to intensify its quest for nuclear weapons, hence the United States slowed the Iraqi nuclear program and inhibited the regional spread of nuclear weapons by restoring Kuwait's freedom.[57] Finally, and most importantly, the deployment of U.S. troops thwarted a serious threat to Israeli security and deflected a threat to the United States that derived from America's commitment to Israel.

If the Arabs living to the east of the Suez canal were united under a single government, Israeli security would be seriously jeopardized. These Asian Arabs are ruled by eleven separate governments. This leaves them unable to act in concert, limiting their collective ability to threaten Israel. Israel might be unable to defend against a single Arab regime that controlled both the oil wealth of the Persian Gulf and the manpower of the eastern front-line states. Such a state would command a net GNP many times that of Israel and might convert this economic superiority into military superiority.

An Iraq that controlled the gulf would be well positioned to establish such an Asian Arab hegemony. Syria, Jordan, Yemen, and Lebanon would then be vastly outmatched by Iraqi power, and might succumb to it. Like Bismarck's Prussia, Iraq would become the enforcer of national union. If so, the GNP of this hegemonic Iraq would be 7.7 times that of Israel.[58] In contrast, the front-line states that fought Israel in 1967 and 1973 held a GNP superiority over Israel of only 1.9:1,[59] and the worst plausible "eastern front" that might challenge Israel absent Iraqi hegemony—a coalition of Syria, Iraq, and Jordan—holds a GNP superiority of only 2.3:1 over Israel.[60] Thus, an Iraqi hegemony in Arab Asia would threaten Israel with a far greater preponderance of resources than it has faced before. If it exploited this preponderance, hegemonic Iraq could probably gain conventional superiority over Israel, and might even find ways to threaten the Israeli nuclear deterrent. Moreover, such a hegemony would concentrate these resources in very hostile hands. The Iraqi Baath party remains committed to the destruction of Israel, hence it seems quite plausible that Iraq would turn against Israel once it gained dominance among the Asian Arabs.

American containment of Iraq therefore serves Israeli security. If Iraq were unchecked, Israel would be compelled to rely far more heavily on America for its security. This would leave Israel's survival more dependent on the whims and vagaries of American domestic politics. The American containment policy saves Israel from this dependent position.

The containment of Iraq also serves American interests, if the United States intends to sustain its security guarantee to Israel. As noted above, the United States could certainly contain further Iraqi expansion, even if Iraq gained hegemony in Arab Asia. However, America's security guarantee to Israel would require greater American effort and involve greater risks.[61] A hegemonic Iraq might have launched a renewed oil embargo to coerce the United States to halt security assistance to Israel.[62] The United States could have weathered such an embargo, but it would have posed a real nuisance. The United States also might have found itself compelled to rescue Israel in a future Arab-Israeli war. This might have required the direct use of American forces, perhaps involving the United States in a regional nuclear conflict. The United States undoubtedly would have succeeded, but perhaps at a high price. These dangers were avoided by containing Iraq before it gained hegemony over its Arab neighbors.

By containing Iraq, the United States also sustained the possibility of an Arab-Israeli peace. Israel will not trade land for peace if it faces a serious military threat from the east since territorial concessions involve some loss of military capability for Israel. Hence the containment of Iraq is a precondition for an Arab-Israeli peace. The possibility of an Arab-Israeli peace seemed remote in 1990, given the aggressive aims embraced by both sides. Nevertheless, both parties may someday pursue peace more seriously, so it seems worthwhile to preserve the conditions that peace requires. The gulf deployment helped sustain these conditions by bolstering Israeli security.

The size of the gulf deployment and the administration's decision for war in January 1991 can still be questioned, however. The administration chose to deploy a very large force in order to put strong military pressure on Saddam Hussein to concede and to prepare an offensive military solution if he did not. In mid-January the administration decided that it had waited long enough and launched the war, which ended with a smashing American victory six weeks later. A strategy of prolonged economic siege also might have forced Iraq to concede, however, and would have required a far smaller force and cost fewer lives. It stood a good chance of success because Iraq is very vulnerable to economic embargo and blockade: it is heavily dependent on revenues from oil exports which supplied 42 percent of Iraq's GNP in 1989 and which are easily interdicted.[63] By one estimate a sustained siege would have reduced Iraq's GNP by 48 percent.[64] Economic sanctions have often failed in the past, but previous economic sanctions have never been so punishing.[65] Iraq would have resisted, but it seems doubtful that this resistance would have lasted for many years had the United States kept up the pressure. Such a siege strategy would have required a force adequate to defend Saudi Arabia from Iraqi attack and to blockade Iraqi ship traffic—perhaps 75,000 to 100,000 U.S. troops—but probably no more than this.

The goals of the gulf deployment were worthy, but the size of the deployment seemed excessive, and its offensive use seemed unnecessary.

Administration officials rejected a long siege strategy on grounds that the United States might have been unable to maintain the unity in the international coalition required to enforce it. But only a small coalition—including just Saudi Arabia, Turkey, and the United States—was required to prevent Iraqi oil exports. The politics of maintaining this small coalition seem manageable. Thus the goals of the gulf deployment were worthy, but the size of the deployment seemed excessive, and its offensive use seemed unnecessary.

What Intervention Forces Does America Require?

The United States has no interests in the Third World that could justify a long and costly intervention. As noted above, the main arguments for past interventions—that interventions protect national security or promote democracy—are not persuasive. Certainly no American Third World interest could justify another engagement as expensive as the Indochina war.

The 1990–1991 Persian Gulf conflict illustrates, however, that the United States does have interests in the Third World that could justify the limited use of force. It also provides a useful yardstick for setting America's intervention force requirements because a more demanding Third World contingency is hard to imagine: Iraq lies halfway around the world, it had the world's fifth-largest army, and it held the advantage of standing on the defensive, already having seized Kuwait. One analyst suggests that the 230,000 U.S. troops in the gulf by early November 1990 were adequate to retake Kuwait; [66] and, as noted above, others argue that a siege strategy requiring only 75,000 to 100,000 troops might have sufficed to free Kuwait. The gulf deployment thus provides a "worst plausible case," and sets a generous standard for meeting the requirements of that case since a smaller force might have been sufficient to achieve American goals. It therefore indicates a maximum requirement for intervention forces.

What specific intervention force requirements does the gulf deployment suggest? Conventional forces can be divided into two types: heavy and light. Heavy forces are designed for combat against heavily-armored opponents; they are most useful in Europe, but can be used in the Third World. America's heavy forces include its armored and mechanized ground forces, and supporting tactical airpower and transport forces. Light forces are optimized for combat against lightly-armored opponents. Such forces are themselves quite lightly armed, and therefore quite strategically mobile. They are more useful for Third World intervention—against guerrillas or small Third World national armies—than for action elsewhere. America's light forces include its light infantry, airborne, airmobile, and amphibious divisions; supporting tactical airpower and transport forces; and the aircraft carrier force. [67]

The gulf deployment included both heavy and light forces. Specifically, the Army deployed the equivalent of six armored and mechanized divisions, one airborne division, and one airmobile division, and the Marines deployed one and two-thirds amphibious divisions. Thus, America's ground units totalled six heavy divisions and three and two-thirds light divisions, with a total complement of about 2,000 tanks. These forces were supported by some 650 Air Force aircraft, about 325 Marine aircraft, and Air Force and Navy transport equipment. In addition, the Navy sent six aircraft carriers to the gulf region, with a complement of roughly 500 aircraft. [68]

This suggests that Third World intervention contingencies create a requirement for six heavy and three and two-thirds light ground divisions, plus supporting tactical airpower and transport, and enough aircraft carriers to deploy six carriers. If so, sizable cuts in American forces are appropriate because U.S. forces now far exceed this requirement.

The gulf deployment provides no argument for cutting American heavy forces, because U.S. heavy force requirements should be pegged to European contingencies, not Third World contingencies. The United States will probably remain committed in Europe, requiring a supporting force of at least six heavy divisions, despite the fading of the Soviet threat. If so, the more demanding European contingency should determine American heavy force requirements; the gulf deployment provides no relevant standard, because it is not the contingency that demands the largest heavy force.

However, a "gulf deployment" standard indicates that U.S light forces can be sharply cut. Since American light forces would have little role in a European war, the case for light forces rests on their utility for Third World contingencies. The gulf contingency absorbed only a modest share of American light forces, which suggests that deep cuts are possible.

If we use the classification scheme outlined above, the total inventory of U.S. light forces in 1990 included the Army's one airmobile, one airborne, and four light infantry divisions, totalling six of the Army's eighteen active divisions; the one light infantry division and five infantry divisions among the Army's ten reserve divisions; all three active Marine divisions, and the Marines' one reserve division; Navy ships designed for amphibious operations; and the Navy's fifteen aircraft carriers and their escort ships.[69] We should also include a share of Air Force and Marine tactical airpower (tacair), and Navy and Air Force transport capability, prorated to reflect the percentage of the active ground forces they support that is light. Together these light forces cost $102.3 billion in FY 1990, or 34 percent of the $300 billion FY 1990 defense budget.[70]

The "gulf deployment" standard suggests that roughly half of these light forces could be safely eliminated. Such a cut would not markedly reduce American capacity to defend Europe and Japan, and would leave the United States with a substantial capacity for Third World contingencies. If four active Army light infantry divisions and one active Marine division were cut, the United States could still retain four active light divisions—an Army airborne division, an Army airmobile division, and two Marine divisions—for Third World contingencies.[71] This four-division force matches the gulf deployment with an extra one-third of a Marine division to spare. It substantially exceeds the American force deployed in the 1989 invasion of Panama (which utilized only one and one-half ground divisions), and is comparable to roughly half the peak American deployment in Vietnam—surely enough for any plausible future Third World contingency.

If the Navy carrier force were cut from fifteen to eight carriers, the United States could still sustain a force of two or three carriers in combat for many months at a time, and could surge a force of six or seven carriers into combat for a few months. Perhaps six carriers would be required to cover American sea lanes early in a Soviet-American confrontation—two carriers each for the Atlantic and Pacific sea lanes, and two more for the Persian Gulf or Northern Norway—hence an eight-carrier force should be adequate for this task. Experience also suggests that Third World contingencies requiring a larger carrier force are very unlikely. The six-carrier gulf deployment has been America's largest carrier deployment since World War II, inside or outside the Third World.[72] An eight-carrier force could sustain a multi-month deployment of this size, although carrier crews would face the hardship of a prolonged tour of duty.

If these cuts were imposed, further proportional cuts in supporting forces would be appropriate. The recommended one-third cut in Marine divisions would also allow a one-third cut in Navy amphibious equipment and Marine tacair. The recommended four-division cut in Army ground divisions would represent a 22 percent reduction in the Army's total eighteen-division FY 1990 structure, allowing a parallel 22 percent cut in Air Force tactical airpower. If total American ground forces were cut from twenty-one to sixteen divisions (a 24 percent cut), sealift and airlift forces could be cut by a parallel 24 percent. Finally, four of the six Army reserve infantry and light infantry divisions and one-third of the Marine reserve division could also be cut; these cuts are proportioned to match the proposed two-thirds cut in active Army light divisions and the one-third cut in active Marine ground units.

Had these cuts been imposed on the FY 1990 defense budget it would have dropped by 17 percent ($51.5 billion), to a total of $248.5 billion. Instead, however, the Bush administration cut American light forces by only one Army division during FY 1991, and has proposed additional cuts that will probably total one additional light army division, two light army reserve divisions, and one aircraft carrier by FY 1995. These cuts would produce a savings of $17.6 billion from FY 1990 spending levels if parallel cuts are made in supporting forces—a significant drop, but far less than the $51.5 billion cut that reductions to a gulf deployment standard would allow. American light forces would still total seven active light ground divisions (four army and three Marine) and fourteen aircraft carriers, some three light ground divisions and six aircraft carriers more than a gulf deployment standard suggests.[73] Thus the Bush budget for light forces substantially exceeds the likely demands of the Third World contingencies that these forces are designed to address.

Fewer dollars, but many lives, could be saved by ending the Bush administration's proxy wars in Cambodia, Afghanistan, and El Salvador, and securing the peace in Angola. The administration's aid to its four main proxies totals only $540 to $600 million per year.[74] But this small expenditure is causing vast human suffering. If the Bush administration values human rights, it should stop these cruel wars as quickly as possible. Toward this goal, it should serve notice that its subsidies are ending, and should press its clients to accept the peace terms that each has been offered. If it did so, the fighting could soon be ended.

Civilians to
Soldiers

Chapter 8

Military Personnel in a Changing World

David Grissmer
Bernard D. Rostker

A Changing World

The year 1990 saw the most dramatic changes since World War II in the basic tenets of U.S. military posture. What initially appeared as a modest series of strategic and conventional arms control agreements in Europe quickly turned into the disintegration of the Warsaw Pact. In short order the world saw the reunification of Germany, the conclusion of a Conventional Armed Forces in Europe (CFE) Treaty, and democratic elections in countries that only a few years before provided troops to the Warsaw Pact. While CFE was nominally a negotiation between the North Atlantic Treaty Organization (NATO) and representatives of the Warsaw Pact, in reality the agreement was not between two coherent multinational military alliances, but a blueprint for the orderly withdrawal of the Soviet Union from Eastern Europe and the downsizing of American forces in Western Europe—forces intended in the post–cold war era as much to reassure Europe about the future of a united Germany as to guard against any military aggression by the Soviet Union. Even the unthinkable is now openly discussed: the dissolution of the Soviet Union itself, the privatization of the Russian economy, and joint Soviet and American action to enforce a new post–cold war world order under the banner of the United Nations.[1]

The authors wish to thank Richard Eisenman, Jennifer Kawata, and William Taylor for their help and support in preparing the drawdown analysis that appears in this chapter. The views expressed in this chapter do not necessarily reflect the opinions or policies of the sponsors of RAND research.

From the fall of the Berlin Wall to the invasion of Kuwait the assumptions that govern the planning of military forces have changed almost monthly. Such a turbulent environment is particularly difficult for personnel planners. This chapter thus focuses on general trends, the implications of these trends, and the options available to manage personnel change, and not on the specifics of the new military programs of the individual services. Topics to be considered are the changing role and posture of American military forces, the implications of these changes for the design of U.S. forces, the options that personnel planners have in managing a drawdown, and the implications of a drawdown for the total force, both active and reserve components.

The Changing Role and Posture of American Forces

Given the rapidly changing situation in Europe, American military planners have started to come to terms with the broad definition of a post–cold war Europe and its implications for the future posture of American forces. While the Congress complained that the fiscal year (FY) 1991 budget, submitted in January 1990, was "out of date," the definition of the future U.S. military posture was proceeding within the Department of Defense.[2] In the Congress a consensus was developing concerning the direction of change, the assignment of appropriate roles and missions, and spending priorities. Under pressure to reduce the budget deficit the Congress put the services on notice that substantial reductions would likely be voted in their military end strength and personnel budgets for the fiscal years starting October 1, 1990.[3] The invasion of Kuwait and the subsequent deployment of American and allied forces changed the specifics of the anticipated congressional action, but if anything Operation Desert Shield reinforced the direction of change contemplated by defense planners inside and outside the Pentagon.[4]

President Bush signaled the need for a new military posture in January 1990 when he proposed that the nation "transition to a restructured military, [following] a new strategy that is more flexible, more geared to contingencies outside of Europe, while continuing to meet our inescapable responsibilities to NATO and to maintain the global balance."[5] For military planners, one of the major components of such a restructuring is the division of responsibilities between the active and reserve components.[6] The chairman of the Senate Armed Services Committee has argued for "much greater reliance on reinforcement with deployable U.S. combat forces to support our allies. More of our forces . . . in the reserves specifically structured for a reinforcement mission [and] employing a concept of flexible readiness—high readiness for certain forces and adjustable readiness for others."[7] Accordingly, the Senate Armed Services Committee in its report on the FY 1991 authorization froze Selected Reserve end strengths awaiting "the recommendations on the force structure and force mix of the military services in the Total Force study."[8] The House Armed Services Committee in its authorization report proposed increasing Selected Reserve end strength by almost 25,000 over that requested by the president for FY 1991.[9] The House Appropriations Committee went further, increasing Selected Reserve end strength by 54,000 over that contained in the budget request.[10]

If the Congress sees the need to increase reserve forces as active forces are reduced, the administration does not necessarily share this view. Secretary of Defense Richard Cheney set the stage by noting that "under the world as it is developing in the 1990s, [we can] assume that we would have significant time, sufficient [warning] time, before a global conflict to reconstitute forces."[11] President Bush, in a speech in August 1990, argued that, "In our restructured forces, reserves will be important, but in new ways. The need to be prepared for a massive, short-term mobilization has diminished. We can now adjust the size, structure, and readiness of our reserve forces. . . . What we need are not merely reductions—but restructuring."[12] Following this theme, the Total Force Policy Study Group noted that "Some of these [active forces] could be transferred to the reserves, manned at significantly reduced levels, or organized into cadre units. Some could be taken out of the force structure entirely as part of our reconstitution strategy."[13]

The assignment of roles and missions to the active and reserve components is the critical first step in defining a new personnel force structure. The range of possible outcomes seems to be very large. In February 1990 before Operation Desert Shield, the Congressional Budget Office (CBO) suggested a number of force reduction options as depicted in table 8–1, that ranged from as little as 100,000 to almost 600,000; a range equal to 23 percent of active duty end

Table 8–1. Congressional Budget Office "Long-Run" Force Reduction Options (Total Military End Strength in Thousands)

Category	1990 End Strength	Required Cuts	Possible Adminis- tration Cuts	Larger Cuts with Cadre	Larger Cuts, More Reserves	Large Cuts
Active Duty Personnel						
Army	744	−77	−132	−199	−240	−272
Air Force	545	−22	−61	−101	−115	−139
Navy	591	−9	−57	−82	−99	−127
Marine Corps	197	0	0	−20	−36	−56
Total	2,076	−107	−251	−401	−491	−594
Selected Reserves						
Army	756	0	−130	0	+75	−149
Air Force	201	0	0	0	+25	−19
Navy	153	0	0	0	+11	0
Marine Corps	44	0	0	0	+14	0
Total	1,155	0	−130	0	+125	−169

Source: Congressional Budget Office, *Meeting New National Security Needs: Options for U.S. Forces in the 1990s*. February 1990, p. 8.

strength. The CBO saw all these force options as providing "adequate numbers of active duty military personnel to handle small military contingencies, such as the recent action in Panama, and adequate active and reserve forces to permit mobilization for a future, large war."[14] The CBO's range of options for the Selected Reserves was even more dramatic, suggesting that, depending upon the particular scheme used to man the reserves, the changing world situation could result in an increase of 125,000 or reductions of almost 170,000, a range of almost 300,000 or 25 percent of the force.

Another indicator of the size and timing of the defense drawdown was provided by the Senate and House Armed Services Committees. Before Operation Desert Shield the Senate Armed Services Committee proposed total active duty end strength levels for each of the military services at the end of fiscal year 1991 and 1995 as presented in table 8–2.

Table 8–2. Senate Armed Services Committee Total Active Duty End Strength Recommendations

	FY 1991 Budget Request	FY 1991 Recommendation	FY 1995 Recommendation
Army	727,500	704,170	510,000
Navy	584,800	568,500	500,000
Marine Corps	196,500	193,735	177,000
Air Force	530,000	510,000	415,000
Total	2,038,800	1,976,405	1,692,000

Source: Committee on the Armed Services, *National Defense Authorization Act for Fiscal Year 1991: Report 101-384.*

Table 8–3. House of Representatives Total Active Duty End Strength Recommendations, by Committee

	FY 1991 Budget Request	FY 1991 Authorizations Committee Recommendation (Pre-Desert Shield)	FY 1991 Appropriations Committee Recommendation (Post Desert Shield)
Army	727,500	675,669	708,769
Navy	584,800	570,501	571,801
Marine Corps	196,500	192,235	196,235
Air Force	530,000	508,500	522,500
Total	2,038,800	1,946,905	1,999,305

Source: *House Report 101-822* and *Report 101-665.*

Before Operation Desert Shield the House Armed Services Committee proposed even deeper reductions, which are presented in table 8–3. The House Appropriations Committee reduced the FY 1991 cuts after the start of Operation Desert Shield as a "realistic compromise of a much longer term drawdown."[15]

While Operation Desert Shield reduced the immediate impact of the drawdown during FY 1991, the administration and the Congress clearly expect that a major reduction and restructuring will take place. The way the Defense Department chooses to reduce its end strength will have a major impact on the cost and readiness of U.S. active and reserve forces in the future.

Strategies for Managing Active Duty Force Reductions

If there is general agreement that changes in the international situation and the budget problems of the early 1990s require a sizable reduction in military forces, there is considerable disagreement on how and where to make the cuts, and much unhappiness about the possibility that such cuts will be a hardship on the people involuntarily separated to meet reduced force levels. Different approaches to reducing force levels can be seen in the "guidance" the Department of Defense received from the two Armed Services Committees of the Congress. The Senate Armed Services Committee gave specific guidance on where the cuts should be made, e.g. "prudently adjusting the intake of new recruits, selectively retiring senior personnel, and selectively releasing first term personnel before completion of their first term of service."[16] The House Armed Services Committee took a less prescriptive stance and emphasized that "the force drawdown [be] accomplished in a balanced and equitable fashion that will preserve the integrity of the military, maintain adequate force readiness, and cushion the blow for adversely affecting career personnel."[17]

History provides little guidance on how to manage a substantial drawdown. Although even the large cuts suggested by the House Armed Services Committee are smaller in size and slower in pace than those taken at the end of World War II, the Korean conflict, or the war in Vietnam, this drawdown is unprecedented because it will affect those who entered the military as volunteers rather than conscripts. At the end of 1990 the United States had the largest number of career enlisted personnel—men and women in their second and subsequent tours—in its history. Moreover, as volunteers, these troops were led to believe that if they performed in a satisfactory manner they would be allowed to complete a normal career and retire with an immediate pension. Some have argued that forcing these people out of the service is a breach of an implied contract. The Army puts the problem this way:

> The United States is not demobilizing a conscript Army after a major conflict, as it often did in the past. It is reshaping a professional, volunteer force. Precipitous acceleration or major modification of the Army's (drawdown) plan would inflict significant hardship on soldiers, civilians, and their families.[18]

Unfortunately, the Army's planned reductions in end strength by about 35,000 active duty soldiers per year through the mid-1990s are substantially less than those imposed by either the Senate or House Armed Services Committee. If the Congress ultimately prevails, the Army and the other services will have to choose between their desire to "retain the correct skills and grades and maintain upward mobility through promotions and selection for schooling and command" and protecting career personnel resulting in a more costly and "out-of-balance" force structure.[19]

The Need to Maintain a Balanced Force

While the desire to protect service men and women promised a full career is laudable, the resulting policy of reducing accessions below that needed to sustain the force over time has very undesirable consequences for the future personnel proficiency and readiness of the U.S. military services. Figure 8–1 shows an ideal military personnel profile with the characteristic shape of an "in-at-the-bottom, up-through-the-ranks" military personnel system.[20] This personnel year-of-service profile is ideal in at least two ways. First, at any time it is consistent with the proper workings of the promotion system, the internal organization of military units, the desired ratio of junior to senior personnel, and the competitiveness of the military pay system. It also minimizes total cost of military personnel. The Air Force notes that an ideal force structure "provides a guideline for personnel policies and management actions, [and] represents a force configuration that

Figure 8–1. Ideal Enlisted Personnel Year-of-Service Distribution

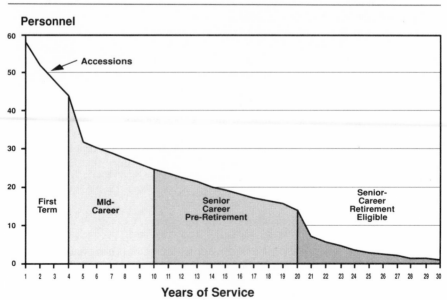

would satisfy all mission requirements, achieve the . . . career progression goals, and be attainable at the least cost."[21]

In addition to providing the right mix of personnel with varying levels of experience, this general force profile will reproduce itself over time, and thus the age and experience of such a force called to war in ten years will be substantially the same as one called to war tomorrow. The Marine Corps, projected to be cut the least during the drawdown, has and will likely continue to have a force profile very close to the ideal. Figure 8–2 shows how the personnel profile of the Marine Corps is likely to change during the 1990s. In each year the Marines will be able to field a balanced force.

The Air Force, conversely, has potentially the most unbalanced personnel profile. That service, when faced with cuts in the late 1980s, sharply curtailed accessions, resulting in a force profile in FY 1990 that was certainly not ideal. Again in 1990, Air Force officials proposed to take most of the pending force reductions through cuts in the number of new recruits accepted in each of the following five years; even if that number falls below that necessary to sustain

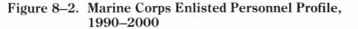

Figure 8–2. Marine Corps Enlisted Personnel Profile, 1990–2000

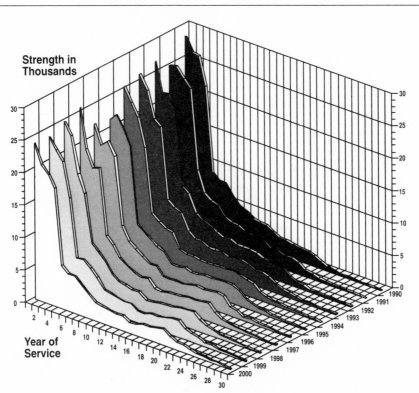

their new end strength. Such a policy, reflected in figure 8–3, will result in an trough moving forward during the decade of the 1990s. Under such a profile, a service would simply trade a short term difficulty for a more serious long term problem. As the CBO notes in such a system:

> Career personnel would have little opportunity for advancement in such a top-heavy force. Indeed, some senior personnel might find themselves performing more and more of the work usually delegated to junior personnel even as the experience levels, and perhaps the pay grade, of these senior personnel advance. Morale almost certainly would suffer and the higher pay following promotion might offer little consolation. [22]

If the Air Force follows a policy of drastically reducing accessions, it will end the 1990s with a far more costly and senior enlisted force structure than once thought desirable. It will even have more senior careerists than first term or mid-career personnel. As these people retire in the early years of next century, the Air Force will suffer an immediate and prolonged loss of experienced personnel. [23] In order to avoid a sharp reduction in total strength at that time, the service will have to increase substantially the number of new people it recruits, increasing the experience imbalance in its personnel structure. Such cycles of boom and bust play havoc with normal career progression and adversely impact job performance and readiness. The research reported in this chapter suggests that a more desir-

Figure 8–3. Air Force Enlisted Personnel Profile, 1990–2001

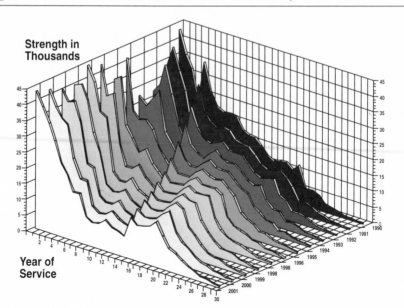

able policy would dampen the cycles by reducing personnel in a more balanced manner.

Force Reduction Options

In general, a military service should maintain accessions at a level close to that required to sustain the force over time, and spread the needed cuts along the entire year-of-service range. The Defense Office Personnel Management Act of 1980 (DOPMA) established for officers an "up-or-out" promotion system and special mechanisms "to assure a sufficient promotion opportunity so as not to adversely affect officer retention . . . [and] mechanisms for increasing the force attrition when such is necessitated by force reductions."[24] The services could apply the same logic and use their enlisted promotion system to identify personnel that would be separated by reducing "high year of tenure" rules. In addition, selective retention boards could be established to review the records of enlisted personnel to determine, independent of the promotion system, who will be asked to leave.

In order to determine the impact that such policies would have on the future personnel profiles of the services, a modified RAND-developed force projection model is used to simulate a number of policy options.[25] The analytic structure of the model is represented in figure 8–4. The analysis starts with the current inventory and projected losses based upon changes in the policy scenario and historical year-of-service continuation rates. This allows estimation of normal losses which, together with end-strength goals and policy rules for managing the drawdown, results in year-by-year projection of involuntary losses, non–prior service

---

**Figure 8–4. Analytic Framework for Drawdown
            Inventory Projection**

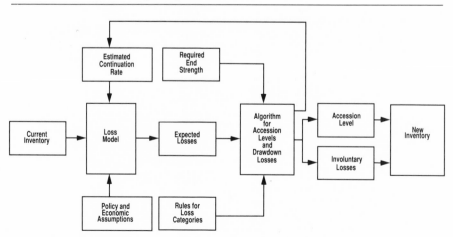

accessions, and the resulting new personnel inventory. The particular rules used to manage the drawdown reduced personnel in those year-of-service groups where there were more people than desirable when compared with their long-term experience before the current drawdown started. The policy options included in the analysis are:

- Cut accessions only. The services would allow the number of accessions to drop to whatever number was necessary to meet immediate end strength goals, thereby avoiding involuntary separations.

- Balance force reductions. The services would maintain accessions close to the level needed to sustain the force over time, with personnel reductions taken from either first term personnel (2–4 years of service), first term and junior career personnel (2–10 years of service), or first term, junior, and senior career personnel (2–15 years of service.)

These studies were based on the assumed end strength reductions represented in table 8–4.

The analysis, as illustrated in figure 8–5, demonstrates that if the services follow a policy of protecting career personnel and taking the required cuts by reducing new accessions, there will be a sharp increase in the seniority of the force.[26]

The force-balancing options simulated in the model and illustrated in figure 8–6 would, by requiring the services to maintain new accessions at a level that would sustain the force over time, reduce the uncontrolled growth in the number of career personnel on active duty.

Table 8–4. Force Reductions Scenario, Authorizations Committee Conference Report

	Percent Reductions from FY 90		Total End Strength	
Service	FY 91	FY 94	FY 90	FY 94
Army	5.6	30.0	702,170	520,000
Air Force	6.4	24.0	510,000	415,000
Navy	3.5	15.0	570,000	501,000
Marine Corps	1.5	10.0	193,735	177,000
Total	4.8	22.0	1,975,905	1,613,000

Figure 8–5. Percent of Force with Ten or More Years of
Service: Accessions-Only Policy

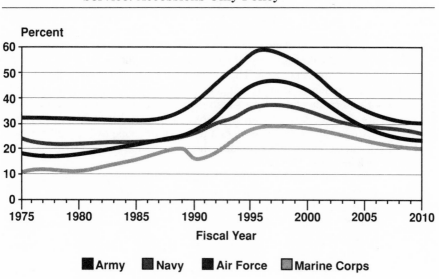

Figure 8–6. Percent of Force with Ten or More Years of
Service: Cuts in YOS 2-14

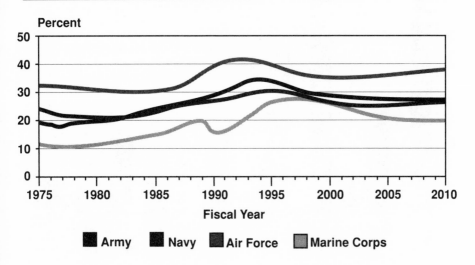

The benefit of such action can be seen by comparing the various options in terms of how the resulting personnel profile differs from the ideal force structure. This is shown in figure 8–7 as the percent of the force in "overage years-of-service" groups. In each case, if the services extend reductions to the entire force, they can substantially reduce the percent of the force that is maldistributed and thus achieve a more balanced and ready force.[27]

Another advantage of a policy of balanced force reductions is that additional budgetary savings are generated. The minimum savings associated with the suggested force reductions are approximately $45 billion over seven years. Figure 8–8 shows the incremental dollars saved during that period from a program of balanced cuts when compared with an accessions-only policy. Since military pay increases sharply with years of service, a policy of reducing even small numbers of career personnel, even after providing them severance pay as provided by the Congress, will increase total savings.

The negative side of taking across-the-board force cuts is the personal costs faced by people forced to leave active service before they would have normally retired. Figure 8–9 shows both voluntary and involuntary reductions for each service during the period FY 1991–1997, given the options discussed above. An

Figure 8–7. Deviations from Ideal Force Structure Under Force-Shaping Options, FY 1991–1995

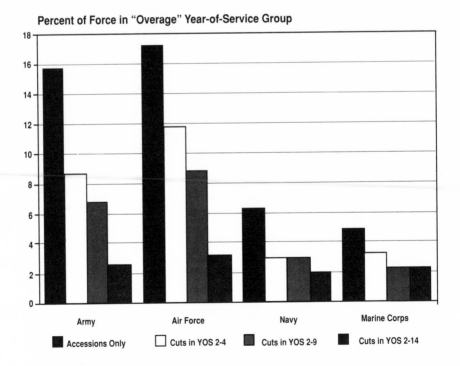

Percent of Force in "Overage" Year-of-Service Group

Army   Air Force   Navy   Marine Corps

■ Accessions Only   ☐ Cuts in YOS 2-4   ■ Cuts in YOS 2-9   ■ Cuts in YOS 2-14

average of approximately 50,000 involuntary separations would be required to implement the force reduction options each year. The largest percentage increase in separations would be in the Air Force, although the largest number of involuntary separations would take place in the Army. In all cases, however, extending cuts into the mid-career force would actually require fewer overall cuts during the drawdown period.[28]

Managing Force Reductions

In order to maintain the long-term viability of their force, the services need to pare their career force. In order to properly manage the officer corps the DOPMA foresaw the possible need for selective continuation boards to choose which officers would be allowed to stay on active duty until retirement, and to compensate those officers "selected out" with severance pay.[29] While severance pay was extended to the enlisted force in October 1990, a general system of managing the enlisted force does not exist in law. Moreover, the severance pay plan may prove to be inadequate given the great disparity that exists between it and the value of the military retirement that an individual would be forced to forfeit, e.g., service members are not vested in their retirement systems and would not receive any retirement income until they retire with at least twenty years of service.[30] This value gap is shown in figure 8–10 and partially explains why the services so strongly oppose the involuntary separation of career personnel before retirement

**Figure 8–8.   Additional Personnel Cost Savings Under Force-
Shaping Options, FY 1991–1997**

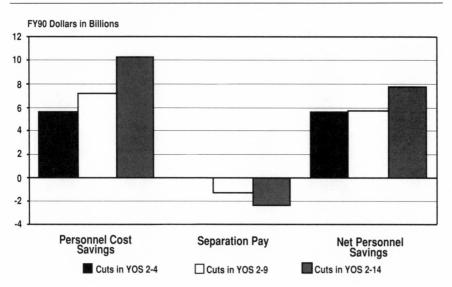

FY90 Dollars in Billions

Personnel Cost Savings   Separation Pay   Net Personnel Savings

■ Cuts in YOS 2-4   ☐ Cuts in YOS 2-9   ■ Cuts in YOS 2-14

eligibility is reached, but why they are willing to force career personnel out after they are eligible to retire, even though this is as much as ten years before they must leave the service. Accordingly, the notion of "keeping faith with career personnel" need not mean that all career personnel must remain on active duty until they are eligible to retire. The United States can "keep faith" if those asked to leave receive vesting rights to their military pensions. Along these lines, it should be noted that the additional savings associated with across-the-board force reductions could be used to pay the costs of initiating early vesting during this drawdown period; that is, vesting could be a temporary policy implemented during the current drawdown, and not a permanent change to the military retirement system.

Impact of the Active Force Drawdown on the Reserve Components

Through the early 1990s, attention has focused on the drawdown of active duty personnel. What has not been generally recognized is that cuts in the active-duty force will adversely impact the ability of the Selected Reserves to maintain their

Figure 8–9. Projected Cumulative Separations Under Force-Shaping Options, FY 1991–1997

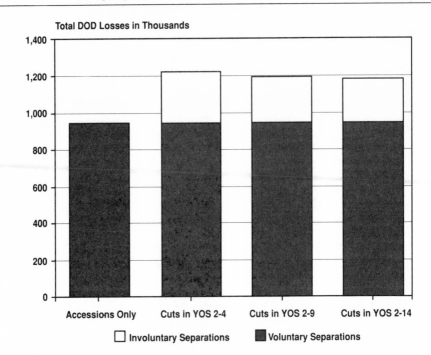

level of experienced personnel and readiness. The relationship between the active forces and the selected reserve forces is presented in figure 8–11.

The flow of personnel from the active forces to the reserve forces constitutes a most critical source of trained and experienced manpower. In fact, as seen in figure 8–12, personnel with prior military service constitute a majority of people who joined the Selected Reserves in FY 1989. Approximately two-thirds of all new enlisted personnel joining the Selected Reserves each year have served for an extended period of time on active duty. The remaining third are recruited directly from civilian life and join units after receiving basic and entry-level technical training. As a result, prior service personnel contribute to the productivity of reserve units to a greater extent than their numbers would indicate. Any significant reduction in the number of prior service people to join the Selected Reserves would have a very negative impact on the capabilities of reserve units and their readiness.

The active and reserve personnel projection models were linked together in order to determine the effects on the reserve forces from the reduction of active forces.[31] First, the expected losses from the active forces under the various force-shaping scenarios were calculated and presented in figure 8–13. Given the size of the drawdown, even if one of the balanced force reduction options is followed,

Figure 8–10. Comparative Annuity Value of Enlisted Retirement Contributions and Separation Pay

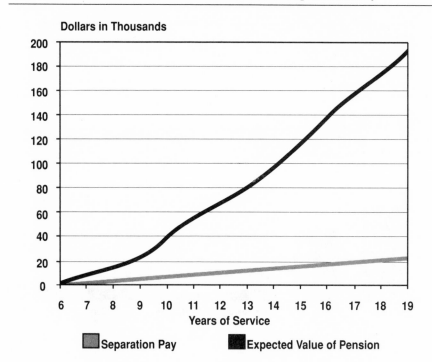

Figure 8–11. A Conceptual Model of Military Personnel Flows

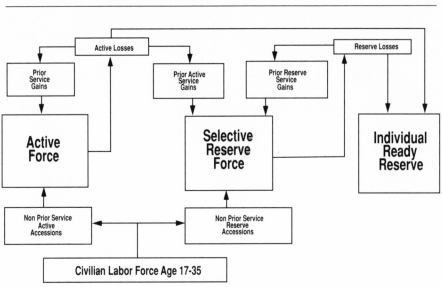

Figure 8–12. Prior and Non-Prior Service Accessions, FY 1989

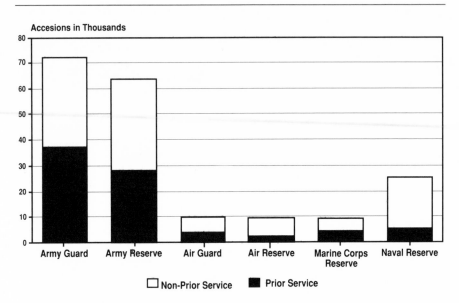

the number of people to leave active service will significantly decline in the years
ahead. Depending upon the way the services reduce their end strength, there
could be a temporary increase in the prior service pool through 1995. However,
that increase will be short lived and regardless of the drawdown option chosen,
the smaller active duty force proposed will generate a much smaller pool of prior
service personnel from which the reserve components can draw experienced personnel in the future.

In the face of the declining pool of prospective prior service Selected Reservists, the services have three options: (1) maintain manning levels by recruiting more people without prior military service, (2) try to attract and retain a larger
proportion of the shrinking pool of prior service personnel eligible to join the
reserves, or (3) reduce reserve end strength. Reducing the prior service/non–
prior service mix will, in the opinion of many, have highly undesirable effects on
the capability and readiness of reserve units. Increasing the "take" from the prior
service pool may be possible for some reserve components, with some additional
incentives.[32] However, while all the services have been successful in recruiting
an increasing proportion of the prior service pool during the last decade, the Army
already is having trouble meeting their prior service goals. Further increases in

**Figure 8–13. Active Duty Losses Under Force-Shaping
             Policy Options**

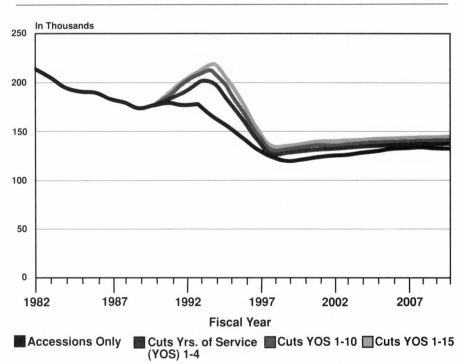

In Thousands

Fiscal Year

■ Accessions Only   ■ Cuts Yrs. of Service   ■ Cuts YOS 1-10   ☐ Cuts YOS 1-15
                     (YOS) 1-4

the flow of prior service personnel into the reserve components may require a mandatory reserve force obligation as a condition of enlistment in an active component.[33]

The last option is to reduce reserve end strength. As noted earlier, the Congress favors increasing the size of the Selected Reserves as part of a new force posture. The Bush administration is considering using the Selected Reserves in "new and different ways" resulting in reduced reserve force levels. Figure 8–14 shows that regardless of what the force planners in Congress and the Defense Department want, the predicted numbers of personnel leaving active duty that are eligible to join the reserves may well place a brake on the overall size of the reserves. If the services want to maintain the proportion of the reserve forces with prior military service, they may have to reduce Selected Reserve end strength.

Conclusion

History provides little guidance for managing the post–cold war U.S. military drawdown. Although projected reductions are much smaller in size and slower in

Figure 8–14. Selected Reserve End Strength with Constant Prior Service/Non-Prior Service Mix as a Percent of FY 1989 End Strength

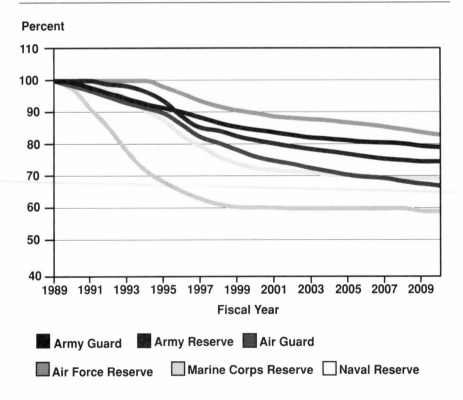

Percent

Fiscal Year

■ Army Guard   ■ Army Reserve   ■ Air Guard

■ Air Force Reserve   □ Marine Corps Reserve   □ Naval Reserve

pace than those at the termination of earlier conflicts (World War II, Korea, and Vietnam), the post–cold war force drawdown is unprecedented because it occurs in peacetime rather than at the end of a conflict, and because it affects a volunteer, rather than a conscript, armed force. Members of the military joined as volunteers with the expectation that good performance would allow a normal career and retirement. If the military services are to maintain a balanced personnel force structure in the years ahead, however, reducing force size will mean involuntary separations of career personnel. While the alternative of cutting junior personnel or reducing accessions may seem politically attractive in the early 1990s, it will increase costs and cause reduced readiness in the future as senior personnel retire without adequate numbers of mid-term personnel to replace them.

If the Congress allows a broader range of cuts in order to maintain a balanced force, it should also assure that there is equity in the separation package. While the cap on separation pay was eliminated and extended to enlisted personnel, the large disparity between severance pay and the value of the foregone pension substantially explains the strong preference of the services to continue senior personnel until they are eligible to retire. Some form of limited and special drawdown retirement vesting would go a long way towards reducing overall costs and equitably treating service personnel forced to leave before retirement.

Finally, any decision concerning the future roles and missions assigned to the Selected Reserves must take account of the delicate balance between the active and reserve forces. In the area of personnel, many would argue that the quality and readiness of the Selected Reserves units is determined by the trained personnel they recruit that have prior service in the active forces. The projected flow of these personnel from smaller active forces will not be sufficient to sustain the experience mix of personnel in the Selected Reserves. Options to increase the incentives for former active duty personnel to join reserve units are likely to result in only limited success. In fact, it is possible that the flow of personnel from the active force to the reserve forces will place a brake on the overall future size of the Selected Reserves.

Senators Review
Desert Shield

Chapter 9

Congress and Defense Decision Making

John Kasich

Nineteen-ninety was a watershed year in Congress' role in defense decision making. The process changed in ways far more fundamental than at previous turning points, such as 1980, when a strong congressional mood for a defense buildup emerged, and 1985, when Congress began the process of ratcheting down the Reagan administration's defense program. Previous episodes were principally characterized by debates over the level of resource inputs; 1990 saw the beginning of a basic reappraisal of U.S. national security strategy.

Clearly, the driving factor in this fundamental shift in congressional attitudes toward national defense was the rapid deterioration of the Warsaw Pact and the reunification of Germany. Those changes were so momentous that even the massive deployment of U.S. forces to Saudi Arabia—the most rapid extended buildup of troop strength overseas since World War II—did not affect the overall downward trend in the size of the U.S. defense establishment. Even in the midst of moving hundreds of thousands of soldiers halfway around the world, for example, the Department of Defense (DOD) announced plans to significantly reduce its logistical infrastructure within the continental United States. This was just one of the ironic counterpoints of the new world order.

As far as congressional decision making is concerned, the first great fallout from the tumultuous changes in the Soviet Union was the breakdown of the consensus on strategic modernization. The consensus was, of course, inherently fragile—as the bruising debates on the MX missile in the early 1980s made clear—and depended on the perception of the Soviet Union as an aggressive adversary of the United States. The fates of the B-2 stealth bomber, rail garrison MX, and the small intercontinental ballistic missile (SICBM) are persuasive tes-

timony to the force of Soviet Foreign Ministry spokesman Georgiy Arbatov's pre-
diction that momentous things would occur when the Soviet Union deprived the
United States of an enemy.

The general feeling of a diminished Soviet threat combined with chronic budgetary problems caused many Republican as well as Democratic members of Congress to advocate a strategic modernization "pause." This argument was
strengthened by the belief that modernization was essentially completed by the
late 1980s. In truth, all three legs of the nuclear triad received substantial shoring
up during the Reagan administration.

During the 1980s, the land-based leg of the triad obtained 500 highly-accurate
MX warheads, as well as accuracy and retargeting improvements to the Minuteman IIIs. A revolution at sea occurred with the deployment of the deep-diving,
silent Trident II submarine equipped with D-5 ballistic missiles. This weapon
system allowed an unprecedented combination of survivability and accuracy. The
air-breathing leg of the triad was augmented by 100 B-1B bombers, while the
venerable B-52 received extensive upgrades, including the capability to carry the
air-launched cruise missile (ALCM-B) and the second-generation advanced cruise
missile (ACM). Finally, strategic command and control communications received
substantial upgrades, including the introduction of systems such as the ground
wave emergency network (GWEN).

In view of the extensive strategic modernization already completed, further
strategic programs met with unprecedented resistance by the Congress. The
most striking example of this was the B-2. While rail garrison and SICBM had
been somewhat controversial from their very inception, the B-2 had led a
charmed existence since its birth in the 1980 presidential campaign as the advanced technology bomber. The heavy veil of secrecy surrounding it not only
inhibited informed debate about its cost and mission, but the glamorous aura of
stealth technology gave rise to perhaps unwarranted expectations about its actual
capabilities.

This aura began to evaporate when portions of the B-2 program were declassified at the end of 1988. In particular, the rising cost of the bomber and
schedule delays caused even strongly pro-defense members of Congress to swal-
low hard at the most expensive weapon system in history. In 1989, the first year
the B-2 was a declassified line item in the budget, there were 145 votes on the
House floor to terminate B-2 production. With the fall of the Berlin wall and the
accelerating decay of the Warsaw Pact, support for the B-2 declined even further.
The House Armed Services Committee, whose membership is generally more
conservative than that of the House as a whole, voted 34 to 20 to end further
production of the B-2. Proponents of the B-2 declined even to offer an amendment
to restore production during floor debate on the defense bill, fearing a strongly
negative vote. The administration program for the bomber narrowly survived in
the Senate. While the House-Senate Conference on the Defense Authorization
Act did not make a clear-cut decision on the B-2, the program was clearly on the
ropes.

The B-2 controversy was also the catalyst for growing congressional interest
in the details of nuclear warfighting strategy. In the MX debate, most of the
controversy was engendered by arguments and counterarguments about the missile's vulnerability and how that would affect crisis stability. Once the B-2 became

controversial because of its high cost, the Air Force placed unprecedented emphasis on U.S. targeting requirements against the Soviet Union as justification for the program. The Single Integrated Operational Plan (SIOP) is based on these targeting requirements and the SIOP, in turn, helps establish the requirements for the design of strategic weapon systems. The Air Force's insistence on SIOP requirements as a justification for the B-2 caused many members of Congress to question the fundamental assumptions—such as damage expectancy—on which the SIOP is based.

The collapse of the Warsaw Pact added more fuel to the controversy: while the details of SIOP targeting remain highly secret, DOD witnesses on several occasions openly described SIOP policy in general terms. Given the need to neutralize enemy nuclear and conventional forces, war-supporting industries, and transportation infrastructure, execution of the SIOP could entail extensive nuclear strikes against such targets in Eastern Europe in the event of general war with the Soviet Union. The political revolutions in Eastern Europe during 1989 and 1990 however, began to raise doubts about U.S. nuclear policy. Congress' perception of this changing strategic picture, combined with the general improvement in U.S.-Soviet relations and the presumably reduced targeting requirements that would obtain under the START Treaty, led many to question both the need for an $800 million bomber and the assumptions of the SIOP that support strategic weapons requirements.

The SIOP requirements for nuclear systems, of course, are simply a subset of the requirements process that drives the procurement of all weapon systems.

By permission of Mike Luckovich and Creators Syndicate

While Congress has begun to debate the former, awareness of the much broader issue of the requirements process for all weapon systems remained only embryonic through 1991. Most congressional controversy over weapon systems, from the ill-fated DIVAD, through the Bradley Fighting Vehicle, to the B-1 bomber focuses narrowly on whether the system "works," i.e., the parts function properly. The embarrassing propensity of complex weapon systems to demonstrate flaws is a heaven-sent opportunity for the press and media-savvy congresspersons to flay the Department of Defense and the defense contractors for their failings, but this phenomenon obscures a more fundamental problem with the way weapon systems are selected.

Given enough time and money, any weapon system can be fixed; the DIVAD can be made more accurate, the Bradley Fighting Vehicle can be given Kevlar armor to protect its occupants, and the B-1's electronic countermeasures can be repaired. But the question then remains whether they are the right systems for the job. Or were the requirements over- or understated in order to buy the kinds of weapon systems the services wanted for parochial reasons? For example, there is unquestionably a need to move an infantry squad around on the battlefield and to give it adequate protection, but is housing a squad in a "fighting" vehicle that looks like a light tank simply placing more requirements on the platform than it can handle at a reasonable cost? In order to shoehorn an infantry squad into an *ersatz* tank, the army was obliged to reduce the standard squad by two men. In other words, the force structure was changed to accommodate a vehicle designed to a possibly overstated requirement.

The point is not to pick on the Bradley, whose actual combat performance has been very good, but to illustrate the importance of defining realistic requirements. When the requirements process is distorted by service parochialism or the desire to force technological development for its own sake, the results may add cost without necessarily meeting a valid mission requirement. The requirement that the F-15 should reach Mach 2.5, for example, cost several hundred million dollars in development funds, although the specification was based on a flawed analysis of the Soviet fighter aircraft threat. While the new generation of Soviet aircraft could fly at over Mach 2, U.S. intelligence analysts neglected the caveat that such performance could only be achieved for short bursts. The Mach 2.5 requirement for the new U.S. air superiority aircraft, however, remained firm. Although the F-15 could reach Mach 2.45, the program manager insisted that the Mach 2.5 requirement be met. The last margin of performance cost hundreds of millions of dollars, even though the plane was unlikely to be flown above Mach 2 in any plausible combat scenario.

Another aspect of the requirements process that finally began to be debated in 1990 was the fact that virtually all U.S. weapon systems were designed to fight in a high-intensity conventional war against the Warsaw Pact in Europe. The U.S. deployment to Saudi Arabia fostered debate about the wisdom of this concentration on a specific threat and a particular geography. Initial shortfalls in sealift, for instance, led Congress to appropriate $900 million for fast sealift ships. There was also widespread congressional concern about the operational suitability of a number of weapon systems in the harsh climates likely to be encountered in Third World contingencies. The rapid deterioration of helicopter rotor blades in the Saudi desert was one instance of the difficulties encountered by high-technology weaponry in the Third World. Contrary to the pronouncements of doomsayers, however, U.S. weapon systems were either sufficiently reliable to meet their mission requirements, or were susceptible to fixes (the rotor blades merely required protective tape). The price, of course, was the initiation of highly intensive and expensive maintenance programs.

The Gulf War may also focus more attention on life-cycle costs of weapon systems. Congress has been as guilty as the services of being caught up in the "glamor" of sophisticated new weapon systems, and neglecting the more mundane issues of reliability and maintainability, which are the main drivers of a system's operation and maintenance (O&M) costs. In the past, Congress essentially accepted at face value the services' claims that follow-on systems, while more expensive to procure than their predecessors, would recoup their investment by virtue of greater reliability and maintainability. Actually, this is rarely the case, and in some instances the operation and maintenance costs of new systems are much higher than those of their predecessors. For instance, the Army advertised the M-1 tank as having lower O&M costs than the M-60 tank it was to replace. In fact, preliminary analyses of Operation Desert Storm indicate that the O&M costs for the M-1 are higher than those of the M-60 by a factor of four.

Any discussion of the congressional role in weapons procurement would be incomplete without some accounting of the growing controversy over special access, or so-called "black" programs. Considerable confusion surrounds this subject; many observers lump together all highly classified intelligence and weapons programs into the category of black programs. This chapter, however, will deal only with DOD, non–intelligence related special access programs. The criteria are outlined in an executive order defining a special access program as "any program imposing 'need to know' or access controls beyond those normally provided for access to confidential, secret, or top secret information."

The 1980s were characterized by a significant expansion in the special access budget. Before that time, the black programs were, according to the open literature on the subject, mainly related to intelligence collection programs, or dealt with concepts in their initial stage of formulation. During the 1980s, however, major weapon systems began to appear in the black budget in larger numbers, and remained "black" until the system was well into low-rate initial production. The most striking example of this was the Lockheed F-117A stealth fighter-bomber. Procurement of sixty units was actually completed before the program was declassified, which led to the curious situation in which the news media reported on flight-test crashes of an aircraft which the Air Force refused to acknowledge even existed.

Obviously, the budgetary share of black programs grew as well. The Congressional Research Service cites nonofficial analyses that estimate that the black budget grew from approximately $9.5 billion in fiscal year (FY) 1981 to a peak of from $24 billion to $35 billion in FY 1989 (if the latter figure is even remotely near the real budget, it means that the special access budget is larger than the annual budgets of most cabinet departments). It is probable that the budget share of black programs began to decline somewhat since the B-2, the most expensive special access program, began to be declassified in FY 1989.

The major argument for black programs is that by denying information about a weapon system in research and development (R&D) to a potential enemy, the enemy is denied the ability to develop countermeasures to the system in a timely manner. Given the protracted development process of modern weapons, denying technical information to an adversary could permit a several year grace period before effective counters to new systems could be fielded.

The secondary, "good government" argument in favor of special access programs is that in bypassing lengthy bureaucratic review, systems can be fielded more cheaply and more quickly than otherwise. Proponents cite the success of the SR-71 reconnaissance plane as an example of how special access programs can cut through red tape.

The counterargument to these assertions is that there is no reason to forego legitimate congressional oversight of cost and schedule information, since it is the taxpayers' money that is being spent. As a practical matter, while the special access world has had successes, the B-2 is a glaring example of how horrendous overruns can accumulate in the absence of proper oversight. The services then use the "sunk cost" argument once the program is out of the black in order to try to prevent the system's cancellation, even if it means throwing good money after bad. For instance, the B-2 has nearly doubled in price, but proponents try to strongarm congressional assent by saying that so much money has been spent on the B-2 that it would be a shame to waste the investment.

Certainly, the Armed Services and Appropriations Committees, which had access to special access data since the inception of the program, should have done a better job of oversight. On the other hand, many members have felt that security restrictions surrounding special access programs hampered their ability to conduct an informed debate. The problem has been compounded by the services' evident desire to rush highly-classified programs into production without public scrutiny.

The Navy's A-12 attack plane is another example of the failure of special access programs to achieve their objectives. Despite the Navy's assurances to Secretary of Defense Cheney in early 1990 that the program was in "great shape," the secretary canceled the program in January 1991. The Navy apparently forgot to mention to Mr. Cheney that the plane was two years behind schedule and $2 billion over cost. The A-12 debacle, the direct result of the withholding of information based on the highly classified status of the airplane, has thrown the Navy's aircraft modernization program into total disarray.

There is increasing congressional impatience with the management of special access programs. The FY 1991 Defense Appropriations Act included language that would provide specific congressional control over special access programs. Heretofore, DOD officials enjoyed considerable discretion over the management of such programs; the classified annexes of previous authorization and appropriation bills dealing with such programs were considered report language that did not have the force of statute, since they could not be made public. The administration, however, announced that President Bush would regard the new provision on special access programs as advisory rather than mandatory on the grounds that there could be no classified public law. As of this writing in early 1991, the status of the provision was at an impasse, with constant jawboning between the executive branch and Congress. Ultimately, the issue may have to be resolved in federal court. Whatever the outcome, the controversy over special access programs can be expected to continue; the House Armed Services Committee tentatively planned to hold hearings on special access reform in 1991.

Congress' authority over weapons procurement—whether special access or otherwise—is unambiguously bestowed upon it by its constitutional mandate "to raise an army and navy," as well as its inherent power of the purse. But to what extent does the authority to buy weapons entail the power to make the strategy that governs their employment? Logically, the two are inseparable. The requirement for a given piece of hardware necessitates a knowledge of the threat and some notion of a strategy for using the forces one is constitutionally charged with equipping. Congress' budding interest in the SIOP indicates a dawning recognition of the importance of overall strategy, a beginning of a break from a myopic concentration on hardware to the exclusion of operational concerns. By early 1991, however, one was obliged to admit that congressional interest in military strategy per se, while growing, remained embryonic. The House and Senate Armed Services Committee chairmen have attempted to jump-start this issue by holding hearings on strategy, but their effect has been minor and fleeting.

Actually, Congress' greatest long-term contribution to a coherent national military strategy was not directly connected to strategy per se, but was instead a bureaucratic reform. The 1986 Defense Reorganization Act, initially resisted by the Pentagon with some rancor, has finally been seen as the most significant change in the military command structure and in civil-military relations in decades. The most important changes embodied in that law are (1) that the president should receive undiluted military advice, and (2) that the position of field commanders should be strengthened. These changes permitted a more rational formulation and implementation of strategy than was previously possible. Traditionally, logrolling and compromises between the services could definitely hamstring the rational employment of military forces in a conflict, as the Desert One fiasco and the Grenada mission made evident. By contrast, the smooth meshing of services in Saudi Arabia was, as the various services themselves attest, a result of the Defense Reorganization Act.

On the debit side of the ledger, one of the perennial charges made against Congress in its role in defense decision making is the alleged congressional penchant for using the defense budget as a "pork barrel" that helps local constituencies at the expense of coherent defense policy. This charge has substance, as exemplified by the strong and continuing legislative resistance to closing military bases in an era of declining defense budgets. In fact, there are some Armed Services Committee members whose principal mission on the committee is the protection of bases, shipyards, or logistics depots in their district, to the neglect of larger policy issues.

There are many more nuances to this issue than might be at first supposed, however, because pork barrel (or to use less judgmental language, "special interest") spending actually involves the interaction of an "iron triangle" consisting of Congress, the military services, and the defense contractors. This concept is somewhat more complex than President Eisenhower's well-known dictum about the two-sided "military-industrial complex," for it is predicated on conflict and compromise between three competing institutions.

One of the most celebrated recent examples of this phenomenon is the V-22 Osprey tilt rotor aircraft. Originally conceived as an assault aircraft for the Marine Corps, it was canceled by Secretary Cheney in 1989 as too expensive. After relentless lobbying by the contracting teams, the Marine Corps, and interested members of Congress (primarily those located in Pennsylvania and Texas, where the Osprey was being built), the V-22 was restored to the budget. In his 1990 budget submission Secretary Cheney again canceled the Osprey, but the iron triangle again prevailed in the budget war of 1990. This is not a comment on whether the V-22 is the most cost-effective system for the mission, but serves only to illustrate that when Congress "adds back" a major weapon system, it usually has help, either overt or covert, from the interested service. In the Osprey's case, the Marine Corps lobbied openly and persistently for the aircraft, raising the issue of the practical (as opposed to theoretical) authority over the military services that is exerted by the Office of the Secretary of Defense. The saga of the V-22 also illustrates the tension inherent in a system of divided government in which no one has the absolute final say: for while the Osprey has been preserved, the secretary of defense has persistently declined to obligate large portions of the funds that Congress has appropriated for the system. The only certainty is that the struggle over the V-22 will be with us for several years to come.

Another salient feature of the pork barrel issue is Congress' preference for production over research and development, that is, the desire to retain a current system in production longer than the Defense Department would prefer, and to delay systems in the R&D phase. From a parochial standpoint, Congress has a clear interest in maintaining major weapon system production, with its attendant infrastructure of plant and logistics, because this preserves large numbers of high-paying, frequently unionized jobs. The disadvantage, from the force-planning standpoint, is that this approach may result in obsolete systems being produced long after they should have been replaced by more modern weapons. Also, congressional addbacks to the procurement accounts generally result in weapons that are produced at inefficient rates. This problem becomes particularly acute as defense budgets decline because the addback money must be obtained from other programs. This action in turn results in more programs operating inefficiently, thereby increasing the unit cost of weapon systems.

There is an advantage to this process, however, in that it tends to counterbalance the services' desire to field follow-on systems quickly. As a general rule, the military services are conceptualizing a replacement system at the moment a weapon enters production. By the time a weapon system is deployed to all field units, its replacement is already well into the development stage. The problem with this process is that there is a tendency for the military service to concentrate on the follow-on system to the detriment of the current system's maturation process. For instance, the Army's self-described top priority in modernization is the fielding of the light helicopter. It has not escaped the attention of Congress that the current helicopter, the Apache, has not yet matured to the point where its mission availability rates are acceptable without intensive maintenance in the field.

Thus, while the concept of divided government frequently draws fire for being cumbersome and protracted in its decision making, the inevitable compromises involved sometimes preserve options that become important later. As an example, in 1989 Secretary Cheney canceled further production of the F-14 aircraft. The DOD's rationale was that the F-14 was too expensive at the projected low rates of production, and that naval aviation funds could be better spent on development of a follow-on system, the Navy advanced tactical fighter (NATF). This decision was reversed, however, as a result of unprecedentedly heavy lobbying by the New York congressional delegation. The addback was widely seen as an example of congressional politics at its worst, but a year's hindsight shows that saving the F-14 may have been the right decision. Because of development delays, deployment of the NATF will be pushed back to the year 2002 at the earliest, while the high tempo of carrier operations in the Persian Gulf area is likely to cause accelerated aging of the current F-14 inventory. Under the circumstances (as well as the fiasco of the A-12 cancellation), preserving the production and subcontractor base for carrier aircraft seems like a prudent hedge against such unforeseen contingencies.

Despite the potential benefits of pork-barrel decisions in certain cases, the overall effect of special interest legislation is to increase delays, inefficiencies, and costs in the defense establishment. Is this situation inevitable? It may well be because special interest legislating is an invariable byproduct of representative government; constituent service is widely regarded as the core function of a member of Congress. Barring the unlikely creation of 535 "at-large" representatives and senators, national priorities will have a hard time being heard over the urgent demands of local constituents fearful of losing their jobs at bases, depots, or defense plants back home.

Can the pork barrel problem at least be diminished? Perhaps after the first major round of base closings in almost two decades is completed, congresspersons in affected districts may discover that there can be a long-term advantage to a short-term misfortune. There is evidence that some impacted communities may actually benefit from having a military facility closed. Communities situated near bases closed in the early 1970s (before Congress made base closing more difficult) have found, in many instances, that they were able to attract industrial parks, civil airports, or cargo hubs, providing steadier employment than the boom-or-bust cycle characteristic of employment in defense. While this is scant consolation for affected workers and the surrounding community in the near term, the fact remains that a smaller military simply cannot maintain the overhead of a large base infrastructure indefinitely, and dramatic changes will occur over the next five years.

There are serious questions over whether the traditional kind of jawboning between Congress and the Department of Defense can remain operative for very long, since the decline of the defense budget (which began in 1985) will continue for the foreseeable future. By the year 2000, the U.S. military budget may fall 25 or even 50 percent from the 1985 baseline. Given those circumstances, a congressional predilection for maintaining large numbers of major programs in production at inefficient rates, at the same time that the services continue to push for frequent new system starts in the R&D budget, could be a formula for collapse of any sort of coherent defense policy.

In addition, there is increasingly a belief, in and out of Congress, that raw military capability, in isolation from technological and economic power, is no longer as important an indicator of national strength as it once was (needless to say, such thinking, whether right or wrong, does constitute an effort to arrive at a "strategy," however haphazardly). While the success of Operation Desert Storm may be a momentary fillip to proponents of the "traditional" school of military power, the trend is toward greater concern for economic competitiveness, industrial base issues, and commercial R&D. Japan's current preeminence in many technology areas, and what that will hold for the competitive position of the United States, are merely harbingers of the difficulties America will face after 1992, when the European Community consolidates into a single trading bloc. Under those circumstances military technologies designed to meet the traditional cold war threat may become as obsolete as horse cavalry.

Neither Congress, nor any other institution, has fully come to grips with the future security environment. Les Aspin (D-Wisconsin), Chairman of the House Armed Services Committee, has, however, attempted to outline a new plan for defense that would emphasize technology base programs within the Pentagon's R&D budget. His plan would sacrifice R&D projects already in the pipeline that are designed to meet the 1980s Soviet threat in order to put technology base programs on a real growth curve. He would also emphasize dual-use technologies that could have significant spin-off potential for civilian use.

This proposal would also consider the possibility of completing research and development of promising military technologies and then placing them "on the shelf" (i.e. not proceeding to production) if they were not immediately needed to counter an emerging threat. This strategy would avoid the problems of concurrency that are frequently experienced when systems are placed in production before the technologies are fully mature. On the other hand, there is considerable question as to whether government contractors could maintain the scientific and engineering personnel while a technology languished in "cold storage" pending its employment in a weapon system.

In conclusion, as the overriding national security issue for the last forty years, the Soviet threat, begins to recede, Congress has become increasingly involved in fundamental issues of strategy, policy, and weapon system requirements. Former "sacred cows," such as nuclear war planning and special access programs, which have traditionally been almost exclusively the province of executive decision making, have come under unprecedented congressional scrutiny. But most members still have to grapple with a basic institutional problem that the decay of the Warsaw Pact has made more acute: however much Congress may be perceived in some circles as skeptical of the Pentagon, or even "anti-defense," it is actually loathe to cancel a weapon or close a base. In some instances, this reluctance may even be sound, but as the decline of the defense budget becomes steeper, Congress' desire to hang on to the present infrastructure may be a case of mortgaging the future to maintain the status quo.

Pershing II
Motors Await Destruction

Chapter 10

Arms Control: Looking Back, Looking Ahead

Lewis A. Dunn

D uring most of 1990, public and official expectations ran high for the arms control process—the negotiation of limited agreements constraining but not eliminating the postwar military competition between East and West. There was good reason, moreover, for such optimism. Spurred on by the broader process of East-West political change, agreements were negotiated to reduce significantly conventional ground forces in Europe (CFE), to destroy all but 5,000 tons of U.S. and Soviet stocks of chemical weapons, and to put in place new verification measures permitting the implementation of the 1974 Threshold Test Ban Treaty (TTBT) and 1976 Peaceful Nuclear Explosions Treaty (PNET). Final agreement on strategic forces reductions under a Strategic Arms Reductions (START) Treaty was thought highly likely in early 1991. In addition, negotiations on short-range nuclear forces (SNF) as well as follow-on negotiations on conventional and strategic forces and nuclear testing were on the horizon. Pursuit of a multilateral chemical weapons ban continued at the Geneva Conference on Disarmament.

But just when arms control appeared to be on the verge of fulfilling its initial promise, serious concerns arose in late 1990 about the accuracy of Soviet data exchanged under the just-signed CFE accord and about Soviet attempts to circumvent the full impact of the accord. In that regard, the redesignation of three Soviet army divisions as "coastal infantry" divisions, accompanied by the claim that treaty-limited equipment in those "new" divisions was excluded from CFE limits, was seen by all other negotiating partners (except Romania, which took no position) as a blatant, unilateral "reinterpretation" of the treaty. These and other Western concerns, in turn, spilled over to further slow the START talks, already slowed by the more basic resurgence of conservative forces and Soviet military (vice Foreign Ministry) influence over the negotiations.

Even before, there were growing questions about arms control's future role in the post-cold war world, though for quite different reasons. Political events in Eastern Europe steadily outpaced the slower process of conventional forces negotiations. While the basic framework of a START agreement was settled in 1987, three additional years were required to hammer out most of the details, and by the end of 1990 there was still no formal agreement. After initial enthusiasm for on-site inspection, the practical realities of implementing intrusive—and costly— inspection procedures have led to second thoughts about how much verification was needed. Besides, Washington and Moscow remained deadlocked in the Defense and Space talks, while the failure of the parties to reach agreement on a final document at the 1990 Non-Proliferation Treaty (NPT) Review Conference cast a shadow over prospects for this treaty's long-term extension in 1995.

It is especially timely, therefore, to step back to reflect on the future role of arms control in a period of great political, military, and economic change and uncertainty. The questions are clear:

- Will concerns about Soviet non-compliance result in an unraveling of East-West arms control?

- Has U.S.-Soviet arms control in any case outlived its usefulness in a period of sharply reduced confrontation if not yet cooperation?

- Assuming that arms control can still contribute to East-West stability, should less emphasis be placed on comprehensive negotiated agreements as opposed to reciprocal unilateral steps or to single-issue deals?

- Should U.S.-Soviet nuclear arms control continue to emphasize limited objectives, or should its goal be a more far-reaching, longer-term transformation of the nuclear relationship between the two superpowers?

- What can arms control do to help lessen the risks of military competition and conflict among developing countries armed increasingly with advanced weaponry?

In thinking about these questions, it is important first to reflect briefly on arms control's conceptual origins, initial agreements, and recent accomplishments.

Arms Control: The Early Years

Arms control as a means to regulate but not eliminate the East-West military competition first took shape in the late 1950s in reaction to lack of progress in talks on comprehensive conventional and nuclear disarmament during the immediate postwar decade. The goals of arms control were more limited: to lessen the risk of war, to lessen the damage should war occur, and to lessen the costs of defense preparations. Both reciprocal actions and formal treaties, unilateral steps and negotiated measures, were seen as approaches to achieve these goals. Taken together, such approaches were regarded by their early proponents as promising alternatives to either unregulated military competition or to continued pursuit of grand designs for general and complete disarmament.[1]

Over the 1960s and 1970s, the results of arms control were mixed.[2] Early agreements such as the 1963 Hot Line Agreement, the 1963 Limited Test Ban Treaty (banning nuclear testing in the atmosphere, the oceans, and outer space), and the 1967 Outer Space Treaty (prohibiting nuclear weapons in space) were useful confidence-building measures. Following the 1962 Cuban missile crisis, these agreements signalled U.S. and Soviet interest in holding in check the risks and scope of their nuclear competition.

Fears of runaway nuclear proliferation, so prominent in the early 1960s, became a self-denying prophecy.

A shared interest in limiting the risks of nuclear war also contributed to successful negotiation of the 1968 Non-Proliferation Treaty. Under the NPT, more than 140 countries committed themselves not to acquire nuclear weapons. For their part, the nuclear weapons states committed themselves to good faith negotiations on nuclear arms control and disarmament, while the industrialized countries agreed both to accept limits on their nuclear exports and to assist developing countries in realizing the benefits of the peaceful atom. Fears of runaway nuclear proliferation, so prominent in the early 1960s, became a self-denying prophecy.

The 1972 Anti-Ballistic Missile (ABM) Treaty helped to head off a costly and destabilizing competition between offensive and defensive forces in the 1970s. In the mid- and late 1980s, it played a similar role in the face of new but technically unsubstantiated claims that a cost-effective U.S. strategic defense was within reach. More importantly, without the ABM Treaty in place, U.S. moves toward deployments of strategic defenses in the 1980s would have all but certainly vastly impeded if not blocked altogether the Soviet reassessment of its most basic foreign and military policy objectives that followed Gorbachev's rise to power—if Gorbachev's own warnings are given credence.[3]

Limits on U.S. and Soviet strategic offensive forces under the 1972 Strategic Arms Limitations Talks (SALT I) Interim Agreement provided a means to regulate the buildup of these forces and enhance predictability for strategic force planners on both sides. But failure to ban multiple independently-targetable reentry vehicles (MIRVs) proved a major weakness that permitted a sharp expansion of the numbers of ballistic missile nuclear warheads on both sides. The 1979 SALT II Treaty provided for equality of launchers and also capped the expansion of Soviet nuclear warheads, but its inability to eliminate or significantly reduce the threat posed by Soviet heavy intercontinental ballistic missiles (ICBMs), its questionable verification provisions, and its inability to deal with the throw-weight inequities highlighted in the Jackson Amendment, contributed to its nonratification.

Conventional arms control made virtually no progress. The Mutual and Balanced Force Reductions Talks (MBFR) dragged on inconclusively from 1973 to

1988. The 1975 Conference on Security and Cooperation (CSCE) agreement at Helsinki began a process of confidence building, but it would be another decade before significant measures were agreed on in that forum.

The arms control record in these early years, however, comprises more than the agreements themselves. Increasingly, the fact and process of East-West arms control negotiations came to have a value in themselves. Particularly in periods of heightened East-West tension, arms control negotiations symbolized to leaders in Washington and Moscow as well as to their allies and friends their shared interest in holding in check their political-military confrontation. With continuing East-West political divisions on the great issues—the division of Europe, conflict in the developing world, human rights, and domestic political and economic freedom—arms control became a central element of the East-West dialogue. Indeed, to the extent that arms control proved a valuable means to lessen the risk of war, that result was probably due as much if not more to the process of negotiation than to the agreements reached.

Post–Cold War Breakthroughs

By the end of the 1970s, however, the very legitimacy of arms control had become increasingly controversial within the United States.[4] Conservative critics argued, for example, that the agreements reached were one-sided in favor of the Soviet Union; that a pattern of Soviet noncompliance reinforced this disadvantage; and that arms control had a soporific effect on the American public, weakening support for needed unilateral defense measures. With many of these critics being prominent officials in the new Reagan administration, traditional supporters of arms control saw little hope for new agreements. Their pessimism was reinforced by the Soviet decision in November 1983 to walk out of the negotiations on intermediate-range missiles and strategic offensive forces reductions in response to successful North Atlantic Treaty Organization (NATO) deployments of cruise and Pershing II missiles.[5]

Confounding the traditional arms controllers, negotiations were in full swing by the end of the 1980s. Paradoxically, the Reagan administration had relegitimized arms control. With progress across the board, it looked increasingly likely that these years—and especially 1990–1991—would come to be regarded as the beginning of the golden age of traditional, negotiated arms control. Consider the initial record.

The Stockholm Accord (1986)

Concluded in September 1986, the accord reached at the Stockholm Conference on Confidence- and Security-Building Measures and Disarmament in Europe (CDE) foreshadowed many of the other conventional and nuclear agreements to follow. Its arms control provisions included notification and observation of a wide range of military exercises and activities. More importantly, the Stockholm accord for the first time provided for mandatory on-site inspection, not only of declared Soviet and Warsaw Pact military exercises, but also on challenge of other military activities that could fall within the CDE notification requirements. In retrospect, Gorbachev's decision during the final days of the negotiations to accept the principle of on-site inspection stands out as an important first step toward greater transparency of East-West military activities.[6]

The INF Treaty (1987)

In December 1987, the United States and the Soviet Union signed the Intermediate- and Shorter-Range Nuclear Forces (INF) Treaty, which eliminated U.S. and Soviet ground-launched missiles with ranges between 500 and 5,500 kilometers. New verification provisions included extensive data exchanges, cooperative measures to assist national technical means (NTM), and a panoply of on-site inspections (baseline, elimination, close out, short-notice, and continuous portal and perimeter monitoring at one missile production facility.)

Militarily, the INF Treaty eliminated the threat posed to Europe by highly accurate, multiple-warhead SS-20 missiles, although the Soviet Union still retained ample strategic systems with which to strike targets in Western Europe. More importantly, looking back three years later, the political significance of INF stands out. Its far-reaching verification measures were another step toward Soviet acceptance of the principle of transparency of East-West military activities. Successful conclusion of the INF negotiations also probably helped in several ways to reinforce the emergence of Soviet "new thinking" on defense and foreign policy, while making it easier for Gorbachev to win military support for the withdrawal of Soviet military power from the heart of Europe.

More specifically, conclusion of the INF agreement cleared the air after the East-West confrontation over the NATO missile deployment in the early 1980s. It was the centerpiece of the December 1987 Washington summit and permitted both sides to move on to other matters. Elimination of NATO's Pershing II missiles also removed what the Soviet leadership perceived as a potential first-strike threat to command and control sites near Moscow. Moreover, by giving up those missiles, the United States and its NATO allies in effect challenged basic Soviet precepts concerning the constancy of class struggle, the implacable hostility of the West, and the need to pursue "absolute security." Finally, elimination of the Pershing IIs made it far harder for Gorbachev's opponents to argue that Soviet security demanded a divided Germany and a continuing military presence throughout Eastern Europe.

The Nuclear Testing Treaties (1990)

Presidents Bush and Gorbachev in June 1990 signed new protocols to the 1974 TTBT and 1976 PNET, culminating several years of negotiations in the Nuclear Testing Talks (NTT) on verification improvements for these treaties. With signature of the new protocols, the Bush administration sought and won Senate advice and consent to ratification. Ratification by the Supreme Soviet occurred in October 1990, and the treaties entered into force in December 1990.

The new protocol for the TTBT includes provision for: (1) nuclear weapons testing only at the Nevada Test Site for the United States and at Novaya Zemlya or Semipalatinsk for the Soviet Union; (2) a right of on-site inspection for tests with a yield between thirty-five and fifty kilotons as well as use of hydrodynamic yield measurement (i.e., direct, on-site measurement of the properties of the shock wave as a function of time) and/or seismic methods in the verified country for tests with a yield of more than fifty kilotons; and (3) various confidence-building measures, notifications, and exchanges of information about nuclear testing programs.

The verification provisions in the protocol to the PNET parallel those of the TTBT concerning permitted measurements, on-site inspection, and notification and exchanges of information. The protocol also contains provisions to deal with possible group explosions with a yield over 150 kilotons.

Ratification of the nuclear testing treaties comprised unfinished business from the early years of arms control. Moreover, since both the Soviet Union and the United States had each stated previously that it was abiding by the 150-kiloton testing threshold of the TTBT, there is likely to be little immediate impact. Over the longer term, however, ratification can be expected to increase pressures on the Bush administration to negotiate a comprehensive test ban treaty (CTBT), or at least to seek more stringent limits on either the numbers or yields of future nuclear tests when the Nuclear Testing Talks resume.

Chemical Weapons Destruction Agreement (1990)

At the June 1990 summit, the United States and the Soviet Union also signed an "Agreement on Destruction and Non-Production of Chemical Weapons and on Measures to Facilitate the Multilateral Convention Banning Chemical Weapons." This bilateral agreement significantly extended the U.S.-Soviet September 1989 Memorandum of Understanding, which entailed exchanges of data on chemical weapons stocks as well as provisions for visits to chemical weapons related facilities in each country.

Among the more important specific provisions in the June 1990 Chemical Weapons Destruction agreement are:

- Cessation of production of chemical weapons.

- Destruction of existing stocks of chemical weapons, to begin by December 31, 1992, with 50 percent to be destroyed by December 31, 1999, and further reductions to an aggregate stock of no more than 5,000 agent tons (metric) by December 31, 2002.

- Exchanges of information concerning plans for destruction as well as updates of information concerning stocks and locations of chemical weapons provided for in the 1989 Memorandum of Understanding.

- Limits on the number (eight) of permitted chemical weapons storage facilities after December 31, 2002.

- Systematic on-site inspection (with detailed provisions to be negotiated by December 31, 1990), including the presence of inspectors and continuous monitoring with on-site instruments to confirm destruction and cessation of production.

- On-site inspection of storage facilities on notification that chemical weapons are no longer stored at a given facility, that destruction under the agreement has been completed, and annually—pending entry into force of the chemical weapons convention (CWC).

- Cooperation in methods and technologies for the safe and efficient destruction of chemical weapon.

- Facilitation of negotiations underway in Geneva on a multilateral CWC, with a commitment to reduce existing stocks to 500 tons by no later than the end of the eighth year after entry into force of such a convention.

- Agreement to propose a conference in the eighth year after entry into force of a CWC to determine whether there is sufficient adherence to a CWC to proceed to total elimination of chemical weapons over the subsequent two years, subject to certain conditions aimed at encouraging such adherence.

It is difficult as yet to draw a bottom line on the Chemical Weapons Destruction and Non-Production Agreement. Its security benefits in greatly reducing Soviet chemical weapons capabilities and enhancing transparency with regard to those capabilities were largely overtaken by the pending withdrawal of the Soviet military and political presence from Eastern Europe. At the same time, the likely benefits of encouraging negotiation of the CWC probably were outweighed by the controversy generated in Geneva at the Conference on Disarmament by the U.S. intention to retain 500 tons of chemical weapons agent, a position President Bush renounced in May 1991. Not least, U.S. and Soviet negotiators proved unable to meet their goal of agreement on a detailed inspection protocol by the end of 1990. Soviet difficulties in putting forward a credible approach to destruction that would meet the accord's timetable and Soviet reluctance to agree to destroy (not convert to peaceful purposes) production facilities emerged as the two major stumbling blocks.

Conventional Armed Forces in Europe Treaty (1990)

Signature of the Conventional Armed Forces in Europe (CFE) Treaty at the November 19–21, 1990 Paris CSCE Summit, followed immediately by questions about Soviet compliance with it, stands out as the most critical arms control event of 1990. Covering the Atlantic-to-the-Urals (ATTU) region, CFE includes:

- Overall ceilings for each side on the numbers of battle tanks (20,000), armored combat vehicles (30,000), artillery pieces (20,000), combat aircraft (6,800), and attack helicopters (2,000) within the ATTU.

- A sufficiency rule, limiting the holdings of any one country in tanks (13,300), armored combat vehicles (20,000), artillery (13,700), combat aircraft (5,150), and attack helicopters (1,500).

- Zonal limits on the ground-force holdings of active-duty units in four geographical areas within the ATTU.

- Measures limiting the amount of equipment on the northern and southern flanks.

- Provision for limited conversion of some tanks and armored combat vehicles to civilian uses.

- Extensive data exchanges (with provisions for updates) on holdings of treaty-limited equipment, by type, unit location, and subordination of so-called objects of verification.

- Other transparency measures, such as notifications of movements to destruction.

- Stabilizing measures, including ceilings on stored equipment; limits on the amount removable from storage; and prenotification requirements for removal of more than 10 percent of the items in permanent storage at a site.

- Intrusive on-site inspections (baseline, of destruction, during a post-destruction 120-day validation period, after that validation period, and of suspect sites).

If eventually brought into force by the parties' ratifications, CFE numerical limits for the first time will establish a parity between NATO and Warsaw Treaty Organization (WTO) forces within the ATTU, while placing significant constraints on Soviet forces in the ATTU. Taken together, the CFE limits on forces, Soviet unilateral withdrawals, and Soviet bilateral agreements with Eastern European countries to remove the Soviet military presence are eliminating the threat of a short-warning, large-scale WTO offensive against NATO. The Soviet Union also will be required to destroy nearly 20,000 pieces of equipment. CFE verification measures will increase significantly the transparency of Soviet military activities in the ATTU. The specific inspections and the overall degree of cooperation with the inspection process will help to provide early warning of the reemergence of an immediate Soviet political and military threat. Technical questions can be raised

By Toles for *The Buffalo News*

about the details of CFE's on-site inspection procedures (e.g., concerning the number of permitted inspections and the focus on "objects of verification" rather than all military formations or sites in the ATTU). Nonetheless, taken as a whole, the on-site inspection procedures will provide unprecedented access to Soviet military units, help NATO to track the continuing reorganization of Soviet military deployments in the wake of unilateral withdrawals, and make it unlikely that any major violation or mobilization would go undetected for long.

On-site inspection procedures will provide unprecedented access to Soviet military units.

Despite these potential benefits, prospects for speedy implementation of CFE were derailed in late 1990 by a series of Soviet actions. At odds with the spirit and in one important instance the intent of the treaty, these actions were:

- During the summer and fall of 1990, the Soviet military greatly accelerated unilateral withdrawals of tanks, artillery pieces, and armored combat vehicles from the ATTU to East of the Urals, thereby avoiding the destruction of this equipment. Though permitted by CFE, these withdrawals (which ultimately totalled about 70,000 pieces of equipment) far exceeded the amounts of equipment that Soviet Foreign Minister Shevardnadze had indicated to NATO would be withdrawn. These withdrawals also were at odds with the spirit of CFE, which envisaged reductions—not simply relocation—of military capabilities.

- Soviet data exchanged when CFE was signed underreported the equipment still remaining in the ATTU. By denying the presence of equipment that could not be shifted East of the Urals by the signature date, the Soviet military sought to circumvent CFE's constraints on that equipment.

- By a variety of force structure changes the Soviet military greatly reduced the number of Soviet "objects of verification," limiting the extent of on-site inspection from that expected by NATO negotiators.

- Most importantly, Soviet military officials redesignated three infantry divisions as "coastal infantry units" and declared that the equipment holdings of these divisions (between 2,500 and 3,500 pieces) was excluded from the limits on equipment under the treaty. In addition, the Soviets claimed that artillery transferred to coastal artillery units in the ATTU and armored combat vehicles transferred to the Strategic Rocket Forces in the ATTU at the time of treaty signing were similarly excluded. This unilateral Soviet reinterpreted of Article III, which set out the counting rules for treaty-limited equipment, had no basis in the negotiating record, which established the parties' clear intent that all such treaty-limited equipment within the ATTU would count against the CFE ceilings.

The United States and its NATO partners protested these Soviet actions, especially the redesignation of "army to coastal" units and the related reinterpretation of what treaty-limited equipment counted under the CFE limits. With the support of the former Warsaw Pact countries, less Romania, NATO also suspended formal follow-on negotiating sessions in the so-called CFE Ia talks on manpower limits and aerial inspections.[7] The Bush administration also indicated that it would not seek Senate ratification of the CFE accord unless these concerns over Soviet transfers of equipment were resolved. For their part, the NATO allies initially supported the tough line, though there were some signs that over time an interest in trying to find a "compromise" could lead to divisions within the Alliance.[8]

Even assuming CFE implementation, the Soviet military will remain a potent force after the three year reductions phase—both within the ATTU and especially East of the Urals. Moreover, the CFE Treaty does not limit modernization, and it only partly constrains equipment in paramilitary forces. Nonetheless, by shifting the balance of Soviet forces to East of the Urals while enhancing warning and transparency, the CFE Treaty adds to Western security. Its successful implementation, with Soviet acceptance of the treaty's intent that all equipment be covered, would make it a definite arms control success.

Confidence- and Security-Building Measures (CSBM) Agreement (1990)

Complementing the CFE Treaty, the Paris summit also produced an agreement to strengthen CSBMs. New measures included:

- Provision for detailed information exchange on land, air, and amphibious forces (excluding naval forces).

- Exchanges of information on major conventional weapon system deployment programs with short-notice inspections to evaluate the information provided.

- A requirement to provide more detailed information as part of the Stockholm-mandated annual exchange of exercise calendars.

- A lowered threshold (40,000 troops) for two-year advance notice of large exercises.

- Improved military contacts and information exchange on military budgets.

- The creation of a mechanism for discussion of unusual military activities.

While some proposed measures were not agreed, these steps further extended the Stockholm agreement and the CSCE confidence-building process. As such, they help to peel back another layer of military activities in Eastern Europe and the Soviet Union.

Strategic Arms Reductions (1991)

At the June 1990 Washington summit, Presidents Bush and Gorbachev made clear their intention to reach agreement on a START Treaty during 1990. This did not prove possible. Nonetheless, by the end of 1990 START's basic contours, though not all the technical details, were in place. With postponement of the February 1991 Summit, conclusion of a treaty was no longer possible in early 1991, but agreement finally was reached in July 1991.

START's basic provisions, to be implemented in three phases over a reduction period of seven years, will:

- Set a limit of 1,600 on the total number of deployed ICBMs, submarine-launched ballistic missiles (SLBMs), and their associated launchers, and heavy bombers (so-called strategic nuclear delivery vehicles (SNDVs)).

- Limit the Soviets to 154 deployed heavy ICBMs (in effect halving their SS-18 force), while banning new types of heavy ICBMs as well as heavy SLBMs or heavy mobile ICBMs.

- Reduce each side's deployed treaty "countable" but not "real" nuclear warheads to 6,000.[9]

- Place a limit of 4,900 warheads on deployed ICBMs and SLBMs, with a further limit of 1,540 on heavy ICBMs and of 1,100 on deployed mobile ICBMs.

- Reduce the aggregate throw weight of deployed ICBMs and SLBMs to approximately 50 percent of existing Soviet systems.

- Permit unlimited long-range non-nuclear air-launched cruise missiles (ALCMs), while not fully counting nuclear-armed ALCMs on heavy bombers against the 6,000 warhead limit.

- Rely on the by now almost traditional mix of verification measures (e.g., data exchanges, notifications, national technical means with a ban on denial of most telemetry, on-site inspection with suspect site inspections subject to agreed conditions, and perimeter and portal monitoring at mobile ICBM factories).

- Place limits on how mobile ICBMs are deployed and limit the number of non-deployed mobile ICBMs to assist verification.

The lasting strategic benefits of the START agreement are likely to be more indirect than direct, more political than military.

During the negotiations, the Soviet side pressed repeatedly for negotiated limits on sea-launched cruise missiles (SLCMs). Eventually, both sides agreed at the Washington summit in June 1990 to a "politically binding" declaration that each side would deploy no more than 880 nuclear-armed long-range (over 600 kilometers) SLCMs. No verification would be entailed.

Several aspects of the START agreement will likely be controversial in future ratification debates. Because not all U.S. and Soviet nuclear warheads are counted under the limit, START will likely result in reductions of only 30 to 35 percent of U.S. and Soviet strategic warheads. Indeed, because of the extended duration of the negotiations, START will serve only to reduce both sides' nuclear weapons to the levels of the early 1980s. In turn, continued Soviet modernization of heavy SS-18 missiles somewhat offsets the benefits derived from cutting in half the number of deployed heavy missiles. Further, there also will be public and congressional debate about the apparent decision in START not to require monitored dismantling of warheads (and to a lesser degree not to place new limits on the special nuclear materials from such warheads.)

For these reasons, the lasting strategic benefits of the START agreement are likely to be more indirect than direct, more political than military. The START warhead cuts set in motion for the first time a process of reducing U.S. and Soviet strategic arsenals. Its reductions of Soviet heavy missiles and 50 percent cut of Soviet ballistic missile warheads—as well as its acceptance of mobile missiles and discounting of bombers—are a step to mutual acceptance of the principle that a gradual restructuring of both sides' strategic offensive forces is needed to reduce sharply, if not eliminate, theoretical first strike instabilities. More broadly, successful agreement would ratify the principle of joint management of future strategic nuclear deployments to enhance stability and prevent them from derailing the process of U.S.-Soviet political realignment.

Deadlock at the 1990 NPT Review Conference

Every five years since the NPT's entry into force in 1975 the parties have gathered to review implementation of its provisions. The fourth such review took place in Geneva from August 23 to September 14, 1990. The inability of the parties to reach a consensus due to differences over nuclear testing issues, however, cast a shadow over the arms control successes of 1990 as well as the prospects for a long-term extension of the NPT in 1995.[10]

During the general debate, virtually all of the parties that spoke emphasized their support for the NPT and its important contribution to global security. In the working committees, agreement was reached on draft language in various areas that would have strengthened global nuclear nonproliferation efforts. This included a commitment by the major nuclear suppliers to require safeguards on all peaceful nuclear activities (so-called full-scope safeguards) as a condition of supply; a call on the International Atomic Energy Agency (IAEA) to consider whether it might undertake "special inspections" of suspected facilities under certain long-unused provisions of its safeguards agreements; compromise language endorsing the idea of a new look at what might be done to strengthen security assurances to non-nuclear weapon states; and formal reference to the declaration made at the conference by the governments of the then two Germanys that a united Germany will continue to renounce nuclear, chemical, and biological weapons.

Failure to agree on nuclear testing issues, however, deadlocked the fourth NPT review conference. Throughout the conference, the Mexican delegate, Ambassador Miguel Marin-Bosch, had argued that achievement of a CTBT must be seen as the preeminent if not sole litmus test of whether the arms control and disarmament obligations of Article VI of the NPT were being met.[11] In effect, Marin-Bosch, with the support of some developing countries, would have linked extension of the NPT in 1995 to conclusion of a CTBT. For its part, the United States, supported only by the United Kingdom, opposed this demand for negotiation of a CTBT and its linkage to NPT extension. For the United States and Britain, pursuit of a CTBT had to be a long-term objective, which they argued was far less important in any evaluation of implementation of Article VI than were the many arms control successes achieved in the late 1980s and early 1990s. Compromise proved impossible.

This deadlock must be viewed as a "warning shot across the bow" of the United States and other NPT supporters. Until 1990, it was possible for Washington to maintain its posture of strong support of the NPT and strong opposition to a CTBT or other drastic curtailments of nuclear testing. Extension of the NPT in 1995 may force a choice. For even though Mexico's approach had the open support of only a few developing countries, virtually all of them considered significant progress toward a CTBT—if not its actual achievement—to be their top disarmament priority for 1995. Absent further progress on limiting nuclear testing, NPT supporters will face a difficult uphill struggle in winning agreement to more than a short treaty extension.

The Future of Arms Control

For nearly all of 1990, the future of arms control seemed assured. Progress was being made across the negotiating fronts. Indeed, the United States and the Soviet Union, and to a lesser degree their allies, had already pledged themselves to begin or continue a sweeping set of follow-on and related negotiations. In their

June 1990 summit statement, for example, Presidents Bush and Gorbachev agreed that following conclusion of START, Washington and Moscow would "pursue new talks on strategic offensive arms, and on the relationship between strategic offensive and defensive arms." Signing of CFE I was to be followed a week later by the opening of CFE Ia, which would deal with provisions for aerial inspection and manpower reductions, with a goal of reaching agreement in time for the 1992 CSCE conference. In turn, at the London NATO summit in July 1990, the NATO allies agreed that "new negotiations between the United States and the Soviet Union on the reduction of short-range nuclear forces should begin shortly after a CFE agreement is signed." Entry into force of the TTBT and PNET was to be followed by resumption of U.S.-Soviet bilateral talks on "step-by-step" reductions of nuclear testing, quite likely beginning in late spring 1991. Further, multilateral negotiations were expected to resume on "open skies," permitting aerial overflights of United States, Soviet Union, and European countries, while negotiation of a global chemical weapons ban was proceeding at the Geneva Conference on Disarmament. Looming on the horizon, despite U.S. opposition, was the prospect of eventual U.S.-Soviet talks on naval arms control.

Is East-West Arms Control Unraveling?

Contrasted with this far-reaching arms control agenda, Soviet actions in CFE had by early 1991 raised the possibility that the East-West arms control process had begun to unravel. CFE ratification was deferred, CFE Ia was on hold, Open Skies talks had yet to resume, and START was slowing down. Whether this downward process continues will depend heavily on Soviet domestic political developments. But it will also be affected by domestic political imperatives in other countries and by the perceived utility of arms control discussions in a period of uncertain East-West relations.

Throughout the fall of 1990, Soviet conservatives steadily reasserted their domestic political power. The resignation of Soviet Foreign Minister Shevardnadze and other prominent reformists and the appointment of conservatives symbolized this shift in the balance of power. At the same time, the continuing clash between Mikhail Gorbachev and Boris Yeltsin as well as between the center and the republics added to the uncertainty of Soviet political life.

Soviet actions in CFE must be viewed in large part as a demonstration of power by the conservatives and the military. The movement of equipment East of the Urals and especially the claimed exclusion from CFE limits of treaty-limited equipment transferred to non-Army units also comprised a symbolic rejection of the arms control deals struck by Shevardnadze, which many military conservatives apparently believed had been undertaken without taking adequate account of their views. Whether Gorbachev supported or simply acquiesced tacitly in the new Soviet approach to CFE is uncertain. Similarly, it remains to be seen whether he is prepared eventually—or has the authority—to reverse the most questionable element of that approach by acknowledging that all treaty limited-equipment in the ATTU is to be counted under the CFE limits.

Interest in Western European and U.S. technological and economic support could provide Gorbachev with an incentive to try to "walk the cat back into the bag." Besides, an acknowledgement that all treaty-limited equipment is to be counted under Article III would have only limited military impact, since the amount of equipment at issue is low, particularly in comparison to that equipment moved East of the Urals. For their part, having reasserted their power and made their point about the need to heed their views more closely in the arms control process, the military and conservatives could be prepared to go along.

Assuming a Soviet walk-back permits CFE implementation to go forward, the broader East-West arms control process would again gather speed. But at least for the short term, progress may continue to be slower than anticipated in 1990. Soviet domestic political upheaval, lingering questions about whether Soviet negotiators "speak for the military," and the many other compelling demands on Gorbachev all are likely to hinder the process.

Absent a Soviet readiness to adopt the position of the other CFE parties on how to count treaty-limited equipment under Article III, prospects for arms control in 1991 appear limited. Some NATO allies may eventually seek purported "compromises" that would permit them to ratify and implement CFE, but the Bush administration gives no sign of support for that approach. Besides, Senate ratification of the CFE Treaty all but certainly would not be forthcoming as long as a strong case existed that the Soviet Union had violated CFE's clear intent. These concerns could spill over to other East-West arms control areas, in all probability weakening political resolve to go forward with follow-on CFE Ia negotiations on manpower and aerial inspections, to pursue the 1992 CSCE meeting, and to finish START in 1991. It may also slow implementation of the bilateral chemical destruction agreement.

Nonetheless, one lesson of the relegitimization of arms control by the Reagan administration is that there are many built-in brakes on the extent of any such unraveling of the East-West arms control process. Both the United States and the Soviet Union continue to have a political and strategic interest in arms control talks as a part of their on-going dialogue. Domestic opinion, in the United States and in Europe, also has traditionally viewed talks between Moscow and Washington as an important barometer of relations between the two superpowers. Congressional interest is still high in some arms control areas such as further limits on nuclear testing and chemical weapons.

Not least, to the extent that it occurs in 1991, an unraveling of the arms control process would exact a price. Failure to implement the CFE Treaty for example, would result in a decreased transparency of Soviet military activities (without CFE's verification package) as well as a lack of legally binding limits on Soviet forces West of the Urals. If the 1992 CSCE meeting in Helsinki is affected, opportunities may be lost to continue to pressure the Soviet Union on human rights and economic issues (under the broad CSCE security agenda) as well as to help stabilize relations among Eastern European countries. An inability to conclude START would entail costs in terms of lessened controls over Soviet strategic forces. Consequently, any arms control slow-down seems likely to be selective rather than across the board, short-term rather than enduring.*

Has U.S.-Soviet Arms Control Outlived Its Time?

The need for U.S.-Soviet arms control was also increasingly questioned for quite different political and military reasons in much of 1990. Assuming a Soviet decision to drop their "reinterpretation" of CFE, these questions could again be raised.

For most of the cold war, arms control negotiations provided the sole venue for serious U.S.-Soviet discussion of security matters. In times of tension, they

---

*This was the case with the disagreements over CFE, resolved in spring of 1991, leading to a signing of the START Treaty in July 1991.

symbolized a mutual commitment to avoid nuclear war while providing essential reassurance to each side's allies. With a sharp improvement in East-West relations—in effect, the end of the traditional cold war—however, it was suggested that arms control negotiations between Moscow and Washington had lost that essential political purpose. At the same time, this line of argument continued, with the radically changed East-West political relationship, there was far less military need to try to negotiate limits or reductions of U.S. and Soviet nuclear armaments. Over time, Washington will come to view Moscow's nuclear forces as no more threatening than those of France or the United Kingdom. Similarly, with a greatly reduced sense of threat, the Soviet Union's significant remaining conventional forces will no longer figure in the political calculations of the United States or other Western governments. Eventually, unilateral national decisions, reinforced by the need to reallocate resources from defense to domestic concerns, will gradually reduce those forces regardless of the status of negotiated agreements.

Over time, Washington will come to view Moscow's nuclear forces as no more threatening than those of France or the United Kingdom.

There are reasons to question this assessment. Despite the changing political climate it is likely to be many decades before U.S. relations with the Soviet Union come to mirror those with either France or the United Kingdom. Uncertainty about the future of the Soviet Union abounds, and a reversal of favorable trends, whether resulting from a breakup of the existing Soviet Union, a military coup, or an anti-Western Russian nationalist restoration, cannot be precluded. Indeed, the resignation of Soviet Foreign Minister Eduard Shevardnadze in December 1990, while warning of the rise of dictatorship in the Soviet Union, exemplified this instability and uncertainty. Consequently, the sizable U.S. and Soviet nuclear forces will continue to cast a shadow over their improving political relationship, raising concerns and requiring—if to a lesser degree—the type of political reassurance that the arms control process provided in the past. The presence of large Soviet conventional forces could well exert a comparable impact.

In addition, the unilateral drawdown of each side's nuclear and conventional forces need not be any more stabilizing than their unilateral buildup. Instead, as budgetary pressures lead to reductions of forces, U.S.-Soviet arms control could prove increasingly necessary to help manage that restructuring in a way that enhances mutual security and stability.

Beyond Traditional Negotiated Agreements?

Assuming that arms control still has a contribution to make in managing the changing East-West political-military relationship, it is an open question whether that contribution has to be made solely via the negotiation of detailed, comprehensive arms control agreements. Recent experience exemplifies the successes but also the limits of that traditional approach.

The START agreement took over eight years to negotiate and exceeded 700 pages. As a result, some of its provisions are being overtaken by the pace of events (e.g., modernization of the remaining Soviet SS-18 missiles has undercut the benefits of a 50 percent reduction of those missiles), while other provisions appear too limited in a changed political climate (e.g., continued acceptance of fixed multiple-warhead land-based missiles.) Similarly, though negotiation of a CFE Treaty took far less time (eighteen months), it, too, was partly outpaced by changes in Eastern Europe, which led to a unilateral drawdown of the Soviet military presence. In turn, the continuing spread of chemical weapons to developing countries will greatly increase the difficulties of winning adherence to an eventual global chemical weapons ban.

Faced with these problems, two solutions have been proposed. One approach is to pursue arms control without negotiated agreements. The second is to seek to negotiate less comprehensive agreements, perhaps only on single issues. Each has a role to play in the future, but neither offers a complete alternative to more traditional arms control negotiations.

Under certain conditions, it may be quicker, less cumbersome, and less intrusive for Washington and Moscow to reach political understandings regarding their respective behavior but not to record those understandings in legally binding detailed agreements. Difficulties in verifying compliance—as well as the intrusiveness of needed monitoring measures—already have led to adoption of this approach for limits on U.S. and Soviet SLCMs, although the Soviets may well seek to reopen the issue of SLCMs in START II. Similarly, NATO proposed elimination from Europe of its nuclear artillery projectiles in return for comparable action by the Soviet Union. Parallel unilateral actions in this case would avoid time-consuming negotiations on verification, the likely result of which would be a highly intrusive but at best only a modestly effective set of verification provisions.

Despite this movement, caution is required with regard to arms control without agreements. In a period of high uncertainty about the long-term Soviet political future, legally binding agreements may offer an important source of stability. Once implemented, their terms probably would be more difficult for new Soviet leaders to disregard, their violation would provide a stronger signal of Soviet backsliding, and the prospects for winning the support of Western publics for appropriate responses would likely be higher if legal obligations had been violated.

Further, some potentially desirable U.S.-Soviet arms control steps (e.g., "deMIRVing" land-based missiles) may be stabilizing only with effective verification means to monitor compliance. Indeed, the emerging verification network of past, present, and future negotiated agreements may itself be an important arms control measure. An overlapping set of data exchanges, notifications, and on-site inspections enhances transparency, reduces uncertainty about Soviet activities, and increases warning of dangerous political-military shifts. This applies equally to politically binding but very detailed provisions for confidence-building measures under the CSCE process.

A comparable blend of potential benefits and limits characterizes attempts to shift from very drawn-out negotiation of detailed, comprehensive treaties or agreements to simpler single-issue agreements. These latter agreements could then be part of a continuing, longer-term arms control process. Rather than seeking an all-inclusive START II treaty, for example, follow-on strategic forces negotiations could seek a series of more limited agreements. At least in theory, any of the following oft-proposed objectives could be pursued in this way: a ban on

MIRVed fixed land-based ICBMs; a ban on mobile ICBMs; a ban on all fixed land-based missiles; a ban on nuclear-armed SLCMs; an additional 50 percent reduction of Soviet missile throw weight; reductions in MIRVed SLBMs; and a reduction to 6,000 "real," not countable, warheads.

Single-issue agreements, however, could prove difficult to reach in practice. Again using START II as an example, each side could fear that the other side would "pocket" an agreement that it wanted (e.g., deMIRVing fixed land-based ICBMs from Washington's perspective) but not negotiate in good faith on other items (e.g., deMIRVing SLBMs from Moscow's vantage point.) In turn, one advantage of many-faceted comprehensive agreements is that they facilitate trade-offs between different systems as well as make it easier for both sides to conclude that the overall mix of advantages and disadvantages is acceptable. For these reasons, single-issue arms control seems unlikely to displace completely more traditional agreements.

Within these limits, a readiness to seek single-issue arms control agreements may sometimes be both desirable and feasible. For instance, the successful conclusion of an agreement to permit aerial inspections under CFE would reinforce the other verification provisions in CFE and add further to Soviet transparency. Or, though stalemated at the end of 1990 by Soviet opposition to intrusive sensors and flexible operational procedures, even a partial Open Skies agreement could set an important precedent for East-West transparency. In both cases, moreover, the potential payoffs of agreement would be enhanced if provision were made for a periodic review and upgrade of sensors—should continuing Soviet domestic political change result in a greater willingness to accept more advanced sensors at a later date. In any event, for the arms control process to be of maximum benefit beyond the early 1990s, some means must be found to reach sound agreements more rapidly than has been generally the case.

Transforming the U.S.-Soviet Nuclear Relationship?

In thinking about the longer-term future of arms control, particularly nuclear arms control, the scope of its objectives also needs to be addressed. From its origins in reaction to the more grandiose and unrealistic disarmament proposals of the 1950s, those objectives have been limited. This approach could be taken again in follow-on nuclear negotiations in START, the Nuclear Testing Talks, and SNF. For example, START II might aim at reductions to 6,000 "real," as opposed to countable, warheads, with a partial or total deMIRVing of fixed land-based ICBMs. Similarly, in seeking step-by-step reductions of nuclear testing, NTT could seek, for example, only a modest further reduction of the nuclear testing threshold to 100 or 75 kilotons. For SNF, the task would be to hold the line at only a partial reduction of SNF missiles in Europe, while keeping air-delivered nuclear weapons out of the negotiations completely.

There are good arguments in favor of this approach. Limited steps are a prudent hedge against political and military uncertainty, especially concerning the increasingly uncertain future of the Soviet Union. They also avoid the need for a costly and difficult restructuring of existing nuclear forces or nuclear testing activities. In any case, more limited objectives may be more consistent with what U.S. and Soviet officials are prepared to negotiate at this stage in their evolving relationship.

Nonetheless, arms control's emphasis on limited objectives had its origins in an era of intense East-West hostility and political-military confrontation. The steady buildup of U.S. nuclear capabilities also was driven by the need to respond to the threat posed by an implacably hostile Soviet Union that possessed over-whelming conventional capabilities in the heart of Europe. By contrast, in the emerging post-cold war era, it may be militarily possible—and politically desir-able—to extend the goals of arms control to include pursuit over time of a more far-reaching transformation of the U.S.-Soviet nuclear relationship. Such a trans-formation would take as its broad goal a sharp reduction in the role of nuclear weapons in East-West security, guided by the proposition that henceforth the sole purpose of these weapons should be to deter the use of other nuclear weapons. Specifics could include, for example:

- Far deeper cuts in strategic offensive forces to residual levels for de-terrence (perhaps to 3,000 "real" warheads, as is most often men-tioned in that regard).[12]

- Restructuring of strategic forces and targeting doctrine to minimize counter-nuclear forces capabilities (e.g., with elimination of fixed land-based ICBMs and a ban on the MIRVing of all remaining missiles, including SLBMs).

- Further evolution of nuclear doctrine from "last resort use" to "no first use."

- Global reductions to residual levels of SNF (perhaps 500 warheads), with provision for monitored destruction of eliminated warheads.

- Tight limits on nuclear testing (initially to perhaps a 20- to 30-kiloton threshold and a quota of several tests per year, but with the right to conduct several other tests per year up to the old 150-kiloton thresh-old if needed to ensure safety and reliability).

- Continuation of ABM Treaty limits, unless amended (e.g., if eventu-ally needed to permit testing and light deployments to manage new Third World missile threats or in response to a heightened risk of accidental or unauthorized launch).

Pursuit of a more ambitious nuclear arms control agenda could pay off in several ways. Sharp reductions in and restructuring of strategic offensive forces would help to eliminate the potential brake on the future evolution of East-West political relations inherent in the levels and types of nuclear arsenals present on both sides in 1990. Reductions of Soviet capabilities also could be a useful hedge against a longer-term political reversal. Not least, such efforts to reduce sharply the role of nuclear weapons in the East-West relationship could contribute signif-icantly to parallel attempts to contain the acquisition and use of nuclear weapons in developing regions. This last point warrants brief elaboration.

The relationship between U.S.-Soviet nuclear arms control and nuclear non-proliferation has long been hotly debated. Skeptics assert that national decisions based on regional security calculations drive proliferation; disarmament propo-nents argue that steps to nuclear disarmament are inseparable from nuclear non-proliferation. The truth appears to lie in between: national decisions are at the heart of proliferation; but those decisions can be influenced by steps taken by the two nuclear superpowers to reverse and reduce their nuclear competition.

More specifically, sharp reductions to residual levels of nuclear forces can reinforce the norm of nonproliferation, the perception that acquisition of nuclear weapons is no longer legitimate. This norm in large part explains why current— as opposed to past—problem countries have chosen not to launch open nuclear weapons programs and deployments. In addition, though short of the demands of the developing countries, tightened limits on nuclear testing that did not preclude an eventual CTBT would increase significantly the prospects for long-term extension of the NPT in 1995. Finally, a second-use, deterrence-only nuclear strategy and doctrine would increase the legitimacy of future U.S. or multilateral efforts to deter the threat or use of nuclear weapons by new nuclear weapons states, whether against U.S. forces, friends, or allies.

Sharp reductions to residual levels of nuclear forces can reinforce the norm of nonproliferation.

Despite these potential payoffs, there are many obstacles to such a sweeping redefinition of nuclear arms control. Bureaucratic inertia, political-military prudence, and practical problems all favor continuing the more traditional incremental approach. Political instability in the Soviet Union and uncertainty about future Soviet policies also reinforce the case for a more cautious approach. At the least, however, the pursuit of more limited arms control measures needs to be increasingly guided and shaped by a broader vision of the potential role of arms control in helping to foster a transformation of the U.S.-Soviet nuclear relationship in the decades ahead.

Arms Control and Regional Conflict

For the most part arms control has focused on East-West problems. To the extent that it has been concerned with regional security problems, arms control's preferred instruments have been multilateral treaties or initiatives. The NPT, the 1987 Missile Technology Control Regime (MTCR), limiting exports of ballistic and cruise missiles and technology to Third World regions, the Biological Weapons Convention banning these weapons, and efforts to negotiate a CWC exemplify that approach. These multilateral arms control measures will remain an important part of future arms control.

A top arms control priority needs to be extension of the NPT in 1995. This treaty has provided a key legal foundation for export controls, while symbolizing the norm of nonproliferation. By legally reflecting the national decisions of Germany, other Western European countries, and the countries of Eastern Europe not to acquire nuclear weapons it is a vital source of stability in a period of great change in Europe. More steps can be taken, as well, to strengthen implementation of the MTCR, from beefed-up national export controls to seeking pledges by China and other potential missile exporters to abide by the regime's limits. After the Gulf War, a tighter MTCR could be especially useful in blocking the spread of more sophisticated missiles than the Scuds fired by Iraq. In turn, successful conclusion of a global chemical weapons ban still holds out the best prospect to contain the proliferation of these weapons. Until then, efforts under the so-called Australia Group to control sales of precursors, technology, and equipment to make chemical weapons will remain the first line of defense.

Looking ahead, however, new thinking is required to identify possible opportunities for region-specific arms control measures and negotiations, from bilateral confidence-building measures to formal agreements restraining weapons developments or deployments. In that regard, the Gulf War has both created new interest at top political levels in such measures and overall a more hospitable climate for their pursuit. Consider a few examples.

Although the leaders of both India and Pakistan have stated that their respective countries possess the capability to make nuclear weapons on short notice, both countries appear reluctant to take the next step across the nuclear threshold to open nuclear arms competition and deployments. Their December 1988 signature of an agreement not to attack each other's nuclear facilities served to symbolize that apparent desire. With the encouragement of interested outsiders, still other nuclear confidence-building measures could be pursued, including commitments not to deploy, test, or use nuclear weapons first. Continued political tensions between Delhi and Islamabad could well preclude conclusion of any such confidence-building agreements. But as in the earlier case of U.S.-Soviet arms control, even the process of discussing them could exert a restraining impact and signal the desire of both countries to contain their nuclear competition.

Following tentative steps to improve political relations between Seoul and Pyongyang, confidence-building measures of another sort could help to lessen the risk of conflict on the Korean peninsula. Possible measures include limits on troop deployments near the demilitarized zone, limits on exercises, notifications of troop movements, stationing of observers at military bases, and observation of exercises. Similar confidence-building measures for conventional forces could contribute to stability between India and Pakistan. Such measures could also be a step to lessen tensions between Israel and some of its neighbors.

Bilateral arms control measures, including limits on capabilities, might also play a part in heading off a nuclear and ballistic missile race between Argentina and Brazil. Particularly given the steady improvement of their political ties over the 1980s, such military competition would serve the interests of neither Buenos Aires nor Brasilia. This is recognized, moreover, by the top civilian leaders in both countries. Nonetheless, both countries are operating sensitive nuclear facilities that could eventually provide them with nuclear weapons materials, and both are conducting ballistic missile development programs. Their November 1990 agreement to renounce acquisition of nuclear weapons, to permit mutual inspection of each other's nuclear facilities, and to negotiate inspection provisions with the IAEA is a major step toward avoiding such an arms race. A follow-on agreement not to deploy ballistic missiles, even though they might still develop them for export, would further lessen the risk of regional military competition and confrontation.

Tacit red lines, demarcating military actions to be avoided by potential enemies, comprise yet another potential regional arms control measure. Within the Middle East, for example, Israel and Syria worked out such restraints to limit Syria's military involvement in southern Lebanon. Tacit or even explicit red lines could also be part of a future security regime in the gulf to limit any new threat from Iraqi forces. Comparable red lines could prove useful in avoiding a future war between India and Pakistan over Kashmir. Should conditions eventually allow, such red lines could pave the way for more formal demilitarization agreements.

In that regard, the 1979 Sinai demilitarization accord between Israel and Egypt, which has been an integral part of the peace between these two former military opponents for over a decade, is a possible example. Still other demilitarization agreements could play a role in political settlements elsewhere in the Middle East, should new U.S. efforts after the Gulf War to restart a Middle East peace process prove successful.

Limits on the transfer of advanced conventional arms to conflict-prone regions also warrant renewed arms control attention in the wake of Iraq's buildup, 1990 invasion of Kuwait, and 1991 defeat by U.S. and coalition forces. Past experience is not encouraging. Use of conventional arms exports as an instrument of East-West confrontation in Third World regions as well as for narrow commercial gain almost always argued against restraint. But with that confrontation giving way to greater cooperation—and with the successful embargo of exports to Iraq after its 1990 invasion of Kuwait—there may be greater readiness in the United States and elsewhere to reconsider some restraints on conventional arms transfers. Even simple agreement by all major suppliers to put the burden of proof on proposals for sales, assessing implications for regional stability and not only commercial gain, would be a step ahead. Systems that would increase power projection capabilities, for example, long-range aircraft, Airborne Warning and Control Systems (AWACS), and refueling aircraft, might also receive close scrutiny. In the gulf, it will be important to maintain restrictions on exports that could assist Iraq to rebuild its advanced conventional, nuclear, or chemical weapons capabilities.

Efforts to institutionalize region-wide forums for discussing political and security issues is another initiative that might make sense in some regions. In Asia, for example, there is growing concern about the possible future buildup of Japa-

By permission of Kirk Anderson

nese military power. China is also viewed with some concern by smaller countries in the region. Though there are important differences between Asia and Europe, an Asian security forum modeled partly on the Europe-wide CSCE could be a means to allay these types of concerns and foster greater political confidence. Should such an "Asian CSCE" also include India and Pakistan, it might help to lessen tensions between them as well as between India and China.

The limits of arms control in containing the risks of regional competition and conflict should not be underestimated. Unlike East-West negotiations, the political conditions in Asia, the Middle East, and elsewhere often are missing or too weak to expect comparable arms control breakthroughs. Longstanding ethnic, political, territorial, religious, economic, and other sources of conflict still dominate relations in most regions. But experience in the 1980s and 1990s also suggests that more modest arms control measures, and the process of arms control discussions, have a growing part to play in other regions of the globe. That, too, comprises part of arms control's future agenda.

Conclusion

Looking back, the arms control process in 1990–1991 took important steps to fulfill the promise of its early proponents who viewed arms control as a means to enhance East-West stability and reduce the risk of war. For a time, unilateral Soviet "reinterpretation" of CFE threatened to undo that agreement and trigger a broader unraveling of the arms control process. Built-in political, strategic, and domestic brakes, however, checked any such unraveling, containing its scope and duration. The CFE dispute was resolved; START was signed.

Looking ahead, uncertainties about future Soviet domestic developments suggest a cautious step-by-step approach for 1991. Arms control is still necessary to help reduce lingering insecurities and foster a continuing process of East-West political rapprochement. A key part of that task could well be longer-term efforts to transform the U.S.-Soviet nuclear relationship, reflecting a post–cold war era in which the role of nuclear weapons in providing security for the United States and its allies can be sharply reduced. By fostering greater transparency of East-West relations, the arms control process can also significantly build confidence and provide warning of any reversal of positive political and military trends. Comprehensive negotiated agreements, reciprocal unilateral steps, and more limited single-issue deals all may play a role.

Looking beyond the East-West dimension, it will be especially important in the 1990s to strengthen and preserve existing multilateral arms control agreements such as the NPT and the MTCR. New agreements such as the CWC are also needed. But greater attention also has to be paid to new region-specific arms control initiatives, possibly taking advantage of the changed climate after the Gulf War. Depending on the region, traditional confidence-building measures, bilateral limits on military activities, bilateral nonproliferation steps, creation of regional security forums, and restraints on transfers of advanced conventional weapons and technology all could be pursued.

So viewed, the future arms control agenda is a full one. Like reports of Mark Twain's death, reports of arms control's imminent demise are premature.

Naval Reservists
in Training

Chapter 11

National Guard and Reserve Forces

Lewis Sorley

S ince World War II reserve force policy has been one of the most conten-
tious, unsettled, complicated, and perplexing aspects of the national defense calculus. During these many years, virtually every aspect of reserve
forces has been the subject of intense debate. The overall philosophy of reserve
force roles and employment; the proper mix between active and reserve forces;
the organization, equipment, and distribution of the reserves; and the readiness
standards and deployment capabilities expected of them—all have been inces-
santly debated, frequently changed, but never settled, at least not for long.

Deployment of U.S. armed forces to Saudi Arabia in the latter half of 1990
dramatically and forcefully brought questions of reserve force policy and capabilities back to center stage. Nearly two decades of Total Force policy, if not philosophy, suddenly seemed like so much rhetoric as Army divisions, made up in part
of "roundout" brigades from the Army National Guard, shipped out for the desert
without their reserve component elements. Meanwhile, three Army National
Guard roundout combat brigades were, however belatedly, mobilized (although
not designated for deployment). Thus, the eventual outcome in terms of the missions assigned such forces—and, should they see combat, their demonstrated
capabilities—had to that point not yet been determined. Whatever the results,
however, they were sure to have great impact on the continuing dialogue concerning reserve force policy.

In this chapter the generic term *reserve forces* will be used, unless otherwise made clear by the
context, to refer to both National Guard and Reserve forces. These consist of the Army National
Guard, Army Reserve, Air National Guard, Air Force Reserve, Naval Reserve, Marine Corps
Reserve, and Coast Guard Reserve.

Then, in a lightning campaign lasting just six weeks and crowned by a dev-astating ground assault that concluded in only four days, coalition forces crushed the Iraqi invaders. Thousands of mobilized Army Reserve and National Guard forces, including two field artillery brigades, took part, as did numerous reserve forces from the other services, in the process making an invaluable contribution to the success of the campaign. The mobilized Army maneuver elements, mean-while, spent the war in a continuation of preparatory training. The examples of both those who deployed and those who did not seem destined to have a major impact on future reserve force policy.

The Postwar Years

Reserve forces, like the rest of the great armed force amassed for the conduct of World War II, were radically and precipitously cut back in the aftermath of that convulsive effort. Thus, when war in Korea unexpectedly confronted the military leadership in June 1950, there were precious few forces in any category, active or reserve, available or ready for deployment. The active forces sent what half-trained, understrength, and ill-equipped units they could scrape together.

Korea

The first Army National Guard units were mobilized in August 1950. Within a year 110,000 Army National Guardsmen had been brought onto active duty, in-cluding eight infantry divisions, three regimental combat teams, and numerous smaller outfits. The first of these forces arrived in Pusan, Korea, in January 1951. Two of the mobilized infantry divisions—the 40th of California and the 45th of Oklahoma—staged through Japan for further training. There a controversy erupted. General Matthew Ridgway, by then commanding the forces in Korea, did not want to bring the two National Guard divisions into combat, preferring instead to break them up and use their personnel as individual replacements. The Army Chief of Staff, General J. Lawton Collins, refused to permit this, and the two divisions eventually entered combat in Korea, where they served admirably.[1]

Although only a partial mobilization of the Army National Guard had been ordered (planners were concerned that Korea might be a feint and that the real challenge would come in Europe, so they held back forces for such an eventual-ity), almost the entirety of the Air National Guard was called. Sixty-six squadrons mobilized, with six of them entering combat in Korea. Another ten were deployed to the European theater.[2]

Overall nearly a million reservists were called to active duty during the three years of fighting. When it was over, the reserve forces came out of the Korean War having maintained the reputation for bravery, patriotism, and competence that most had earned during World War II.

Post–Korean War Reserve Policy

Symptomatic of the roller-coaster ride that has constituted reserve force policy over the years was a post-Korean War suggestion by a senior defense official that the primary mission of the National Guard in the atomic era should be civil de-fense.[3] Fortunately this was not agreed to, and thus substantial combat forces existed so that, in the midst of the Berlin crisis of 1961, President John F. Kennedy could mobilize more than 300,000 reserve forces to demonstrate to Soviet leader Nikita Khrushchev that the United States could not be intimidated. The following year, Kennedy again turned to the reserve forces, mobilizing some 14,000 during the brief but intense Cuban missile crisis.

Over the years reserve forces have also periodically been mobilized to deal with crises other than military threat. President Eisenhower called up nearly 10,000 troops during school integration disturbances in Little Rock, Arkansas; President Kennedy mobilized about the same number when James Meredith was being enrolled as the first black to attend the University of Mississippi; and the following year Kennedy summoned more than 16,000 reserve forces when racial disturbances erupted in Alabama cities. Less than two years later President Johnson called up some 4,000 troops during voter registration protests in Selma, Alabama. And in 1970 President Nixon called up more than 26,000 troops to get the mail delivered during a postal strike.[4]

Once it became apparent that the president was not going to call up the reserves, they became a haven for those seeking to avoid military service.

In the early 1960s Secretary of Defense Robert McNamara became convinced that the reserve forces were too large, preferring fewer forces maintained in a higher state of readiness. Thus, in a 1963 reorganization more than 800 units, including four divisions, were eliminated from the Army National Guard. An effort by McNamara to merge all units of the Army Reserve into the National Guard was blocked by Congress. The drawdown of reserve forces continued, however, with a total of fifteen divisions inactivated by September 1967, leaving the Army National Guard with eight divisions.[5]

By this time U.S. involvement in the Vietnam War was reaching massive proportions. One of the most fateful decisions of that entire war had taken place in July 1965. In a tense meeting of the National Security Council, Secretary of Defense McNamara recommended mobilization of the reserves. President Johnson turned him down.

General Creighton Abrams was then Army vice chief of staff. It fell to Abrams to build from scratch the units required for deployment to Vietnam, units that in many cases existed in the reserve forces, just out of reach. As year after year went by without being able to mobilize the reserves, the Army's leadership and experience levels were progressively diluted and depleted. And, forced to take much of what was needed "out of its hide," the Army decimated the forces stationed in other theaters. The proud Seventh Army in Europe became, as General

Bruce Palmer later said, "singularly unready, incapable of fulfilling its NATO mission."[6]

The impact on the reserve forces was equally severe. Once it became apparent that the president was not going to call up the reserves, they became a haven for those seeking to avoid military service. This was an agonizing situation for the committed and dedicated long-term reservists who had to stand by and watch what they had built disintegrate in front of their eyes. It was many years before the impact of this debacle began to diminish.

In the aftermath of the 1968 Tet offensive in Vietnam, some limited mobilization of reserve forces was finally authorized by President Johnson. For the Army, at least, it became more of an ordeal than an asset. While some units responded professionally, and a few even deployed to Vietnam and served ably there, overall the mobilization was marred by numerous protests, refusals to report, class action suits by reservists challenging the legality of their mobilization and the war that occasioned it, and similar byplay, which served to further undermine confidence in the reserve forces. None of this was the fault of reserve force leaders. Rather it was the predictable, even inevitable, result of President Johnson's refusal to mobilize earlier.

The Total Force Policy

Following five years in Vietnam, the last four as commander of U.S. forces there, General Abrams returned to the United States to become Army chief of staff. Having experienced at first hand the negative impact of the failure to mobilize reserve forces for Vietnam, he was determined to ensure that the mistake would not be repeated.

Abrams reached an agreement with Secretary of Defense James Schlesinger that whatever savings in manpower Abrams could achieve through headquarters reductions and other economies could be applied to increasing the Army's combat power. Schlesinger also agreed to work to stabilize the Army's end strength. Abrams in return would try to produce sixteen combat divisions from the same end strength numbers that then sufficed, if that, for only thirteen.

Under Abrams' stewardship a number of Army headquarters were eliminated and many others, including his own, were drastically cut back. The manpower savings were still insufficient, however, to fill sixteen divisions to an acceptable level. A partial solution was to organize a number of active Army divisions with two active force brigades instead of the usual three, and "round out" those divisions with a brigade from the reserve forces. Later, some brigades were similarly organized, with two active force battalions rounded out by a third battalion from the reserve forces.

Abrams' first assignment as a general officer had been as deputy assistant for reserve forces in the office of the Army chief of staff. There he had developed an appreciation for the dedication and competence of the reserve forces and their leadership, and they had developed a reciprocal confidence in Abrams, in his fairness and professionalism. Now, as chief of staff, Abrams was determined to help the reserve forces achieve the standards being asked of them. He set up a complex of readiness regions, assigning active duty general officers to head them up and tasking them with just one responsibility—to do everything possible to help the reserve forces.

All of this contributed to what came to be called the "total force policy," an approach first articulated by Secretary of Defense Melvin Laird and later formalized under Secretary Schlesinger. That policy, which viewed the active and reserve forces as a single fighting force, was one factor leading to increasing reliance on reserve forces, especially in the case of the Army, in the 1970s and 1980s.

This reliance is such that some military capabilities exist solely in the reserve forces, and are thus unavailable without at least partial mobilization (or, in what seems a rather pathetic resort for a superpower, appeals to individual reservists to volunteer for active duty). Examples include naval minesweeping, water purification, and naval combat search and rescue. Many other capabilities exist primarily in the reserves. Thus, in theory, and in declarative policy as well, the United States cannot go to war without its reserve forces. The extent to which some mission capabilities have been assigned to the reserves means that they have become "integral to future war-fighting efforts, not just a force to be held in reserve or used for augmenting active forces. The reserves have become essential to meeting future operational requirements despite an historical reluctance on the part of the United States to mobilize reserve units for military operations."[7]

Abrams took these steps very deliberately, determined to stem the decline in authorized Army manpower and at the same time ensure that the Vietnam experience could not be repeated. "They're not taking us to war again without calling up the reserves," Abrams declared on many occasions.[8]

Eventually, although not until a number of years after Abrams' death, these initiatives, skillfully implemented and augmented by his successors, came to fruition. The result was Army reserve forces that were more capable, better trained and equipped, more closely integrated with the active force, and better supported by that force than ever before. Still there remained, especially on the part of those with no firsthand experience at the interface between active and reserve forces, the same antagonisms and suspicions that have historically marred the relationship. And these antagonisms, again as usual, cut both ways. The active military leadership remained uneasy about the ability of reserve forces to measure up to the unprecedented demands set for them, while reserve leaders felt active force willingness to provide them with adequate resources was becoming increasingly tenuous.

The uneasiness of senior uniformed leaders about this reliance on reserve components was not lessened by testimony such as that presented in April 1988 by General Accounting Office (GAO) official Richard Davis. "Most of the Army's support forces are in the reserves," Davis said, "and a large proportion of this force do not have sufficient personnel, necessary skills, or the equipment required to perform their wartime missions."[9]

Active force military leaders must have felt they were on a slippery slope. The initial commitment to greater reliance on reserve forces had been motivated by a desire to tie the nation and its military forces more closely together in any future conflict, and to build a force appropriate to the strategic requirements of the day. Colonel Harry Summers, who served at the time on a special study group reporting directly to General Abrams, later underscored this point.

It is important to note that it was the requirements of U.S. national security, not manpower or fiscal constraints as some have erroneously assumed, that was the genesis of the Total Army concept. The National Guard and the Army Reserve returned to the importance they enjoyed in World War I, World War II, and the Korean war.[10]

In the 1980s, however, precisely those manpower and fiscal constraints have undeniably been major factors in extending and accelerating the ever-growing reliance on reserve forces.

The combined strength of the reserve components of the various services increased every year during the decade of the 1980s, from a grand total of about 1,300,000 in September 1979 to a total of over 1,660,000 in September 1989. Those totals include the Selected Reserve, the Individual Ready Reserve, the Inactive National Guard, and the Standby Reserve. In the category of greatest interest, the Selected Reserve (which includes the units that would be called first in a mobilization), the totals also increased each year during the decade as seen in figure 11–1, from over 807,000 in 1979 to more than 1,170,500 in 1989.[11]

Analysis by component shows that most of the increase took place in the Army. The Army National Guard increased by 117,000 over the period, and the Army Reserve by 172,000, together accounting for more than 80 percent of the total increase.[12]

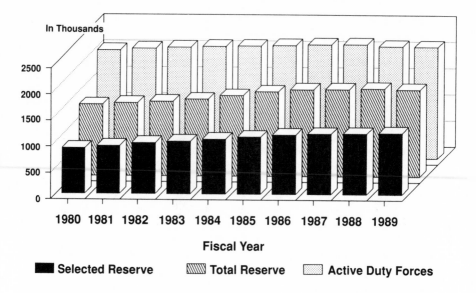

Data for active duty forces from Richard B. Cheney, *Annual Report to the President and Congress* (Washington D.C.: USGPO, January 1990).
Data for reserve forces from DOD, *Reserve Manpower Statistics, FY 1989* (Washington D.C.: Directorate for Information, Operations, and Reports, OSD`

Overall, there are some 1.7 million people in the various reserve components of all the services. The Army continues to be, as it historically has been, the service most reliant by far on its reserve forces. By 1990 the combined elements of Army forces were about a million strong, with three-quarters of that number in the Selected Reserve, the organized troop units and individuals considered essential to wartime missions. The extent of reliance on these forces was illustrated by the fact that half the Army's combat forces, and more than two-thirds of its combat support and combat service support, were to be found in the reserve components. The Army National Guard included ten combat divisions, two of which were armored and two mechanized. In the Army Reserve were two infantry brigades, three artillery brigades, and two special forces groups. Seven reserve forces brigades were designated to round out active force divisions.[13]

Of the other services, the Air Force was next most reliant on its reserve forces. Indeed, the Air National Guard and the Air Force Reserve had long been regarded as among the most competent and ready of all reserve forces, in part because what they did in uniform often equated with their primary jobs in civil life. Nevertheless, a very much smaller proportion of overall Air Force capability resided in its reserve forces than was the case for the Army. Dependence of the Navy, Marine Corps, and Coast Guard on their reserves was in turn much less than that of the Air Force.

Roundout Units

Designation of certain reserve component elements as roundout units for active duty divisions and brigades brought many advantages. Along with the assignment came added resources, both equipment and training assets. Some reserve forces with missions as early deploying units, for example, received issues of first-line equipment before some elements of the active force. This included such state-of-the-art major systems as the M-1 Abrams tank and the Bradley infantry fighting vehicle.

Not everyone was convinced that giving such high priority to reserves was a good idea. Active units waiting their turn for new equipment, in particular, were likely to resent having to get in line behind the reserves. Others raised the perennial issue that reserve forces by their very nature could not be as ready as active duty forces, citing the obvious and unavoidable disparity in available training time as a major factor. Many thoughtful and dedicated leaders of reserve forces acknowledged that matching the readiness and deployability requirements of the active forces was probably beyond the capabilities of most reserve component units. So long as the discussion was confined to these narrow issues, the outcome was predictable.

It was equally so when only cost considerations were taken into account. Reserve forces are cheaper to maintain than active forces, and virtually everyone acknowledges that this is so, at least in the narrowest sense. Thus, if the only issue is budgetary, there are strong reasons for shifting missions and resources from the active to reserve forces. Defense planning is a calculus, however, and markedly unsuited to single-factor analysis. Thus, such questions as the relative deterrent effect of active and reserve forces, or the necessity for forward deployment, require much richer analyses than simple considerations of cost or capability, no matter how important those aspects may be.

By the late 1980s, much of the dialogue on the active-reserve force mix focused on costs. This led important elements of the Congress and, to a lesser extent, of the civilian defense leadership, to emphasize reliance on reserve forces. At the same time, active duty military leaders became increasingly concerned with practical aspects of force utilization and effectiveness such as readiness and deployability. They manifested growing caution about the wisdom of relying on reserve forces to such an extent that the Army, in particular, could not go to war without them.

Lost in this dialogue, or relegated to peripheral importance, was one factor General Abrams viewed as crucially important: the role played by reserve forces as a link between the military establishment and the American people. When Abrams declared that he was going to fix it so the political leadership would never again be able to take the Army to war without the reserves, he had in mind more than just the contributions of reserve forces in terms of experience, commitment, and capabilities, valuable as those are. He also believed that mobilized reserve forces brought with them the support, concern, and compassion of the American people for their armed forces.

In addition, mobilization was sure to precipitate a general debate over the policies requiring such forces, the kind of open debate conducted before the fact that is essential to the effective conduct of war, leading either to a unified approach on the part of the people, the government, and the armed forces, or to a decision not to commit those forces. Failure to mobilize reserve forces in the crucial days of the war in Vietnam, Abrams seems to have concluded, was a major factor in the erosion of public support for the troops who were fighting that war.

Total Force Policy and the Iraqi Invasion of Kuwait

When President Bush decided to deploy military forces to the Middle East in the wake of Iraq's August 1990 invasion of Kuwait, nearly 50,000 reserves were called to active duty. These included combat support and combat service support elements, but no combat units. Nearly half the total were Army, with the next largest contingent from the Air Force. Among the units activated were medics, cargo handlers, and specialists in strategic and tactical airlift, minesweeping, transportation, maintenance, ammunition, chemical decontamination, construction, supply, military police, communications, and water purification.

This looked like a faithful operationalization of the total force concept, but closer review showed this not to be entirely the case. Two Army divisions that included roundout brigades were among the forces chosen to deploy. The 24th Infantry Division (Mechanized), stationed at Fort Stewart, Georgia, had for a number of years had the 48th Infantry Brigade (Mechanized) of the Georgia National Guard as its third brigade. The 1st Cavalry Division, based at Fort Hood, Texas, had similarly been rounded out by assignment of the 155th Armored Brigade of the Mississippi National Guard as its third brigade. In both cases the National Guard elements had trained extensively with their active duty parent units and established close ties through liaison, shared experiences, and a tutorial relationship. When the marching orders came down, however, these roundout units were left behind.

Failure to call up the roundout brigades for the 24th Infantry and 1st Cavalry Divisions shocked the reserve forces. For nearly two decades they had been told by both military and civilian defense leadership that the Total Force policy was real, not just rhetoric or public relations. The demanding missions assigned to early deploying reserve forces, along with the equipment and training priorities they enjoyed, seemed to confirm what they were being told.

When the first real test of the policy arose, however, units that had worked hard to measure up were left behind. It was a devastating blow. Commanders who had urged their soldiers on, stressing that the active force could not get by without them in any future conflict, suddenly found themselves completely undermined. And those soldiers who had responded to the challenge must have wondered why they bothered. In effect these first-line reserve forces had done everything asked of them, indeed done everything the active Army had enabled them to do, and then were told when the crisis came that their effort was still not good enough.

"We were disappointed" not to be called up, publicly admitted the commander of the 155th Armored Brigade with impressive understatement. Others were not so restrained in their reaction. The "Letters" pages of *Army Times,* a reliable barometer of what is troubling the troops, provided examples. "Total Force double-cross—that is what General Colin Powell has done to the Total Force policy," wrote a captain from Michigan. "The 48th Mech should have gone." Some members of the brigade ripped the 24th Infantry Division patches from the pockets of their uniforms and sent them to division headquarters to show how they felt about being left behind.

A study of the 48th Brigade (commissioned after the 24th Infantry Division had deployed without the brigade) was conducted at the Army War College's Strategic Studies Institute. The results were suppressed. "Our investigation indicates a unit-wide feeling of disappointment and deep frustration due to years of extra drills and annual training exercises to prove that the 48th was prepared to serve with the parent division," said the report, which also acknowledged that the 48th Brigade was "recognized as the best-trained and equipped brigade in the Reserve Components."[14]

The authors of the study next quoted a speech by General Carl Vuono, the Army chief of staff, to the National Guard Association meeting in Reno, Nevada. "First of all," said Vuono, "let me assure you that the roundout concept is alive and well. Both the brigades and their parent divisions have benefited enormously from this concept, and I am confident that the 48th [Infantry Brigade] and the 155th [Armored Brigade] would fight with valor and distinction if called upon." But, he went on to say, the prospective employment of these units was based on a contemplated period of additional training before deployment, and the limited call-up authority—then 180 days—did not allow for such training and subsequent deployment.[15]

Many members of the Congress were dismayed and angered by the rebuff of the uncalled roundout brigades.

According to the suppressed report, many who heard Vuono's speech were unpersuaded by his rationale. That is unsurprising since many serving reservists undoubtedly agreed with the assessment of a very senior reserve force general officer who maintained that "the 48th Brigade's readiness is equal to, or very close to, that of the 24th Division," and that furthermore it has more stability of leadership. They undoubtedly also knew that it had never been the plan to deploy the 48th Brigade simultaneously with the active elements of the division, since the strategic lift to deploy them all at once simply did not exist. Thus, there was a built-in time for training while the available lift recycled. Quoting a civilian defense official's comments on the redraft of an interim report on Total Force Policy to be sent to the Congress, the War College study noted that the remarks were clearly supportive of "Under Secretary [of Defense] Wolfowitz and Chairman [of the JCS, General] Powell's new force structure plan—contingency corps Atlantic and Pacific forces, and Reconstitution forces—which relegates [reserve component] combat forces to support of an increasingly irrelevant European war scenario."[16]

Further lack of confidence at high levels in the readiness of reserve combat elements was revealed by Defense Secretary Cheney's remarks in early November 1990. "The Guard and Reserve provide a very significant component for our military capability," said Cheney. "But I'm not eager to send units that aren't fully ready."[17]

Not just the troops involved, but also many members of the Congress, were dismayed and angered by the rebuff of the uncalled roundout brigades. This was predictable, of course, since the reserve components maintain a vigorous lobbying effort and enjoy strong support in the Congress. Senator Sam Nunn (D-Georgia) and Congressman "Sonny" Montgomery (D-Mississippi) wrote a joint letter to Secretary of Defense Cheney noting his exclusion of reserve force combat units from duty in the Middle East and encouraging him to "integrate the use of such combat units in Operation Desert Shield early on in the order of employment." They also rejected the idea that reserve forces might not have been activated because, with the overall limitation on the period they could be held on active duty, necessary training would consume too much of that time to permit subsequent deployment. "If selected units need additional training," observed the two legislators, "we wonder why these units cannot train under other training authorities . . . so that their training time would not count against the six month activation limit under 10 USC 673b."[18]

In a separate letter Congressman Montgomery told Secretary Cheney that "if we believe in the Total Force Policy, we ought to be mobilizing combat units and not just be concentrating on support units."[19] Congressman Les Aspin (D-Wisconsin), chairman of the House Armed Services Committee, returned from a visit to U.S. forces in the Persian Gulf region and also wrote to Cheney, saying he was "deeply concerned about [his] decision *not* to call up any reserve component combat forces." Aspin reminded the secretary that for a decade the nation had been investing substantial resources in upgrading the caliber of the reserves, that the Congress had approved a comprehensive package of educational benefits and other incentives to attract and retain high quality recruits to the reserve forces, that reserve component units were receiving top-of-the-line equipment, and that opportunities for such forces to receive realistic training had been greatly enhanced.

This was not done idly, Aspin emphasized, but rather to clearly demonstrate Congress's strong commitment to the Total Force. "Unfortunately," he added, "the extent of [the Department of Defense (DOD)] commitment is far less clear, particularly in light of some of the decisions made with respect to the reserve callup." What Aspin had in mind, as he made apparent in a series of pointed questions, was failure to mobilize the roundout brigades and send them with the deploying divisions. And, he wanted to know, "why in the Air Force have we called up only the 'lifters' and not the 'shooters,' despite the unparalleled records of many Air Force Reserve or Air National Guard A-10, F-15, and F-16 fighter squadrons?"

Aspin also reminded Cheney that while DOD witnesses throughout the year had repeatedly affirmed the importance of an ongoing review of Total Force policy, force mix, and military force structure to designing the force of the future, "the department's reserve callup actions to date call into question the validity of the entire Total Force study effort." Representatives Montgomery, Beverly Byron, and Dave McCurdy, all members of the House Armed Services Committee, cosigned Aspin's letter.[20]

Aspin, Byron, and Montgomery then jointly issued a White Paper entitled "Iraq, Saudi Arabia, and the Reserve Components: Missing Lessons for a Future Force Structure." The press release they used to distribute the document was headlined "Anti-Reserve Bias Behind Combat Unit Absence." After reviewing the president's decisions on troop deployments to Desert Shield, and the familiar advantages and disadvantages of reserve forces, the report suggested that failure to deploy the roundout brigades meant "the viability of the whole roundout concept may be considered suspect. This would carry profound implications for the organization of the Armed Forces of the United States in the future."[21] That state-ment may be viewed as a complaint, or merely an observation. It mirrors the obvious concerns of the Army's leadership, however motivated, as evidenced in the chief of staff's ordering a study—one predating Operation Desert Shield—of whether an Army expeditionary corps could be deployed and sustained without reliance on reserve force support or augmentation.

Throughout the 1980s the Congress had willingly supported ever-increasing Army dependence on reserve forces. Yet when the payoff was in prospect and the Army backed away from using the combat maneuver elements of those forces, this seemed to prejudge whether the investment in reserves had been a prudent one. Thus, urged the congressional authors of the White Paper, the re-serve combat forces should be committed, thereby providing a factual rather than conjectural basis for determining their capability for such missions in the future.

Later Reaction

After the first wave of reaction, a more moderate assessment of the roundout brigades and their readiness status began to appear. In January 1990 Lieutenant General Herbert R. Temple, Jr., then chief of the National Guard Bureau, had written that the goal was "to insure that Guard units can deploy to meet contin-gency missions with little or no additional training," something he concluded was being accomplished in most cases. Temple conceded, however, that "it would be unreasonable to expect that [Army National Guard] readiness levels should be collectively the same as a regular unit. If this were so," he acknowledged, "one could certainly argue that we are wasting vast resources in maintaining any reg-ular forces."[22]

In the first wave of reaction, senior reserve component leaders had pointed out that the 48th Infantry Brigade had been rated combat ready by the active forces, that it had years of experience training with the 24th Infantry Division, and that it received its readiness ratings and evaluations from the commander of that division. "If any attempt is now made to say that the unit is not deployable or needs major training," said one source, "then the issue becomes that of the integrity of the readiness rating process."

A senior officer in the Army's leadership addressed that issue. Both active and reserve component units are rated under the same system, he observed, but it may be that the system is not fine-grained enough to measure some key aspects of unit capability. He cited in particular the experience of commanders in inte-grating the complex of maneuver, fire support from multiple sources, intelligence, logistics, and other inputs and actions that characterize the modern battlefield. After the Iraqi crisis is over, this officer predicted, the readiness rating scheme for reserve components would probably be reviewed.

In 1990, he also observed, the Army's leadership still accepted Abrams's view that involvement of the reserve components is a good thing in terms of keeping deployed forces from becoming isolated from the larger public, but they saw that as only one factor among many to be considered. Besides, he noted, there was never any question about calling up the support forces, and that served the purpose of ensuring the linkage.

When the roundout brigades of the Army National Guard were eventually activated, they were scheduled for very extensive supplemental training. This included, for the 48th Infantry Brigade, a period of forty-one days at the National Training Center at Fort Irwin, California, the longest time any unit had ever spent there, later extended to forty-five days. These units would then be subjected to testing before a decision was made as to whether they qualified for deployment, something of course not done in the case of the active forces units previously dispatched to the gulf. Observing these developments, a senior National Guard officer could only conclude that "being equal is apparently not good enough."

There is, however, some evidence that, after the initial reaction of dismay at being left behind, the activated roundout brigades themselves developed a more dispassionate view of the training and readiness realities. The *Army Times,* in an editorial accompanying a very favorable feature story on the pre-deployment training of these units, provided a straightforward assessment. "The advocates who claim these citizen-soldiers are capable of everything full-time soldiers are, with no additional training, should be sobered by reality," said the paper. "The Guardsmen themselves know what they need, and are damn thankful to get it."[23]

The issue of the hidden agenda, this time from the standpoint of reserve forces, also came under scrutiny by the editorial writer, who observed that "some of the Guard's advocates have not made the transition from peacetime politics to a wartime footing that the Guard brigades are making." Instead, "to some conspiracy theorists in Washington, sending soldiers to a combat zone has more to do with the competition for budgets than the life and death of young Americans."[24]

This concern is shared by the active leadership. The Army saw itself in 1990 as simultaneously operating on three "vectors": conducting Operation Desert Shield, maintaining worldwide readiness, and reshaping the force in response to newly emerging realities. The reserve components were, at least as some senior active force officers perceived it, most interested in the impact of all this on the third vector.

Thus, each component has expressed concern that the primary consideration of the other has been for budget and structure advantage in the inevitably reduced overall force of the near future. Lieutenant General F. J. Brown is a recently retired officer whose command of a Continental United States (CONUS) army brought him into extensive contact with the reserve components. He spoke to this mutual distrust and the need to improve understanding and tolerance between active and reserve forces in a thoughtful commentary. Those in the Army reserve components, he acknowledged, feel "a deep-seated frustration bordering on resentment that the [active component], in command in peace and war, simply doesn't understand the problems of [reserve component] units. By and large," he concluded, "they are right."[25]

General Brown characterized the reserve components as "remarkably ready part-time soldiers" who were achieving "unprecedented peacetime military competence" for such forces. But their improving readiness, he noted, while paralleling the increasing capability of active forces, trailed the active levels of combat readiness by some ten to fifteen years. Brown may well have reflected the prevailing active force outlook, later operationalized in the extensive training scheduled for the activated roundout brigades and their leadership, when he concluded that "as a result of lack of time for training, and marginal effectiveness of the Army school courses for the [reserve components], many [reserve component leaders], particularly more senior officers, are not competent in execution of AirLand Battle doctrine." "Put simply," he said, "for reasons largely beyond their control, they are trying very hard, but they don't know what they don't know."

This is, he added, "almost a generational problem."[26] His words seemed prophetic when the commander of the 48th Brigade was replaced during the unit's training.

Contending Viewpoints

Even without a practical test in the gulf, it seemed obvious that Congress was not going to be easily dissuaded from the path of increasing reliance on reserve forces. The fiscal year (FY) 1991 defense authorization bill made that clear. While major reductions in active force manpower were mandated, only modest cuts in reserve forces were made, and two reserve components—the Air National Guard and the Air Force Reserve—received increases in their authorized end strength. The Congress also rejected administration proposals to cut spending on the reserve components, even shifting some funds, equipment, and tasks from the active to reserve forces. The conference committee report on the bill admonished the administration itself to follow this lead: "The Department of Defense should shift a greater share of force structure and budgetary resources to the reserve components of the armed forces."[27]

It was the military *leadership who did not want the reserves.*

Congressman Montgomery also read to a number of audiences a statement by an Army general. "Roundout is a fact of life," he quoted. "The 48th Brigade, Georgia Army National Guard, is the third brigade of my division. . . . I expect them to fight alongside us. They have demonstrated [their capability] through three demanding rotations at the National Training Center . . . they are, in fact, combat ready."[28] Then Montgomery revealed the punch line: the quotation was from General H. Norman Schwarzkopf, commander of U.S. forces in Saudi Arabia, who had made the statement when, in an earlier assignment, he commanded the 24th Infantry Division. The implied question was obvious: What's different now?

The situation was infused with irony. When General Abrams sought to intertwine active and reserve forces so inextricably that the Army could not be sent to war again without the reserves, what he was worried about was unwillingness on the part of the civilian leadership to call up the reserves when they were needed. He sought to make it impossible for some future president to respond to crisis as Lyndon Johnson had done, denying the Army access to the reserve forces on whose mobilization every contingency plan had been based. But now, when the issue again was joined, it was the *military* leadership who did not want the reserves, preferring instead to leave the roundout brigades at home and to replace them with active Army brigades drawn from other units.

There were precursors to this decision, events that predated the August 1990 Iraqi invasion of Kuwait and which at least in retrospect provide important insights into the thinking of senior Army officers. Army chief of staff General Vuono convened a study group in January 1989 to look at the feasibility of supporting a three-to-five-division contingency force without calling up reserve forces. The conclusion was that it could be done, but that the assets needed would have to be redeployed from other theaters of operation. Subsequently, the GAO related a senior Army official's comment that the study "showed how close to the margin the Army is in relying on its reserve forces."[29]

Earlier, when Vuono headed up the Army's Training and Doctrine Command, another general, then chief of the ROTC Cadet Command, had complained to him that "our service is literally choking on our reserve components." The issue was the amount of resources being allocated to reserve forces, and the results being attained in deployment readiness. "Roundout is not working," Vuono was told.[30] Although those observations were four years old at the time of the Iraqi invasion, they may well have influenced Vuono's outlook on the whole issue of heavy dependence on reserve forces when he became chief of staff.

Vuono's study initiatives do not necessarily reflect only a lack of confidence in the reserve forces, however. They probably also stem in part from residual concern that in time of need the president might, no matter'how crucial the reserves have been made to the active forces, nevertheless fail to call them, or at least delay doing so to the detriment of deployed active forces.

For some years the Association of the United States Army (AUSA), a private organization that often reflects official Army thinking on doctrinal and policy issues, has been urging caution in the matter of increasing reliance on reserve forces. "This ballooning reliance on the Reserve Components places unprecedented demands on them and has reached the point where careful analysis is required before additional assignments are transferred," AUSA said in a widely circulated "Defense Report" in 1986. Two years later the warnings had become more urgent. "Attempting to solve the current budgetary dilemma by transferring too many additional early missions to the Army Reserve and the National Guard," said AUSA, "will yield dangerously illusory benefits at the risk of imperiling our deployed forces and the nation's strategic interests."[31]

The Changing Strategic Environment and the Total Force Policy

There is an additional factor that may explain the change in official attitudes toward the reserves, the radically changed international environment. In March 1990 the president issued a report on "National Security Strategy" that contained other precursors of possible change in the roles and missions of reserve forces, and in the dependency of active forces on them. Noting that for nearly two decades under the Total Force policy a significant portion of the nation's total military power had resided in the reserve forces, the report predicted that "various elements of that policy—the balance between active and reserve forces, the mix of units in the two components, the nature of missions given reserve forces—are likely to be adjusted as we respond to changes in the security environment."[32]

The diminished threat, agreements on conventional forces in central Europe, the unpredictable but obviously dramatic effect of the collapse of the Soviet empire—all have no doubt had significant impact on the thinking and long-range planning of senior civilian officials and military officers alike. Coupled with predictable decreases in authorized military forces and in the resources provided the defense establishment, these events of necessity would impel responsible military leaders to review the whole range of defense policy and the supporting force structure. It would be understandable if, as a result of such review, those leaders concluded that it was no longer necessary to ask reserve forces to meet the demanding standards of readiness and deployability that had been dictated by the Soviet threat.

General John Foss, commanding general of the Army's Training and Doctrine Command, outlined some of the new thinking in late 1990. Explaining that projection of combat power would in the future be the primary mission, he called that a "fundamental change" because such power would be projected from the United States, with consequent reduction in the forward-deployed forces that have characterized the American defense posture for a number of years.[33] It seems apparent that a change of this importance would have a major, if as yet unspecified, impact on the structure, size, and missions of the reserve forces.

What also seems to have happened is that events in the Persian Gulf intruded on the ongoing process of reassessment. Military leaders who were in the process of charting a new force structure, indeed a new vision and supporting rationale for the defense establishment, found that endeavor interrupted by the need for a massive deployment of forces. Perhaps even before the Iraqi invasion of Kuwait, or perhaps as a result of confronting the issue in the midst of crisis, those leaders may have concluded that—absent the Soviet threat which had led to giving reserve forces unprecedentedly demanding readiness tasks and goals in the first place—it was no longer necessary to ask so much of those forces. No doubt some senior officers found it easier to reach such a conclusion because they harbored longstanding mistrust of reserve forces, regardless of the overt support for the Total Force they had felt constrained to exhibit when that was the order of the day.

One more factor, indeterminate in its impact but nevertheless real, may have come into play. In a period of declining defense resources, inevitable competition for increasingly scarce assets would make the active military leadership begrudge reserve forces the support it was easy to give them in an earlier period of resource plenty. The overall active military establishment is slated for a 25 percent decrease by 1995, and many observers think it will decline even more, perhaps much more. It would be understandably difficult for active duty military leaders to agree to further allocation of missions or assets to reserve forces at a time when they will be scrambling to protect whatever they can of the active forces.

Some reserve force leaders see this reality reflected in the initial failure to mobilize the roundout brigades. One general officer on Pentagon duty, referring to General Powell and General Vuono, said, "The Chairman and the Chief are of one mind on this. If we give up force structure to the reserves, and if they prove they can do the job, then we'll lose that structure to them." On this reading, then, it was not fear that the reserve combat forces would not be up to the job, but fear that they would be that motivated excluding the roundout brigades when the first divisions deployed.

General William C. Westmoreland, former Army chief of staff, has been driving this "turf" issue. Two years ago, at the annual conference for retired four-star Army generals, he gave a speech in which he argued that the "BS" of the Total Force had to be abandoned. The president, he insisted, had to have units that he

could use unencumbered by the Congress. In this, Westmoreland was continuing ✓
to argue a position he had maintained, unsuccessfully, as far back as his retirement
from active duty in 1972. At that time he framed the issue in terms of readiness,
telling the president, in a valedictory letter, that "only Regular Army forces in
being can achieve the levels of readiness required." His solution was to consider
the Regular Army a cadre that could be expanded in an emergency and thus
"serve as a hedge against the high risk associated with the heavy reliance on the
Reserve Components."[34]

In this Westmoreland staked out one end of the spectrum of active force
attitudes toward reserve forces, essentially one of disdain. One of his predecessors, General George C. Marshall, staked out the other end, coincidentally also
in his final report as Army chief of staff. Marshall wrote to the secretary of war
that "probably the most important mission of the regular Army is to provide the
knowledge, the expert personnel, and the installations for training the citizen-
soldier, upon whom, in my opinion, the future peace of the world largely
depends."[35]

While such leaders as Marshall and Abrams have stressed both the potential
of reserve forces and the obligation of the active force to enable them, their
outlook is far from representative. The more likely common attitude is that identified by a group of student researchers at the National War College in the early
1980s. Surveying their classmates, among whom were officers representing all
the services, they reported as a typical view that "Guard and Reserves should be
confined to serving as fillers for active units."[36]

Ironically, at the same time the future generals and admirals attending the
National War College were expressing this view, the president of the National
Defense University—of which the War College forms a part—was on record with
the conviction that "geopolitical conditions and economic constraints no longer
permit us to think of the Guard and Reserve as merely forces of last resort; we
must recognize them as indispensable to our ability to defend the nation."[37] Nearly
a decade passed between the juxtaposition of these opposing views and the Iraqi
invasion of Kuwait. A new generation of military leadership was in the saddle, and
events revealed how they came down on this issue.

Senior civilian officials in the Defense Department concede that it was the
recommendation of the uniformed military leadership not to call the roundout brigades along with their affiliated divisions. But they also maintained that this was
a function of the fact that under the rules then applicable the call-up could only
have been for a period of 180 days—too short a time, they said, to get the reserve
forces trained and deployed and still be able to utilize them. Congress later extended the allowable period of active duty to 360 days, and the three roundout
brigades were subsequently mobilized, although the causal factors undoubtedly
included the backlash from reserve force commanders and congressional reaction
as well as the extension of allowable duty. "Calling reserves is *essential* to getting
congressional support," recently acknowledged an Army general in the Pentagon.

The Future of the Total Force

In early 1991, prior to any deployment of combat reserve forces, prior even to
any actual combat involving U.S. forces in the Middle East, public calls for abandonment of the Total Force policy were beginning to be heard. Lawrence Korb,

a respected defense analyst and former civilian official of the Defense Department, was among the first to raise the issue. "We must live with the Total Force policy for now," he wrote, "but after this crisis is over it should be discarded as we develop a post–cold war military strategy." In arguing his case, Korb disputed the view of the military leadership of the Vietnam era that calling the reserves would have rallied the American people behind the war, calling that a "proposition of dubious validity."[38]

Korb's interpretation of the leadership's views seems too narrow, however. The contention of Vietnam-era leaders was that such a mobilization would force the issue of the war onto the public agenda before major deployments were ordered, and that the ensuing debate would either result in cohesive backing for war or demonstrate that such backing could not be achieved. In the latter case, presumably, the administration would have been dissuaded from going ahead with its plans for greater involvement.

Those expectations seem to have been validated by events of 1990. President Bush called up reserve forces, including a substantial number of combat reserve forces in a second call. A major debate began. Congressional hearings featured witnesses such as Henry Kissinger, calling for early military action, and two former chairmen of the joint chiefs of staff, Admiral William Crowe and General David Jones, calling for patience and additional time to allow the economic sanctions imposed on Iraq to have their full effect. A continuing discussion of the matter, focused on a succession of resolutions, took place in the United Nations. In all, this seems to have constituted an unprecedented examination of all the factors bearing on the use of military force, and all this before the fact—before, that is, commitment of the deployed forces to actual combat.

How all this played out remained to be seen. Under pressure to sustain a force approximately double that originally assembled in the desert, the Army alerted three National Guard maneuver brigades for mobilization, including both the roundout brigades for the divisions already deployed and another which played that role for a third active division, the 5th Infantry, not at the time tabbed for Middle East service. There seems little doubt that congressional pressure was also a factor in these call-ups. Immediately after the DOD failure to call the 48th Infantry and 155th Armored Brigades, the reserve forces establishment went into action, working behind the scenes—primarily with members of Congress—to urge the Army to make good on its Total Force commitments.

The mobilized brigades were scheduled to be sent to the National Training Center, a desert environment at Fort Irwin, California, for additional preparation before a decision was made on whether to deploy them to the Middle East. Before a further decision could be made as to whether to deploy them to the gulf, the war was over.

But even in the aftermath of the Gulf War, as so often before, that will not be the end of it. The larger defense establishment, along with the nation's allies, will for years to come be absorbed in assessing and responding to the new realities of a radically changed international environment. Whatever role for reserve forces lies ahead, it seems certain that, as so often in the past, it will involve both challenges and opportunities sufficient to require their best efforts.

What that outcome ought to be seems rather clear. Under the combined pressures of the traumatic impact of having been denied the use of reserve forces during most of the war in Vietnam, post–Vietnam War recovery as an institution, severe budgetary constraints, an undiminished primary Soviet and surrogate threat, and a plethora of new or increasingly demanding missions such as narcotics interdiction and counterterrorism, the armed forces in general and the Army in particular placed unprecedentedly demanding requirements on their reserve components. In some cases, in fact, reserve forces were expected to be as ready to deploy as active forces, and even more ready than some elements of the active force.

The reserves responded, by and large, in an exceptional way, reaching new levels of readiness and deployability. For combat support and combat service support forces, their performance, when activated, was often indistinguishable from that of the active forces, in part a reflection of the frequent congruence between what they did in civil life and their military duties. For combat maneuver forces these equivalent capabilities did not, however, equate to the best of the active forces (two National Guard field artillery brigades deployed and served well in combat). That is not a criticism of those forces, nor of their leadership, but simply a recognition of the inevitable impact of part-time involvement in missions for which there is no civil counterpart.

The radically changed threat environment will inevitably bring about corresponding changes in the size, composition, and disposition of U.S. military forces, active and reserve alike. It seems obvious that this new reality will permit the armed forces to revise what have been unrealistic, if understandable, requirements on the reserve forces. In the future reserves are much more likely to be just that—reserves, to be brought in to supplement the active forces when that is required.

The Army seems intent on generating one, or possibly two, corps that could be deployed without the necessity of reserve component augmentation. The motives for this initiative are understandable—assurance that the forces would be available when required, full control over their levels of manning and training, and independence from a political decision to call the reserves. But there are hazards as well. Any involvement of U.S. forces amounting to a corps is going to be a significant one. That inevitably brings up the issue of domestic support for the operation, and the Abrams view that an important means of ensuring such support—or of dissuading the political leadership from the commitment if that support cannot be engendered—is the involvement of reserve forces.

If Army leaders remain alert to this factor, they may well conclude that the deployable corps need not be totally independent of the need for reserve support. They could then provide for involvement of combat support or combat service support reserves, thus preserving that vital link without any significant degradation in readiness or deployability.

The Total Force Policy has much to recommend it and, with appropriate modification in requirements for the reserve components, should continue to evolve and mature in the coming years. The necessity to get the fullest return on scarce resources virtually mandates that. But its most important contribution, one not yet fully realized, can be increased understanding, trust, sympathy, and cooperation between active and reserve forces.

**General Powell
and General Moiseyev**

Chapter 12

U.S.-Soviet Security Cooperation in the Post–Cold War Era

Andrey Kokoshin

D ramatic changes in international relations, including relations between the militarily most powerful nations, the Soviet Union and the United States, shed new and different light on superpower interaction in the field of national and international security. German reunification, for instance, created a peculiar situation in which Soviet and American troops found themselves on the territory of the same state, no longer separated by political borders which had been in existence for decades.

By the end of 1990, it was widely accepted that the United States and the Soviet Union were no longer opponents, no longer implacable enemies in cold war hostilities. But to visualize how they might interact as partners under the new conditions of the post–cold war era, it is important to have at least a general perception of the emerging world system.

A World Transformed

The most significant change of the late 1980s and early 1990s was the fundamental transformation of sociopolitical regimes in the nations of central and southeastern Europe and in the Soviet Union itself, and the implications of that change for U.S.-Soviet relations. When the Soviet leadership, headed by Mikhail Gorbachev, declared the preeminence of human values over class interests, the Soviet Union took an important step in the de-ideologization of the its foreign policy. Concurrent with this trend has been some de-ideologization of American foreign policy, which was rather highly ideological at several periods after World War II. The Soviet Union did not become a rival of the United States in the economic sphere. Here, the major competition is among the United States, Western Europe, and Japan. As a result of these shifts, many of the factors contributing to the Soviet-

American confrontation of the postwar era have lost their substance and momentum.

In the past, changes of this scope and importance happened as a by-product of violent sociopolitical revolutions, major wars between states and coalitions of states, or civil wars. The very fact that these changes are taking place, on the whole, in a peaceful setting is in itself one of the prominent features of the system of international relations in the early 1990s.

It is important to note that removing the sources of U.S.-Soviet confrontation *per se* does not necessarily create room for constructive interaction between the two countries in the realm of international security. To obtain this, a number of other prerequisites, both of an objective and subjective nature, are needed.

The process of radical transformation of political systems and societies is not yet over. Each country in central and southeastern Europe may go through several different stages of internal political development before it acquires a level of internal political stability similar to that enjoyed by the United States or most countries of Western Europe. At some point these countries might deviate substantially from the path of democratic development, producing regimes that could be quite aggressive against some of their neighbors.

More significantly, the situation in central and in southeastern Europe has the potential to create new conflicts between the Soviet Union and the United States, and between the Soviet Union and some countries of Western Europe, involving the United States through the North Atlantic Treaty Organization (NATO). One can agree with Joseph Kruzel that the waning influence of the Soviet Union in this area will allow long-simmering disputes to surface. Several issues could lead to the possibility of the United States and the Soviet Union being drawn to opposite sides of such a conflict.[1]

As the world changes in ways that make U.S.-Soviet security cooperation more necessary, changes within the Soviet Union exert pressures that may make cooperation more difficult to achieve. In the 1980s the Soviet Union experienced tremendous economic and social difficulties. In the 1990s it faces the additional problem of preserving its political integrity. Analysis of trends in the Soviet Union provides ample evidence to forecast that the Soviet Union might not be the same unitary state in the future as it has been since 1922 or as Tsarist Russia had been for several centuries before 1917.

Supercentralization of political and economic power is in all probability a thing of the past. The Communist party's monopoly is shrinking at all levels—union, republic, and local. New political parties are emerging and some of them, particularly in the union republics, have a strong nationalistic orientation. These forces are elaborating their own approaches to the problems of defense and foreign policy for their republics and the union at large. Some of them demand ever greater sovereignty.

Notwithstanding the future status of the Soviet Union—federation, confederation, or a combination of both—it is clear that the central government's authority to command foreign and domestic policy will never again be as complete as it was from the 1920s to the mid-1980s. A substantial number of the new political leaders in the majority of republics favor a new union with common defense arrangements, a unified foreign security policy, and a single, unified armed forces, including, most importantly, the Strategic Rocket Forces and the Navy with its nuclear component. The attempt to divide the armed forces, especially the nuclear component, among the republics could have catastrophic consequences.

It is the supercentralization of authority that enabled the Soviet Union to allocate massive funds for foreign and domestic objectives, comparable in many respects to the level expended by the United States and its allies, who were economically much stronger. This ability of the Soviet central government to channel immense resources to foreign and military activities in accordance with certain ideological guidelines gave rise to the Soviet Union's global political presence and influence. Although it was diminishing in the early 1990s, the Soviet global position might be instrumental for constructive U.S.-Soviet cooperation in future conflict resolution and crisis management.

Radical revision of the scope and essence of Soviet commitments in various parts of the globe began several years ago and seems to have been inevitable. This change would have occurred even if the Soviet Union had preserved its unitary status because sentiment was growing that Soviet national priorities should be changed in favor of domestic economic, environmental, and social problems. Domestic issues became the main theme of discussions on national security in the Supreme Soviet of the USSR and in the Supreme Soviet of the Russian Federation.

It is essential that the United States and the Soviet Union develop a deep mutual understanding of their security interests.

Politicians and the public are increasingly inclined to believe that Soviet national security demands refocusing on the traditional Eurasian perimeter of Russia along with a reduction of Soviet commitments beyond this perimeter, especially in Latin America and Africa. This way of defining the foreign policy domain as related to national security seems to be rather simplistic because it ignores the functional dimension of national security. In any case, this Eurasian approach will be an important part of the Soviet public mentality for the foreseeable future and has the potential of reducing the global area in which fruitful cooperation may be pursued.

As far as the armed forces are concerned, a number of important trends are noticeable. In all probability, the armed forces will be reduced, possibly by as much as one-half, during the 1990s. Some experts and members of the Supreme Soviet of the USSR strongly believe that step-by-step measures should be taken to introduce a professional volunteer army not only for officers but for enlisted forces as well.

The whole structure of the armed forces ought to be revised, particularly that of the ground forces. The traditional Soviet emphasis on heavily armed tank and motorized-rifle divisions is coming under increasing criticism, even by many military experts. Increasingly, suggestions are made to have an optimal combination of troops for territorial defense using highly mobile units, which can reinforce territorial troops and provide a flexible and reliable defense in any part of the union.[2] The transformation of the Soviet armed forces into a real "defensive defense" mode of operations will be more likely and more likely to be permanent with reciprocal movements from the West, from the People's Republic of China, Japan, and other countries bordering the Soviet Union.

Changes are expected in the Soviet Navy as well, though its functions in connection with Soviet interests in the world's oceans should be preserved. There is a high probability that the Soviet Union will in the 1990s have a very different kind of general purpose naval force from the one it maintained in the 1970s and 1980s. This force could be much more oriented to extended coastal defense while retaining the capability to perform the high-seas mission of protecting the vital economic interests of the Soviet Union (or the Union of National Republics which could replace the Soviet Union).

It is most probable that if the Soviet Union and its armed forces continue to exist in a real federal status, the forces will be able to participate in crisis settlements and conflict resolution together with the United States and other Western countries under United Nations auspices. It is more difficult to imagine such collaboration if instead of the Soviet Union there is some kind of a loose confederation or a "League of States." (< I S)

Common Problems, Cooperative Solutions

To prevent being drawn into the many crises that threaten the international system in the 1990s and beyond, it is essential that the United States and the Soviet Union develop a deep mutual understanding of their security interests in central and southeastern Europe, as well as broad cooperation on other security matters. It is a mistake, however, to think that the notion of common U.S.-Soviet interests is simply a product of changes in the Gorbachev era. The issue of concurrent and parallel interests of the Soviet Union and the United States was widely discussed during the past decades, and not only during the détente years of the early 1970s.[3]

In defining common interests it is important to recall both recent experience and cooperation in earlier times, not only in World War II, but also in older, less well known historical periods. It is worth noting, for example, that during the American Civil War, two Russian squadrons under the command of Admiral Lesovsky and Admiral Popov were sent, one to New York and the other to San Francisco. These ships demonstrated Russian political support for President Lincoln in his fight against the Confederacy. While in the United States, Russian squadrons exerted pressure on the Confederates, threatening to use force.[4]

Understanding this rich history of security cooperation between the Soviet Union and the United States could help to reveal avenues of potential cooperation in the changing world of the 1990s. And while one cannot forget that the interests of the two superpowers are not completely symmetrical, spheres of common and parallel interests have broadened in the 1990s. There are many issues on which the Soviet Union and the United States could find the necessary common ground for cooperative enterprises.

The Gulf Crisis: Lessons about Cooperation

In its response to the Iraqi invasion of Kuwait, the United States was once again shown to be the only power in the West militarily and politically capable of projecting and maintaining a large contingent of troops many thousands of miles from home. Budget constraints, however, also proved to be real, and once again German and Japanese financial might was evident, though neither country, as the United States saw it, was willing to use its resources to defray American expenses in this region. It showed once again that the United States was still the leader of the West, but very much dependent on new forces.

The United States and the Soviet Union proved to be good partners, then, in trying to settle the crisis. They discovered an ability to cooperate in a new way, first of all within the framework of the United Nations Security Council. At the same time, some differences were revealed, largely stemming from the significant difference in the geopolitical positions of the two countries.

The Soviet Union is located next to the Moslem world. More to the point, part of this world is within Soviet borders. Russia traditionally had good cultural and diplomatic relations with Moslem countries despite some severe conflicts and wars. And that tradition, combined with the geographic proximity of the Moslem world to the Soviet Union, accounted in part for the relatively more restrained approach of the Soviet Union.

The specificity of the Soviet attitude towards the Iraq crisis seemed to be instrumental for the United States because it gave Washington the opportunity to search other channels to confront the crisis while preserving a united front against aggression.

The high level of militarization of Saddam Hussein's Iraq is rooted in the policies of a number of states, as well as in the prolonged confrontation in the Middle East, which has involved both superpowers. The United States always tried to exclude the Soviet Union from the region while the Soviet Union strove to weaken American positions there. Saddam Hussein profited by the conflict of goals.

In retrospect, both nations should have had much greater levels of interaction in the Persian Gulf area. They should have signalled to Hussein, as well as to all other actors in the region, that a united front of the international community, with the United States and the Soviet Union at its head, would stand firmly in opposition to any aggression. It cannot be denied that this would have helped to deter the aggression.

Joint action, as we know, was not initiated. This is probably because the U.S. and Soviet governments in spite of the improvements in their relations, unfortunately were unwilling to create an adequate Soviet-U.S. mechanism for interaction in international crisis situations that could include, among other complexities, rather candid and confidential exchanges of information and assessments of the political and military situations in different regions. That type of candid exchange, along with more active cooperative measures, could be important as new regional powers develop in the future and later regional conflicts arise.

Cooperation in Naval Issues

Political and military measures taken to reinforce international security could not be put into practice without some participation by the naval forces of both the United States and the Soviet Union. During the Iran-Iraq War in September of 1987 the Soviet Union proposed the establishment of an international naval squadron under a United Nations flag to maintain safety of navigation in the Persian Gulf. This proposal, which seemed promising, was not supported by the United States and its allies, although some Western politicians and experts showed some interest in it. The 1990 Persian Gulf crisis further showed the necessity for such cooperative naval efforts. And representatives of the Soviet Navy demonstrated once again in 1990 the willingness to discuss seriously the idea of a United Nations Naval Force with the participation of Soviet vessels.[5]

Ideally, the preparations for joint naval actions to preserve peace and stability should begin before crises erupt. Such preemptive preparation, including joint maneuvers and exercises on the high seas occurring under normal conditions, could allow for the joint familiarization of the forces.

Soviet-American naval interaction could be carried out on the basis of mutual respect for the vital interests of United States and the Soviet Union in the world's oceans. But defining these interests cannot be left solely to the members of the naval services of the two sides. Political leaders must come together and thoughtfully explicate the goals and missions of the cooperative forces along with the basic interests of each side in the world ocean.

The huge military potential of the two superpowers plays repeatedly against their long-term interests.

Soviet naval interests encompass both military and civilian concerns. From the military perspective, the Soviet Union is concerned with maintaining the defense of its coastlines and the security of the sea-based component of Soviet nuclear forces. The civilian perspective is no less vital. Normal performance of the Soviet economy is greatly dependent on sea communications between eastern and western parts of the Soviet Union through the Arctic Ocean, the Indian Ocean, and the Pacific. Fisheries in various parts of the world ocean provide a considerable percentage of the total Soviet food supply. Major Soviet tanker fleets transport the bulk of crude oil and oil products, which are a major source of hard currency for the Soviet Union. Respect for those interests, as well as a further fleshing-out of U.S. and Soviet concerns, would be a vital starting point for cooperation in the naval arena.

The Diffusion of Power

Several Soviet and American historians correctly point out that Soviet and American leadership missed historic opportunities for cooperation in the area of international security immediately after World War II. At that time Soviet-American cooperation would have been a cooperation of two giant states that enjoyed overwhelming superiority, in terms of force and influence, over any other state except perhaps the United Kingdom. To underline the unique role of the superpowers some scholars argue that these two giants were the only real sovereign states after World War II.[6]

But the changing distribution of power had radically transformed the international system even prior to the developments of 1989 and 1990. New centers of power had risen both regionally and globally, and they issued a challenge to the United States and the Soviet Union in many areas, although the pattern of this challenge differed from what had taken place at earlier stages of international relations before World War II. These fresh centers of power are in fact lagging behind the United States and the Soviet Union in the military dimension. But it is evident that this criterion of power is of much less significance in the 1990s for the developed nations of the North than it used to be. Moreover, the huge military potential of the two superpowers imposes a great economic burden and plays repeatedly against their long-term interests.

The development of new centers of power took place while the military dimension of power was diminishing and economic, technological, and other "civilian" dimensions were gaining more significance. This was belatedly recognized in the Soviet Union and contributed to the crisis of the late 1980s despite the fact that the emphasis on economic development was always in every element of the official ideology.

The diffusion of power has been a significant factor in the growing interdependence of states and societies. Once political leaders and the public understand the economic, ecological, political, and military aspects of this phenomenon, the traditional confrontation of states can be transformed in a positive way. It should not be forgotten though, that interdependence also brings additional conflicts and problems through deeper penetration of different international issues into the lives of societies that are less prepared to become an integral part of the international community.

Proliferation

It seems apparent that the above-mentioned processes of sociopolitical change are different in various parts of the world. In the Third World the role of military power is not decreasing and in fact continues to be an important instrument both domestically and internationally. Despite acute economic and social problems, military expenditures are increasing and military industries are developing in some countries of the Third World. To justify these actions they point to nations of the developed North where no serious reductions of military outlays were made until the very late 1980s.

There are sufficient grounds to believe that the world community is on the threshold of a new cycle of rising dangers from the proliferation of nuclear, as well as bacteriological and chemical, weapons. There is unfortunately the attendant probability that nuclear weapons might be used somewhere in the South. This prospect appears even more ominous given the accelerating proliferation of various types of ballistic missiles, which began at the end of the 1980s.

Halting the proliferation of nuclear and other weapons of mass destruction is a traditional area of common interest for the Soviet Union and the United States. This point of agreement existed even at the height of the cold war. There have been some achievements and some failures in this area. As to the latter, they could at least be partially explained by the cold war conditions under which countries seeking nuclear status had substantial room to maneuver for that purpose.

Scholars and politicians long ago understood that an international regime for the nonproliferation of weapons of mass destruction depended not just on the technology and economy of a particular state, but also on the political situation, on the nature of the state and its political leadership, on its political aims, ambitions, and philosophy. This makes the issue of mutual Soviet-American efforts to resolve regional conflicts and crises of extreme importance in connection with the issue of nonproliferation.

Conflict resolution, especially resolution of conflicts that could push opposing sides to acquire nuclear weapons, should be the first priority. In some cases this process must be accompanied not only by political settlement but by agreements that would provide changes in structures and compositions of confrontation forces according to "defensive concepts." Certainly, this shift would be different in different cases and regions. However, the experience of the restructuring of conventional forces in Europe in 1990 might be helpful. For this purpose a great deal of joint intellectual effort is needed to formulate the criteria and conditions for strategic stability at the regional level in the different regions of concern.

Strategic Nuclear Issues

A nonproliferation regime for nuclear weapons or ballistic missiles depends to a significant extent on the progress the superpowers make in nuclear and chemical weapons reductions. It also depends on the prospects of other countries joining this process. Slow progress in this area has been a strong criticism of the nonproliferation regime in place since 1968.

The START I Treaty will not satisfy the demands of these members of the world community. Only a quick advance to a START II Treaty would contribute significantly to an overall strengthening of the nonproliferation regime.[7] Decisive actions in the area of tactical nuclear weapons reductions would also be very desirable in this sense, especially reductions in sea-based tactical nuclear weapons.

The comprehensive nuclear test ban treaty, which the Soviet Union has been unsuccessfully seeking to conclude, would also be helpful in this regard. The last several American administrations have rejected proposals for such a treaty, going so far as to criticize Soviet efforts such as its unilateral moratorium on nuclear testing.

The Soviet moratorium on nuclear explosions was held for more than five hundred days. The Soviet Union almost enacted another such moratorium in 1990 (performing only one test at the Novaya Zemlya test site) due to strong public pressure against nuclear testing.[8] Despite calls by the Soviet Union and the larger international community for some sort of reciprocal action on the part of the United States, U.S. testing continued unabated, and U.S. political leaders rejected efforts to move on a comprehensive test ban treaty.

Many experts on both sides agree now that there is no serious need for tests of the reliability of existing warheads. The bulk of explosions are for other purposes—such as the creation of new weapons—which becomes even more irrelevant under the new conditions of political relations between the Soviet Union and the United States.

Some states of the South, and in particular those which are on the nuclear threshold, are very sensitive to the nuclear powers' political hints that nuclear arsenals of the North are to deter countries of the South.[9] Therefore it is quite important to be very delicate on all matters concerning the transformation of the nuclear strategy of NATO, the United States, and the Soviet Union.

Arms Transfers

Limiting the transfer of arms and military technologies is an issue of overriding importance. Unfortunately, Soviet-American negotiations on limitations of arms transfers, which started in the late 1970s under the direction of Lev Mendelivich and Leslie Gelb, were suspended when Soviet-American relations later deteriorated.

Since then a number of weapons suppliers have emerged and grasped strong positions in the world weapons markets. Moreover, Third World countries now have their own military industries. Thus, Soviet-American mutual efforts now might not be as productive as they could have been if they had been made earlier. Nevertheless, every potentially efficacious step should be explored. The new features emerging in Soviet-American relations give grounds for hope that the two states will not only put some limits on their own activities, but will also be able to influence other nations' weapons transfers to various parts of the world or establish joint arms transfer policies with respect to some areas.

Without Soviet-American interaction it would be nearly impossible to set up an efficient and badly needed international framework in this realm. The United States and the Soviet Union should begin creating the framework for such international cooperation. Such a framework might be based on a working body of standing members in the United Nations Security Council, who themselves are major weapons suppliers. Mutual efforts to resolve conflicts or to secure nonproliferation of nuclear or chemical weapons and to regulate weapons transfers are possible only along with regular exchanges of information and assessments. Some steps were taken in this direction through diplomatic channels, but this should be considered only as an initial stage of interaction.

It goes without saying that this is a most delicate and sensitive procedure, which is proved by the experience of such exchanges during World War II when the United States and the Soviet Union fought the common enemy for several years. Yet, now as then, such exchanges are absolutely urgent. Some Soviet experts suggest that a joint Soviet-American information system, including the use of special satellites, should be set up to warn about signs of crisis development, like that in the Persian Gulf. It is said that the United States and the Soviet Union should share their information with other standing members of the United Nations Security Council.

Conclusion

While forming a new structure of Soviet-American relations in the international security area, it is important to be aware of conflicts and disagreements inevitable in such a partnership.

The United Nations still is not a very popular organization for the United States or the Soviet Union. A considerable part of the public in both countries would probably prefer to focus on maintaining international security exclusively through their own forces. But for the international community at large, U.S.-Soviet cooperation within the United Nations is much more attractive, although almost no one seems to fear Soviet-American condominium.

Besides, U.N. structures, properly developed, could stabilize the Soviet-American relationship itself under certain conditions. It seems prudent, then, to direct cooperative Soviet-American security efforts into U.N. channels, thereby setting a good example for its other members. At the same time, the strictly bilateral cooperation of the United States and the Soviet Union in many areas, where it has proved necessary and effective, should be maintained and expanded.

Comment: The DOD Annual Report to Congress, FY 1992

Mark Wayda

T he *Annual Report of the Secretary of Defense* for fiscal year (FY) 1992 is the first payment on a promissory note issued by Secretary of Defense Richard Cheney in the previous year's *Annual Report*. The report for FY 1991 clearly expressed the feeling held within the Bush administration—and by many outside of it—that it was just too soon after the onset of changes in the international political system to begin adjusting defense strategy and force posture. A prolonged and sober assessment was required of trends in the global security environment, predominantly but not exclusively related to the changes in Eastern Europe and the Soviet Union. The FY 1992 report begins to make those assessments and lay out changes in the U.S. defense posture to bring it in line with the new security challenges.

As one reads the *Annual Report* it is helpful to keep in mind that it is a planning document published by the Department of Defense (DOD). The goal of the Defense Department is to provide the president with the maximum range of options for any conceivable contingency without exceeding the political and budgetary constraints as determined by the larger foreign policy decision-making process. When the president (or the president in conjunction with Congress) decides on a military course of action, it is the job of the Defense Department to make that happen. It is not the function of the Department of Defense to make the policy decisions to use or not to use military capabilities in any given contingency. The secretary of defense is subordinate to, and acts in support of, the executive.

On the other hand, the secretary of defense helps establish the agenda of policy options available to the president. Military commanders better understand that some tasks are more amenable to military solutions than others, and that military expertise should have a place in decision making even by the executive.

It should be the responsibility of the secretary of defense to inform the policy-making process by providing expert advice as to what is and is not rightly a problem calling for a military solution.

The purpose of these preliminary comments is to help provide a framework within which to understand the DOD *Annual Report*. These comments are an acknowledgement that some of the criticisms may seem misplaced, relating to broader political decisions than normally the purview of the secretary of defense. But they are also an indication that the secretary of defense plays a role in shaping those larger political decisions—by assessing the threat to U.S. national security, determining U.S. vital interests, and directing defense procurement into specific programs to provide particular capabilities. It is in that sense that the secretary of defense shares the president's responsibility for the foreign policy of the United States.

Assessment of the Threat

The assessment of the external threat to vital U.S. security interests is often the most interesting aspect of the DOD *Annual Report*. It provides insights into the thinking of the defense establishment on the broad issues that shape the design of more specific military programs. In so doing it exposes the parameters—the bounds of what is possible—for change in the military posture of the United States.

The Soviet Threat

The Soviet Union has posed a number of different military threats to U.S. interests: direct conventional aggression against Western Europe or the Middle East, the projection of force into various Third World regions, and strategic weapons targeted at the United States and its allies. On two of those dimensions, Secretary Cheney concludes the likelihood of volitional aggression by the Soviet Union is virtually nil. Assessing the impact of unilateral Soviet troop withdrawals, the democratization of Eastern Europe, and the overall decline in the Soviet economy, he concludes that "the threat of a short-warning, global war starting in Europe is now less likely than at any time in the last 45 years."* He further indicates the Soviet capacity to project conventional military power beyond its borders will continue to weaken.

Nevertheless, the Soviet Union still possesses impressive military capabilities. Its conventional forces are some of the largest and best-equipped in the world, and it retains a significant and expanding strategic nuclear capability. Those capabilities continue to pose a threat to U.S. interests. Initially, Cheney worries that the continuing economic malaise in the Soviet Union threatens to re-empower conservative and military constituents at the expense of the liberal reformist pol-

---

*Richard Cheney, *Annual Report to the President and the Congress* (Washington, D.C.: U.S. Government Printing Office, January 1991), p. vii. Subsequent references to the *Annual Report* will be made in the text by page number.

icies of Mikhail Gorbachev. Cheney already notes a growing influence of the Soviet military over the central government. Were the military to continue to gain power, the impetus to reform the Soviet economy would disappear, and a general pall would be cast over the future of U.S.-Soviet relations, "not necessarily a return to the worst days of the cold war, but it would prevent movement to a thorough-going across-the-board state of cooperation with the Soviet Union" (*Annual Report*, p. vii).

Secretary Cheney also warns of the possible consequences of the continuing slide of the Soviet Union into civil disorder. The twin forces of ethnic nationalism and economic frustration threaten to submerge the Soviet Union in unrest and violence that might spill over into Central and Western Europe, requiring the use of U.S. forces to maintain the territorial and political integrity of Western European states. And if revolutionary forces were to come into possession of Soviet nuclear weapons, the risk to U.S. national interests grows significantly.

Regardless of the scenario, Soviet strategic forces remain a threat, virtually unchanged in the era of new thinking. In fact, as the secretary notes, the Soviet Union has continued to modernize and expand its strategic forces, enhancing their capabilities and increasing the threat to U.S. interests. Prudence dictates efforts to maintain a robust nuclear capability to balance and deter Soviet forces.

The Soviet threat has changed, and it has remained the same. The risk of short-warning attacks and the consequent need to respond within days or weeks has been replaced by a much more slowly developing threat. Caution is still the watchword as the military capabilities of the Soviet Union remain impressive, but the need to respond quickly and to retain a large forward-deployed force for that purpose has been significantly reduced. "The extent of the changes, and particularly the elimination of the threat of a massive, short-warning invasion of Europe, has enabled the Department [of Defense] to work towards refining a new strategy for the emerging world security environment and has mandated a reassessment of many of the imperatives that have shaped our defense strategy for the past four decades" (*Annual Report*, p. 1).

Non-Soviet Threats

On the day of the Iraqi invasion of Kuwait, President Bush announced the broad outlines of a new national security strategy balancing continuing security requirements and the need to reduce spending on defense. That strategy contained four major components:

1. Maintaining forward presence in key areas
2. Responding effectively to crises
3. Retaining the capacity to rebuild forces as necessary
4. Maintaining an effective deterrent

The Iraqi invasion of Kuwait and the resultant U.S.-led effort to reverse the Iraqi occupation was the first practical test of that new strategy for responding to regional threats. Long-cultivated but hastily arranged approval for forward deployment of U.S. forces resulted in a near-immediate deployment of U.S. troops to the region to prevent a further Iraqi thrust into Saudi Arabia. Among the goals cited for the U.S. action was the desire to blunt aggression, and deter potential future aggressors by demonstrating the U.S. ability and willingness to act.

Secretary Cheney, then, surveyed the globe for threats to stability that might call for U.S. action under the new defense strategy. In a virtual reprise of the FY 1991 *Report,* he cites the potential for instability in Latin America, Korea, Japan, East Asia, South Asia, and sub-Saharan Africa, the growing problems of narcotics trafficking, terrorism, and the proliferation of weapons of mass destruction and more conventional heavy forces as areas of concern for the Department of Defense, threatening U.S. interests and potentially requiring the deployment of U.S. military forces. Given those threats, Secretary Cheney indicates that the United States "must maintain its capability to respond to major regional contingencies" (*Annual Report,* p. 3). And that means the "peace dividend" must not arise at the price of force projection and forward deployment.

There appears, though, to be a fundamental disconnect between the litany of global ills outlined by the secretary and the U.S. security interests put at risk. In short, the list of hot spots does not correspond with a list of instances in which the United States would use force. Does the secretary really mean to say that the United States would spend American lives to guarantee Pakistani control of Kashmir? Or the victory in Cambodia of whichever group the United States happens to be supporting at the time? What interests, in reality, justify the use of U.S. forces in such conflicts, especially given the assessment that the risk of Soviet involvement in or benefit from such conflicts is nil? If the zero-sum world of global East-West competition has given way to a post–cold war world, the United States may wish to be somewhat more circumspect in its use of military force.

Not that military power has no role in a post–cold war world. The Iraqi invasion of Kuwait proved that situations will arise in which, in a democratic society, the choice will be made to use military force. Prudence demands that preparations be made in advance to carry out the military mission in the most effective, least costly manner possible. That is perhaps the best lesson to be learned from the Iraq-Kuwait war.

But at some point political and budgetary realities step in, and it becomes impossible to prepare to the fullest for all possible contingencies. The real question must be whether the secretary has gone beyond what is feasible, given the economic and political realities of the 1990s. The United States learned in the 1970s the folly of claiming too many countries or issues as being in its vital interest. If he were to make a sober assessment of what is truly in the interest of the United States—what is important enough to risk U.S. lives—the secretary could begin to avoid a 1990s strategy-resource mismatch.

Collective Security

Alliance relations have long been a key component of U.S. defense strategy, and they retain their importance in the new defense strategy announced by President Bush. The partnerships in security maintained by the United States in the postwar era were critical assets leading to the eventual victory of the United States over communism, and will continue to be important as they promote stability and security, providing a U.S. presence in many regions of the world and, demonstrating U.S. resolve.

NATO

The North Atlantic Treaty Organization (NATO) has been the cornerstone of U.S. alliance policy. Standing immediately opposed to the largest mass of then-hostile Soviet troops in Europe, NATO played a particularly important role leading to the movements that have changed the face of Europe since 1989.

Post–cold war Europe continues to need a strong and cohesive NATO, but as the secretary indicates, it will be a NATO different from that which existed during the height of the cold war. NATO will respond to the changing situation in Europe, becoming more of a political than a military instrument. It will promote stability and security, but its military forces will be reduced. Although it must be understood that, in keeping with the pillars of the new defense strategy as outlined by the president, "NATO forces, while reduced in number, will continue to be structured to demonstrate cohesion and resolve and make the risks of aggression unacceptable" (*Annual Report,* p. 9).

Overseas Bases

The president's defense strategy features a forward-deployed U.S. troop presence, making overseas bases a key component of U.S. security policy. Cheney indicates that maintaining a permanent presence is critical both to upholding treaty obligations and to deterring regional actors who might threaten stability and security. Responding to the changing security environment, however, Secretary Cheney notes the number of troops held permanently on station, especially in Europe, Japan, and Korea, will be reduced.

Security Assistance

For years military analysts have written about arms transfers and the effect they have in expanding the influence of supplier nations. Nowhere was that more clearly demonstrated than in Operation Desert Shield. Cheney explains how U.S. security assistance programs, carried on largely out of the spotlight, were critical in paving the way for the impressive cooperative international response to the Iraqi aggression against Kuwait. "Both the deployment and the remarkable U.S. success in marshalling foreign support for (Operation Desert Shield) would have been far more difficult without the political-military groundwork established by security assistance programs" (*Annual Report,* p. 11). During the cold war such influence creation played a role in the U.S. global anti-Soviet, anti-communist security strategy. In the post–cold war world, the maintenance of informal relationships through security assistance remains vital to the U.S. defense strategy of presence and deterrence.

In addition, Secretary Cheney notes a host of additional benefits of security assistance programs: among others, protecting friends from external aggression, promoting democracy, and controlling drug trafficking.

In some cases, however, these benefits compete rather than complement. Most recently in Kuwait, concerns have surfaced that in its zeal to protect Kuwait from external aggression and to promote regional stability, the United States has turned a blind eye to undemocratic regimes and unjust practices. In the new world order the welfare of individuals apparently still takes a back seat to the requirements of sovereignty and security.

In addition, arms sales appear to be fundamentally at odds with President Bush's goal of reducing regional arms races. As nations enhance their military capabilities through the acquisition of weapons and other military equipment, they create feelings of increasing insecurity in their neighbors, leading to a desire by these neighbors to redress the perceived imbalance by acquiring greater military capability. This cycle ultimately reduces the perception of security in the region. That security dilemma, long recognized by security analysts, dooms Bush administration arms control efforts until political preconditions can be put in place. The continuing sale of military equipment complicates the process of creating those political preconditions.

Defense Budget and Force Structure

The process of determining the FY 1992 defense budget began with a senior-level reevaluation of U.S. defense strategy and security requirements for the mid- to late 1990s. The FY 1992 *Annual Report* begins the restructuring of the U.S. defense establishment promised in the previous year's *Annual Report,* in a manner consistent with the new defense strategy.

The FY 1992 budget features slow real declines in defense expenditures, less than 1 percent in FY 1992 and slightly more over the next several years. By the end of 1995, the force structure will be reduced by 25 percent from its FY 1990 levels. The number of Army divisions will be reduced from twenty-eight (eighteen active) to eighteen total (twelve active) with two cadre divisions. All four of the Navy's battleships will be retired. The number of aircraft carriers will drop from sixteen to twelve with one additional training carrier, and the number of carrier air wings will drop from fifteen to thirteen. The total number of ships will decline from 545 to 451. The Air Force will be cut from thirty-six tactical fighter wings (twenty-four active) to twenty-six (fifteen active), and the number of strategic bombers will decline from 268 to 181.

In addition, Cheney proposed cancellation of several programs including the Trident submarine, P-7A antisubmarine aircraft, the Navy advanced tactical fighter, the Air Force advanced tactical aircraft, and others, and maintained the previously recommended cancellation of the V-22 Osprey, M-1 tank, F-15E, F-14D, and Apache helicopter. The SSN-21 attack submarine, the C-17 transport and B-2 bomber programs will be stretched out and total production targets reduced. The big winners in the proposed budget include counternarcotics programs with a recommended 40 percent increase in funding.

Arms Control

While arms control is mentioned throughout the report, usually preceded by the phrase "despite the promise of," it receives relatively short shrift by Secretary Cheney. Essentially, he notes that it is continuing and may or may not produce results, and while concluding agreements can enhance U.S. national security, it would not render defense planning and force acquisition unnecessary.

Missile Defense

As in previous editions of the *Annual Report,* the strategic defense initiative (SDI) is conceived as a significant component of the overall defense posture. There is a traditional treatment of SDI which includes the notion that the Soviet Union, in spite of internal political changes and the prospects for arms control, will retain an enormous and very capable strategic nuclear force. SDI is seen as a prudent hedge against such a capability.

The 1992 *Annual Report* also contains a new approach to SDI. Motivated by the proliferation of ballistic missile technology, and spurred by the experience of missile attacks in the Persian Gulf War, Cheney emphasized a shift in focus for SDI to a capability to counter such threats. Global Protection Against Limited Strikes (GPALS) is a scaled-down version of the Phase I SDI architecture. It is intended to provide a more immediate defense against the types of missile strikes deemed most likely to face the United States—small strikes from Third World countries or accidental launches from the Soviet Union. In addition, Cheney suggests that going ahead with a GPALS SDI system puts the United States in a position to explore research and development of advanced SDI systems if the international environment permits or demands.

Conclusion

Significant changes continue to take place in the international security environment. Some of the old threats that were the drivers of U.S. security policy have faded, others have been more persistent, and still others have risen anew. It is fair to say the *Annual Report* has captured the volatile nature of the international system.

The report projects a slower pace of change in defense policy, however, citing the unpredictability of the international system and the potential requirement to respond with military force to a crisis somewhere in the world. What of note, then, does Secretary Cheney offer in this *Annual Report?* While the security environment remains uncertain, there are discernible trends. During the cold war, U.S. strategy was based on the assumption that a war immediately threatening the vital interests of the United States could break out within a matter of days or hours. The requirement was to be prepared to counter such a strike at the point of attack.

In the 1990s, the immediacy of the threat is gone. The Soviet Union, while it retains a formidable military capability, cannot muster it to threaten U.S. interests without a significant lag time during which the United States could prepare to blunt an attack. Regional powers, while possessing increasingly capable military forces, are not able to strike at vital U.S. interests with enough force in a short enough time to require high levels of readiness and counter-capability at the many points of potential instability. In short, the United States can afford to reduce its ready forces and supplement them with reserve or reconstitution forces.

The president's defense strategy is an attempt to guide U.S. policy into that new security environment. The secretary's *Annual Report* begins to put in place the force posture to enact that strategy, stressing a numerically reduced ready capability, a minimal yet sufficient defense infrastructure, and continued technological modernization. While it is possible to quibble, as I have, with the pace at which capabilities are scaled down or the diminished nature of the threat is recognized, the overall direction of the report must be judged as sound.

Defense Chronology, 1990

January

1   The first of the U.S. troops sent to Panama in Operation Just Cause return to the United States.

2   A North Atlantic Treaty Organization (NATO) C-130 arrives in Hungary as part of an agreement to test procedures for an "Open Skies" regime.

3   Manuel Noriega surrenders to U.S. military authorities in Panama.

3   The United States proposes withdrawing up to 6,000 troops from South Korea.

3   Congresswoman Patricia Schroeder announces that, prompted by the battle experiences of women in Operation Just Cause, she is preparing legislation to authorize the use of women in combat.

4   The Ford Foundation releases a study of U.S. defense contractors indicating that the military's emphasis on low-volume high-cost products puts those industries at a competitive disadvantage, especially with Japanese manufacturers.

5   President Bush acknowledges that the U.S. invasion of Panama has damaged U.S. political ties with nations in the region.

8   Secretary of Defense Richard Cheney orders major reviews of U.S. military strategy and weapons systems in an attempt to assess the proper direction for U.S. defense policy in a changing security environment.

8   The White House, reacting to a strong negative response by Latin American nations, postpones plans to send a carrier battle group (CVBG) to monitor drug traffic off the coast of Colombia.

9   The Pentagon reports that 220 Panamanian civilians were killed during the U.S. invasion.

9   The Congress releases budget documents on the Navy's A-12 advanced fighter. The documents show the unit cost at nearly $100 million, five times the unit cost of the A-6, the aircraft it is to replace.

10   Secretary Cheney says the revolutions in Eastern Europe do not reduce significantly the strategic threat posed by the Soviet Union and do not justify a reduction in funds for the Strategic Defense Initiative (SDI).

10   The Defense Intelligence Agency reports that the Soviet Union is maintaining large stocks of ammunition in Eastern Europe as its troops withdraw to the east.

10   South Korea announces that it and the United States will reduce the size of their joint military operations as an overture to North Korean president Kim Il Sung.

11   The White House confirms that it is reassessing U.S. Afghan policy in light of the failure of U.S.-backed *mujahideen* rebels to make significant military gains since the withdrawal of Soviet troops from Afghanistan.

11   Secretary Cheney announces plans to cut 42,000 jobs from the Pentagon as part of an effort to cut costs and increase efficiency.

11   The Pentagon institutes a hiring freeze.

12   A NATO study reports that despite some reduction in overall defense spending, the Soviet Union continues to upgrade its conventional and nuclear weapons.

13   The Air Force proposes eliminating its 450 Minuteman II missiles as a budget-cutting option.

15   The Air Force announces that Col. Marcelite J. Harris will become the first black woman to achieve the rank of Air Force brigadier general.

15   Czechoslovakia and the Soviet Union begin talks on the withdrawal of Soviet troops from Czech territory.

15   Round IV of the Nuclear Testing Talks begins in Geneva. The Bush administration, in an apparent policy reversal, announces that it will not engage in negotiations to limit further underground nuclear tests pending evaluation of new protocols on the Peaceful Nuclear Explosions Treaty (PNET) and Threshold Test Ban Treaty (TTBT).

16   JCS chair Colin Powell meets with Soviet Chief of the General Staff Mikhail Moiseyev, opening a three-week CSCE conference on military doctrine.

17   Deputy National Security Adviser Robert Gates departs for Manila in a show of support for the Aquino government.

17   Greece agrees to allow U.S. bases to remain on its territory at least through 1990 while a referendum and negotiations on the subject continue.

18   The Navy declares that the problems with its Trident II missile that caused it to spin out of control have been corrected, putting the system on track for deployment in March.

18 Soviet Foreign Minister Eduard Shevardnadze announces Soviet intentions to remove all its military forces from Asian countries outside the Soviet Union. No timetable for withdrawals was given, but Pentagon officials report all of the Soviet MiG-23s and half of its TU-16 bombers have been removed from Cam Ranh Bay.

19 The Bush administration decides to support increased high-technology sales to formerly communist East Bloc nations.

19 The Navy reverses its policy on marijuana use, announcing that recruits who test positive will be barred from service.

22 The Navy plans to reevaluate procedures for assigning clearance for access to nuclear weapons after dozens of sailors and Marines, cleared for such access, are found to be psychologically unstable.

23 The twenty-first annual REFORGER exercises begin.

24 The Pentagon imposes a three-month freeze on military construction pending a White House review of military priorities.

24 Belgium announces that it will withdraw its 25,000-person force from West Germany by year's end.

25 The United States drops its demand to inspect physically military sites in Eastern Europe as a condition of verification of a CFE agreement.

25 President Bush presents his new antidrug plan, proposing a greatly expanded role for the military.

25 The United States orders the withdrawal of the last of its minesweepers from the Persian Gulf. After the withdrawal of the three minesweepers, a total of twenty U.S. warships, including the aircraft carrier *Enterprise,* remain on station in the Indian Ocean region.

26 The Army proposes closing or streamlining up to 126 military installations in the United States as part of a Pentagon-ordered restructuring and budget reduction.

29 Secretary Cheney presents the FY 1991 defense budget to the Congress. The budget represents a mixed bag of spending increases and cuts, with a net real decrease of 2.6 percent from FY 1990 levels. The federal budget's biggest winner is NASA, with a 23 percent increase in funding.

31 U.S. intelligence agencies report the Sandinistas are preparing sites in Nicaragua for Soviet SA-2 surface-to-air missiles and Cuba is receiving additional Soviet MiG-29 fighters.

31 A U.S. Coast Guard patrol boat fired on a Cuban cargo ship suspected of carrying drugs.

31 In his State of the Union address, President Bush calls on the Soviet Union to join in massive troop cuts in Europe and to ease German unification.

February

2 A federal jury finds General Electric guilty of cheating the Army out of $8 million on a battlefield computer system.

5 The Navy announces that the guided-missile cruiser *Normandy* will replace the battleship *Iowa,* scheduled to be mothballed later in the

year, as the flagship of the naval group to be homeported at the new base at Stapleton, Long Island, New York.

6   The Defense Planning Guidance, long-range planning instructions for U.S. military leaders, is released. It reassesses the Soviet threat to the Persian Gulf, claiming it is no longer necessary for U.S. forces to deter a Soviet invasion of Iran.

6   Negotiations on a chemical weapons ban resume in Geneva.

6   Honduras threatens to "demilitarize" a U.S. installation if U.S. military aid to that country is reduced.

7   Secretary of State James Baker, meeting with Soviet Foreign Minister Shevardnadze, offers new proposals to cut nuclear, non-nuclear, and chemical weapons.

7   The Navy reports that a significant decrease in Soviet submarine and other naval operations may result in reductions in U.S. anti-submarine warfare (ASW) efforts.

8   NATO officials present a conventional weapons reduction proposal that, for the first time, includes cuts in combat aircraft and helicopters.

8   The Soviet Union drops its demand for linkage between U.S. SDI efforts and a Strategic Arms Reductions Talks (START) treaty.

8   President Bush declares that development of new strategic nuclear weapons remains critical to U.S. national security.

8   General Maxwell Thurman, CINCSOCOM, testified to Congress that the government of El Salvador is unable to defeat its rebel Marxist revolutionaries and that negotiation is the only solution to the conflict there.

9   The Air Force halts reliability tests and deliveries on the advanced medium-range air-to-air missile (AMRAAM) because fixes to earlier problems only resulted in greater problems.

12   President Bush rejects a Soviet proposal on equal limits for American and Soviet troops in Europe, saying that U.S. troops are needed in Europe as a stabilizing force, even if the Soviet Union were to withdraw its forces completely.

12   The Soviet Union proposes "open seas" and "open space" policies to NATO, exchanges of data on the movement of naval forces and satellite launches.

13   The Soviet Union abandons its demand for equal U.S. and Soviet troop levels in Europe.

13   The last of the U.S. troops sent to Panama for Operation Just Cause are withdrawn.

14   Secretary Cheney begins a ten-day tour of Asia, seen by many as a prelude to a series of U.S. military drawdowns in the region.

15   A British defense minister discloses that the U.S. Bentwaters Air Base in Suffolk will house F-15E nuclear-armed fighter-bombers.

15   The United States and South Korea announce a drawdown of U.S. forces in Korea and a transition to a South Korean–dominant military relationship.

19   Defense Secretary Cheney tells the government of the Philippines that the United States is willing to abandon its military bases there if the costs of those bases become too high.

20   The Bush administration announces that it will give Egypt 700 M60A1 tanks withdrawn from Europe. Egypt agrees to destroy one Soviet-made T-54 or T-55 in its inventory for every U.S. tank it receives.

21   Due to continuing cooperation between Soviet and Eastern European intelligence agencies, the Bush administration slows the relaxation of restrictions on the sale of advanced technology to Eastern Europe.

21   Polish prime minister Tadeusz Mazowiecki declares that Soviet troops should remain in Poland until questions about German claims to Polish territory are resolved.

21   France approves the sale of a nuclear reactor to Pakistan, ending a fourteen-year embargo enacted due to fears of Pakistani diversion of such technology into weapons production.

22   Defense Secretary Cheney tells the Japanese minister of defense that U.S. defense strategy in the Far East remains unchanged despite announced reductions in personnel levels. The Japanese leadership approves of U.S. plans to cut troops in Asia by 10 percent.

25   The United States and Singapore begin talks on increased U.S. use of military bases in Singapore.

26   The Supreme Court refuses to consider a challenge to the military's bar on homosexuals in the services.

26   Mikhail Gorbachev agrees to Vaclav Havel's demands that the withdrawal of Soviet troops from Czechoslovakia be accelerated.

27   Northrop Corporation pleads guilty to criminal fraud charges and is fined $17 million.

28   The Soviet Union warns that it will back out of a START agreement if the United States begins testing an SDI system.

March

1   CIA director William Webster says the reduction in the Soviet military threat is permanent, even if Mikhail Gorbachev were to be replaced by a hard-liner. Defense Secretary Cheney takes issue with that assessment, arguing that it reduces Congress's willingness to fund requested defense programs.

1   In response to political changes in Eastern Europe, NATO cancels Hilex 14, a high-level crisis management exercise scheduled to begin March 4.

2   Vietnamese officials offer to allow foreign military forces, including those of the United States, to use its naval and airfield complexes at Cam Ranh Bay.

4   The Soviet Union refuses to abandon its doctrine of "counter-preparation," though it pledges to employ the doctrine only in response to attack.

5   The Bush administration warns that Soviet-made SS-23 missiles in East Germany, uncovered by U.S. military intelligence, may violate the provisions of the INF Treaty.

5   The Pentagon reports that U.S. and West German officials have completed plans to remove thousands of U.S. nerve gas artillery shells from a base in Clausen near the Franco-German border.

6   General John Chain, commander-in-chief of the Strategic Air Command, testifies to Congress that regardless of events in the Soviet Union, the U.S. military will require the B-2 stealth bomber and a mobile ICBM, linking support of a START agreement to strategic modernization.

6   The Bush administration announces that Libya has renewed production of small amounts of chemical weapons and has stepped up efforts to enter full-scale production.

6   The SR-71 Blackbird supersonic reconnaissance aircraft is retired from service.

7   Two Army sergeants are indicted for using military mails to smuggle cocaine from Panama to the United States.

8   The Pentagon steps up its efforts to combat drug smuggling, ordering additional ships and aircraft into the Caribbean.

8   The Pentagon proposes selling 1,300 AIM-7 air-to-air missiles to Japan.

8   The United States announces it will sell Patriot air defense missiles to Israel to help counter the threat of the spread of ballistic missiles.

10   The Soviet Union closes its Semipalatinsk nuclear testing site, reducing the number of tests and moving them to Novaya Zemlya.

11   The United States conducts its first underground nuclear test of 1990.

12   The Bush administration announces plans to shift $300 million from the defense budget to aid the newly elected government of Nicaragua and to disband the contras.

12   The first Soviet troops leave Hungary as part of an agreement to remove all Soviet troops from that country by the end of June 1991.

13   Secretary of State Baker protests the Soviet refusal to allow x-rays of three missile containers, claiming the refusal is a violation of the 1987 INF Treaty.

14   The "two plus four" talks between the two Germanys and the four World War II allies open. They will address German reunification and European security.

14   The Navy reveals that because of problems leading to the shutdown of the Rocky Flats nuclear weapons plant, it may be unable to equip more than the first two Trident submarines with a full complement of twenty-four eight-warhead D-5 missiles.

14   A suspected Libyan chemical weapons production plant is put out of commission by a fire of unknown origin.

15   Mexico protests the deployment of U.S. troops at the U.S.-Mexican border as part of a drug control effort.

15   Defense Secretary Cheney orders the Army to provide justifications for its proposed $42 billion Light Helicopter (LH).

16   Defense Secretary Cheney warns that drastic cuts in the defense budget would strip the United States of its status as a superpower.

18   The Soviet military begins maneuvers in Lithuania, one week after the region declared its independence from the Soviet Union.

19   NATO cancels its EAGLE coordinated troop movement exercises due to the changing European political situation.

20   The services seek authority from Congress to force officers from the ranks to help meet their manpower reduction goals.

22   The State Department begins an investigation of Soviet SS-23s in Czechoslovakia to determine whether they violate the INF Treaty.

23   The Pentagon requests that President Bush exempt the military from federal, state, and local clean air laws, claiming that compliance with such laws risks national security.

23   The Navy accepts delivery of the first fully upgraded F-14D.

24   The Soviet Union discloses to the United States that it had transferred SS-23 missiles to Bulgaria as well as Czechoslovakia and East Germany prior to signing the 1987 INF Treaty that required the elimination of those missiles from the Soviet arsenal.

26   The *Major Aircraft Review,* a Pentagon review of the four largest DOD aircraft programs, reaffirms the military need for the B-2 bomber, the C-17 airlifter, the Advanced Tactical Fighter (ATF), and the Navy A-12, and concludes that all can be afforded within the scope of declining defense budgets.

27   The Pentagon reports that Libya has successfully tested an in-flight refueling procedure for its military aircraft, greatly extending their range.

29   Six people are arrested in Great Britain and charged with attempting to smuggle triggers for nuclear explosive devices to Iraq.

29   The Navy certifies the Trident II missile and deploys it aboard the USS *Tennessee.*

29   The People's Republic of China (PRC) refuses to assure the United States that it will limit its sales of ballistic missiles to the Middle East.

30   Margaret Thatcher and Helmut Kohl agree that NATO nuclear weapons should continue to be based in Germany after reunification.

30   The Bush administration withdraws its assessment that a fire at a Libyan chemical weapons plant had rendered the facility inoperable. Instead, the administration expresses concern that the fire may have been a hoax designed to reduce Western concerns over Libyan chemical weapons production.

31   Suspected communist guerrillas fire machine guns at a bus carrying U.S. service personnel in Honduras. Seven are injured.

April

1   The Bush administration, in a move seen as an expression of the president's displeasure with Soviet pressure on Lithuania, cancels a trip to the Soviet Union by the Army chief of staff, Carl Vuono.

1   General John Foss, commander of the Training and Doctrine Command (TRADOC), orders Army planners to develop more rigorous marksmanship tests for the infantry.

2   President Saddam Hussein of Iraq warns that he has acquired chemical weapons and will use them against Israel if Israel threatens Iraq.

2   NATO scraps plans to develop and deploy a successor to the Lance missile.

3   The Air Force reveals that a total of fifty-seven F-117A stealth fighters have been built with total program costs approaching $6.6 billion.

3   The Pentagon reports that the first combat mission for the F-117A stealth fighter, a bombing mission in Operation Just Cause, failed when pilot error caused a critical target to be missed by hundreds of yards.

4   Secretary of State Baker and Foreign Minister Shevardnadze open talks to prepare for a June summit.

4   Defense Secretary Cheney orders a fundamental review of the Navy's Seawolf submarine and Arleigh Burke destroyer programs.

6   The Joint Chiefs' annual net assessment of the military threat facing the United States concludes that nuclear weapons in Europe remain a valuable component of U.S. military forces.

7   Former national security adviser John Poindexter is convicted of all five felony charges filed against him in his Iran-contra trial.

9   The United States grants an export license to sell a Cray computer to India despite warnings that it could be used to produce nuclear weapons and ballistic missiles.

9   The White House steps back from predictions that a strategic arms reductions agreement would be ready for signature at the June summit, noting that the talks had deadlocked.

10   The Pentagon releases results of a test in which a laser radar was able to distinguish between a reentry vehicle and a decoy.

10   U.S. and Soviet negotiators meet to prepare an agreement to reduce chemical weapons for signature at the June summit.

11   A member of the 82d Airborne division is charged with the murder of a civilian during Operation Just Cause.

11   British customs officials seize components of what they call a huge gun capable of firing a shell hundreds of miles. The shipment was bound for Iraq.

14   Defense Secretary Cheney rejects a Soviet proposal to cut sea-based nuclear weapons.

16   The January 11 DOD hiring freeze is relaxed, allowing promotions, but not new external hires.

17   The Pentagon announces that it continues to outspend its NATO allies and Japan for military expenditures.

18   The Army rejects the recommendation of the Defense Advisory Committee on Women in the Services (DACOWITS) to permit women in combat roles for a four-year test period.

19   The General Accounting Office (GAO) issues a report warning that the Army's AH-64A Apache helicopter gunship has such serious performance and maintenance problems that the Army should cancel the program and end production of the remaining 132 Apaches ordered but not yet delivered.

20   President Bush nominates Lt. Gen. Carl Stiner to become commander-in-chief of the U.S. Special Operations Command (USSOCOM).

20   The United States initiates a new military aid program to Peru to

arm and train Peruvian military personnel to combat leftist guerrillas and drug traffickers.

23   The Air Force offers to cancel its rail garrison plan for MX missiles
and slow development of small ICBMs to reduce its expenditures.

23   The Air Force confirms the existence of hairline cracks behind the
engines of the B-2 bomber.

24   The Navy presents Congress with a list of ninety-four bases and
other facilities the service will consider for closure or realignment.

24   The Air Force's over-the-horizon/backscatter (OTH/B) radar system in Maine begins operation predominently in an antidrug role.

24   The PRC and the Soviet Union sign an agreement to reduce troop
levels at their border.

25   Responding to a slow but continuing buildup of North Korean
troops close to the South Korean border, U.S. intelligence sources
reduce the estimated warning time of a North Korean attack to
twenty-four hours.

25   Defense Secretary Cheney orders the Air Force to reinstate plans
for the rail garrison MX.

25   Belgium, the Netherlands, and Luxemburg announce plans to join
the Missile Technology Control Regime (MTCR).

26   Defense Secretary Cheney cuts planned B-2 procurement from
132 aircraft to seventy-five.

26   President Bush names General Michael Dugan to replace the retiring General Larry Welch as Air Force chief of staff.

26   The sixth round of the Conventional Armed Forces in Europe
(CFE) talks and the latest round of the U.S.-Soviet chemical weapons talks end.

27   The Army, in its new six-year spending plan, calls for an end to
production of the M-2 Bradley Fighting Vehicle, 1,800 units short
of the planned 8,500.

28   The F-117A stealth fighter makes its first air-show appearance at
Carswell Airshow '90.

30   The USS *Coral Sea* is retired after forty-two years of service.

May

1   The Air Force resumes testing of the B-2 bomber following a
scheduled five-month modification period.

2   President Bush cancels the Follow-on-to-Lance (FOTL).

3   Secretary of State Baker announces to a meeting of NATO foreign
ministers that the United States will withdraw some nuclear artillery from Europe and that it seeks negotiations to remove all
ground-based short-range nuclear forces (SNF) from Europe.

3   NATO adopts proposals to ease German unification and make the
inclusion of a unified Germany in NATO acceptable to the Soviet
Union.

7   Two Colombian drug dealers are arrested as they attempt to purchase 120 Stinger antiaircraft missiles.

7   U.S. and Greek negotiators resume talks over the status of U.S.
military facilities in Greece.

8 Defense Secretary Cheney tells a meeting of NATO defense ministers that European security requires the deployment of a new generation of air-launched tactical nuclear missiles.

10 The NATO Nuclear Planning Group concludes it is necessary to maintain a nuclear deterrent force in Europe as a counter to continued Soviet nuclear modernization.

11 A Soviet team inspects B-1 bombers at Grand Forks AFB as part of a pre-START verification procedure.

11 The Pentagon begins a test of SDI technologies involving a giant sensor aboard a Boeing 767. The sensor is designed to track warheads in space.

12 Two U.S. airmen are murdered in the Philippines. Philippine rebels vow to increase attacks on U.S. personnel until the United States pulls out of its military bases in that country.

14 U.S. and Philippine negotiators begin talks over the future of U.S. bases in the Philippines.

14 The PRC cancels plans to modernize its F-8 jet fighters, reneging on a $550 million arms deal with the Grumman Corporation that was part of a series of long-term military ties between the PRC and the United States.

15 Vice Admiral John Nyquist testifies to Congress that Aegis radar systems, like those already in service on some ships in the U.S. Navy, can detect stealth aircraft.

15 The Air Force unveils the competing designs for the advanced technology fighter (ATF), the proposed replacement for the F-15.

16 The Soviet Union suspends its partial withdrawal of troops from East Germany due to an unavailability of housing for those troops in the Soviet Union.

17 President Bush and Chancellor Helmut Kohl agree that a unified Germany should remain in NATO and that the four World War II victors should retain some of their residual rights to control the political course of Germany.

17 The United States drops its long-standing requirement that its NATO allies increase their defense budgets by 3 percent each year.

17 A team of U.S. scientists reports that a small gamma ray detector can distinguish between nuclear and non-nuclear cruise missiles by detecting the output of gamma rays from the warhead.

19 Secretary of State Baker and Foreign Minister Shevardnadze agree to numerical limits on cruise missiles, clearing the way for conclusion of a strategic arms reductions agreement. They also reach full agreement to cut chemical weapons stocks to 20 percent of the current U.S. total. The United States also agrees to an immediate unilateral cessation of chemical weapons production.

21 Western analysts report that the Soviet Union has begun moving nuclear weapons out of the Baltics for fear of ethnic disturbances there.

20 West Germany agrees to subsidize the withdrawal of Soviet troops from German territory.

22 The Air Force establishes the Air Force Special Operations Command (AFSOC).

22   The Bush administration announces that a split between the United States and the Soviet Union over German military power and disposition of weapons to be controlled has threatened to delay completion of a conventional forces reduction agreement until 1991 or later.

23   The Army reveals the existence of a barge-based helicopter unit that has been operating in the Persian Gulf for two and a half years. The unit flew almost exclusively night missions over water as part of the effort to protect gulf shipping from Iranian gunboats.

23   NATO defense ministers declare for the first time that the Warsaw Pact no longer poses a military threat. In response the ministers announce plans to reduce NATO readiness and scale back NATO training programs.

23   Defense Secretary Cheney acknowledges that safety problems with U.S. nuclear artillery shells in Europe were discovered in 1988 and that the shells were repaired secretly.

24   The Navy suspends all live firings of sixteen-inch guns on its four battleships following tests that indicate the April 1989 explosion of a sixteen-inch gun aboard the USS *Iowa* could have been accidental. The Navy reopens the investigation into the *Iowa* explosion.

26   Defense Secretary Cheney meets with nuclear experts to determine the safety risks of the nuclear short-range attack missile (SRAM-A) inventory and whether those missiles should be taken off alert until alleged safety problems are addressed.

28   The Soviet Union begins to dismantle its radar facility at Krasnoyarsk.

28   For the first time in thirty-six years, North Korea returns the remains of five U.S. service personnel killed during the Korean War.

29   A U.S. reconnaissance satellite gathers the first photographic evidence of the deployment of indigenous North Korean ballistic missiles.

30   Mikhail Gorbachev arrives in Washington for a four-day summit meeting with President Bush. While a START agreement was not completed in time for their signature at this meeting, they expect to issue a statement of understanding on cuts in strategic weapons.

30   The United States and Greece agree on terms to allow U.S. military installations to remain in that country for the next eight years. Hellenikon AB, near Athens, is to be closed as announced by Secretary Cheney in January as part of a DOD cost-cutting plan.

31   The Defense Department dispatches a six-ship Marine amphibious group to the Liberian coast to protect and evacuate American citizens threatened by advancing rebel forces.

31   The United States concedes to the Soviet Union the right, under a START regime, to continue modernization of its SS-18 ICBM.

June

1   The United States and the Soviet Union sign an agreement to eliminate most of their chemical weapons stockpiles.

2   U.S. and Soviet negotiators agree to future talks on a second treaty on strategic nuclear arms.

2   The Philippines announces plans to purchase twenty-four F-16s to replace their F-5s.

4   The Navy releases a report indicating that more than twenty nations have submarine forces that might pose a significant threat to the United States.

5   The British American Security Information Council reveals that although NATO has decided to forgo modernization of its land-based nuclear forces, it has deployed American nuclear-armed sea-launched cruise missiles (SLCMs). The Pentagon denies the report.

5   Foreign Minister Shevardnadze announces that the Soviet Union will remove some of its short-range nuclear forces from Central Europe.

6   President Bush agrees to lift restrictions on the sale of advanced telecommunications equipment to the formerly communist countries of Eastern Europe.

7   The Warsaw Pact announces that the West is no longer an ideological enemy of the East.

7   Congress and the Pentagon reach agreement to cover a shortfall in the DOD payroll accounts. Under the agreement, $58 million will be shifted from the MX, Midgetman, Trident, and Seawolf programs.

8   Secretary Cheney orders all SRAM-As removed from strategic aircraft pending completion of an inquiry into the risks that the weapons could accidentally explode.

8   NATO foreign ministers officially declare an end to cold war hostilities with the eastern bloc.

9   The White House informs the Defense Department that it will no longer lobby Congress for funds for antisatellite (ASAT) weapons.

9   East German Defense Minister Rainer Eppelmann announces that East Germany will withdraw from the Warsaw Pact immediately upon the unification of Germany.

10   Lawrence Garret, secretary of the Navy, responding to test delays and high cost estimates, orders a special review of the A-12 aircraft program.

11   The Supreme Court rules that the Constitution does not give states the right to interfere with the call-up of National Guard units for duty overseas.

11   Two Soviet SU-27s land for the first time in North America at Elmendorf AFB, Anchorage. They are en route to a Canadian air show.

12   Mikhail Gorbachev agrees to allow a unified Germany to remain in NATO but continues to see some role for Germany in the Warsaw Pact. Western leaders reject any German participation in the Warsaw Pact.

13   The Soviet Union announces it will destroy unilaterally sixty short-range nuclear missile launchers in Eastern Europe.

13   The Army announces plans to deactivate the 2d Armored Division at Fort Hood, Texas, as part of a plan to save $1.2 billion. The 9th

Infantry Division at Fort Lewis, Washington, is also to be deactivated.

14   NATO and Warsaw Pact representatives announce they are close to an agreement to limit the number of tanks and other armored vehicles each side can have in Europe, a significant step toward a complete CFE agreement.

14   Soviet Defense Minister Dmitri Yazov claims that the Soviet Union could agree to a unified Germany only if it were to become a member of a collective European security system that would replace both NATO and the Warsaw Pact.

15   Nicaraguan president Violetta Barrios de Chamorro announces a one-third reduction in the size of the Nicaraguan Army.

15   Captain Marsha Evans becomes the first woman to command a U.S. naval station when she assumes command of the Treasure Island base in San Francisco Bay.

16   U.S. intelligence reports that Libya is constructing a second chemical weapons production facility.

17   Officials in the Bush administration indicate that the president is unwilling to abandon the long-standing NATO doctrine allowing the first use of nuclear weapons.

19   Defense Secretary Cheney sends to Congress a proposal to reduce the armed forces by 25 percent over five years.

20   An explosion and fire damage the aircraft carrier USS *Midway* off the coast of Japan and kill at least two sailors.

22   Checkpoint Charlie, the most famous point of entry between east and west Berlin, is removed.

22   Northrop unveils the YF-23, its entry in the competition for the ATF, the Air Force replacement for the F-15.

23   Pentagon officials report that the Navy's A-12 attack plane, under development by General Dynamics and McDonnell Douglas, is well behind schedule and faces continually increasing costs.

24   The Navy withdraws long-standing objections to Soviet commercial shipping in Puget Sound.

25   The United States and South Korea agree to move the headquarters of the U.S. Army in Korea out of Seoul to the provinces.

25   Naval Station New York officially relocates from Brooklyn to Staten Island.

26   Germany requests that U.S., British, and French troops remain in Berlin until all Soviet troops are out of the territory of East Germany.

26   The Hungarian parliament votes overwhelmingly to withdraw from the Warsaw Pact.

26   U.S. troops begin moving chemical weapons out of West Germany.

27   Iraqi president Saddam Hussein warns that war in the Middle East is inevitable unless the United States takes steps to curb anti-Palestinian actions by Israel.

27   NATO agrees to retain its first-use policy regarding nuclear weapons.

27   The Soviet Union formally agrees to limits on its tanks and other

armored vehicles in Europe, clearing the way for a CFE agreement by year's end.

27   Donald Gregg, the U.S. ambassador to South Korea, warns against unilateral U.S. troop withdrawals from the South, saying that the North would view such an act as an invitation to invade.

28   Iraqi president Saddam Hussein declares that his country does not possess nuclear weapons.

29   The Air Force announces it is withdrawing one of its two tactical fighter squadrons—twenty-four F-4Gs—based at Clark Air Base in the Philippines.

29   The Institute for Defense Analysis releases the results of a study that concludes the V-22 Osprey could perform its military functions more effectively than helicopter alternatives and at a lower cost.

29   Secretary Cheney orders the Air Force to discontinue flights of WC-130 "Hurricane Hunters" by October 1, turning those responsibilities over to the Department of Commerce.

30   The Bush administration proposes the withdrawal of the nearly 1,400 U.S. nuclear artillery shells from Europe.

July

1   President Bush proposes a change in NATO's flexible-response doctrine, which entails a quick nuclear response to a Soviet invasion of Western Europe. Instead the president wants to make the use of nuclear weapons a "last resort."

2   The United States and Singapore reach agreement allowing the United States to operate ships and aircraft out of that country.

3   Defense Secretary Cheney reaffirms his opposition to the V-22 Osprey in spite of the results of a study by the Institute for Defense Analysis that indicates the aircraft would be both effective and economical.

3   North and South Korea agree to hold talks aimed at settling their long-standing military disputes.

3   The Energy Department increases by 50 percent, to $28.6 billion, its estimate of the cost of cleaning up radioactive and toxic wastes at weapons-manufacturing facilities.

3   France announces plans to attend, for the first time, talks on curbing the proliferation of nuclear weapons.

4   President Bush pledges to provide economic aid to the Soviet Union if it follows through with promised defense cuts and market reforms.

5   The United States and South Korea complete a $4 billion deal to co-produce F/A-18 fighters starting in 1992.

6   NATO leaders pledge to alter profoundly their political and military thinking in response to the change in the European and global security environments.

7   The Army reveals live-fire test results which show that the ADATs air defense system is extremely vulnerable, putting its two-person crew at risk.

8   Pakistan calls for a South Asian nuclear nonproliferation pact.

9   The United States gives final approval for a $3 billion deal for General Dynamics to sell 315 M1 tanks to Saudi Arabia.

9   The Bush administration announces plans to sell 200 AMRAAMs to Spain for $132 million.

10   Henry F. Cooper, former U.S. arms negotiator, is named the first civilian head of the Strategic Defense Initiative Organization (SDIO).

11   Army Secretary Michael Stone announces that the Army will close up to fifty ROTC programs across the country as part of the Army's long-term budgetary reduction.

12   The last of fifty-nine F-117A stealth fighters is delivered to the Air Force.

12   A Pentagon spokesperson reaffirms the commitment of Defense Secretary Cheney to the A-12 despite its severe schedule and cost difficulties.

14   The General Accounting Office (GAO) releases a study of Air Force radar jamming devices including the Airborne Self-Protection Jammer (ASPJ). The study concludes that the four systems—ASPJ, ALQ-184, ALQ-135, and ALQ-131—were all defective and that most of the units have been grounded or put in storage.

16   The Soviet Union drops its objections to a unified Germany remaining a member of NATO.

16   President Bush revamps the President's Foreign Intelligence Advisory Board (PFIAB), reducing the membership from fifteen to six and naming John Tower as its chair.

17   U.S. military engineers from Subic Bay Naval Station join a rescue effort for victims of an earthquake that killed over 200 people in the Philippines.

17   Both East and West Germany agree to accept the postwar German-Polish frontier.

18   The United States drops its long-standing recognition of a three-part coalition of forces—including the Khmer Rouge—in Cambodia.

18   The Soviet Union and Hungary accept NATO's offer to establish diplomatic ties.

19   The Army resumes experimental destruction of chemical weapons stocks after a nearly three week pause due to technical problems.

20   A federal appeals court vacates all of Oliver North's convictions in connection with the Iran-contra scandal, ordering the lower court to reexamine all of the evidence against North.

21   The Navy's newest aircraft carrier, the USS *George Washington,* is christened.

21   The Navy cancels its contract with Lockheed for the P-7A ASW aircraft.

22   Secretary Cheney orders SDIO to conduct a study of and make recommendations for SDI's role in countering the threat of Third World ballistic missiles.

23   Iraq masses nearly 30,000 elite troops at the Kuwaiti border. U.S. officials report that a lack of visible logistical support lines suggests

the buildup is merely a show of force and not the precursor to an invasion.

23   The Pentagon announces plans to move U.S. chemical weapons from West Germany to Johnston Atoll, a small island in the Pacific where the Army has been operating an experimental incinerator for destruction of chemical weapons.

24   The U.S. naval squadron in the Persian Gulf and those of the United Arab Emirates hold short-notice exercises as a signal to Iraqi president Saddam Hussein to avoid starting a conflict with Kuwait.

25   President Mubarak of Egypt announces that the crisis in the Persian Gulf appears to be easing as Iraq and Kuwait agree to meet to attempt to settle their differences over territory and oil prices.

26   General John Galvin, SACEUR, seeks congressional approval to close 100 military installations in Europe.

27   The Bush administration takes "Looking Glass," a SAL airborne command post charged with directing a nuclear war in the aftermath of a Soviet nuclear attack off round-the-clock alert.

29   U.S. Army troops participate in raids on marijuana fields in California.

30   U.S. officials explain that despite the slaughter and breakdown of order in Liberia, U.S. troops would not become involved because U.S interests are not at risk.

31   The Soviet Union petitions the United States for permission to launch Proton rockets from Cape Canaveral.

31   Five Central American nations, Costa Rica, El Salvador, Guatemala, Honduras, and Nicaragua, meet to discuss reducing the size of national military establishments.

August

1   The DOD Inspector General and the Office of the Secretary of the Navy begin probes of the troubled A-12 program.

2   Iraq invades Kuwait. The United States condemns the invasion and orders the aircraft carrier *Independence* and its escorts to the Middle East.

2   Soviet Foreign Minister Shevardnadze announces that the Soviet Union will cease production of its rail-mobile SS-24 ICBM.

2   President Bush presents his plan to restructure the U.S. military by 1995, making it smaller, with a quick-response capability.

3   The Pentagon provides President Bush with a list of options for defending Saudi Arabia from Iraqi troops occupying Kuwait. The list includes air attacks but does not include a massive deployment of U.S. troops.

5   President Bush announces that he will not settle for anything less than the complete withdrawal of Iraqi troops from Kuwait and the restoration of the Kuwaiti royal family to power.

5   Secretary Cheney departs for Saudi Arabia to consult on the defense of the country from Iraqi troops and to attempt to arrange for the use of Saudi military installations by U.S. forces.

6   President Bush proposes the creation of a multinational naval force to enforce a U.N.-imposed embargo on Iraq. The naval buildup in the region continues as the United States, France, Great Britain, and the Soviet Union order additional warships into the area. U.S. military officials are planning to deploy aircraft and support forces to Saudi Arabia, pending Saudi approval.

7   King Fahd of Saudi Arabia approves the deployment of U.S. military forces on Saudi soil. President Bush orders air assets and ground forces to that country—the beginning of Operation Desert Shield.

8   The first 4,000 American troops arrive in Saudi Arabia. Secretary Cheney reports that the U.S. troop deployment could ultimately reach 90,000.

8   Great Britain becomes the first foreign nation to join the United States in its effort to resist Iraq.

8   U.S. military officials warn Iraq that the use of chemical weapons would result in a swift and severe retaliation. Four thousand U.S. Marines are deployed near the Kuwaiti border near the town of Khafji. Eight Air Force Reserve C-5A cargo jets are called to active duty in the gulf. Saddam Hussein declares the annexation of Kuwait.

9   France dispatches an independent naval force and ground units to the Persian Gulf. The U.N. declares the Iraqi annexation of Kuwait void. The Pentagon reports that it will take a month to complete the planned deployment of U.S. troops to the gulf. The Defense Intelligence Agency reports that more Iraqi troops are en route to Kuwait, bringing the total to 170,000. The Pentagon increases the number of U.S. troops to be dispatched to as many as 250,000.

9   Israel announces that its Arrow antitactical missile is ready for its first test. The Arrow is the Israeli contribution to the U.S. SDI program, with 80 percent of the costs of the program being provided by the United States.

11   The Defense Department mobilizes the Civil Reserve Air Fleet, calling on commercial airlines to provide airlift for troops and equipment to the gulf.

13   President Bush declares the naval blockade of Iraq a success as ships refuse to challenge the U.S. ships on station. A fourth aircraft carrier, the *John F. Kennedy,* and the battleship *Wisconsin,* are en route to the crisis area.

14   President Bush offers financial aid to Jordan's King Hussein to ensure his compliance with the U.N. embargo of Iraq, also warning that U.S. warships could blockade Jordanian ports if it fails to comply. Saddam Hussein announces the withdrawal of Iraqi forces from Iran and the freeing of Iranian prisoners of war. The United States considers a partial mobilization of reserves to augment the gulf deployment.

15   The Pentagon announces that it will deploy F-117 stealth fighters to the Persian Gulf. The Philippines warns the United State not to use its military installations in that country for operations in the Persian Gulf.

16   The Pentagon announces that 45,000 Marines will be sent to the gulf to supplement the thousands of troops already committed. The White House orders U.S. naval forces in the gulf to begin intercepting commercial shipping to and from Iraq and Kuwait.

17   Mikhail Gorbachev announces plans to professionalize the Soviet armed forces by reducing conscription and relying more on volunteers.

18   The first U.S. service person to die in the Persian Gulf, Air Force Staff Sergeant John Campisi, is buried. He was struck by a truck on a darkened Saudi runway.

20   The United Arab Emirates agrees to allow U.S. forces to operate from its military installations.

21   The nine-nation Western European Union pledges increased naval support in the Persian Gulf.

22   President Bush orders 40,000 reservists to active duty. The Pentagon halts the deactivation of the 2d Armored Division at Fort Hood, Texas, and dispatches it to Saudi Arabia. The first elements of the 24th Mechanized Infantry Division arrive in Saudi Arabia. U.S. units based in Europe also begin moving to the gulf. Saudi officials divert thousands of barrels of jet fuel and diesel from export, supplying them to U.S. forces.

23   Saudi Arabia permits U.S. forces to hold large-scale exercises in that country. The first such exercises take place. Two Iraqi MiG-23s fire on a pair of U.S. F-15s in Saudi airspace; the F-15s do not return fire.

24   Secretary Cheney halves the procurement plans for the Army's Light Helicopter (LH).

25   The U.N. Security Council approves the use of force by the naval forces in the gulf to enforce the embargo against Iraq.

25   The Pentagon announces plans to deploy F-111 bombers from Great Britain to Saudi Arabia.

26   Despite the authorization of the Security Council, the Soviet Union says it will not participate in military action against Iraq.

27   President Bush says he is pessimistic about the chances for a diplomatic solution to the gulf crisis.

27   The YF-23, the McDonnell Douglas–Northrop entry in the competition for the Air Force's ATF, completes its first flight.

27   The Defense Department reports that the first of a series of tests of sensors for its Brilliant Pebbles SDI system was only partially successful because the telemetry terminated prematurely.

28   The United States agrees to end low-level flights—below 300 meters—over West Germany.

28   The Bush administration decides to sell $6 to $8 billion in weapons, including F-15 fighters and Stinger antiaircraft missiles, to Saudi Arabia.

29   The Bush administration reports that Libya, Cuba, Mauritania, Yemen, North Korea, and Sudan are violating the U.N.-imposed embargo of Iraq.

29   A C-5A bound for Saudi Arabia crashes in West Germany, killing thirteen U.S. soldiers.

29   The Navy announces that the carrier *Lexington,* used for training, will be decommissioned in mid-1991.

30   President Bush says the presence of hostages in Iraq will not limit U.S. military options.

31   General H. Norman Schwarzkopf, the commander of Desert Shield, says U.S. forces will not strike first.

31   A U.S. soldier charged with murder in the killing of an unarmed civilian during the 1990 invasion of Panama is found not guilty.

September

2   Israel requests Patriot air defense missile systems from the United States.

3   Two Italian warships in the Red Sea sail at high speed through the center of a U.S. carrier battle group forcing the carrier, the *Saratoga,* and its escorts to scatter. The incident underscores the lack of communication and coordination among the multinational naval forces in the Middle East.

4   Secretary of State Baker tells Congress that the United States and the Arab nations should band together in a sort of Middle Eastern security arrangement structured like NATO to contain Iraqi aggression.

4   U.S. forces in the Middle East seize an Iraqi freighter carrying tea from Sri Lanka.

5   The White House downplays concerns over the presence of Soviet military advisors in Iraq, claiming instead that the Soviet Union is to be praised for its cooperation in building a multinational coalition against Iraq.

5   The Navy lifts the ban, imposed at the reopening of the investigation into the 1989 *Iowa* explosion, on live firings of sixteen-inch guns, authorizing the USS *Wisconsin,* on station in the Middle East, to use its sixteen-inch guns.

6   U.S. troop levels in the Persian Gulf top 100,000. Saudi Arabia agrees to pay billions of dollars in windfall oil revenues to the United States as payment for U.S. efforts to contain Iraqi aggression. The embargo against Iraq weakens as several nations suggest sending food and medical supplies as humanitarian aid.

6   The State Department approves the sale of rocket parts to Brazil despite concerns that it will aid Iraq in developing long-range ballistic missile capabilities.

7   The Bush administration announces plans to sell 385 M1-A2 tanks to Saudi Arabia.

8   The chief Soviet negotiator at the CFE talks suggests dramatic cuts in U.S. forces in Western Europe, including a ceiling of about 80,000 troops.

9   Presidents Bush and Gorbachev hold a one-day summit in Helsinki. The Gulf crisis dominates the discussions, with the two leaders warning Iraq more could be done if the sanctions fail to reestablish

the pre–August 2 status of Kuwait, though they differ on the use of force to settle the crisis.

9   Representatives of the twenty navies that have committed ships to the anti-Iraq coalition meet in Bahrain to establish a joint command.

10   The Air Force reports that its deployment of forces to the Persian Gulf is nearly complete.

10   The West German government agrees that a unified Germany would pay $8 billion to underwrite the removal of 360,000 Soviet soldiers from East Germany.

12   The Air Force reports a total of fifteen tactical fighter wings (equivalent) on station in the Persian Gulf.

13   John Betti, the undersecretary of defense for acquisition, says that the crisis in the gulf is not changing the DOD position on the V-22 Osprey.

14   Air Force chief of staff General Michael Dugan says the Joint Chiefs have decided that U.S. forces will rely heavily on air strikes against Iraq if war breaks out.

16   National Security Advisor Brent Scowcroft reports that the remarks by General Dugan about plans for an air strike to drive Iraq from Kuwait are not supported by the Bush administration.

17   Defense Secretary Cheney dismisses Air Force chief of staff General Michael Dugan for revealing military plans for a war against Iraq.

18   Negotiations on the future of U.S bases in the Philippines open as the United States announces it is prepared to make a ten-year phased withdrawal from its military facilities in the Philippines.

18   France agrees to reduce its troop levels in Germany after unification.

18   The Pentagon announces plans to scale back or end operations at 150 overseas military installations of various sizes.

18   The Pentagon discloses that it has monitored a tremendous buildup of Iraqi troop strength in Kuwait and southern Iraq over the past ten days, bringing the total number of Iraqi troops arrayed against U.S. forces in Saudi Arabia to 360,000. Rules of engagement for U.S. pilots in the Persian Gulf are clarified to stress that pilots have the option to determine if a situation is threatening and if so, to fire upon enemy aircraft. The Soviet Union lends a large transport ship to the United States to aid in transporting equipment to the Persian Gulf. West Germany pledges 3.3 billion DM to aid the anti-Iraq effort. Turkey extends its defense agreement with the United States, including basing rights for installations that could serve as staging areas for actions against Iraq.

20   The United States and Great Britain agree to place British defense forces in the Persian Gulf under the command of the U.S. CINCCENTCOM.

21   General Merrill McPeak is named to replace Michael Dugan as Air Force chief of staff.

23   Saddam Hussein threatens to destroy Middle Eastern oil fields and draw Israel into a war if the sanctions against Iraq begin to threaten

Iraqi security. The United States announces that military equipment continues to arrive in Iraq, despite the U.S.-led naval blockade.

23   Iran purchases fourteen Soviet MiG-29s.

24   The Pentagon releases the 1990 edition of *Soviet Military Power,* warning that despite changes in the Soviet Union, it retains an overwhelming military capability and remains a threat to the United States.

24   East Germany withdraws from the Warsaw Pact.

25   The U.N. Security Council votes to extend the embargo against Iraq to cover air traffic to and from the country. The Pentagon announces plans to send the aircraft carrier *Independence* into the Persian Gulf.

25   The Senate ratifies the 1974 Threshold Test Ban Treaty and the 1976 Peaceful Nuclear Explosions Treaty.

25   Secretary Cheney extends the DOD civilian hiring freeze through the end of the year.

25   U.S.-Peruvian negotiations over U.S. military aid to assist in the drug war collapse.

26   A former Israeli intelligence officer, General Ahron Yariv, warns that given Iraq's sophisticated air defense system, ground forces, not air power, will play the decisive role in any war with Iraq.

26   Secretary Cheney orders a withdrawal of 40,000 U.S. troops from Europe over the coming year.

26   The CIA releases documents showing that South Africa has done extensive nuclear weapons related research and possessed enough material for an atomic explosive device more than a decade ago.

27   The United States assures Israel that it would mount a vigorous response to an Iraqi attack on Israel. Soviet Chief of the General Staff, General Mikhail Moiseyev, warns that a military conflict in the gulf would bring Iran and Iraq into an alliance and could escalate to a world war.

28   U.S. intelligence sources report that Iraq has produced a stockpile of biological weapons.

29   Air Force documents reveal that the B-1's tail-mounted missile warning system fails in low-level flights.

29   The Lockheed entry into the Air Force ATF competition, the YF-22, makes its first flight.

30   An F-15 crashes in Saudi Arabia while on a routine exercise flight, killing two. Saddam Hussein announces he will seek a dialogue with France over the crisis in the gulf.

October

1   The House of Representatives passes a resolution supporting President Bush's actions in the gulf. Military officials report that the Pentagon has not placed nuclear weapons in the gulf.

1   Retired Air Force General Curtis Lemay dies at the age of eighty-three.

1   The Bush administration asks Congress to approve a package of continued aid to Pakistan despite the administration's inability to certify that Pakistan has not developed nuclear weapons.

1   The Department of Energy announces plans to close its weapons production facility at Fernald in Ohio.

2   The Senate passes a resolution in support of President Bush's actions in the gulf.

2   A meeting of the thirty-five nation Conference on Security and Cooperation in Europe (CSCE) ends with an agreement to play a larger role in the newly emerging Europe.

2   Allied control of Berlin ends.

3   The United States and the Soviet Union agree in principle on major provisions of a treaty to reduce conventional forces in Europe.

3   The division of Germany ends.

4   The Pentagon reveals that Iraq has a stockpile of fuel-air explosives.

4   U.S. officials report that the Soviet Union has begun to redeploy thousands of weapons systems out of the area to be covered by a CFE treaty, reducing the number of Soviet weapons that will have to be destroyed under the terms of any such treaty.

4   Henry F. Cooper, head of the SDI program, reveals that the Bush administration is planning for a scaled-down version of SDI to defend against an accidental missile launch or an attack by some Third World country.

5   Brazil reveals that it uncovered and stopped a plan by several military officials to develop atomic weapons.

7   The United States announces plans to inspect Soviet SS-23s now held by the recently unified German government.

8   Pakistan rejects a U.S. request that it open its nuclear facilities to international inspection.

9   Saddam Hussein announces that Iraq possesses a missile capable of reaching Israel and threatens to use it if war breaks out. The U.S. Army restricts night maneuvers in Saudi Arabia in an attempt to limit the growing number of accidents there.

9   The Soviet Parliament ratifies the 1974 Threshold Test Ban Treaty and the 1976 Peaceful Nuclear Explosions Treaty.

9   The Air Force grounds its B-1 fleet following a training mishap in which an engine exploded.

10   The Marine Corps calls up the first increment of its reservists, assigning them to Hawaii as replacements for Marines sent to Saudi Arabia as part of Desert Shield.

11   The United States freezes $500 million in aid to Pakistan pending Pakistani curtailment of programs believed designed to facilitate the production of nuclear weapons.

11   The Air Force grounds all training flights in the Persian Gulf for twelve hours and orders a review of the flying program in an attempt to reduce the number of accidents. Elements of the 3rd Armored Cavalry Regiment and the 1st Cavalry Division, including

units equipped with M-1 tanks and Bradley Fighting Vehicles, begin arriving in Saudi Arabia.

12 The U.S. Army War College releases a study concluding that U.S. forces in the gulf are ill-prepared for war with Iraq's experienced forces.

14 The number of U.S. troops in the gulf passes 200,000.

15 The first law is enacted to compensate U.S. civilians killed or injured by radiation from the U.S. atomic weapons production and testing programs.

15 The State Department reports that Egyptian troops in Saudi Arabia will be supplied by the United States with Stinger antiaircraft missiles.

17 House and Senate budget conferees agree on a DOD fiscal year (FY) 1991 budget that includes limits on the B-2 program, a $2 billion cut from the Bush administration request for SDI, nearly full funding for the V-22 Osprey despite repeated DOD efforts to cancel the program, and severe cuts in the tactical air-to-surface missile (TASM) program.

17 Soviet president Gorbachev communicates a gulf peace plan to President Bush calling for an Iraqi withdrawal from Kuwait in exchange for a cash payment as compensation for the economic ills Iraq claims have been caused by Kuwaiti oil overproduction.

17 The French-German Brigade, the first mixed army brigade in Europe, is commissioned.

18 Defense Secretary Cheney visits an underground Soviet air defense command center.

18 The Soviet Union announces it will stop deploying nuclear weapons on ships and aircraft operating in the Baltic Sea.

18 China agrees to sell Pakistan a nuclear reactor despite Pakistani refusal to open its nuclear facilities to international inspection under the terms of the Nonproliferation Treaty (NPT).

19 Pentagon officials disclose that Iraqi forces are training to operate 150 Hawk antiaircraft missile batteries captured from Kuwait. The Pentagon announces plans to send 400 to 500 M-1A1 tanks from a NATO prepositioned storage facility to Saudi Arabia.

19 Defense Secretary Cheney warns Congress that he intends to recommend that the president veto the defense appropriations bill because it fails to mirror DOD requests.

19 The second B-2 stealth bomber makes its first flight.

21 Saddam Hussein pledges not to invade Saudi Arabia.

22 The Navy confirms that the Aegis cruiser *San Jacinto*, deployed to the Middle East, is the first Navy ship to be armed solely with SLCMs.

23 Iraq releases fourteen Americans and vows to release all of the French citizens it is holding.

23 The United States assesses that Pakistan possesses an atomic weapon.

24 The Soviet Union conducts its first nuclear test of 1990.

25   Secretary Cheney announces that an additional 100,000 U.S. troops could be sent to Saudi Arabia to augment the over 200,000 troops already deployed.

27   U.S. military sources report that Iraq has mined the waters off Kuwait to discourage an amphibious attack.

29   The Bush administration reveals it plans to meet with allies in the gulf and in Europe to discuss offensive military options against Iraq. Soviet president Gorbachev reports that his envoy to Iraq sees signs of flexibility in the Iraqi position, holding out the hope for a peaceful solution to the crisis.

30   A steam pipe ruptures on board the USS *Iwo Jima,* killing ten sailors, bringing to forty-two the number of U.S military personnel killed in the Persian Gulf since the buildup began.

31   A Hungarian official announces that the Warsaw Pact will cease to exist in 1991.

November

1   President Bush denies he is attempting to prepare the United States for war, but expresses impatience with Saddam Hussein and the effects of U.N. sanctions. Saudi officials announce that Syria plans to send additional troops to Saudi Arabia, ending speculation that Syria's commitment to the coalition is weakening. A fourth U.S. aircraft carrier, the *Midway,* arrives on station in the Middle East. Thousands of Marines take part in amphibious assault exercises.

3   The Pentagon plans to call up as many as 100,000 combat reservists for service in the Persian Gulf.

4   Iraq warns that it will fight rather than relinquish Kuwait. Defense officials reveal that software fixes to protect U.S. aircraft against HAWK missiles captured by Iraq were in effect within seventy-two hours of the initial U.S. deployment to Saudi Arabia.

4   Soviet officials report that Soviet troops may leave the newly unified Germany well before the agreed 1994 deadline.

5   Secretary of State Baker and Saudi King Fahd agree on a command and control structure for U.S. and Saudi forces in the event of war against Iraq. Turkey's President Ozal rules out the notion of Turkish troops opening a northern front against Iraq in the event of war.

5   The Supreme Court lets stand a circuit court ruling that the Army must allow the reenlistment of Staff Sergeant Perry Watkins, discharged due to his sexual preference.

6   China indicates that it will not veto a potential U.N. resolution to authorize the use of force against Iraq.

7   The *Journal of the American Medical Association* publishes a study comparing death rates between civilians and members of the peacetime Army. The study concludes that civilians die at a rate of 215 per 100,000 while members of the Army die at a rate of 109 per 100,000.

7   The United States informs the Philippines it will remove all fighter aircraft from that country within a year.

7   Japanese prime minister Toshiki Kaifu withdraws a bill to authorize sending Japanese troops to the gulf. Saddam Hussein orders the release of 100 German and twenty European and American hostages. The United States drafts a U.N. resolution to authorize the use of force against Iraq. Egyptian president Hosni Mubarak calls for an additional several months before any military option is exercised in the gulf, giving sanctions more time to work.

8   President Bush orders an additional 150,000 U.S. troops to the Persian Gulf to give the coalition forces an offensive military option. The Soviet Union says that the use of force cannot be ruled out, signaling a willingness to support a coalition military effort against Iraq. Saddam Hussein orders the release of an additional 100 hostages. President Bush orders a second battleship, the *Missouri,* and its support ships to the Middle East.

9   The Pentagon cancels plans to rotate troops in the Persian Gulf, announcing that troops sent to the region will remain for the duration of the crisis.

9   Secretary Cheney says that Third World ballistic missile arsenals justify a continued investment in SDI.

11   The Iraqi ambassador to the United States concedes that U.S.-led forces have the capacity to level Iraq.

12   President Bush pledges to consult with Congress on efforts in the Persian Gulf.

13   The United States and Singapore sign an agreement allowing U.S. ships and aircraft to use military facilities on the island.

13   Great Britain announces plans to close two of its four air bases in Germany.

14   Defense Secretary Cheney calls up another 72,000 National Guard and reserve troops for Desert Shield.

15   U.S. and Saudi forces begin a massive six-day mock assault on Saudi beaches. The Pentagon says it has no plans to revive the draft to meet personnel requirements of the gulf crisis. Iraq invites the International Atomic Energy Agency to verify that Iraq's stock of enriched uranium has not been used to produce weapons.

15   The United States announces it is prepared to provide economic aid to the Soviet Union if the Soviet economy collapses.

16   The last of 102,000 chemical artillery shells removed from Germany arrives in Johnston Atoll where it will be destroyed.

16   President Bush vetoes legislation that would have imposed sanctions on nations using chemical weapons and companies that aid in the development of chemical and biological weapons.

18   Saddam Hussein offers to free all hostages starting December 25 and continuing through March 25, provided the U.S.-led coalition does not initiate a military conflict. A major U.S. military amphibious exercise in the Persian Gulf is thwarted by heavy winds. Secretary of Defense Cheney warns that a vigorous congressional debate on the use of force could weaken the image of U.S. resolve in Iraqi eyes.

18   NATO and Warsaw Pact nations sign the CFE Treaty.

20   The Warsaw Pact agrees to dissolve the military elements of the alliance.

21   The Army freezes the release of officers and enlisted personnel from all units to maintain personnel levels through the gulf crisis.

22   President Bush visits the troops in Saudi Arabia for Thanksgiving dinner. Eight Iraqi generals are reportedly executed after a failed coup attempt.

23   Congressional leaders insist the Bush administration must have congressional approval prior to the initiation of hostilities against Iraq.

24   Iraq begins to mobilize 150,000 army reservists.

25   Defense Secretary Cheney says that an Iraqi withdrawal from Kuwait would not satisfy the United States because of a persistent Iraqi threat to develop nuclear weapons. The United States asks the United Nations to set January 1 as a deadline for Saddam Hussein to comply with U.N. Security Council resolutions regarding Kuwait.

26   Pakistan announces it will seek to open talks with the United States to settle a dispute over Pakistani nuclear proliferation.

27   Soviet Defense Minister Yazov authorizes Soviet troops to use force in self defense in the non-Russian republics.

27   The IAEA reports that Iraq's stock of fissionable material has not been diverted to weapons programs.

28   Brazil and Argentina renounce the production of nuclear weapons.

29   The U.N. Security Council approves the use of force against Iraq if it fails to comply with Security Council resolutions regarding Kuwait before January 15.

30   The Pentagon announces plans to deploy an additional 300 aircraft to the Persian Gulf region, raising the number of U.S. aircraft in the region to 1,200.

December

1   The Pentagon announces that the gulf crisis makes it impossible to achieve the first round of cuts in the congressionally mandated five-year, 25 percent reduction in the armed forces. The Soviet Union reports that if war were to begin, it would not send troops.

2   President Bush vetoes the FY 1991 authorization bill for U.S. intelligence agencies because of a requirement that Congress be informed of covert actions other countries are asked to perform.

3   The five permanent members of the Security Council pledge not to attack Iraq if it withdraws unconditionally from Kuwait. Secretary Cheney says Iraq is capable of outlasting sanctions against it.

3   The upgrade of the U.S.-Soviet hotline is completed.

4   The Navy dismisses two admirals and a captain for mismanaging the A-12 program.

4   Turkish president Ozal grants permission for the United States to use a key air base in Turkey for operations against Iraq should war begin. Iraq announces that all Soviet citizens in Iraq are free to

leave the country. The first European-based U.S. troops to be deployed to the gulf depart Germany.

5 CIA director Webster testifies that sanctions will begin to erode Iraqi combat readiness within nine months.

5 U.S. officials report that Syria has been attempting to purchase advanced weaponry with the $1 billion it has received for participating in the anti-Iraq coalition in the gulf.

5 President Bush lifts a ban on sales of weapons and other military equipment to Chile. The ban was imposed in 1976.

7 The Bush administration warns that any military action against Iraqi forces will center on a massive ground campaign.

7 Secretary Cheney orders SRAM-A missiles removed from strategic aircraft permanently due to concern that aircraft fires could detonate the non-nuclear material surrounding the fissionable core of the warhead, widely scattering plutonium.

7 The Defense Department releases its proposed six-year budget plan including significant cuts in personnel and weapons systems.

8 Pentagon officials report that during a December 2 test firing of three Iraqi missiles, U.S. equipment failed to detect the missiles until about a minute before they reached their targets.

9 Saddam Hussein releases the foreign hostages held in Iraq. President Bush says that the release of Americans held as human shields in Iraq makes the decision to use force less complicated. The aircraft carrier *Ranger* departs for the Middle East.

10 President Bush signs the TTBT and the PNET.

11 The Pentagon estimates the number of Iraqi troops in Kuwait at 500,000.

11 Salvadoran officials request sophisticated U.S. equipment to counter new Soviet surface-to-air missiles being used by rebels in El Salvador.

12 President Bush announces that U.S. and Soviet negotiators are close to agreement on a START treaty, setting the stage for a treaty signing at a proposed February summit.

12 Undersecretary of Defense for Acquisition John Betti resigns in the wake of criticism over his failure to reform the defense acquisition process.

13 Navy Secretary Lawrence Garrett recommends putting the F-14D back into production as the Navy's fighter of the future.

13 President Bush rejects suggestions that he reward Saddam Hussein for releasing U.S. hostages. In two separate actions federal district court judges reject challenges to the authority of President Bush to deploy troops to the Middle East.

14 Former commander-in-chief of U.S. air forces in Europe, General Charles Donnelly, tells Congress that the United States would lose 100 aircraft flying 20,000 sorties in the first ten days of a war with Iraq.

15 A Defense Contract Audit Agency review of the Navy's A-12 program reveals that the Navy overpaid A-12 contractors by several hundred million dollars.

17 U.S. negotiators report they are two sessions away from concluding a treaty with the Philippines on the future of Clark Air Base and Subic Naval Base.

18 President Bush says that even if Iraq withdrew from Kuwait, an international peacekeeping force, including U.S. forces, would be required in the region. Secretary of State Baker says that a partial Iraqi pullout from Kuwait would not satisfy the Security Council resolutions and would not prevent the coalition from using force to push Iraq completely out of Kuwait. Saddam Hussein announces that further peace talks are futile and that he will not relinquish Kuwait.

19 Lt. Gen. Calvin Waller, the second-ranking officer in Operation Desert Shield, says U.S. forces will not be ready to launch an offensive on January 15. French president Mitterand supports the U.S. position that an Iraqi withdrawal from Kuwait must be complete.

19 Turkey requests multinational air forces be sent to help defend against possible skirmishes with Iraqi forces.

20 President Bush tells a congressional delegation that he may postpone an attack against Iraq until March.

20 Soviet Foreign Minister Eduard Shevardnadze resigns, warning that the Soviet Union is drifting toward dictatorship.

20 The Air Force grounds its B-1 bomber fleet for recurring engine failures, the fifth fleet grounding in two years.

21 Israel successfully tests its Arrow antimissile system.

22 President Bush says U.S. troops in Saudi Arabia are ready to respond immediately to an Iraqi provocation.

23 Defense Secretary Cheney says that some members of the twenty-eight nation coalition arrayed against Iraq will not take part in offensive operations to eject Iraqi forces from Kuwait.

24 McDonnell Douglas completes assembly of the first C-17.

25 The Gulf Cooperation Council ends its summit by warning Iraq to withdraw from Kuwait.

26 Diplomatic contacts between the United States and Iraq resume in Iraq. Little hope remains for a peaceful solution to the crisis.

28 The aircraft carriers *America* and *Theodore Roosevelt* depart for the Middle East.

31 Baghdad indicates it is willing to negotiate with the United States to achieve a compromise solution to the gulf crisis. Iraq begins calling seventeen-year-olds to military service. Iran declares neutrality if war breaks out. U.S. troop levels in the gulf reach 325,000.

Worldwide U.S. Force Deployments, 1991

U.S./Western Hemisphere
1 Airborne Division
1 Air Assault Division
4 Armored Divisions
6 Mechanized Infantry Divisions
10 Infantry Divisions
3 USMC Divisions
23 Combat Brigades
24 USAF Tactical Fighter Wings

Desert Shield/Desert Storm[4]
Ground Assets
4 Armored Divisions
1 Mechanized Division
3 Infantry Divisions
2 USMC Divisions
1 Airborne Division
1 Air Assault Division
5 Combat Brigades
1 Special Forces Group

Naval Assets
6 Aircraft Carriers
7 Helicopter Carriers
2 Battleships
1 Command Ship
15 Cruisers
12 Destroyers
14 Frigates
4 Minesweepers
44 Auxiliary and Support Ships

Air Assets
18 USAF Tactical Fighter Wings
6 USN Tactical Fighter Wings
1 USMC Tactical Fighter Wing
2 Bomb Wings
4 Tactical Airlift Wings
2 Air Refueling Wings
48 Additional Tankers
2 Tactical Air Control Wings
2 Air Medical Evacuation Squadrons

Pacific Command
East Pacific (3rd Fleet)
4 Aircraft Carriers
5 Helicopter Carriers
21 Destroyers
43 Frigates
36 Attack Submarines
20 Amphibious Ships
7 USN/USMC Tactical Fighter Wings

Atlantic Command
North Atlantic (2nd Fleet)
5 Aircraft Carriers
5 Helicopter Carriers
9 Cruisers
35 Destroyers
50 Frigates
49 Attack Submarines
18 Amphibious Ships
10 USN/USMC Tactical Fighter Wings

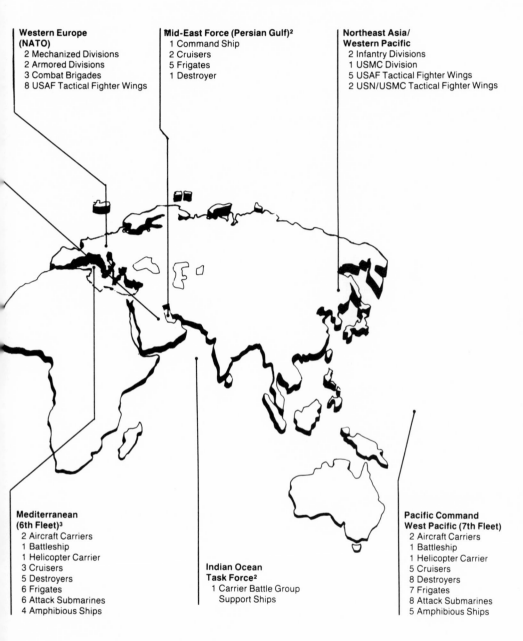

Western Europe (NATO)
- 2 Mechanized Divisions
- 2 Armored Divisions
- 3 Combat Brigades
- 8 USAF Tactical Fighter Wings

Mid-East Force (Persian Gulf)[2]
- 1 Command Ship
- 2 Cruisers
- 5 Frigates
- 1 Destroyer

Northeast Asia/ Western Pacific
- 2 Infantry Divisions
- 1 USMC Division
- 5 USAF Tactical Fighter Wings
- 2 USN/USMC Tactical Fighter Wings

Mediterranean (6th Fleet)[3]
- 2 Aircraft Carriers
- 1 Battleship
- 1 Helicopter Carrier
- 3 Cruisers
- 5 Destroyers
- 6 Frigates
- 6 Attack Submarines
- 4 Amphibious Ships

Indian Ocean Task Force[2]
- 1 Carrier Battle Group
  Support Ships

Pacific Command West Pacific (7th Fleet)
- 2 Aircraft Carriers
- 1 Battleship
- 1 Helicopter Carrier
- 5 Cruisers
- 8 Destroyers
- 7 Frigates
- 8 Attack Submarines
- 5 Amphibious Ships

Notes:

[1]Compiled from numerous private and public sources.

[2]Indian Ocean & Persian Gulf surface units rotate out of the Pacific Fleets.

[3]Mediterranean surface units rotate out of the Atlantic Fleet.

[4]These assets are the major deployments for Operation Desert Shield and Desert Storm. In some cases, only part of a listed asset was deployed, and this list does not include many auxiliary and support components. A full Order of Battle can be found in *Defense and Foreign Affairs*, January-February 1991, pp. 12-32. These assets were drawn from the other theaters and fleets and do not represent assets in addition to those attributed to those regions.

Defense
Publications

T his bibliography cites the major books published during calendar year 1990
on U.S. national security affairs. Books are grouped in the following categories: arms control, conventional forces and strategy, defense budget
and political issues, history, the North Atlantic Treaty Organization (NATO), nuclear strategy and weapons, other regional issues, personnel, terrorism and other
issues, yearbooks and data bases.

Arms Control

Arms Control Verification & the New Role of On-Site Inspection. Lewis A. Dunn and Amy
E. Gordon, eds. Lexington, Mass.: Lexington Books. 288 pp. Provides a balanced
assessment of the capabilities and limitations of on-site inspection.
Arms Industries: New Suppliers and Regional Security. Ralph Sanders. Washington, D.C.:
National Defense University. 198 pp. Examines the growth in arms suppliers and the
implications of that expansion for efforts to curb global weapons proliferation.
Beyond 1995: The Future of the NPT Regime. Robert E. Pendley and Joseph F. Pilat, eds.
New York: Plenum Publishing. 276 pp. Examines the problems facing the NPT regime
and assesses the likelihood of it surviving past 1995.
Conventional Force Reductions: A Dynamic Assessment. Joshua M. Epstein. Washington,
D.C.: The Brookings Institution. 275 pp. Outlines the effects of various arms control
proposals on the European conventional balance.
Engines of War: Merchants of Death and the New Arms Race. James Adams. New York:
The Atlantic Monthly Press. 307 pp. Examines arms transfers, indigenous armament
industries, and the effects of arms acquisition on political and military stability in both
regional and global contexts.

EURATOM and Nuclear Safeguards. Darryl A. Howlett. New York: St. Martin's Press. 336 pp. Explores the role of EURATOM and its nuclear safeguards in the creation and maintenance of the nuclear nonproliferation regime.

The Guns Fall Silent: The End of the Cold War and the Future of Conventional Disarmament. Ian M. Cuthbertson and Peter Volten, eds. Boulder, Colo.: Westview Press. 201 pp. Examines the strategic military implications of the revolutions in Eastern Europe and the breakdown of the bipolar European security system.

Icarus Restrained: An Intellectual History of Nuclear Arms Control, 1945–1960. Jennifer E. Sims. Boulder, Colo.: Westview Press. 264 pp. Traces the sources of modern arms control thinking to the postwar period.

The Korean Peninsula: Prospects for Arms Reduction Under Global Détente. John Q. Blodgett, Cha Young-Koo, and William J. Taylor, Jr. Boulder, Colo.: Westview Press. 275 pp. Explores the state of security in the Northeast Asian region and the prospects for regional arms control.

National Implementation of the Future Chemical Weapons Convention. Thomas Stock and Ronald Sutherland, eds. New York: Oxford University Press. 192 pp. Explores the national requirements of the projected Chemical Weapons Convention.

The New Nuclear Rules: Strategy and Arms Control After INF and START. James L. George. New York: St. Martin's Press. 194 pp. Recommends reductions in new weapons procurement to bring strategic weapons acquisition in line with professed arms control goals.

The Nuclear Seduction: Why the Arms Race Doesn't Matter—And What Does. Charles Deber, William A. Schwartz, et al. Berkeley, Calif.: University of California Press. 307 pp. Members of the Boston Nuclear Study Group, these authors attempt to focus the debate over the risk of nuclear war away from so-called marginal issues to the factors of greatest risk: U.S. intervention in the Third World throughout the cold war.

Regaining the High Ground: NATO's Stake in the New Talks on Conventional Armed Forces in Europe. Barry M. Blechman, William J. Durch, and Kevin P. O'Prey. New York: St. Martin's Press. 217 pp. Examines the political and military implications of conventional force reductions in Europe.

Security at Sea: Naval Forces and Arms Control. Richard Fieldhouse, ed. New York: Oxford University Press. 320 pp. An examination of the process and prospects of naval arms control.

START and the Future of Deterrence. Michael J. Mazarr. New York: St. Martin's Press. 208 pp. Examines the future of nuclear deterrence.

The Superpowers and Nuclear Arms Control: Rhetoric and Reality. Dennis Menos. Westport, Conn.: Praeger Publishers. 200 pp. Examines superpower involvement in arms control in the nuclear age, arguing that they have only a minimal interest in achieving agreements.

Tacit Bargaining, Arms Races, and Arms Control. George W. Downs and David M. Rocke. Ann Arbor, Mich.: University of Michigan Press. 256 pp. Compares techniques of arms control from formal negotiation to tacit bargaining.

Unconventional Approaches to Conventional Arms Control Verification: An Exploratory Assessment. Henry van der Graaf and John Grin, eds. New York: St. Martin's Press. Examines verification procedures for conventional weapons reduction agreements beyond CFE I.

Verification: Monitoring Disarmament. Francesco Calogero, Marvin L. Goldberger, and Sergei P. Kapitza, eds. Boulder, Colo.: Westview Press. 266 pp. Examines methods of verification, their prospects for success in ongoing arms control negotiations, and the larger prospects for reductions in weapons arsenals.

Verification of Conventional Arms Control in Europe: Technological Constraints and Opportunities. Richard Kokoski and Sergey Koulik, eds. Boulder, Colo.: Westview Press. 322 pp. Explores the full range of methods available for verification of conventional arms reductions in Europe.

The Vienna Conference on Security and Cooperation in Europe: A Turning Point in East-West Relations. Stefan Lehna. Boulder, Colo.: Westview Press. 224 pp. Examines the November 1986–January 1989 session of the CSCE, its outcome, and the direction it outlined for a Europe in flux.

Conventional Forces and Strategy

Alternative Conventional Defense, Volume 1. Hans Gunter Brauch, ed. Bristol, Penn.: Crane Russak. 200 pp. Reacting to the sea changes underway in defense technologies and the political and military security environment globally and in Europe, this volume explores alternative means to defend Central Europe and their political and military consequences.

Armoured Warfare. J. P. Harris and F. H. Toase, eds. New York: St. Martin's Press. 224 pp. Examines the role of armored warfare in twentieth century military strategy.

Bound to Lead: The Changing Nature of American Power. Joseph S. Nye, Jr. New York: Basic Books. 292 pp. In this latest entry in the declinism debate, Nye assesses alternative futures and the role of U.S. policy in their emergence, contending there will be a continuing requirement for U.S. military capability.

Command, Control and the Common Defense. C. Kenneth Allard. New Haven, Conn.: Yale University Press. 317 pp. Examines the unique character of each military service and the need for a unifying strategic conception.

Deception Operations: Studies in the East-West Context. David Charters and Maurice Tugwell, eds. New York: Brassey's. 432 pp. Examines the use of deception in political and military operations.

The Evolution of Modern Land Warfare: Theory and Practice. Christopher Bellamy. New York: Routledge, Chapman, and Hall. 320 pp. Surveys the evolution of warfare in Europe from the Napoleonic Wars to the 1990s, arguing that U.S. military planners should have greater knowledge of the experiences of Russia, China, and other Asian countries.

Firepower in Limited War. Robert Scales, Jr. Washington, D.C.: National Defense University Press. 291 pp. Examines conventional operations and the essential role of artillery, helicopters, and fixed-wing aircraft in combat operations.

Insurgency & Terrorism: Inside Modern Revolutionary Warfare. Bard E. O'Neill. Washington, D.C.: Brassey's. 185 pp. Examines insurgency as a form of warfare.

The Lessons of Modern War. Anthony H. Cordesman and Abraham R. Wagner. Boulder, Colo.: Westview Press. This three-volume set explores the Arab-Israeli conflicts (vol. 1, 394 pp.), the Iran-Iraq War (vol. 2, 647 pp.), and the Afghan and Falklands conflicts (vol. 3, 371 pp.).

LIC 2010: Special Operations & Unconventional Warfare in the Next Century. Rod Paschall. New York: Brassey's. 166 pp. Predicts the future of low-intensity conflict.

Maritime Strategy and European Security. Eric Grove. London: Pergamon-Brassey's. 168 pp. Examines the effects of strategy and arms control on naval efforts to achieve security in Europe.

Military Misfortunes: The Anatomy of Failure in War. Eliot A. Cohen and John Gooch.

New York: The Free Press. 296 pp. Explores reasons for failure by competent military organizations.

Military-Technological Choices and Political Implications: Command and Control in Established NATO Posture and a Non-Provocative Defence. John Grin. New York: St. Martin's Press. 300 pp. Explores the interplay of technological development and military posture in the creation of a European defense structure.

Narrow Seas, Small Navies, and Fat Merchantmen: Naval Strategies for the 1990s. Charles W. Koburger, Jr. Westport, Conn.: Praeger Publishers. Analyzes U.S. naval power in light of what is seen as a new threat posed by lesser navies and the requirements of low-intensity conflict.

Operation Just Cause: Panama, December 1989; A Soldier's Eyewitness Account. Clarence E. Briggs, III. Harrisburg, Penn.: Stackpole Books. 176 pp. Examines the changing rules of engagement involved in the Panama operation with an attempt to draw lessons from Panama for civil-military relations in future contingencies.

Operation Just Cause: The U.S. Intervention in Panama. Peter G. Tsouras and Bruce W. Watson. Boulder, Colo.: Westview Press. 246 pp. A comprehensive analysis of Operation Just Cause, its historical basis, and its implications for U.S.-Panamanian relations and U.S. foreign policy.

Tanks, Fighters & Ships: U.S. Conventional Force Planning Since WW II. Maurice A. Mallin. Washington, D.C.: Brassey's. Examines the process of force planning, the various weights given to different inputs by various planners, varying threat perceptions, and the related outputs.

Uncertainty and Control: Future Soviet and American Strategy. Stephen J. Cimbala. New York: St. Martin's Press. 191 pp. Looks at the attempts made, or not made, by the United States and the Soviet Union to control the escalation of a war between them should deterrence fail.

United States Overseas Basing: An Anatomy of the Dilemma. James R. Blaker. Westport, Conn.: Praeger Publishers. Analyzes the entire system of overseas bases, assessing the value of individual bases and the base structure as an interactive whole.

The U.S. Army in a New Security Era. Sam C. Sarkesian and John Allen Williams, eds. Boulder, Colo.: Lynne Rienner Publishers. 325 pp. Examines the present make-up and mission of the U.S. Army and its alternative missions and structures for the future.

U.S. Bases Overseas: Negotiations with Spain, Greece, and the Philippines. Diane B. Bendahmane and John W. McDonald, Jr., eds. Boulder, Colo.: Westview Press. 224 pp. Looks at the future of overseas U.S. military installations.

War, Peace, and Victory: Strategy and Statecraft for the Next Century. Colin S. Gray. New York: Simon & Schuster. 442 pp. Argues for a reevaluation of military strategy and national interests in light of the changing global security environment and increasingly tighter defense budgets.

Defense Budget and Political Issues

Blank Check: The Pentagon's Black Budget. Tim Weiner. New York: Warner Books. 273 pp. Focuses on the problems with management of special access programs.

Controlling the Sword: The Democratic Governance of National Security. Bruce Russett. Cambridge, Mass.: Harvard University Press. 201 pp. Examines trends in and influences of public opinion on U.S. national security policy.

Fighting for Peace: Seven Critical Years in the Pentagon. Caspar Weinberger. New York: Warner Books. 464 pp. An examination of defense decision making during Caspar Weinberger's years as secretary of defense.

Making Defense Reform Work. James A. Blackwell, Jr., and Barry M. Blechman. Washington, D.C.: Brassey's. 278 pp. A report card on the progress achieved on the recommendations of the Packard commission and the direction provided by the Goldwater-Nichols Act.

A Question of Balance: The President, the Congress, and Foreign Policy. Thomas E. Mann, ed. Washington, D.C.: The Brookings Institution. 265 pp. Examines executive-legislative relations in a number of issue areas including arms control, war powers, and intelligence.

Superpowers in Economic Decline: U.S. Strategy for the Transcentury Era. Richard Cohen and Peter A. Wilson. Bristol, Penn.: Crane Russak, 276 pp. Suggests that U.S. national security depends on restraining defense spending in the short term to restore long-term economic security.

Too Good to Be True: The Outlandish Story of Wedtech. James Traub. New York: Doubleday. 379 pp. Tracks the growth of Wedtech and the subsequent influence peddling procurement scandal.

U.S. Defense Policy in an Era of Constrained Resources. Robert L. Pfaltzgraf, Jr., and Richard H. Shultz, Jr., eds. Lexington, Mass.: Lexington Books. 416 pp. Examines the range of choices facing U.S. defense decision makers as they attempt to establish a new long-term strategy accounting for both changes in the international environment and fiscal austerity.

U.S. National Security Policy Groups: Institutional Profiles. Cynthia Watson. Westport, Conn.: Greenwood Press. 320 pp. Explores the expansion of organizations through which the American public has sought to participate in the formulation of national security strategy.

History

Admiral Arleigh Burke: A Biography. E. B. Potter. Washington, D.C.: Sidney Kramer Books. 494 pp. An examination of the life and military career of Arleigh Burke.

Air Wars and Aircraft: A Detailed Record of Air Combat, 1945 to the Present. Victor Flintham. New York: Facts on File Publications. 415 pp. Examines aerial engagements in the postwar period, detailing orders of battle, aircraft markings, and the context of political and military crises surrounding the battles.

Ashes to Ashes: The Phoenix Program and the Vietnam War. Dale Andrade. Lexington, Mass.: Lexington Books. 285 pp. A detailed recital of the vital statistics of the attempt to neutralize the Viet Cong infrastructure during the war in Vietnam.

As I Saw It. Dean Rusk. New York: W. W. Norton. 672 pp. Memoirs of the Rusk years in U.S. defense policy.

Brute Force: Allied Strategy and Tactics in the Second World War. John Ellis. New York: Viking Penguin. 643 pp. Begins with the premise that victory in war depends on long-term economic capabilities and the ability to outproduce the opponent in military hardware. This book explores the application of that principle by the allies in World War II.

General of the Army: George C. Marshall, Soldier and Statesman. Ed Cray. New York: W. W. Norton. 847 pp. A detailed biography of General Marshall.

John Foster Dulles and the Diplomacy of the Cold War. Richard Immerman, ed. Lawrence-
ville, New Jersey: Princeton University Press. 287 pp. An archivally based reassessment of Dulles' impact on U.S. foreign policy.

Korean War Almanac. Harry G. Summers, Jr. New York: Facts on File Publications. 330
pp. Provides a detailed chronology of the Korean conflict and examines its political
and military components.

Military Crisis Management: U.S. Intervention in the Dominican Republic, 1965. Herbert
G. Schoonmaker. Westport, Conn.: Greenwood Press. 168 pp. A study in U.S. crisis
management. Looks at the U.S. intervention in the Dominican Republic, examining
the role of U.S. military forces and civil-military relations.

The Rockets' Red Glare: When America Goes to War, the President and the People. Richard
J. Barnet. New York: Simon & Schuster. 475 pp. Examines the struggle between
U.S. presidents and the public over the issues of war and peace for 200 years of
American history.

Scream of Eagles: The Creation of Top Gun and the U.S. Air Victory in Vietnam. Robert
Wilcox. Washington, D.C.: Sidney Kramer Books. 320 pp. Explores the circumstances that led to the creation of the Top Gun flight school and its impact on the air
war in Vietnam.

A Substitute for Victory: The Politics of Peacemaking at the Korean Armistice Talks. Rosemary Foot. Ithaca, N.Y.: Cornell University Press. 248 pp. Analyzes the political and
military context of the negotiations leading to the Korean armistice.

Vietnam: The Decisive Battles. John Pimlott. Washington, D.C.: Sidney Kramer Books.
200 pp. Examines many of the critical battles of Vietnam War.

The Vietnam War as History. Elizabeth Jane Errington and B. J. C. McKercher, eds. Westport, Conn.: Praeger Publishers. The collected proceedings of the 15th Military History Symposium held at the Royal Military College of Canada in March 1989, this
book examines the causes and consequences of the Vietnam War.

Where Eagles Land: Planning and Development of U.S. Army Airfields, 1910–1941. Jerold
E. Brown. Westport, Conn.: Greenwood Press. 231 pp. Examines the factors that
explain the choice of air base locations.

The Wrong War: American Policy and the Dimensions of the Korean Conflict, 1950–1953.
Rosemary Foot. Ithaca, N.Y.: Cornell University Press. 296 pp. Examines the evolution of U.S. policy during the Korean War.

NATO

Alliance Strategy and Navies: The Evolution and Scope of NATO's Maritime Dimensions.
Robert S. Jordan. New York: St. Martin's Press. 175 pp. Provides a basic understanding of the maritime foundations of NATO's defense posture.

Allies in Crisis: Meeting Global Challenges to Western Security. Elizabeth D. Sherwood.
New Haven, Conn.: Yale University Press. 245 pp. Examines the way NATO has
agreed to manage out-of-area concerns to minimize strains on the alliance.

The Bundeswehr and Western Security. Stephen F. Szabo. New York: St. Martin's Press.
288 pp. Looks at the West German armed forces, prior to unification, as the linchpin
of Western defense.

The Central Front. Michael Dewar and Brian Holden Reid, eds. London: Brassey's. 200

pp. Examines strategies for defending Western Europe in an era of revolutionary change.

Conflict Termination in Europe: Games Against War. Stephen J. Cimbala. Westport, Conn.: Praeger Publishers. Considers the problem of conflict termination in Europe, arguing that NATO lacks a well thought out policy for conflict termination.

The Declining Hegemon: The United States and European Defense, 1960–1990. Joseph Lepgold. Westport, Conn.: Greenwood Press. Examines the notion of national decline as it impacts on U.S. relations with NATO, particularly in the areas of extended deterrence and conventional defense.

Europe After an American Withdrawal: Economic and Military Issues. Jane M. O. Sharp, ed. New York: Oxford University Press. 528 pp. Explores issues of burden sharing and commitment through the vehicle of a hypothetical U.S. withdrawal from Europe.

European Security in the 1990s: Deterrence and Defense After the INF Treaty. Walter Laqueur and Leon Sloss. New York: Plenum Publishing. 230 pp. Assesses the future of European security given the effects of the INF Treaty and the emergence of the post–cold war security environment.

The German Nuclear Dilemma. Jeffrey Boutwell. Ithaca, N.Y.: Cornell University Press. 288 pp. Examines German attitudes toward NATO nuclear strategy and an independent German nuclear force in the post-cold war era.

The Military Committee of the North Atlantic Alliance: A Study of Structure and Strategy. Douglas L. Bland. Westport, Conn.: Praeger Publishers. Examines the development of structures for allied civil-military relations, focusing on the Military Committee and its role in shaping NATO.

Military Power in Europe: Essays in Memory of Jonathan Alford. Lawrence Freedman, ed. New York: St. Martin's Press. 220 pp. Explores questions of military power in Europe in a time of revolutionary change.

NATO at Forty: Confronting a Changing World. Ted Galen Carpenter, ed. Lexington, Mass.: Lexington Books. 304 pp. Analyzes the viability and relevance of the NATO alliance in light of the changes that have taken place in U.S.-Soviet relations.

NATO's Changing Strategic Agenda. Colin McInnes. Cambridge, Mass.: Unwin Hyman. 208 pp. Examines the issue of defense of the central front in light of the changing European security environment.

Organizing Western Europe. Clive Archer. New York: Edward Arnold. 224 pp. Explores the structures, workings, and roles of Western European political and politico-military organizations, including NATO.

Reforging European Security: From Confrontation to Cooperation. Kurt Gottfried and Paul Bracken, eds. Boulder, Colo.: Westview Press. 226 pp. Examines the requirements of security in Europe in the post–cold war era.

Rethinking European Security. Furio Cerutti and Rodolfo Ragionieri. Bristol, Penn.: Crane Russak. 200 pp. An examination of European security issues in the post–INF treaty era.

Shifting into Neutral? Burden Sharing in the Western Alliance in the 1990s. Christopher Coker, ed. London: Brassey's. 176 pp. Explores burden sharing in the 1990s from the perspective of players on both sides of the Atlantic.

The Western Alliance After INF: Redefining U.S. Policy Toward Europe and the Soviet Union. Michael R. Lucas. Boulder, Colo.: Lynne Rienner Publishers. 350 pp. Examines the debate between proponents of the military-dominant and economics-dominant schools of thought within NATO and the Warsaw Pact.

Nuclear Strategy and Weapons

Alternative Security: Living Without Nuclear Deterrence. Burns H. Weston, ed. Boulder, Colo.: Westview Press. 284 pp. Presents alternative security arrangements to nuclear weapons based strategies such as mutually assured destruction.

The Army's Nuclear Power Program: The Evolution of a Support Agency. Lawrence H. Suid. New York: Greenwood Press. 130 pp. Examines the growth and decline of the Army's nuclear power program and the development of U.S. atomic capability.

At the Heart of the Bomb: The Dangerous Allure of Weapons Work. Debra Rosenthal. Reading, Mass.: Addison-Wesley. 244 pp. Explores the personality traits of those who work in the U.S. weapons labs.

Beyond Deterrence: The Political Economy of Nuclear Weapons. Frank L. Gertcher and William J. Weida. Boulder, Colo.: Westview Press. 362 pp. Examines root justifications for nuclear weapons and suggests a more critical analysis for the nuclear defense debate.

Deterrence and Defense in a Post-Nuclear World: Emerging Soviet and American Strategies. Gary L. Guertner. New York: St. Martin's Press. 240 pp. Explores conventional alternatives to nuclear-dependent theater defenses.

First Strike Stability: Deterrence After Containment. Stephen J. Cimbala. Westport, Conn.: Greenwood Press. Analyzes the problem of military uncertainty resulting from the political and military vacuum created in Europe by the lifting of the cold war international structure, and its impact on first strike stability.

The Future of Nuclear Weapons: Issues for the U.S. into the 21st Century. Patrick J. Garrity and Steven Am Maaranen, eds. New York: Plenum Publishing Corp. 425 pp. Authors from many different national perspectives assess the role of nuclear weapons in the post-cold war world.

International Nuclear Trade and Nonproliferation: The Challenge of the Emerging Suppliers. William C. Potter, ed. Lexington, Mass.: Lexington Books. 448 pp. Examines the cases of eleven new nuclear suppliers and policy options to control the diversion of nuclear materials into weapons programs.

Life Beyond the Bomb: Global Stability Without Nuclear Deterrence. Elman Schmähling, ed. New York: St. Martin's Press. 224 pp. Examines the role of nuclear weapons in the maintenance of global security.

National Security and International Relations: The Search for Security. Peter Mangold. New York: Routledge, Chapman, and Hall. 144 pp. Assesses attempts to ensure security in the twentieth century, looking for alternatives to such approaches as the competitive acquisition of nuclear weapons.

Nuclear Ambitions: The Spread of Nuclear Weapons 1989–1990. Leonard S. Spector. Boulder, Colo.: Westview Press. 450 pp. The fifth volume of Spector's series on the proliferation of nuclear weapons.

Omnicide: The Nuclear Dilemma. Lisa Marburg Goodman and Lee Ann Hoff. Westport, Conn.: Praeger Publishers. Examines the biological and psychological roots of the nuclear competition and its psychic impact on the population at large.

Security Without Nuclear Weapons? Different Perspectives on National Security. Regina Cowen Karp. New York: Oxford University Press. 412 pp. Examines the rise of the current security order, the role of nuclear weapons in that order, and new ways of thinking about security in the nuclear age.

Selling Strategic Defense: Interests, Ideologies, and the Arms Race. Erik K. Pratt. Boulder, Colo.: Lynne Rienner Publishers. 175 pp. Examines the origins of U.S. ballistic missile defense programs since 1945, exposing the process of decision making in the strategic arena.

The Soviet Union and the Politics of Nuclear Weapons in Europe, 1969–1987. Jonathan Haslam. Ithaca, N.Y.: Cornell University Press. 256 pp. Explores the Soviet decision to deploy SS-20s in Europe and the effect of that decision on superpower relations and nuclear planning in Europe.

Still the Arms Debate. Robert A. Levine. Brookfield, Vermont: Dartmouth Publishing Company. 453 pp. Explores the details of U.S. strategic policy.

The Strategic Nuclear Balance: Volume 1: And Why It Matters. Peter V. Pry. Bristol, Penn.: Crane Russak. 360 pp. Examines and critiques various qualitative and quantitative methods used to compare U.S. and Soviet strategic nuclear capabilities.

The Strategic Nuclear Balance: Volume II: Nuclear Wars: Exchanges and Outcomes. Peter V. Pry. Bristol, Penn.: Crane Russak. 350 pp. Uses exchange models—a form of simulation analysis—to examine the strategic nuclear balance.

Other Regional Issues

Alternative to Intervention: A New U.S.–Latin America Security Relationship. Richard J. Bloomfield and Gregory Treverton, eds. Boulder, Colo.: Lynne Rienner Publishers. 160 pp. Explores the underlying causes of U.S. intervention in Latin America and assesses the prospects for an alternative security arrangement that would satisfy the needs of the United States and the nations of Latin America.

Land of the Morning Calm: Korea and American Security. A. James Gregor. Lanham, Md.: University Press of America. 142 pp. Discusses Korea's future and its implications for regional security and U.S. security policy.

New Directions for American Policy in Asia. Bernard K. Gordon. New York: Routledge, Chapman, and Hall. 160 pp. Examines the strategic, political, and economic environment of the Asian-Pacific region, U.S. policy toward the region, and the prospects for U.S.-Asian relations in the future.

The Persian Gulf War: Lessons for Strategy, Law, and Diplomacy. Christopher C. Joyner, ed. Westport, Conn.: Greenwood Press. 272 pp. Examines the state of the Persian Gulf following the Iran-Iraq war. Useful context for understanding Desert Shield and Desert Storm.

Power and Leadership in International Bargaining: The Path to the Camp David Accords. Shibley Telhami. Irvington, N.Y.: Columbia University Press. 280 pp. Examines the context and history of the Camp David accords and the lessons of the accords for international relations and strategic conflicts.

Sovereignty and Security in the Arctic. Edgar Dosman, ed. New York: Routledge, Chapman, and Hall. 240 pp. Examines the superpower rivalry and its implications for sovereignty and security in the Arctic.

Soviet Naval Power in the Pacific. Derek da Cunha. Boulder, Colo.: Lynne Rienner Publishers. 200 pp. Examines the buildup of Soviet maritime power in the Pacific and the responses of the United States and various regional actors.

Subregional Security Cooperation in the Third World. William T. Tow. Boulder, Colo.: Lynne Rienner Publishers. 140 pp. Explores the strategic and economic implications of the rise of subregional security organizations replacing more traditional organizations such as ASEAN.

The $36 Billion Bargain: Strategy and Politics in U.S. Assistance to Israel. A. F. K. Organski. Irvington, N.Y.: Columbia University Press. 315 pp. Examines the U.S. relationship with Israel, asserting that U.S. aid is motivated by strategic interests in the region, not by a concern for Israel's continued existence.

The United States and the Defense of the Pacific. Ronald D. McLaurin and Chung-In Moon. Boulder, Colo.: Westview Press. 353 pp. Examines U.S. security concerns and preparations in the Asian Pacific rim.

Personnel

Financial Aid for Veterans, Military Personnel and Their Dependents, 1990–1991. Gail Ann Schlachter and R. David Weber. San Carlos, Calif.: Reference Service Press. 291 pp. Lists and describes the many sources of funding available for veterans and military personnel.

The Hollow Army: How the U.S. Army is Oversold and Undermanned. William Darryl Henderson. Westport, Conn.: Greenwood Press. 184 pp. Assesses the quality of soldiers in the all-volunteer force and the active duty force structure.

Leadership: Quotations from the Military Tradition. Robert A. Fitton, ed. Boulder, Colo.: Westview Press. 382 pp. Quotations and readings on military leadership.

The Moral Equivalent of War? A Study of Non-Military Service in Nine Nations. Donald Eberly and Michael Sherraden, eds. Westport, Conn.: Greenwood Press. 248 pp. Examines nonmilitary national service programs, assessing the social, economic, and individual success of such programs.

Terrorism and Other Issues

The Anatomy of Terrorism. David E. Long. New York: The Free Press. Exposes the structures of terrorist motivation and support and suggests methods of preventing and defending against terrorist acts.

Combating Terrorism. G. Davidson Smith. New York: Routledge, Chapman, and Hall. 336 pp. Argues that combating terrorism requires an understanding of the structure and motivations of particular terrorist groups and responses targeted to those specific structures and goals.

The Cult of Counterterrorism: The "Weird World" of Spooks, Counterterrorists, Adventurers, and the Not-Quite Professionals. Neil C. Livingstone. Lexington, Mass.: Lexington Books. 464 pp. An insider's look at the world of counterterrorism.

International Terrorism: Characteristics, Causes, Controls. Charles W. Kegley, Jr., ed. New York: St. Martin's Press. 352 pp. A comprehensive treatment of the terrorism question.

Origins of Terrorism. Walter Reich, ed. New York: Cambridge University Press. 289 pp. A multidisciplinary exploration of the motivations and psychologies of terrorism.

Qaddafi, Terrorism, and the Origins of the U.S. Attack on Libya. Brian L. Davis. Westport, Conn.: Praeger Publishers. 213 pp. Examines the historical context that led finally to the U.S. bombing of Libya in 1986.

Terrorism and Guerrilla Warfare: Forecasts and Remedies. Richard Clutterbuck. New York: Routledge, Chapman, and Hall. 224 pp. Examines the state of terrorism and guerrilla warfare in the early 1990s, the methods employed to combat terrorism, and directions terrorists may take in the future.

Terrorism: The North Korean Connection. Joseph S. Bermudez, Jr. Bristol, Penn.: Crane

Russak. 192 pp. Consolidates and explains the available open-source information on North Korean ties to terrorist organizations.

The Ties That Bind: Intelligence Co-operation Between the UKUSA Countries. Desmond Ball and Jeffrey T. Richelson. Cambridge, Mass.: Unwin Hyman. 420 pp. Examines the workings of the UKUSA agreement between the United States, the United Kingdom, Canada, Australia, and New Zealand, which created a global network of security and intelligence cooperation.

U.S. Foreign Intelligence: The Secret Side of American History. Charles D. Ameringer. Lexington, Mass.: Lexington Books. 480 pp. Examines the U.S. intelligence system and the balance that must be struck between its strategic value and the threat posed to democratic institutions by its requirement of secrecy.

Yearbooks and Databases

The American Defense Annual 1990–1991. Joseph Kruzel, ed. Lexington, Mass.: Lexington Books. 387 pp. Survey of 1989's events with forecasts of issues likely to assume significance in future strategic thinking.

Military and Strategic Policy: An Annotated Bibliography. Benjamin R. Beede. Westport, Conn.: Greenwood Press. 334 pp. Focuses on the mid-1960s through the post–Vietnam War era.

Military Periodicals: United States and Selected International Journals and Newspapers. Michael E. Unsworth, ed. Westport, Conn.: Greenwood Press. Examines the histories of selected unclassified periodicals devoted to military and naval subjects.

The Naval Institute Guide to Combat Fleets of the World. Bernard Prezelin. Annapolis: Naval Institute Press. 1040 pp. A comprehensive accounting of naval forces and capabilities of more than 165 nations.

The Scientific Measurement of International Conflict: Handbook of Datasets on Crises and Wars, 1945–1988 A.D. Claudio Cioffi-Revilla. Boulder, Colo.: Lynne Rienner Publishers. 75 pp. A detailed compendium of the international conflict datasets of the Data Development for International Relations (DDIR) project.

Shield of Republic/Sword of Empire: A Bibliography of United States Military Affairs, 1783–1846. John C. Fredriksen. Westport, Conn.: Greenwood Press. 446 pp. A bibliography of military history covering the period from the American Revolution to the Mexican war.

Cross-Reference by Author

Adams, James. *Engines of War: Merchants of Death and the New Arms Race.*
Allard, C. Kenneth. *Command, Control and the Common Defense.*
Ameringer, Charles D. *U.S. Foreign Intelligence: The Secret Side of American History.*
Andrade, Dale. *Ashes To Ashes: The Phoenix Program and the Vietnam War.*
Archer, Clive. *Organizing Western Europe.*
Ball, Desmond and Jeffrey T. Richelson. *The Ties That Bind: Intelligence Co-operation Between the UKUSA Countries.*
Barnet, Richard J. *The Rockets' Red Glare: When America Goes to War, the President and the People.*
Beede, Benjamin R. *Military and Strategic Policy: An Annotated Bibliography.*
Bellamy, Christopher. *The Evolution of Modern Land Warfare: Theory and Practice.*

Bendahmane, Diane B. and John W. McDonald, Jr., eds. *U.S. Bases Overseas: Negotiations with Spain, Greece, and the Philippines.*

Bermudez, Joseph S., Jr. *Terrorism: The North Korean Connection.*

Blackwell, James A., Jr., and Barry M. Blechman. *Making Defense Reform Work.*

Blaker, James R. *United States Overseas Basing: An Anatomy of the Dilemma.*

Bland, Douglas L. *The Military Committee of the North Atlantic Alliance: A Study of Structure and Strategy.*

Blechman, Barry M., William J. Durch, and Kevin P. O'Prey. *Regaining the High Ground: NATO's Stake in the New Talks on Conventional Armed Forces in Europe.*

Blodgett, John Q., Cha Young-Koo, and William J. Taylor, Jr. *The Korean Peninsula: Prospects for Arms Reduction Under Global Détente.*

Bloomfield, Richard J. and Gregory Treverton, eds. *Alternative to Intervention: A New U.S.-Latin America Security Relationship.*

Boutwell, Jeffrey. *The German Nuclear Dilemma.*

Brauch, Hans Gunter, ed. *Alternative Conventional Defense, Volume 1.*

Briggs, Clarence E., III. *Operation Just Cause: Panama, December 1989; A Soldier's Eyewitness Account.*

Brown, Jerold E. *Where Eagles Land: Planning and Development of U.S. Army Airfields, 1910–1941.*

Calogero, Francesco, Marvin L. Goldberger, and Sergei P. Kapitza, eds. *Verification: Monitoring Disarmament.*

Carpenter, Ted Galen, ed. *NATO at Forty: Confronting a Changing World.*

Cerutti, Furio and Rodolfo Ragionieri. *Rethinking European Security.*

Charters, David and Maurice Tugwell, eds. *Deception Operations: Studies in the East-West Context.*

Cimbala, Stephen J. *Conflict Termination in Europe: Games Against War.*

————. *First Strike Stability: Deterrence After Containment.*

————. *Uncertainty and Control: Future Soviet and American Strategy.*

Cioffi-Revilla, Claudio. *The Scientific Measurement of International Conflict: Handbook of Datasets on Crises and Wars, 1945–1988 A.D.*

Clutterbuck, Richard. *Terrorism and Guerrilla Warfare: Forecasts and Remedies.*

Cohen, Eliot A. and John Gooch. *Military Misfortunes: The Anatomy of Failure in War.*

Cohen, Richard and Peter A. Wilson. *Superpowers in Economic Decline: U.S. Strategy for the Transcentury Era.*

Coker, Christopher, ed. *Shifting into Neutral? Burden Sharing in the Western Alliance in the 1990s.*

Cordesman, Anthony H. and Abraham R. Wagner. *The Lessons of Modern War.*

Cray, Ed. *General of the Army: George C. Marshall, Soldier and Statesman.*

Cuthbertson, Ian M. and Peter Volten, eds. *The Guns Fall Silent: The End of the Cold War and the Future of Conventional Disarmament.*

da Cunha, Derek. *Soviet Naval Power in the Pacific.*

Davis, Brian L. *Qaddafi, Terrorism, and the Origins of the U.S. Attack on Libya.*

Deber, Charles, William A. Schwartz, et al. *The Nuclear Seduction: Why the Arms Race Doesn't Matter—And What Does.*

Dewar, Michael and Brian Holden Reid, eds. *The Central Front.*

Dosman, Edgar, ed. *Sovereignty and Security in the Arctic.*

Downs, George W. and David M. Rocke. *Tacit Bargaining, Arms Races, and Arms Control.*

Dunn, Lewis A. and Amy E. Gordon, eds. *Arms Control Verification & the New Role of On-Site Inspection.*

Eberly, Donald and Michael Sherraden, eds. *The Moral Equivalent of War? A Study of Non-Military Service in Nine Nations.*

Ellis, John. *Brute Force: Allied Strategy and Tactics in the Second World War.*

Epstein, Joshua M. *Conventional Force Reductions: A Dynamic Assessment.*

Errington, Elizabeth Jane and B. J. C. McKercher, eds. *The Vietnam War as History.*

Fieldhouse, Richard, ed. *Security at Sea: Naval Forces and Arms Control.*

Fitton, Robert A., ed. *Leadership: Quotations from the Military Tradition.*

Flintham, Victor. *Air Wars and Aircraft: A Detailed Record of Air Combat, 1945 to the Present.*

Foot, Rosemary. *A Substitute for Victory: The Politics of Peacemaking at the Korean Armistice Talks.*

———. *The Wrong War: American Policy and the Dimensions of the Korean Conflict, 1950–1953.*

Fredriksen, John C. *Shield of Republic/Sword of Empire: A Bibliography of United States Military Affairs, 1783–1846.*

Freedman, Lawrence, ed. *Military Power in Europe: Essays in Memory of Jonathan Alford.*

Garrity, Patrick J. and Steven Am Maaranen, eds. *The Future of Nuclear Weapons: Issues for the U.S. into the 21st Century.*

George, James L. *The New Nuclear Rules: Strategy and Arms Control After INF and START.*

Gertcher, Frank L. and William J. Weida. *Beyond Deterrence: The Political Economy of Nuclear Weapons.*

Goodman, Lisa Marburg and Lee Ann Hoff. *Omnicide: The Nuclear Dilemma.*

Gordon, Bernard K. *New Directions for American Policy in Asia.*

Gottfried, Kurt and Paul Bracken, eds. *Reforging European Security: From Confrontation to Cooperation.*

Gray, Colin S. *War, Peace, and Victory: Strategy and Statecraft for the Next Century.*

Gregor, A. James. *Land of the Morning Calm: Korea and American Security.*

Grin, John. *Military-Technological Choices and Political Implications: Command and Control in Established NATO Posture and a Non-Provocative Defence.*

Grove, Eric. *Maritime Strategy and European Security.*

Guertner, Gary L. *Deterrence and Defense in a Post-Nuclear World: Emerging Soviet and American Strategies.*

Harris, J. P. and F. H. Toase, eds. *Armoured Warfare.*

Haslam, Jonathan. *The Soviet Union and the Politics of Nuclear Weapons in Europe, 1969–1987.*

Henderson, William Darryl. *The Hollow Army: How the U.S. Army is Oversold and Undermanned.*

Howlett, Darryl A. *EURATOM and Nucelar Safeguards.*

Immerman, Richard, ed. *John Foster Dulles and the Diplomacy of the Cold War.*

Jordan, Robert S. *Alliance Strategy and Navies: The Evolution and Scope of NATO's Maritime Dimensions.*

Joyner, Christopher C., ed. *The Persian Gulf War: Lessons for Strategy, Law, and Diplomacy.*

Karp, Regina Cowen. *Security Without Nuclear Weapons? Different Perspectives on National Security.*

Kegley, Charles W., Jr., ed. *International Terrorism: Characteristics, Causes, Controls.*

Koburger, Charles W., Jr. *Narrow Seas, Small Navies, and Fat Merchantmen: Naval Strategies for the 1990s.*

Kokoski, Richard and Sergey Koulik. eds. *Verification of Conventional Arms Control in Europe: Technological Constraints and Opportunities.*

Kruzel, Joseph, ed. *The American Defense Annual 1990–1991.*

Laqueur, Walter and Leon Sloss. *European Security in the 1990s: Deterrence and Defense After the INF Treaty.*

Lehna, Stefan. *The Vienna Conference on Security and Cooperation in Europe: A Turning Point in East-West Relations.*

Lepgold, Joseph. *The Declining Hegemon: The United States and European Defense, 1960– 1990.*

Levine, Robert A. *Still the Arms Debate.*

Livingstone, Neil C. *The Cult of Counterterrorism: The "Weird World" of Spooks, Counter- terrorists, Adventurers, and the Not-Quite Professionals.*

Long, David E. *The Anatomy of Terrorism.*

Lucas, Michael R. *The Western Alliance After INF: Redefining U.S. Policy Toward Europe and the Soviet Union.*

Mallin, Maurice A. *Tanks, Fighters & Ships: U.S. Conventional Force Planning Since WW II.*

Mangold, Peter. *National Security and International Relations: The Search for Security.*

Mann, Thomas E., ed. *A Question of Balance: The President, the Congress, and Foreign Policy.*

Mazarr, Michael J. *START and the Future of Deterrence.*

McInnes, Colin *NATO's Changing Strategic Agenda.*

McLaurin, Ronald D. and Chung-In Moon. *The United States and the Defense of the Pacific.*

Menos, Dennis. *The Superpowers and Nuclear Arms Control: Rhetoric and Reality.*

Nye, Joseph S., Jr. *Bound to Lead: The Changing Nature of American Power.*

O'Neil, Bard E. *Insurgency & Terrorism: Inside Modern Revolutionary Warfare.*

Organski, A.F.K. *The $36 Billion Bargain: Strategy and Politics in U.S. Assistance to Israel.*

Paschall, Rod. *LIC 2010: Special Operations & Unconventional Warfare in the Next Century.*

Pendley, Robert E. and Joseph F. Pilat, eds. *Beyond 1995: The Future of the NPT Regime.*

Pfaltzgraf, Robert L., Jr., and Richard H. Shultz, Jr., eds. *U.S. Defense Policy in an Era of Constrained Resources.*

Pimlott, John. *Vietnam: The Decisive Battles.*

Potter, E. B. *Admiral Arleigh Burke: A Biography.*

Potter, William C., ed. *International Nuclear Trade and Nonproliferation: The Challenge of the Emerging Suppliers.*

Pratt, Erik K. *Selling Strategic Defense: Interests, Ideologies, and the Arms Race.*

Prezelin, Bernard. *The Naval Institute Guide to Combat Fleets of the World.*

Pry, Peter V. *The Strategic Nuclear Balance: Volume I: And Why It Matters.*

———. *The Strategic Nuclear Balance: Volume II: Nuclear Wars: Exchanges and Outcomes.*

Reich, Walter, eds. *Origins of Terrorism.*

Rosenthal, Debra. *At the Heart of the Bomb: The Dangerous Allure of Weapons Work.*

Rusk, Dean. *As I Saw It.*

Russett, Bruce. *Controlling the Sword: The Democratic Governance of National Security.*

Sanders, Ralph. *Arms Industries: New Suppliers and Regional Security.*

Sarkesian, Sam C. and John Allen Williams, eds. *The U.S. Army in a New Security Era.*

Scales, Robert, Jr. *Firepower in Limited War.*

Schlachter, Gail Ann and R. David Weber. *Financial Aid for Veterans, Military Personnel and Their Dependents, 1990–1991.*

Schmähling, Elman, ed. *Life Beyond the Bomb: Global Stability Without Nuclear Deterrence.*

Schoonmaker, Herbert G. *Military Crisis Management: U.S. Intervention in the Dominican Republic, 1965.*

Sharp, Jane M. O., ed. *Europe After an American Withdrawal: Economic and Military Issues.*

Sherwood, Elizabeth D. *Allies in Crisis: Meeting Global Challenges to Western Security.*

Sims, Jennifer E. *Icarus Restrained: An Intellectual History of Nuclear Arms Control, 1945–1960.*

Smith, G. Davidson. *Combating Terrorism.*

Spector, Leonard S. *Nuclear Ambitions: The Spread of Nuclear Weapons 1989–1990.*

Stock, Thomas and Ronald Sutherland, eds. *National Implementation of the Future Chemical Weapons Convention.*

Suid, Lawrence H. *The Army's Nuclear Power Program: The Evolution of a Support Agency.*

Summers, Harry G., Jr. *Korean War Almanac.*

Szabo, Stephen F. *The Bundeswehr and Western Security.*

Telhami, Shibley. *Power and Leadership in International Bargaining: The Path to the Camp David Accords.*

Tow, William T. *Subregional Security Cooperation in the Third World.*

Traub, James. *Too Good to be True: The Outlandish Story of Wedtech.*

Tsouras, Peter G. and Bruce W. Watson. *Operation Just Cause: The U.S. Intervention in Panama.*

Unsworth, Michael E., ed. *Military Periodicals: United States and Selected International Journals and Newspapers.*

van der Graaf, Henry and John Grin, eds. *Unconventional Approaches to Conventional Arms Control Verification: An Exploratory Assessment.*

Watson, Cynthia. *U.S. National Security Policy Groups: Institutional Profiles.*

Weinberger, Caspar. *Fighting for Peace: Seven Critical Years in the Pentagon.*

Weiner, Tim. *Blank Check: The Pentagon's Black Budget.*

Weston, Burns H., ed. *Alternative Security: Living Without Nuclear Deterrence.*

Wilcox, Robert. *Scream of Eagles: The Creation of Top Gun and the U.S. Air Victory in Vietnam.*

Notes

Chapter 1
After the Storm:
Perspectives on the Gulf War

1. Peter D. Feaver and Mark Wayda, "The Risk of Letting the Warriors Run a War," *Christian Science Monitor,* January 24, 1991, p. 19.

2. Norman Friedman, "The Air Campaign," *Naval Institute Proceedings* 117, no. 4 (April 1991), p. 49.

3. Gen. Michael Dugan (USAF Ret.), "First Lessons of Victory," *U.S. News & World Report,* March 18, 1991, p. 32.

4. Caleb Baker and George Leopold, "Air Force Urges JSTARS Finish Testing Before Production," *Defense News,* March 19, 1991, p. 44.

5. Edward H. Kolcum, "Joint-STARS E-8s Return to U.S.; 20-Aircraft Fleet Believed Assured," *Aviation Week and Space Technology,* March 11, 1991, p. 20.

6. Barbara Starr, "Satellites Paved Way to Victory," *Jane's Defense Weekly,* March 9, 1991, p. 330.

7. Interview, *Jane's Defense Weekly,* February 9, 1991, p. 200.

8. Eric Schmitt with Michael Gordon, "Unforeseen Problems in Air War Forced Allies to Improvise Tactics," *New York Times,* March 10, 1991, p. 1.

9. Tim Weiner, "Stealth Fighter Revived," *Philadelphia Inquirer,* March 31, 1991, p. 1.

10. William Matthews, "Cheney Credits Predecessors for Success," *Navy Times,* April 8, 1991, p. 26.

11. Theodore H. Moran, "International Economics and Security," *Foreign Affairs* (Winter 1990/91), p. 84.

12. VAdm. J. Metcalf III (USN Ret.), "The Last Great Air Battle," *Naval Institute Proceedings* 17, no. 3 (March 1991), p. 26.

13. John T. Correll, "The Force at War," *Air Force Magazine*, March 1991, p. 6.

14. *New York Times*, March 1, 1991, p. A8.

15. Peter Applebome, "Georgia's Guardsmen Return From a War They Didn't Fight," *New York Times*, March 27, 1991, p. 1.

16. *Foreign Relations of the United States, 1926*, Vol. I, Department of State, Washington, D.C., p. xxvi.

Chapter 2
Toward the Post–Cold War World:
Structure, Strategy, and Security

1. Speech to the House of Commons, March 1, 1848, quoted in Jasper Ridley, *Lord Palmerston* (London: Constable, 1970), p. 334.

2. An unpublished paper by Professor Terry L. Deibel of the National War College, "Strategies Before Containment—Patterns for the Future," has influenced my thinking on this point.

3. See Felix Gilbert, *To the Farewell Address: Ideas of Early American Foreign Policy* (Princeton, N.J.: Princeton University Press, 1961), especially pp. 19–43.

4. Gordon S. Wood, *The Creation of the American Republic, 1776–1787* (Chapel Hill: University of North Carolina Press, 1969), pp. 135–36, 448–49, 548–49.

5. Americans were quick to react to the possibility of British and French expansion into Texas and California in the 1840s; they deliberately "tilted" toward Russia during the Crimean War; Lincoln's Emancipation Proclamation can be understood as a successful attempt, by moral means, to turn the European balance of power against the Confederacy; and Theodore Roosevelt played an explicit balancing role in the diplomacy of the Russo-Japanese War, first favoring Japan, and then Russia.

6. "A steadfast concern for peace can never be maintained except by a partnership of democratic nations," Woodrow Wilson told the Congress in asking for a declaration of war against Germany in April 1917. "No autocratic government could be trusted to keep faith with it or to observe its covenants." (Arthur S. Link, ed., *The Papers of Woodrow Wilson: Volume 41 (January 24-April 6, 1917)* [Princeton, N.J.: Princeton University Press, 1983], p. 524).

7. See N. Gordon Kevin, *Woodrow Wilson and World Politics: America's Response to War and Revolution* (New York: Oxford University Press, 1968).

8. For an argument that the great powers have already, in effect, abolished war as a rational instrument of policy, see John Mueller, *Retreat From Doomsday: The Obsolescence of Major War* (New York: Basic Books, 1989).

9. I have adapted this analogy from Heinz R. Pagels, *The Dreams of Reason: The Computer and the Rise of the Sciences of Complexity* (New York: Simon and Schuster, 1988), p. 227.

10. *Public Papers of the Presidents: Harry S. Truman, 1947* (Washington, D.C.: U.S. Government Printing Office, 1963), p. 178. See also John Lewis Gaddis, *Strategies of Con-*

tainment: A Critical Appraisal of Postwar American National Security Policy (New York: Oxford University Press, 1982), pp. 65–66.

11. Or, as the editors of *The Economist* recently put it, "the trend is towards both fission and fusion, with plenty of tension between the two" ("Go Forth and Unify," *The Economist,* October 6, 1990, p. 16). I am indebted to Geoffrey Dabelko for bringing this reference to my attention.

12. For example, Wendell L. Willkie, *One World* (New York: Simon and Schuster, 1943).

13. On the importance of communications in the collapse of communism, see Zbigniew Brzezinski, *The Grand Failure: The Birth and Death of Communism in the Twentieth Century* (New York: Charles Scribner's Sons, 1989), pp. 254–55.

14. See, on this point, Gaddis, *Strategies of Containment,* pp. 28–29, 58–61.

15. To be sure, General Charles DeGaulle terminated France's formal military association with NATO in 1966. But by that time, it had become clear that West Germany was so firmly linked to NATO that it could pose no future threat. And we now know that, in certain areas at least, informal French military cooperation with NATO members has never ceased. See especially, on this last point, Richard H. Ullman, "The Covert French Connection," *Foreign Policy* 75 (Summer 1989), pp. 3–33.

16. The term "soft power" comes from Joseph S. Nye, Jr., *Bound to Lead: The Changing Nature of American Power* (New York: Basic Books, 1990), especially p. 188. See also Nye, "Soft Power," *Foreign Policy* 80 (Fall 1990), pp. 153–71.

17. Theodore S. Hamerow, *From the Finland Station: The Graying of Revolution in the Twentieth Century* (New York: Basic Books, 1990), pp. 210–25, 300–309.

18. See *New York Times,* February 22, 1990; also Timothy Garton Ash, *The Uses of Adversity: Essays on the Fate of Central Europe* (New York: Random House, 1989), pp. 191–93.

19. Michael Doyle, "Kant, Liberal Legacies, and Foreign Affairs" *Philosophy and Public Affairs* 12 (Summer and Fall 1983), pp. 205–35, 323–53; also Doyle, "Liberalism and World Politics," *American Political Science Review* 80 (December 1987), pp. 1151–69.

20. See, for example, A. W. DePorte, *Europe Between the Super-Powers: The Enduring Balance,* 2d ed. (New Haven, Conn.: Yale University Press, 1986), pp. 186–87; also Michael Howard, "1989: A Farewell to Arms?" *International Affairs* 65 (Summer 1989), especially pp. 409–10. But many authors have found events to be moving faster than their word processors recently. An obvious example is John Lewis Gaddis, "One Germany—in Both Alliances," *New York Times,* March 21, 1990.

21. Celestine Bohlen, "Ethnic Rivalries Revive in East Europe," *New York Times,* November 12, 1990.

22. John F. Burns, "In Quebec, Yet Another Splintering," *New York Times,* July 29, 1990.

23. See Bernard Lewis, "The Roots of Muslim Rage," *The Atlantic,* September 1990, pp. 47–60.

24. For an excellent account, see Thomas L. Friedman, *From Beirut to Jerusalem* (New York: Farrar, Straus, and Giroux, 1989).

25. See William H. McNeill, "Winds of Change," in Nicholas X. Rizopolous, ed., *Sea-Changes: American Foreign Policy in a World Transformed* (New York: Council on Foreign Relations Press, 1990), p. 176. The nation did, after all, survive the infatuation of earlier generations with Elvis Presley and the Beatles.

26. There is growing evidence, as well, that the standard of living for the middle class

in the United States is no longer improving. See "American Living Standards: Running to Stand Still," *The Economist,* November 10, 1990, pp. 19–22.

27. I refer here to recent controversies over the alleged use of quotas to ensure equal access to education and employment, and to the imposition on many college campuses of both formal and informal restrictions on freedom of speech in an effort to avoid offending particular groups of people. See, on this issue, "Race on Campus," a special issue of the *New Republic,* 204 (February 18, 1991); and Dinesh D'Souza, "Illiberal Education," *The Atlantic,* March 1991, pp. 51–79.

28. See William F. Buckley, Jr., *Gratitude: Reflections On What We Owe To Our Country* (New York: Random House, 1990).

29. Reagan's "Martian" scenario is discussed in John Lewis Gaddis, "How the Cold War Might End," *The Atlantic,* November 1987, pp. 90–91.

30. Joseph S. Nye, Jr., "Nuclear Learning and U.S.-Soviet Security Regimes," *International Organization* 16 (Summer 1987), pp. 371–402; Robert Jervis, *The Meaning of the Nuclear Revolution: Statecraft and the Prospect of Armageddon* (Ithaca: Cornell University Press, 1989).

31. Alfred E. Eckes, Jr., *A Search for Solvency: Bretton Woods and the International Monetary System, 1941–1971* (Austin: University of Texas Press, 1975); Robert A. Pollard, *Economic Security and the Origins of the Cold War, 1945–1950* (New York: Columbia University Press, 1985); G. John Ikenberry, "Rethinking the Origins of American Hegemony," *Political Science Quarterly* 104 (Fall 1989), pp. 375–400.

32. Henry R. Nau, *The Myth of America's Decline: Leading the World Economy into the 1990s* (New York: Oxford University Press, 1990), pp. 77–128, makes a strong argument that it was really the Marshall Plan that created the system of price stability, liberalized trade, and minimally regulated markets from which postwar prosperity resulted.

33. See Bruce G. Blair and Henry W. Kendall, "Accidental Nuclear War," *Scientific American,* December 1990, pp. 53–58.

34. McNeill, "Winds of Change," pp. 187–92.

35. Since 1945 there have been at least thirty-six major regional crises—Iran (1946), Greece (1947), Czechoslovakia (1948), Berlin (1948), Korea (1950–53), East Berlin (1953), Indochina (1954), Quemoy-Matsu (1954–55), Hungary (1956), Suez (1956), Lebanon (1958), Quemoy-Matsu (1958), Berlin (1958–59), U-2 Incident (1960), Bay of Pigs (1961), Berlin (1961), Sino-Indian conflict (1962), Cuba (1962), Dominican Republic (1965); India-Pakistan War (1965), Vietnam (1965–75), Six-Day War (1967), Czechoslovakia (1968), Sino-Soviet border incidents (1969), India-Pakistan War (1971), Yom Kippur War (1973), Iran (1978–81), Afghanistan (1979–88), Sino-Vietnamese War (1979), Nicaragua/ El Salvador (1979–90), Iran-Iraq War (1980–88), Falklands War (1982), Lebanon (1982–84), Korean airliner incident (1983), Panama (1989), and the Persian Gulf crisis and war (1990–91)—not one of which has led to a world war.

36. See John Lewis Gaddis, *The Long Peace: Inquiries into the History of the Cold War* (New York: Oxford University Press, 1987), pp. 215–45.

37. For example, Paul Kennedy, *The Rise and Fall of the Great Powers: Economic Change and Military Conflict from 1500 to 2000* (New York: Random House, 1987); David P. Calleo, *Beyond American Hegemony: The Future of the Western Alliance* (New York: Basic Books, 1987); Clyde V. Prestowitz, Jr., *Trading Places: How We Are Giving Our Future to Japan and How to Reclaim It* (New York: Basic Books, 1989).

38. The dangers are clearly stated in two recent articles by John J. Mearsheimer, "Why We Will Soon Miss the Cold War," *The Atlantic,* August 1990, pp. 35–50; and "Back

to the Future: Instability in Europe After the Cold War," *International Security* 15 (Summer 1990), pp. 5–56.

39. An extreme, but prominent, example of such celebration is Francis Fukuyama, "The End of History?" *The National Interest* 16 (Summer 1989), pp. 3–18.

40. Seweryn Bialer, "Russia vs. the Soviet Union," *U.S. News,* November 5, 1990, pp. 46–47.

41. See, on this point, George F. Kennan, "Communism in Russian History," *Foreign Affairs* 69 (Winter 1990/91), especially pp. 181–84.

42. It may be that preoccupation with European developments prior to August 1990, prevented the United States and the Soviet Union from sending sufficiently discouraging signals to Saddam Hussein.

43. One of my students, Ed Merta, has pointed out in a seminar essay that the Persian Gulf crisis is only one of many examples throughout history—ranging from ancient Greece through the aftermath of World War II—of how imperial decline destabilizes international relations: "The structure of the new world has yet to emerge clearly, but the consequences of the old one's demise are clear: the joint restraint on armed conflict exerted by the United States and Soviet Union has disappeared as domestic concerns preoccupy both and the uncertain West tries to redefine its strategic interests."

44. W. W. Rostow, *The Stages of Economic Growth: A Non-Communist Manifesto* (Cambridge: Cambridge University Press, 1962), p. 164. For a strong critique of this theory, see D. Michael Shafer, *Deadly Paradigms: The Failure of U.S. Counterinsurgency Policy* (Princeton, N.J.: Princeton University Press, 1988).

45. See Hamerow, *From the Finland Station,* especially pp. 349–53; also Brzezinski, *The Grand Failure,* pp. 250–51.

46. Doyle, "Kant, Liberal Legacies, and Foreign Affairs," part 2, pp. 351–53.

47. James Chase has suggested, persuasively in my view, that this attitude goes back to Lyndon Johnson's attempt to fight the Vietnam War without asking for sacrifices on the home front. See Chase, *Solvency: The Price of Survival* (New York: Random House, 1981), p. 15.

48. See Robert Gilpin, *The Political Economy of International Relations* (Princeton, N.J.: Princeton University Press, 1987), pp. 334–37. It is worth noting that, with all their complaints about taxes, Americans still pay far less than do the citizens of most other industrial countries. For 1989 comparisons, see *The Economist,* October 27, 1990, p. 24.

49. Richard Lacayo, "Why No Blue Blood Will Flow," *Time,* November 26, 1990, p. 34.

50. I am indebted to Robert Jervis and John Mueller for suggesting this point.

51. Not the least of the unfortunate consequences of the Persian Gulf crisis is the extent to which it has distracted attention from the problems of the Soviet Union and Eastern Europe.

52. See the editorial, "The Russians Are Coming," *The Economist,* October 20, 1990, pp. 11–12.

53. The best assessment is Michael J. Hogan, *The Marshall Plan: America, Britain, and the Reconstruction of Western Europe, 1947–1952* (Cambridge, Mass.: Cambridge University Press, 1987), especially pp. 430–45.

54. See Timothy Garton Ash, "Germany Unbound," *New York Review of Books,* November 22, 1990, pp. 11–15. The Conference on Security and Cooperation in Europe, which is now little more than a framework for negotiations, suffers from a deficiency opposite to that of NATO and the European Community: it includes *all* of the states of

Europe, from the largest to the most microscopic, and it requires unity in order to act, which in most cases ensures that it will not.

55. See Gaddis, *The Long Peace,* especially pp. 222–23, 239–40; also Mueller, *Retreat From Doomsday,* pp. 217–44.

56. For an eloquent explanation of the advantages adherence to international law can offer, see Daniel Patrick Moynihan, *On the Law of Nations* (Cambridge, Mass.: Harvard University Press, 1990).

57. See Gina Kolata, "Japanese Labs in U.S. Luring America's Computer Experts," *New York Times,* November 11, 1990.

58. McNeill, "Winds of Change," pp. 184–87, sets this problem within a long-term historical context.

59. See note 52. Recent large increases in the emigration of Soviet Jews to Israel have, of course, already increased tensions in the Middle East.

60. For a more pessimistic view, see McNeill, "Winds of Change," pp. 178–79.

61. John Lewis Gaddis, "Great Illusions, the Long Peace, and the Future of the International System," in Charles W. Kegley, Jr., ed., *The Long Postwar Peace* (New York: Harper Collins, Inc., 1990), pp. 39–41.

62. My understanding of "solvency" here echoes that of Walter Lippmann: "If its expenditures are safely within its assured means, a family is solvent when it is poor, or is well-to-do, or is rich. The same principle holds true of nations." (*U. S. Foreign Policy: Shield of the Republic* [Boston: Little, Brown, 1943], p. 10). For a thoughtful elaboration of this principle, see Chace, *Solvency, passim.*

63. Gaddis, *Strategies of Containment,* pp. 135–36.

64. Eisenhower's "Farewell Address," delivered on January 17, 1961 and printed in *The Public Papers of the Presidents of the United States: Dwight D. Eisenhower, 1960* (Washington, D.C.: U.S. Government Printing Office, 1961), pp. 1035–40, is well worth regular re-reading.

65. One striking indication of this lack of consensus is the polarization of the international studies community into optimistic and pessimistic schools of thought. The optimists include Francis Fukuyama, Richard Rosecrance, Joseph S. Nye, Jr., and John Mueller; but there is an equally conspicuous and equally influential group of pessimists, among them Paul Kennedy, David Calleo, Clyde Prestowitz, and John Mearsheimer. (Specific references to the work of all of these individuals appear elsewhere in these notes.) The optimists tend to stress the role of integrative phenomena in current world politics; and the pessimists the role of fragmentationist phenomena. The differences in mood are so stark, though, that the proverbial man from Mars might legitimately wonder whether these two groups of analysts are writing about the same planet.

66. *The Federalist* (New York: Modern Library, n.d.), p. 336.

Chapter 3
The Economics of Defense in the 1990s

1. John Kenneth Galbraith, "Military Power and the Military Budget," in Robert H. Haveman and Robert D. Harrison, eds., *The Political Economy of Federal Policy* (New York: Harper & Row, 1973), p. 115.

2. *DOD Budget: Comparison of Undated Five-Year Plan with President's Budget* (Washington, D.C.: U.S. General Accounting Office, 1990), p. 6.

3. Stephen Cain, *Analysis of the FY 1992–93 Defense Budget Request* (Washington, D.C.: Defense Budget Project, 1991), table 1.

4. Statement of Robert D. Reischauer, Director, Congressional Budget Office, before the Committee on the Budget, U.S. House of Representatives, February 27, 1991, pp. 1–24. See also the statement of Charles A. Bowsher, Comptroller General, before the House of Representatives Committee on the Budget, *Cost and Financing of Operation Desert Shield,* January 4, 1991.

5. Barton Gellman and Steven Mufson, "There'll Be Hell to Pay, But No One Knows How Much Yet," *Washington Post Weekly,* January 21, 1991, p. 22.

6. See *Underestimation of Funding Requirements in Five Year Procurement Plans* (Washington, D.C.: U.S. General Accounting Office, 1984).

7. Congressional Budget Office, *Effects of Weapons Procurement Stretch-Outs on Costs and Schedules* (Washington, D.C.: U.S. Government Printing Office, 1987), p. 17.

8. Stanley Hoffmann, "Watch Out for a New World Disorder," *International Herald Tribune,* February 26, 1991, p. 14.

9. U.S. Congressional Budget Office, *The Economic and Budget Outlook: Fiscal Years 1991–1995* (Washington, D.C.: U.S. Government Printing Office, 1990), p. 66.

10. David Evans, "Budget Pressure, End of Cold War Bringing Changes," *Chicago Tribune,* October 29, 1989, p. 1; "Sen. Nunn on Vision of Military," *New York Times,* April 20, 1990, p. A10.

11. Lawrence J. Korb, "How To Reduce Military Spending," *New York Times,* November 21, 1989, p. 23.

12. Andrew Rosenthal, "Plan for Closing Military Bases Alarms Capitol," *New York Times,* January 27, 1990, p. 1.

13. Statement of Charles L. Schultze before the Joint Economic Committee, December 19, 1989, p. 6.

14. U.S. Office of Management and Budget, *Budget of the United States Government, Fiscal Year 1992* (Washington, D.C.: U.S. Government Printing Office, 1991), part 2, p. 58.

15. See Murray Weidenbaum, *Small Wars, Big Defense* (New York: Oxford University Press, 1991).

Chapter 4
Strategic Forces

1. Quoted in John D. Morrocco, "Defense Department Grapples with Massive Spending Cuts," *Aviation Week and Space Technology,* November 27, 1989, p. 16; Peter Almond, "Pentagon Budgeters Collide with Changes in Eastern Europe," *Washington Times,* November 21, 1989, p. 5.

2. MX estimates are for fifty missiles deployed on twenty-five trains. SICBM estimates are for 500 missiles deployed on hard mobile launchers on three Minuteman bases. All figures are in then-year (TY) dollars. Procurement cost estimates come from the U.S. Air Force Public Affairs Office, November 1990. O&S estimates are derived from Michael E. Brown, "The U.S. Manned Bomber and Strategic Deterrence in the 1990s," *International Security* 14, no. 2 (Fall 1989), pp. 34–35.

3. For more discussion of MX and SICBM survivability, see *Department of Defense Authorization for Appropriations for Fiscal Years 1988 and 1989,* hearings before the Sen-

ate Armed Services Committee, 100th Cong., 1st Sess., February–April 1987, pt. 4; 1891–93, 1931–32; Barry E. Fridling and John R. Harvey, "On the Wrong Track? An Assessment of MX Rail Garrison Basing," *International Security* 13, no. 3 (Winter 1988/89), pp. 113–41; Ivo H. Daalder, *Strategic Defence Deployment Options: Criteria and Evaluation* (London: Macmillan, forthcoming).

4. Matthew Bunn, "SS-18 Modernization: The Satan and START," *Arms Control Today* 20, no. 6 (July/August 1990), pp. 13–17; Mary Dejevsky, "Moscow to Halt Production of Rail-Mobile Missiles," *The Times* (London), August 3, 1990; International Institute for Strategic Studies (IISS), *The Military Balance, 1990–1991* (London: IISS, Autumn 1990), pp. 29, 221.

5. For a thorough discussion of the development of the D-5, see Graham Spinardi, "Why the U.S. Navy Went for Hard-Target Counterforce in Trident II (And Why It Didn't Get There Sooner)," *International Security* 15, no. 2 (Fall 1990), pp. 147–90.

6. John D. Morrocco, "Second Trident II Test Failure Points to Missile Design Flaw," *Aviation Week and Space Technology,* August 21, 1989, p. 26; IISS, *Military Balance, 1990–1991,* p. 12.

7. IISS, *Military Balance, 1990–1991,* pp. 29, 222; "Joint U.S.-Soviet Summit Statement," *Survival* 30, no. 3 (May/June 1988), pp. 267–72.

8. Over two dozen B-52Gs with conventional and maritime assignments were retired in 1990 as well.

9. Barbara Amouyal, "Air Force Extends B-52's Operational Life 30 Years," *Defense News,* October 29, 1990, p. 13.

10. "Air Force Starting Flight Tests of B-1B Defensive Avionics System," *Aviation Week and Space Technology,* October 15, 1990, pp. 50–51; Tony Capaccio, "Air Force Admits to New B-1 Problems," *Defense Week,* October 1, 1990, p. 1.

11. The discussion that follows is based on Michael E. Brown, "The Case Against the B-2," *International Security* 15, no. 1 (Summer 1990), pp. 129–53. Also, see Brown, "U.S. Manned Bomber," pp. 8–17. The best exposition of the case for the B-2 can be found in Donald Rice, "The Manned Bomber and Strategic Deterrence: The U.S. Air Force Perspective," *International Security* 15, no. 1 (Summer 1990), pp. 100–128.

12. See the comments by General John T. Chain, Jr., the commander-in-chief of the Strategic Air Command, in R. Jeffrey Smith, "General Disputes Cheney on Need for B-2 Bomber," *Washington Post,* May 5, 1990, p. 15.

13. Testimony before the House Armed Services Committee, March 1990; quoted in Richard H.P. Sia, "Aspin Challenges Rationale for B-2," *Boston Globe,* March 7, 1990, p. 6.

14. For more on the B-2's technical problems, see U.S. General Accounting Office, *B-2 Program Status and Current Issues,* GAO/NSIAD-90–120 (Washington, D.C.: U.S. Government Printing Office, February 1990).

15. See Brown, "Case Against the B-2," pp. 144–49.

16. These estimates are in TY dollars. For more details, see Ibid.

17. See David F. Bond, "Congressional Debate on B-2 Turns to Arms Control Impact," *Aviation Week and Space Technology,* July 31, 1989, p. 24; John D. Morrocco, "Opposition to B-2 Threatens Viability of Strategic Triad," *Aviation Week and Space Technology,* March 19, 1990, pp. 49–51.

18. Philip Finnegan, "Budget Pact Slows Some Weapons," *Defense News,* October 22, 1990, p. 8; "Pentagon Wins Accord for $288 Billion in 1991," *International Herald*

Tribune, October 24, 1990, p. 4; "B-2 Tangle," *Aviation Week and Space Technology,* October 29, 1990, p. 17.

19. Congress also approved $107.4 million ($34 million more than the Defense Department requested) in long-lead procurement funds, which will be used to start work on the next batch of ACMs.

20. In TY dollars. For more on the ACM program, see "Full-Rate Production of ACM to Begin in 1992," *Aviation Week and Space Technology,* January 29, 1990, p. 32.

21. John D. Morrocco, "Problems with Rocket Motor Delay Initial Flight of SRAM II," *Aviation Week and Space Technology,* January 29, 1990, pp. 31–32; David J. Lynch, "SRAM II Being Hampered by Propellant Problems," *Defense Week,* January 22, 1990, p. 1.

22. Many of these launchers will be armed with conventional and antiship SLCMs, however. See IISS, *Military Balance, 1990–1991,* pp. 12–13, 216.

23. For more details, see Peter Adams, "Brilliant Pebbles Ready for First Flight in Summer," *Defense News,* February 2, 1990, p. 3; Vincent Kiernan, "Technology to Deploy Brilliant Pebbles 'At Hand,' SDIO Says," *Space News,* February 12, 1990, p. 4.

24. See Ibid. Also, see "First HEDI Test Flight Termed a Success Despite Early Detonation," *Defense Daily,* January 29, 1990, p. 146; James R. Asker, "SDI Seeks Increased Funds to Push Near-Term Projects," *Aviation Week and Space Technology,* February 5, 1990, pp. 29–30; R. Jeffrey Smith, "Pentagon Increases SDI Push," *Washington Post,* February 18, 1990, p. 1.

25. See Asker, "SDI Seeks Increased Funds"; Smith, "Pentagon Increases SDI Push." Also, see James R. Asker, "SDIO Believes Brilliant Pebbles Could Cut Cost of Missile Defense by $14 Billion," *Aviation Week and Space Technology,* February 26, 1990, pp. 62–63; James R. Asker, "Congress Raises ABM Treaty Concerns on Strategic Defense Deployment," *Aviation Week and Space Technology,* June 25, 1990, p. 30; "Administration Sees No SDI Redirection," *Aviation Week and Space Technology,* October 22, 1990, p. 28.

26. For more discussion of Soviet attitudes and programs, see Jeanette Voas, *Soviet Attitudes Toward Ballistic Missile Defense and the ABM Treaty,* Adelphi Paper No. 255 (London: IISS, Winter 1990/91).

27. See Dan Boyle, "Countering Stealth: Progress in OTH Skywave Radar," *International Defense Review* 23, no. 6 (June 1990), pp. 712–13; George Leopold, "Air Force Rejects Cruise Missile Detection Role for OTH-B Radar," *Defense News,* March 12, 1990, p. 41.

28. For a thorough discussion of the alternatives, see William P. Delaney, "Air Defense of the United States: Strategic Missions and Modern Technology," *International Security* 15, no. 1 (Summer 1990), pp. 181–211.

29. For an overview of this issue, see John W.R. Lepingwell, "Soviet Strategic Air Defense and the Stealth Challenge," *International Security* 14, no. 2 (Fall 1989), pp. 64–100.

30. "U.S.-Soviet Summit Joint Statement on START and START Follow-On Negotiations," June 1990, pp. 1–5.

31. The two sides also agreed not to deploy new types of heavy ICBMs, mobile heavy ICBMs, heavy SLBMs, or rapid reload launchers.

32. The two sides agreed that ICBMs and SLBMs would not be flight tested with more warheads than the official attribution numbers agreed to at the Washington summit of December 1987.

33. These provisions only apply to nuclear-armed ALCMs with ranges in excess of 600 kilometers. Non-nuclear ALCMs are not limited by this agreement, provided that they are distinguishable from nuclear ALCMs. The two sides also agreed that they would not deploy nuclear-armed ALCMs with multiple, independently-targetable warheads.

34. This understanding only applies to nuclear-armed SLCMs with ranges in excess of 600 kilometers. The two sides also agreed that they would not deploy nuclear-armed SLCMs with multiple, independently-targetable warheads.

35. IISS, *Military Balance, 1990–1991,* p. 211.

36. See Desmond Ball and Robert C. Toth, "Revising the SIOP: Taking War-Fighting to Dangerous Extremes," *International Security* 14, no. 4 (Spring 1990), pp. 65–92.

37. Quoted in Ibid., p. 70.

38. Michael M. May, George F. Bing, and John D. Steinbruner, "Strategic Arsenals after START: The Implications of Deep Cuts," *International Security* 13, no. 1 (Summer 1988), pp. 93–94. Also, see Ball and Toth, "Revising the SIOP," pp. 71–72; Bond, "Congressional Debate," p. 24; Morrocco, "Opposition to B-2," pp. 50–51; Rice "Manned Bomber and Strategic Deterance," p. 109.

Chapter 6
Seapower

1. In December of 1990 the U.N. passed a resolution threatening Iraq with the use of force in the event it did not withdraw from Kuwait. Although Britain supported this threat, numerous newspaper reports suggested that other U.S. allies did not.

2. When Ireland gained its independence from the United Kingdom, for example, it agreed to allow the Royal Navy to use its Irish bases in wartime. Britain withdrew from this agreement in 1938, and paid heavily in wartime for the lack of patrol plane stations in Ireland.

3. The reader is reminded of the common cry, on the Left, during the Vietnam War: "One Vietnam, two Vietnams, many Vietnams." That meant that the United States could deal with one Vietnam, but not two. The problem was averted because most Third World observers did not relish what was happening to North Vietnam. It seems likely that the United States deliberately hit Libya rather than Syria in 1986 because Libya was an easier target, and thus a demonstration attack on it would be more convincing. The Syrians could not know how well U.S. forces would do against its own air defenses (which, incidentally, were comparable with those of Libya).

4. Antitorpedo measures are decoys for acoustic homing torpedoes. They have no effect on straight-running (unguided torpedoes), but it can be argued that a submarine has to come very close to be sure of hitting its target with such weapons. Competent ASW forces ought to be able to enforce an appropriate keep-out zone. The problem became acute in the early 1980s when the Soviets introduced wake-following torpedoes that were unaffected by standard acoustic decoys. That in turn led to a program for surface ship torpedo defense (SSTD). The central problem in torpedo defense (i.e., in hard kills of torpedoes rather than in decoying them) is false alarms: each is so costly in ordnance expended that defensive measures tend to swamp a ship's offensive capability. For current programs and systems, see Norman Friedman, *Naval Institute Guide to World Naval Weapons Systems* (Annapolis, Md.: U.S. Naval Institute, 1989).

5. Larger ships need not cost much more, since so large a proportion of a ship's

total cost is in its combat system. Typically, larger ships cost proportionately more because more electronics and weapons are added to fill the larger available volume, but that need not be the case. One way out would be to change design standards so that larger unused spaces would be required outboard of, or around, vital spaces such as magazines and combat information centers. The new Israeli Lahav-class typifies the opposite approach, in which the hull shrinks to the tightest possible fit around the combat system. That looks economical, but it almost certainly makes for limited survivability and seakeeping. For a description of the Israeli ship, see R.Adm. Israel Leshem (Israeli Navy), "Current Israeli Naval Programmes: A Status Report," *Military Technology*, October 1990, pp. 79–98.

6. World War II IFF was largely, though by no means entirely, visual, and the requirement for IFF led to intense efforts to teach troops and sailors to recognize aircraft. The U.S. Government published a *Recognition Journal* specifically to help in this effort, and the journal was filled with horror stories of IFF failure (friendlies killed by friendlies) to supply motivation for what was, after all, a boring task. See the reprint of the six issues published in 1990 by the U.S. Naval Institute (Annapolis, Md.).

7. For an account of the Maritime Strategy, see this author's *The U.S. Maritime Strategy* (London: Jane's Information Group, 1989).

8. For a good explanation of the importance of the decisive battle, see W. H. Honan, *Bywater: The Man Who Invented the Pacific War* (London: Macdonald, 1990), particularly "Keston Pond Maneuvers." Honan regards the question of forcing a decisive battle under unfavorable terms as the single key issue in Pacific strategy. He stops just short of saying that the United States had to attack Saipan in 1944 for just this reason. Japanese strategy was also to fight a decisive battle, but under much more favorable circumstances. For a sense of allied objections to the Maritime Strategy, see the discussions in J. Pay and G. Till, eds., *East-West Relations in the 1990s: The Naval Dimension* (London: Pinter Publishers), particularly pp. 221–231. This book is the record of a conference at the Royal Naval College, Greenwich (February 1989).

9. The British invented carrier operations in World War I largely as a means of forcing the German fleet out into a decisive battle. Between wars, they formed a Committee on Harbour Attack (i.e., on ways of dealing with an enemy fleet that refused action). For details of World War I British carrier strategy as a means of forcing battle, see Norman Friedman, *British Carrier Aviation* (London: Conway Maritime Press, and Annapolis, Md.: Naval Institute Press, 1988).

10. For immediate post–1945 U.S. naval strategy, see M. J. Palmer, *The Origins of the Maritime Strategy* (Annapolis, Md.: Naval Institute Press, 1990). Palmer's book was originally published by the U.S. Naval Historical Center. See also Norman Friedman, *Post-war Naval Revolution* (London: Conway Maritime Press and Annapolis, Md.: Naval Institute Press, 1986), which shows considerable commonality between U.S. and British post-war thinking.

11. This division, now so common that it is little noticed, probably first appeared in the annual Defense Department reports.

12. The division of naval forces was formalized in a handbook on naval force planning, NWP-1, which was issued in 1974.

13. A Seawolf-class submarine carries about twice as many torpedoes (or cruise missiles) as a Los Angeles–class submarine, a number generally estimated as fifty. Later Los Angeles–class submarines carry twelve vertical tubes specifically for Tomahawk missiles, so in a land-attack sense they carry about three-quarters as many weapons as a Seawolf-class. However, because the vertical tubes are external, the weapons cannot be changed

or serviced after the submarine leaves port; a Los Angeles–class loses flexibility compared to a Seawolf-class. For ship characteristics, see A. D. Baker, III, and J. Labayle-Couhat, *The Naval Institute Guide to Combat Fleets of the World 1990–91* (Annapolis, Md.: Naval Institute Press, 1990).

14. Budget policy in 1990 is tending towards a ceiling of twelve operational carriers, although the Navy is fighting to keep fourteen.

15. It appeared in 1990 that each A-12 would have cost about $100 million, or about three times as much as its predecessor, the A-6. The main argument for the A-12 was that, given its much better performance against enemy air defenses, one A-12 would have been more than equal to three A-6s in ordnance actually delivered on target. At an average cost of about $40 million, an eighty-airplane air wing costs about $3.2 billion. Airplanes last about twenty years, or about half the lifetime of a ship, so in theory a carrier's air wing should cost about $6 to $7 billion in all. The ship herself costs about $3 billion. These are all approximate figures in 1990 dollars, but they well illustrate the fact that net aircraft costs (APN) are not too different from net shipbuilding costs. By way of comparison with the carrier, an Arleigh Burke–class destroyer (well into the production run) should cost about $700 million, and a Seawolf-class submarine something between $1 and $2 billion (depending on whose estimate is used). 1990 estimates for the unit price of a B-2 bomber are not too far from the estimated cost of a destroyer.

16. The important difference is that a Los Angeles–class submarine requires only one reactor refueling during its lifetime.

Chapter 7
The United States and the Third World:
Policies and Force Requirements

1. The administration also began an intervention in Peru in early 1990, and has sustained lesser American involvement in civil conflicts in Guatemala and the Philippines. On Peru see James Brooke, "U.S. Will Arm Peru to Fight Leftists in New Drug Push," *New York Times*, April 22, 1990, p. 1; and Tom Wicker, "This Is Where I Came In," *New York Times*, April 23, 1990, p. A19.

2. See Dennis M. Gormley, "The Direction and Pace of Soviet Force Projection Capabilities," *Survival* 24, no. 6 (November/December 1982), pp. 266–276; and Michael T. Klare, *Beyond the "Vietnam Syndrome": U.S. Interventionism in the 1980s* (Washington, D.C.: Institute for Policy Studies, 1981), pp. 110–133.

3. Calculated from Ruth Leger Sivard, *World Military and Social Expenditures 1989* (Washington, D.C.: World Priorities, 1989), pp. 47–49.

4. I develop these arguments in "Why Europe Matters, Why the Third World Doesn't: American Grand Strategy After the Cold War," *Journal of Strategic Studies* 13, no. 2 (June 1990), pp. 1–51, at pp. 19–24.

5. A survey is Stanley Karnow, *In Our Image: America's Empire in the Philippines* (New York: Random House, 1989), pp. 323–433. See also Raymond Bonner, *Dancing with a Dictator: The Marcoses and the Making of American Policy* (New York: Times Books, 1987), pp. 96–99, 108–141, on Nixon administration policies.

6. R. M. Koster, "In Panama, We're Rebuilding Frankenstein" (op-ed), *New York Times*, December 29, 1989, p. A35; and Larry Rohter, "Commander of Panama's Security Force Resigns," *New York Times*, January 4, 1990, p. A12.

7. Michael Massing, "New Trouble in Panama," *New York Review of Books,* May 17, 1990, pp. 43–49, at pp. 43 and 45. Herrera was himself eased out in August 1990, was jailed on suspicion of plotting to overthrow the government in October 1990, then escaped, and led an attempted coup on December 4. Eric Schmitt, "U.S. Helps Quell Revolt in Panama," *New York Times,* December 6, 1990, p. 1.

8. Koster, "In Panama."

9. Dennis Gilbert, *Sandinistas* (New York: Basil Blackwell, 1988), pp. 3, 83.

10. Ibid., pp. 14, 81–104.

11. Ibid., p. 161.

12. Ibid., pp. 168–169.

13. Anthony Lewis, "Out of this Nettle," *New York Times,* March 2, 1990, p. A33.

14. See Bruce Cumings, *The Origins of the Korean War* (Princeton, N.J.: Princeton University Press, 1981), pp. 68–100, 135–151.

15. See Peter W. Stanley, *A Nation in the Making: The Philippines and the United States, 1899–1921* (Cambridge, Mass.: Harvard University Press, 1974), pp. 51–57; and Karnow, *In Our Image,* pp. 325–330, 340, 345.

16. Robert Trudeau and Lars Schoultz, "Guatemala," in Morris J. Blachman, William M. LeoGrande, and Kenneth Sharpe, eds., *Confronting Revolution: Security Through Diplomacy in Central America* (New York: Pantheon, 1986), p. 28.

17. See Walter LaFeber, *Inevitable Revolutions: The United States in Central America* (New York: W.W. Norton. 1983), pp. 148–195.

18. These eleven episodes are summarized in William Blum, *The CIA: A Forgotten History* (Atlantic Highlands, N.J.: Zed Books, 1986), pp. 67–76, 79–91, 108–113, 117–123, 170–74, 181–191, 195–205, 232–243, 272–274.

19. John Robinson, "Reagan says foes of contra aid are inviting 'strategic disaster'," *Boston Globe,* March 5, 1986, p. 3.

20. Lindsey Gruson, "Threats and Party Backlash for El Salvador Chief," *New York Times,* September 16, 1990, p. 10; and Lindsey Gruson, "Political Violence Up in Guatemala in Recent Months," *New York Times,* November 13, 1988, p. 14.

21. Casualty data are from Ruth Leger Sivard, *World Military and Social Expenditures 1991* (Washington, D.C.: World Priorities, 1991), pp. 22–25, except Afghanistan casualties, which are construed from John F. Burns, "Afghans: Now They Blame America," *New York Times Magazine,* February 4, 1990, pp. 24, 27, and Angolan amputees, which are from United Church of Christ, "Why is the U.S. Prolonging War in Angola?" (advertisement), *New York Times,* October 5, 1989, p. A22.

22. Murray Hiebert, "Going it Alone," *Far Eastern Economic Review,* October 5, 1989, p. 16; and Steven Erlanger, "Vietnamese Force Helping Cambodia, Diplomats Assert," *New York Times,* February 23, 1990, p. A8.

23. Robert Pear, "Phnom Penh, Eye on West, Tries to Shed Image as Hanoi Puppet," *New York Times,* January 8, 1990, p. 1; and John McAuliff and Mary Byrne McDonnell, "The Cambodian Stalemate: America's Obstructionist Role in Indochina," *World Policy Journal* 7, no. 1 (Winter 1989–1990), pp. 71–106, at pp. 72–75.

24. Craig R. Whitney and Jill Tolliffe, "Ex-Allies Say Angola Rebels Torture and Slay Dissenters," *New York Times,* March 11, 1989, p. 1; and Craig R. Whitney, "A Onetime Backer Accuses Savimbi," *New York Times,* March 12, 1989, p. 9.

25. William Minter, "Who is Jonas Savimbi?" *Africa News,* July 11, 1988, pp. 6–7; and Radek Sikorski, "The Mystique of Savimbi," *National Review,* August 18, 1989, pp. 34–37.

26. Sikorski, "The Mystique," p. 36.

27. See Reed Kramer, "Lobby Gets Results for Savimbi," *Africa News,* November, 1989, pp. 1–3.

28. John F. Burns, "U.S. Is Cutting Off Arms Supplies to a Major Afghan Rebel Faction," *New York Times,* November 19, 1989, p. 16.

29. Ahmed Rashid, "Fundamental Differences," *Far Eastern Economic Review,* September 14, 1989, p. 23. See also Barbara Crossette, "As Accord on Afghan Future Nears, Refugees Live in Fear and Hardship," *New York Times,* August 19, 1990, p. 14, describing a "mysterious campaign of terror in the name of Islamic fundamentalism" being carried out against Afghans and Westerners in Pakistan by *mujahideen* extremists.

30. Burns, "U.S. Is Cutting Off Arms Supplies," p. 16.

31. Ahmed Rashid, "Gang Warfare," *Far Eastern Economic Review,* September 14, 1989, p. 23. Akhunzada's death is noted in John F. Burns, "Afghan President Marks His 11th Year in Power," *New York Times,* April 29, 1990, p. 12.

32. John F. Burns, "Misery Replaces Hope in a Battered Afghanistan," *New York Times,* December 17, 1989, p. 26; and Rashid, "Gang Warfare."

33. Amnesty International, *El Salvador: "Death Squads"—A Government Strategy* (London: Amnesty International, 1988), pp. 10n, 37–40; and "What is ARENA?" *Central America Reporter,* January–February 1989 (pullout section), p. 3.

34. "What is ARENA?", p. 3. Strangely, the Reagan administration responded by removing Pickering and granting D'Aubuisson a visa to visit the U.S. Martin Diskin and Kenneth E. Sharpe, "El Salvador," in Blachman, LeoGrande, and Sharpe, *Confronting Revolution,* p. 78.

35. The Bush administration has shown a studied unconcern for these clients' sordid human rights records, often whitewashing their abuses. See Human Rights Watch, *The Bush Administration's Record on Human Rights in 1989* (New York: Human Rights Watch, 1990), pp. 1–16, 21–26, 43–50, 89–100.

36. Steven Erlanger, "Cambodia Peace Effort: A Bit More Realism," *New York Times,* January 19, 1990, p. A6; and Michael Fields and Murray Hiebert, "Regime of Last Resort," *Far Eastern Economic Review,* January 25, 1990, pp. 8–9. Criticizing this scheme is Michael J. Horowitz, "Toward a New Cambodia Policy," *American Spectator,* June 1990, pp. 24–26, at p. 24; and Michael J. Horowitz, "The 'China Hand' in the Cambodia Plan," *New York Times,* September 12, 1990, p. A31.

37. Horowitz, "The 'China Hand.'"

38. Erlanger, "Vietnamese Force Helping Cambodia," p. 1.

39. Economist Intelligence Unit, *Country Report: Angola, Sao Tome & Principe,* no. 1, 1989, pp. 6–7.

40. Economist Intelligence Unit, *Country Report: Angola, Sao Tome & Principe,* no. 3, 1989, p. 7.

41. Kramer, "Lobby Gets Results," pp. 1–2.

42. Literacy in Angola is 39 percent, compared with 47 percent for Africa as a whole, 62 percent for the developing world as a whole, and 72 percent for the world as a whole. Ruth Leger Sivard, *World Military and Social Expenditures 1987–88* (Washington, D.C.: World Priorities, 1987), pp. 46, 48.

43. Clifford Krauss, "Superpowers Seeking an Angola Agreement," *New York Times,* September 17, 1990, p. A3.

44. In December 1990 the Angolan government and UNITA agreed on a plan to resolve the war through free elections. "Guerrillas Report Pact With Angola," *New York Times,* December 15, 1990, p. 6. In January 1991 the Angolan government reportedly agreed to a timetable for these elections. Kenneth B. Noble, "Angola Accepts Plan to End Its 15-Year War," *New York Times,* January 24, 1991, p. A7.

45. A cease-fire was agreed in May 1991. Alan Riding, "Angola Agrees to Cease-fire with Guerillas," *New York Times,* May 2, 1991, p. 1.

46. Economist Intelligence Unit, *Country Report: Pakistan, Afghanistan,* no. 4, 1989, pp. 17–18.

47. Afghanistan had a literacy rate of only 24 percent and a GNP per capita of $351 in 1984, compared with a GNP per capita of $752 for the developing world, and $2,911 for the entire world. Sivard, *World Military and Social Expenditures 1987–88,* pp. 46, 48.

48. Economist Intelligence Unit, *Country Report: Guatemala, El Salvador, Honduras,* no. 2, 1989, p. 14; Christopher Orsinger, "A Trail of Missed Opportunities," *Progressive,* February 24, 1990, p. 23; Ruben Zamora, "For El Salvador, Democracy Before Peace" (op-ed), *New York Times,* January 24, 1990, p. A23; and LeoGrande, "After the Battle," pp. 350–351.

49. LeoGrande, "After the Battle," p. 349.

50. LeoGrande, "After the Battle," pp. 352–353. For example, during 1990 the administration opposed congressional efforts to punish the Salvadoran government for protecting Army death squads by halving American aid to El Salvador.

51. Had Iraq retained Kuwait it would have still controlled fewer net economic resources than Saudi Arabia, its next proximate target: in 1986 the combined GNPs of Iraqi and Kuwait totalled only $62.3 billion, compared with a Saudi GNP of $77.1 billion (Sivard, *World Military and Social Expenditures 1989,* p. 48). However, even without Kuwait Iraq would have held military superiority over Saudi Arabia, because the monarchic character of the Saudi political system inhibits the Saudi elite from converting its economic resources into military strength; this would require arming more Saudi citizens, which would put at risk the political monopoly of the Saudi royal family. As a result Saudi armed forces number only 67,500, and could not defend alone against Iraqi forces, which numbered some 1,000,000 in 1990 (International Institute for Strategic Studies, *The Military Balance 1990–1991* [London: IISS, 1990], pp. 105, 115). The other Arab gulf states all have far smaller economies and far weaker military forces than Saudi Arabia, and would be defenseless if Saudi Arabia were overrun.

52. On the Iraqi Baath see Samir al-Khalil, *Republic of Fear: The Inside Story of Saddam's Iraq* (New York: Pantheon, 1989), pp. 149–182, 189–191.

53. Figures are for 1989, and are from *Basic Petroleum Data Book,* vol. 10, no. 3 (September 1990), section 4, table 2e; section 10, table 6; and section 14, table 2, except figures for Bahrain's oil production, which are for 1987 and are from Rose Schumacher, et al., eds., *World Economic Data,* 2d ed. (Santa Barbara: ABC-Clio, 1989), p. 12. Had Iraq retained only Kuwait, it would have controlled 6.9 percent of world oil production.

54. Iraq's GNP would have grown from $38 billion to $175 billion, a 461 percent increase. These figures are for 1986, and are from Sivard, *World Military and Social Expenditures 1989,* p. 48.

55. Sivard, *World Military and Social Expenditures 1989,* pp. 47–48. The United States is followed by the Soviet Union (15 percent), Japan (10 percent), Germany (6 percent), France (4 percent), Italy (3 percent), and Britain (3 percent).

56. In December 1990 Middle East Watch estimated that Iraqi forces had killed about 1,000 Kuwaitis since their invasion, and held another 3,000 in detention. Judith Miller, "Atrocities by Iraqis in Kuwait: Monitors Differ on the Scope," *New York Times,* December 16, 1990, p. 1. As noted above, the American-supported regimes in El Salvador and Guatemala have committed far greater atrocities.

57. As matters developed, the United States also retarded the Iraqi nuclear program more directly, by using airpower to destroy Iraqi nuclear facilities during the 1991 gulf war.

58. Sivard, *World Military and Social Expenditures 1989,* pp. 48–49. I assume that all eleven Asian Arab states are united under Iraqi rule.

59. Ruth Leger Sivard, *World Military and Social Expenditures 1976* (Leesburg, Va.: WMSE Publications, 1976), p. 22. Figures are for 1973, and include Egypt, Syria, Iraq, and Jordan as the Arab combatants for both wars. Iraq deployed only token forces in both wars; if Iraq is therefore excluded, the Arab advantage falls to 1.3:1.

60. Sivard, *World Military and Social Expenditures 1989,* p. 48.

61. Some might solve this problem by ending America's security relationship with Israel. I would oppose this because I think the Christian West owes atonement for its recurrent barbarism toward the Jewish people over the past millennium, and this debt of atonement includes an obligation to help ensure the survival of Israel. My views are summarized in a letter to the editor, *Atlantic Monthly,* October 1990, pp. 15–16. In any case, the United States will remain committed to Israel absent profound change in American domestic politics, and American policy should reflect this reality. However, it does seem appropriate for American leaders to remind Israeli leaders that the American gulf deployment is a major service to Israel, was largely required by America's security guarantee to Israel, and therefore merits a major quid-pro-quo from Israel—for example, a more positive Israeli response to American efforts to mediate an Arab-Israeli peace than the Shamir government has so far provided.

62. Many observers have suggested that the gulf deployment is justified by the need to "maintain American access to oil." However, American access to Persian Gulf oil would be jeopardized rather little by an Iraqi hegemony in the gulf if the United States had no security relationship with Israel. Iraq would then have little reason to impose an embargo, because Iraq and the United States have few disputes that do not derive from the Arab-Israeli conflict. Thus the "oil access" rationale for the deployment grows mainly from America's security guarantee to Israel, since this guarantee supplies the motive for an Arab hegemon who controlled the gulf to use its control over oil supplies coercively.

63. Central Intelligence Agency Directorate of Intelligence, *Handbook of Economic Statistics, 1990* (Washington, D.C.: U.S. Government Printing Office, 1990), pp. 34, 104.

64. Gary C. Hufbauer and Kimberly A. Elliott, "Sanctions Will Bite—and Soon" (op-ed), *New York Times,* January 14, 1991, p. A17.

65. A recent survey of 115 twentieth-century sanctions efforts found only three efforts that reduced the GNP of the target state by over 10 percent, and none that achieved a reduction of as much as 16 percent. Gary Clyde Hufbauer and Jeffrey J. Schott, assisted by Kimberly Ann Elliott, *Economic Sanctions Reconsidered: History and Current Policy* (Washington, D.C.: Institute for International Economics, 1985), pp. 64–77.

66. Barry R. Posen, *Political Objectives and Military Options in the Persian Gulf,* Defense and Arms Control Studies Working Paper (Cambridge: Center for International Studies, Massachusetts Institute of Technology, November 5, 1990), p. 8; and on the force already in the gulf in early November, Michael Gordon, "U.S. Says Its Troops Won't Be Rotated Until Crisis Is Over," *New York Times,* November 10, 1990, p. 1.

67. I classify the carriers as "light" because they represent a tradeoff of mobility for firepower; carrier airpower is more mobile than ground-based tactical airpower when ground bases are not available, but ground-based airpower can deliver far more sorties per dollar than carrier-based air.

68. These figures are for January 1991, and are construed from Gordon, "U.S. Says Its Troops Won't Be Rotated;" "Major Military Units in the Persian Gulf Area," *New York Times,* January 20, 1991, p. E2; and International Institute for Strategic Studies, *Military Balance 1990–1991,* pp. 19, 22.

69. Force structure data are for June 1, 1990, and are from International Institute for

Strategic Studies, *Military Balance 1990–1991,* pp. 17–27. During FY 1991 one light infantry division is being cut from this force; see Michael R. Gordon, "Cheney Would Cut 5
Army Divisions and Back the B-2," *New York Times,* January 30, 1990, p. 1. I have excluded the U.S. infantry division in Korea and the one U.S. "motorized infantry" division
from this list of light forces because they both have substantial armored capability and thus
lie somewhere between "heavy" and "light." One of the Navy's fifteen carriers is always in
long- term overhaul; hence the Navy has only fourteen deployable aircraft carriers.

70. These cost figures are extrapolated from William W. Kaufmann, *Glasnost, Perestroika, and U.S. Defense Spending* (Washington, D.C.: The Brookings Institution, 1990),
table 15, p. 68. In my accounting, a 6/18 share of Air Force active and reserve tactical
airpower costs are prorated to light forces, to match the light forces' share of the Army's
active ground forces, since tacair's main mission is to support Army ground forces and a
slice of tacair should therefore be assumed to support the light ground forces. All Marine
tacair costs are classified as light since all the Marine divisions that they support are classified as light. A 9/21 share of airlift and sealift costs is prorated to the light forces, to
match the share of total active ground divisions (including the Marine divisions) that are
light, since the airlift and sealift forces are tasked to support ground and air forces overseas, and a slice of these lift forces should therefore be assumed to support the light
forces.

71. The U.S. would also retain its infantry division now in Korea, providing an additional presence in the Third World.

72. The United States never deployed more than four carriers off Korea during the
Korean War, and these carriers were half the size of today's carriers. (Karl Lautenschlager, "Korean War Carrier Forces" [unpublished memorandum, February 1990], and Karl
Lautenschlager, "Korean War Carrier Deployments" [unpublished memorandum, February
1990]). The United States kept five carriers in Southeast Asia during much of the Indochina
war, but this deployment also involved some smaller carriers, and the United States could
have used fewer carriers by relying more heavily on ground-based tactical airpower. The
United States deployed only four carriers off Lebanon in 1983, and used only two carriers
in its 1986 raid on Libya. Moreover, most serious Third World contingencies involve aggression by one Third World state against another. If so, the threatened state should be
willing to provide basing for American ground-based tactical airpower, limiting the need for
carrier airpower.

73. On FY 1991 see Gordon, "Cheney Would Cut 5 Army Divisions," p. 1; on FY
1995 see "FY 1992–93 Department of Defense Budget Request," Office of Assistant Secretary of Defense, News Release, February 4, 1991. The news release indicates that four
active army divisions will be cut between FY 1991 and FY 1995, but does not indicate the
type of division to be cut. I have assumed that the Army will continue to maintain a force
composed of one-third light divisions, as it did in FY 1990. If so, the Army will include
eight heavy and four light divisions in FY 1995, for a net cut of two light divisions from its
FY 1990 level, and one light division from its FY 1991 level.

74. U.S. aid was $7–$20 million to the non-communists in the Khmer Rouge coalition
for FY 1991; $315 million to the Salvadoran government for FY 1990; and over $200 million
to the Afghan *mujihadeen* for FY 1990. Steven Erlanger, "Favored Cambodians Lose U.S.
Aid," *New York Times,* April 10, 1991, p. A3; Robert Pear, "House Amendments Would
Halve Aid for El Salvador," *New York Times,* May 23, 1990, p. 1; Clifford Krauss, "Afghan
Rebels Take Garrison Town, U.S. Reports," *New York Times,* April 2, 1991, p. A7. U.S.
aid to UNITA, previously $60 million, will be reduced to $20 million for FY 1992. "House
Votes for Plan for More Covert Aid to Angolan Rebels," *New York Times,* June 12, 1991,
p. A8.

Chapter 8
Military Personnel in a Changing World

1. For example, Richard Kugler has argued that, "The transition of the Warsaw Pact from a hollow alliance to complete dismantlement thus must be accompanied by appropriate security guarantees to those nations regarding Germany's military forces and the preservation of recent borders. NATO provides the best institutional framework for making such guarantees credible" (*NATO's Future Role in Europe: Toward a More Political Alliance in a Stable 1 1/2 Bloc System*, R-3923-FF, [Santa Monica, Calif.: The RAND Corporation, May 1990], pp. xi–xii). See also, President George Bush, Remarks by the President to the Aspen Institute Symposium (The White House, Office of the Press Secretary), August 2, 1990.

2. Senator Sam Nunn, floor speech, March 22, 1990. He complained that the "FY 1991 defense budget is based on 1988 threat and a 1988 strategy." See also, Secretary of Defense Richard Cheney, speech at the National Press Club, March 22, 1990. The FY 1992 through 1997 defense program was "taking into account the dramatic events in the Kremlin and Eastern Europe as well as a number of other assumptions about arms control and the future course of democratization in Europe. . . . If our critics would actually look at what we are doing in the department to restructure our forces for the future, they would see a complete rethinking of mission and strategy. Major program reviews, long-term program reviews, . . . reevaluating our force structure and long-term national requirements" (News Release no. 129–90, Office of the Assistant Secretary of Defense [Public Affairs], pp. 2–3).

3. "End strength" is authorized by the Congress and refers to the total number of service men and women that may be employed by each service on the last day of the fiscal year. Just prior to the Iraqi invasion of Kuwait the House Armed Services Committee provided the following assessment of the future: "With the crumbling of the Warsaw Pact, the diminished threat in Europe, and the enormous Federal deficit, the nation can no longer afford to maintain a large cold war era standing military on foreign soil. By mid-decade, the size of the active force—just over two million men and women in uniform today—may well shrink by at least 25 percent" (Committee on the Armed Services, *National Defense Authorization Act for FY 1991*, Report 101–665, U.S. House of Representatives [Washington D.C.: U.S. Government Printing Office], p. 263.) Also see the Committee on the Armed Services, *National Defense Authorization Act for FY 1991*, Report 101–384, United States Senate (Washington, D.C.: U.S. Government Printing Office).

4. Secretary Cheney recently noted that "we now face in the Persian Gulf, in the Middle East, exactly the kind of situation that we had been focusing on as we developed the strategy and the adjustments to the new world situation" (Remarks before the International Institute for Strategic Studies [The Homestead, Hot Springs, Virginia], September 6, 1990, p. 3).

5. As quoted by Senator Nunn in his floor speech, "Defense Budget Blanks," March 22, 1990.

6. For a general discussion of the history of the Total Force Policy, see Martin Binkin and William W. Kaufmann, *U.S. Army Guard & Reserve: Rhetoric, Realities, Risks* (Washington, D.C.: The Brookings Institution, 1989).

7. Senator Nunn, floor speech, "Implementing A New Military Strategy: The Budget Decisions," April 20, 1990.

8. *Senate FY 1991 Defense Authorization Report*, p. 161.

9. *House FY 1991 Defense Authorization Report*, p. 267.

10. Ibid., p. 50.

11. Secretary Cheney, Speech before the International Institute for Strategic Studies, September 6, 1990, p. 2.

12. President George Bush, Remarks to the Aspen Institute Symposium, August 2, 1990, pp. 2–4.

13. Department of Defense, *Total Force Policy Interim Report to the Congress,* September 1990, p. 12. The administration's FY 1992–1993 DOD budget shows that, "By the end of FY 1995, active military end strength will fall . . . 24 percent below its post–Vietnam peak . . . (reached) in FY 1987, . . . (and) reserve personnel levels will drop . . . (to) 21 percent below FY 1987." Department of Defense, *Statement of the Secretary of Defense before the Senate Armed Service Committee,* February 21, 1991, p. 18.

14. CBO, *Meeting New National Security Needs: Options for U.S. Forces in the 1990s,* February 1990, p. 2.

15. House Report 101–822, p. 51. More recently the administration's FY 1992–1993 DOD budget shows the following active military end strength for FY 1995: Army 536,000, Navy 510,000, Marine Corps 171,000, and Air Force 437,000. Department of Defense, *Statement of the Secretary of Defense before the Senate Armed Service Committee,* February 21, 1991, Briefing chart #8.

16. *Senate FY 1991 Defense Authorization Report,* p. 157.

17. *House FY 1991 Defense Authorization Report,* p. 264. The CBO, in a recent study *Managing the Reduction in Military Personnel* (July 1990), also identified the two approaches available to defense personnel planners to reduce the active duty force: the "accession-heavy" approach and the "across-the-board" approach.

18. *Army Focus,* September 1990, p. 26. It should be noted, however, that even under the draft all officers and enlisted personnel in their second and subsequent tour of service were volunteers.

19. *Army Focus,* September 1990, p.17.

20. A. P. Smith points out that as early as 1679, the secretary of the admiralty regulated the annual entry of officers into the British Navy, and that by 1779 career structures, retention rates, and promotion probabilities were regularly analyzed for the Royal Marines. The systematic collection of the statistics used in personnel planning dates from 1820 in the British Navy, and the basic personnel planning models were discussed in 1899 in the *Naval Proceeding of the American Navy.* See A. P. Smith, "Defense Manpower Studies," *Operational Research Quarterly* 19, no. 3. For a discussion of manpower structures and personnel planning models, see Richard C. Grinold and Kneale T. Marshall, *Manpower Planning Models* (New York: North Holland Press, 1977).

21. Each service has its own ideal distribution depending upon its mission and the need for junior or senior personnel. The Army and Marine Corps desire a more junior force because of their need for combat soldiers. The Navy and Air Force prefer a more senior force because of the requirement for technical personnel to maintain aircraft and other equipment. See *United States Air Force Personnel Plan. Volume Three: Airman Structures,* September 12, 1975, p. C-2.

22. CBO, *Managing the Reduction in Military Personnel,* (Washington, D.C.: U.S. Government Printing Office, July 1990), p. 5.

23. This would not be the first time that the Air Force had such a problem. In the 1950's the Air Force, "allowed most airmen to remain in the service as long as they desire. Once past initial reenlistment point, airmen were not removed from the service except for cause until they reach retirement eligibility." This resulted in the "Korean Hump" and the "large experience deficits once the Korean War hump disappeared [and] required that the Air Force change its method for managing the enlisted force" (*United States Air Force Personnel Plan. Volume Three: Airman Structures,* September 12, 1975, pp. A-1/8).

24. House Report No. 96–1462, p. 14.

25. Coroazon Francisco, David Grissmer, Richard Eisenman, and Jennifer Kawata, *The Active Force Policy Screening Model (POSM)* (Santa Monica, Calif.: The RAND Corporation, forthcoming).

26. The CBO, among others, has noted that "continued cuts in accessions would lead to top-heavy forces. [And], as senior personnel became more expensive to support, they could find their assignment becoming more elementary" (CBO, *Managing the Reduction in Military Personnel*, pp. v–vi).

27. Figure 8–7 measures the degree of maldistribution as the percent of the force in "overage year-of-service" groups. Since for every person in an overage year-of-service group there is a person missing from an "underage" year-of-service group, the true degree of maldistribution is twice that shown.

28. Senior career personnel, those with between nine and fourteen years of service, have more expected future man years than do junior personnel. Thus, senior personnel whom are cut early in the drawdown period will save several man years over the drawdown. Junior personnel, many of who will be getting out in the near future, will save man years mainly in the current year, resulting in the need to cut additional personnel in the following year in order to achieve end strength goals.

29. DOPMA provides for separation pay equal to one month's basic pay for each year of service as "a contingency payment for an officer who is career committed but to whom a full military career may be denied." Such a payment in 1980 was seen as "an adequate readjustment pay to ease his reentry into civilian life" (House Report No. 96–1462, pp. 31–32).

30. "These payments (severance payments) would be much smaller than the total value of retirement benefits that would be earned by an individual who completed twenty years of military service. The proposed severance payments, however, would offer fairer treatment than is available under current law, which provides severance payments only for officer personnel. . . . As an alternative to severance payments, or possibly as part of a package that included modest payments, the Congress could provide early vesting in the military retirement system" (CBO, *Managing the Reduction in Military Personnel*, p. 12).

31. Jennifer H. Kawata, David W. Grissmer, and Richard Eisenman, *The Reserve Force Policy Screening Models*, R-3701-JCS/RA/FMP (Santa Monica, Calif.: The RAND Corporation, June 1989).

32. For an analysis of prior service supply, see M. Susan Marquis and Sheila Nataraj Kirby, *Reserve Accessions among Individuals with Prior Military Service: Supply and Skill Match*, R-3892-RA (Santa Monica, Calif.: The RAND Corporation, January 1990).

33. The Army and Navy have had programs that typically required two or three years of active service coupled with a mandatory reserve term of three or four years. The Air Force has the "Palace Chase" program that allows a serviceman to trade active duty time for an increased reserve commitment.

Chapter 10
Arms Control:
Looking Back, Looking Ahead

1. On the origins and goals of arms control, see Donald G. Brennan, ed., *Arms Control, Disarmament, and National Security* (New York: George Braziller, 1961); Thomas Schelling and Morton Halperin, *Strategy and Arms Control* (New York: The Twentieth Century Fund, 1961).

2. For a review of the arms control record, including an assessment of the various

charges and countercharges made against the arms control process, see Albert Carnesale and Richard Haass, eds., *Superpower Arms Control: Setting the Record Straight* (Cambridge, Mass.: Ballinger Publishing Co., 1987).

3. See, for example, Philip Taubman, "Gorbachev Irritated by U.S. Assertions on 'Star Wars,'" *New York Times,* December 15, 1987.

4. This section draws on materials prepared by my colleagues Richard Davis, Amy Gordon, Sandy Hallenbeck, and Timothy Pounds on the negotiations discussed in this section.

5. This pessimism predominates in Strobe Talbott, *Deadly Gambits: The Reagan Administration and the Stalemate in Nuclear Arms Control* (New York: Alfred A. Knopf, 1984).

6. For a discussion of inspections under the CDE accord, see Don O. Stovall, "The Stockholm Accord: On-Site Inspections in Eastern and Western Europe," in Lewis A. Dunn, ed., *Arms Control Verification and the New Role of On-Site Inspection* (Lexington, Mass.: Lexington Books, 1990).

7. Michael Z. Wise, "Conventional Arms Talks Suspended in Vienna," *The Washington Post,* February 22, 1991.

8. The preceding discussion draws on conversations with my colleague Sandy Hallenbeck as well as presentations by U.S. officials.

9. The START agreement places a limit of 6,000 warheads on each side's strategic offensive nuclear forces. However, because of the use of so-called counting rules, some strategic nuclear warheads will be discounted. For example, heavy bombers carrying free-fall nuclear bombs and short-range attack missiles (SRAMs) will be counted as carrying only one warhead. Similarly, up to 150 ALCM-carrying heavy bombers will be counted as carrying ten ALCMs, even though such bombers could conceivably carry more.

10. Article X provides that twenty-five years after its entry into force, the parties to the NPT will gather to decide whether to extend the treaty "indefinitely or for a fixed period or periods."

11. Article VI of the NPT states: "Each of the Parties to the Treaty undertakes to pursue negotiations in good faith on effective measures relating to cessation of the nuclear arms race at an early date and to nuclear disarmament, and on a treaty on general and complete disarmament under strict and effective international control."

12. See, for example, George F. Bing, Michael M. May, and John D. Steinbruner, "Strategic Arsenals after START: The Implications of Deep Cuts," *International Security* 13 (Summer 1988), *passim.*

Chapter 11
National Guard and Reserve Forces

1. National Guard Bureau, *A Brief History of the Militia and the National Guard* (Washington, D.C.: NGB Office of Public Affairs, July 1986), pp. 50–51.

2. Ibid., p. 51.

3. Ibid., p. 52.

4. *Washington Post,* August 23, 1990.

5. *Brief History of the Militia and the National Guard,* p. 53.

6. General Bruce Palmer, Jr., *The 25-Year War: America's Military Role in Vietnam* (Lexington: University Press of Kentucky, 1984), p. 175.

7. U.S. General Accounting Office, *Reserve Force: DOD Guidance Needed on Assigning Roles to Reserves under the Total Force Policy* (Washington, D.C.: USGAO, December 1989), p. 2.

8. General John W. Vessey, Jr., Interview, March 8, 1988.

9. Richard A. Davis, "Readiness of Army Guard and Reserve Support Forces," Statement before the Subcommittees on Readiness, Sustainability and Support and Manpower and Personnel, Committee on Armed Services, April 13, 1988, p. 1.

10. Colonel Harry G. Summers, Jr., *On Strategy: The Vietnam War in Context* (Carlisle Barracks: Strategic Studies Institute, U.S. Army War College, 1981), p. 113.

11. Department of Defense, *Reserve Manpower Statistics, FY 1989* (Washington, D.C.: Directorate for Information Operations and Reports, OSD, September 30, 1989), p. 2.

12. Ibid., p. 4.

13. Association of the United States Army, *The Active and Reserve Components: Partners in the Total Army* (Arlington, Va.: Institute of Land Warfare, AUSA, December 1989), p. 11.

14. Strategic Studies Institute, U.S. Army War College, *Is Roundout a Myth? A Case Study of the 48th Infantry Brigade* (draft), p. 15.

15. Ibid., p. 16.

16. Ibid., p. 17.

17. *The New York Times,* November 11, 1990.

18. Letter dated October 15, 1990. The reference is to the provision of law allowing the President to call up to 200,000 from the reserve forces for up to ninety days, with an extension for another ninety days, on his own authority.

19. Letter dated August 24, 1990.

20. Letter dated September 6, 1990.

21. White Paper dated October 15, 1990; distributed by news release from the HASC dated October 16, 1990.

22. Lt. Gen. Herbert R. Temple, Jr., Chief, National Guard Bureau, letter to Lt. Gen. LaVern E. Weber (USA Ret.), Executive Director, National Guard Association of the United States, January 26, 1990.

23. *Army Times,* December 31, 1990.

24. Ibid.

25. "The Evolving Total Force," Paper presented at the Fletcher School of Law and Diplomacy, Tufts University, October 21, 1989.

26. Ibid.

27. *Army Times,* November 12, 1990.

28. Remarks, National Guard Association of Georgia, September 15, 1990, for example.

29. *Reserve Force: DOD Guidance Needed on Assigning Roles to Reserves under the Total Force Policy,* pp. 4 and 36.

30. *Washington Post,* August 24, 1990.

31. Association of the United States Army, Defense Reports 86–25 and 88–8.

32. *National Security Strategy of the United States* (Washington, D.C.: The White House, March 1990), p. 27.

33. *Army Times,* November 26, 1990.

34. Richard B. Crossland and James T. Currie, *Twice the Citizen: A History of the United States Army Reserve, 1908–1983* (Washington, D.C.: Office of the Chief, Army Reserve, 1984), p. 216.

35. Edward J. Philbin and James L. Gould, "The Guard and Reserve: In Pursuit of Full Integration," in Bennie J. Wilson, III, ed., *The Guard and Reserve in the Total Force: The First Decade, 1973–1983* (Washington, D.C.: National Defense University Press, 1985), p. 46.

36. James W. Browning, II, et al., "The U.S. Reserve System: Attitudes, Perceptions, and Realities," in Wilson, *The Guard and Reserve in the Total Force*, p. 83.

37. Lt. Gen. Richard D. Lawrence, "Foreword," in Wilson, *The Guard and Reserve in the Total Force*, p. xi.

38. *Christian Science Monitor*, October 1, 1990.

Chapter 12
U.S.-Soviet Security Cooperation
in the Post–Cold War Era

1. Joseph Kruzel. "Whence the Threat to Peace? U.S. Security Interests in the Post–Cold War Era," *American Defense Annual 1990–1991* (Lexington, Mass.: Lexington Books, 1990), p. 3.

2. The territorial formations existed in the Soviet Union before World War II due to Mikhail Frunze's military reforms after the civil war of 1918–1922. There were also several national divisions in different republics; some of them ceased to exist within several years after World War II.

3. See, for example, Sergey Rogov, *Sovetskiy Soyuz, SSHA: Poiski Bilansa Interesov* (On the Soviet Union and the United States. In search of a Balance of Interests) (Moscow: Mezdunarodniye Otnoschenia, 1989), p. 304.

4. At the same time this action had significant political and military meaning for Russia. Having foreseen Britain's (and France's) war against Russia because of Poland, the Russian government thought it would be expedient to threaten Great Britain's sea communications (V. Potemkin, ed., *Istoria Diplomatsii* [History of Diplomacy] [Moscow: OGIZ, 1941], p. 468).

5. The functions of the United Nations Naval Forces, as proposed by the same Soviet naval experts, would be prevention of regional armed conflicts; provision of security of sea lines of communications in areas of armed conflicts; and operations against piracy, terrorism, and narcotics transactions. See, for example, I. Stolyarov, *VMS OON: V Interesah Mira*, Morskoy Sbornik (United Navy. In the Interests of Peace, Naval Proceedings), November 11, 1990, pp. 69–70.

6. See the analysis of such views, especially Kenneth Waltz, in Hayward R. Alker, Jr., Thomas J. Biersteker, and Takashi Inoguchi, ed., *The Decline of Superstates: The Rise of the New World Order?* (Paris: World Congress of Political Science, International Political Science Association, July 1985).

7. There are already several Soviet studies that show that with a START II agreement, both sides could reduce their stockpiles to between 2,000 and 2,500 strategic warheads each, eliminating some categories of strategic nuclear weapons for the sake of strategic stability and mutual security. Some other experts would prefer to have more warheads after the implementation of START II—between 3,000 and 4,000, especially if the other three major nuclear powers will not be energetic enough in their efforts to limit their nuclear forces.

8. The Soviet Union actually had a unilateral moratorium on nuclear testing in 1990 (only one nuclear test in Novaya Zemlya) due to the actions of the antinuclear movement around Semipalatinsk.

9. See, for example, Air Commodore Jasit Singh, Director of the Institute for Defense Studies and Analysis, India, Presentation at the 5th International Colloquium, organized by the Group de Bellerive, Geneva, June 20–21, 1990, in Sadruddin Aga-Khan, ed., *Nonproliferation in a Disarming World*, p. 142.

Index

About the Contributors

Robert D. Blackwill teaches East-West relations, defense policy, and arms control at the Kennedy School of Government at Harvard University. He is a former Special Assistant to President Bush for European and Soviet Affairs on the staff of the National Security Council and previously served as ambassador and chief negotiator at the negotiations with the Warsaw Pact on conventional forces in Europe. He is the author of many articles on European security and East-West relations and coeditor of *Conventional Arms Control and East-West Security* (1989) and *A Primer for the Nuclear Age* (1990).

Michael E. Brown is senior research fellow in U.S. security policy at the International Institute for Strategic Studies. He is the author of *Flying Blind: Decision Making in the U.S. Strategic Bomber Program,* to be published by Cornell University Press in 1991, and his articles on strategic forces have appeared in *International Security, Survival,* and *Orbis.*

Lewis A. Dunn, assistant vice president and manager of the Negotiations and Planning Division, Science Applications International Corporation, is a former assistant director of the U.S. Arms Control and Disarmament Agency, and ambassador to the 1985 Nuclear Nonproliferation Treaty Review Conference. He has written numerous articles on national security and arms control and the book *Controlling the Bomb,* and is coeditor of *Arms Control Verification and the New Role of On-Site Inspection.* He is presently managing projects on arms control policy, verification, nuclear and missile proliferation, and long term defense planning.

Norman Friedman is a widely published naval and defense analyst. He has served as a consultant to the Department of the Navy, to the Department of

Defense, and to a variety of defense contractors. Among his numerous books on naval issues are *The U.S. Maritime Strategy, The Postwar Naval Revolution,* and the biennial *Naval Institute Guide to World Naval Weapons Systems* (first edition 1989). He is currently visiting professor of operations research at University College, London, and was formerly deputy director for National Security Affairs of the Hudson Institute.

John Lewis Gaddis is distinguished professor of history and director of the Contemporary History Institute at Ohio University. He has also taught at the U.S. Naval War College, the University of Helsinki, and Princeton University. His books include: *The United States and the Origins of the Cold War; Russia, the Soviet Union, and the United States; Strategies of Containment;* and *The Long Peace.*

David Grissmer is the deputy director of the Defense Manpower Research Center at the RAND Corporation and the former director of Policy Research at the General Research Corporation. His research focuses on both the active and reserve forces and the appropriate joint structure of those forces. He has authored numerous articles and reports on military manpower.

John Kasich is a four-term congressman from Ohio serving on the House Armed Services Committee and the House Budget Committee. He has been deeply involved in reform of DOD spending practices, led congressional efforts to eliminate funding for the B-2 bomber, and played a key role in passage of legislation that will allow the closing of unneeded military bases.

Andrey Kokoshin is the director of the Institute for the USA and Canada, Soviet Academy of Sciences. He has been actively involved in efforts to promote mutual understanding between the Soviet Union and the United States, including a mutual appreciation of each other's security concerns.

Bernard D. Rostker is the director of the Defense Manpower Research Center at the RAND Corporation and former director of Selective Service. He has spent the bulk of his career in manpower planning and analysis in civilian and military offices, and is the author of numerous articles and research reports on military manpower, mobilization planning, and combat systems analysis.

Lewis Sorley is a former soldier and civilian official of the Central Intelligence Agency. A graduate from the U.S. Military Academy, he also holds a Ph.D. from Johns Hopkins University and has been on the faculty at West Point and the Army War College. He is writing a biography of the late General Creighton Abrams, which will be published by Simon and Schuster in the autumn of 1991.

Stephen Van Evera is an assistant professor in the political science department at the Massachusetts Institute of Technology and a former managing editor of *International Security.* He has published articles on American defense policy and grand strategy, and is writing a book on the causes and prevention of war.

Murray Weidenbaum, a former chairman of the Council of Economic Advisers and corporate economist at the Boeing Company, is Mallinnckrodt Distinguished University Professor and director of the Center for the Study of American Business at Washington University in St. Louis. He is the author of *Economic Impact of Vietnam Spending* (1968), *Economics of Peacetime Defense* (1974), and various articles on defense economics.

About the Editor

Joseph Kruzel is a senior associate at the Mershon Center and associate professor of political science at Ohio State University. He served as a member of the U.S. delegation to SALT I and as a consultant to the U.S. Senate and the Department of Defense. Professor Kruzel taught previously at Harvard and Duke universities. He has written and lectured extensively on arms control and U.S. defense strategy.